AF361596

THREE ENCOUNTERS

DAVID
FARRELL
KRELL

THREE
ENCOUNTERS

Heidegger Arendt Derrida

INDIANA UNIVERSITY PRESS

This book is a publication of

Indiana University Press
Office of Scholarly Publishing
Herman B Wells Library 350
1320 East 10th Street
Bloomington, Indiana 47405 USA

iupress.org

The paper used in this publication meets the minimum requirements of
the American National Standard for Information Sciences—Permanence
of Paper for Printed Library Materials, ANSI Z39.48–1992.

Manufactured in the United States of America

First Printing 2023

Cataloging information is available from the Library of Congress.

ISBN 978-0-253-06553-7 (hdbk.)
ISBN 978-0-253-06554-4 (pbk.)
ISBN 978-0-253-06555-1 (web PDF)

*for my parents
and my children*

CONTENTS

PREFACE

MANY OF MY STUDENTS OVER THE YEARS HAVE pressed me with questions about Martin Heidegger, Hannah Arendt, and Jacques Derrida, knowing that I had met them and worked with them on at least a few occasions. It seems that I was among the very few of my generation and nationality who had the chance to meet with Heidegger, although many of my generation knew Arendt, and many of my younger colleagues met and worked with Derrida. In the first two cases, a "memoir" appeared to be justified. However, since I knew Derrida best of the three, I decided to write about all three encounters, but only after long hesitation. Two things, perhaps three, held me back.

To start with the third obstacle, I felt that I should let such a project wait until I began to feel closer to my death. An absurd conceit! At least for the young. In any case, absurd or not, I feel that it is now time to write.

The second obstacle will sound abstract and merely "bookish," but it did cause me to walk away from the project. Hershel Parker, in his extraordinarily detailed account of Herman Melville's life, raises a strange warning flag several times—indeed, he seems to be obsessed with the worry.[1] He notes that when Melville was writing *Redburn* in 1849, he "dipped into" his own biography for material without realizing how "dangerous" a confrontation with one's own life story must be. Only years later, when writing *Pierre, or, The Ambiguities*, did Melville come to recognize the perils of autobiography. What sorts of perils? In Melville's case, the dangers involved certain memories of his childhood, which was largely a childhood of deprivation resulting from a beloved yet inept father's inability to provide for his children. The ghost of an incompetent yet loved father haunted Melville, especially when he was writing *Pierre*, and even more so as he realized that his life as a professional writer was damaging the lives of his own children, some of whom came to disastrous ends, and all of whom bore a certain resentment toward their illustrious—and

---

1 Hershel Parker, *Herman Melville: A Biography*, 2 vols. (Baltimore: Johns Hopkins University Press, 1996), 1:645, 650, 693; 2:11, 37–38, 91, and elsewhere, for the following.

impoverished—father. Parker's obsession struck me as odd, and I did not understand it well, but it did cause me to shy from anything that smacked of autobiography.

Which brings me to the first obstacle, the most potent one. Derrida's work on the genre of autobiography, exposing all the traps that it sets for an author, "traps on all sides," as he liked to say, surely discouraged me the most. Among my friends and colleagues with whom I discussed the possibility of a memoir, one voice urged me strongly to resist the temptation. It was a voice coming from a careful student of Derrida's works, a student more insightful and better informed than I was about the perils of memoir, someone who felt affection for me and had my best interests at heart.

Disregarding the voice of that friend and all the other obstacles, I began the project and was immediately stymied by something I did not expect. When I started to research the documents that took me back five or six decades in my life, I discovered that I often did not recognize the person I met in my own letters and journals. The feeling was more intense than merely not recognizing him, however; I felt a certain aversion toward this ambitious young man. Of course, it is Heidegger, Arendt, and Derrida who are to be remembered here, not me. Yet how to suppress the recollecting ego? The narrative itself, even if it should silence the "I remember," would keep calling the narrating ego back. I can only hope that what is gained by such a recording of memories compensates for what may seem like too much ego, especially because the memories I most want to record are highly personal. I am of course interested in the *ideas* of these three philosophers—otherwise, I would have had nothing to do with them then or now, nor they with me. Yet in each case, it was the quality of the person that struck me in our meetings and conversations; that is what I felt, and still feel, is worth recounting and recording. This is perhaps especially true of Derrida, if only because I was much older when I met him and because our friendship extended over two decades, whereas I knew Heidegger only during the two or three final years of his life, and Arendt for only two very short (but quite wonderful) years. The obvious answer to these qualms of mine is to let the reader decide.

An early reader of this book commented that they would like to see more about the narrator, especially his life choices—such as where and how he lives—as far as these three encounters have affected those choices. I am happy to say that another book of mine does, in both text and photographs, what this book is reluctant to do.[2]

* * *

I met Martin Heidegger and Hannah Arendt very early in my professional life, when I was thirty, five years after I had completed my doctoral studies. I began to correspond with Jacques Derrida when I was thirty-nine and met him when I was forty-one. Heidegger died some three years after I met him, Arendt only two years after I met her. Derrida and I remained in close touch until the period of his illness—our correspondence dwindled after 2000, and I did not see him from that point until his death four years later. The fact that I knew Heidegger and Arendt so briefly and so early in my adult life, whereas I knew Derrida over decades and much more closely, accounts for the "unevenness" of the present undertaking. It is also clear to me that many other people in the English-speaking world knew at least one of these three philosophers much more intimately than I did and that there will be many other published memoirs. For the privilege of having known these philosophers, and because so many students and colleagues have asked me about my encounters with all three, I have decided to write these pages.

Recently someone asked me, in my daughter Salomé's presence, whether there was a common thread or theme in my "scholarly" work.

—No, I replied, it's all over the place.

Salomé responded immediately.

—Not true: you've always been as much interested in the *lives* of thinkers as in their ideas.

She may have been thinking of my work on Nietzsche in the 1990s, both the book of photographs and the novel.[3] It is certainly true that I have always been troubled by Heidegger's scorn for biography—his notion of the ostensibly perfect biography of Aristotle being "Aristotle was born, worked, and died." Now that Heidegger's own biography has returned to haunt him and us, my doubts seem justified. To put all this more positively, I felt strongly drawn to Derrida's emphasis on the conjunction *and* in

---

2 See David Farrell Krell, *A Black Forest Walden: Conversations with Henry David Thoreau and Marlonbrando* (Albany: State University of New York [SUNY] Press, 2022).

3 D. F. Krell and Donald Bates, *The Good European: Nietzsche's Work Sites in Word and Image* (Chicago: University of Chicago Press, 1997), and Krell, *Nietzsche: A Novel* (Albany: State University of New York Press, 1996).

the common phrase, "the life and work of x," *la vie* et *l'œuvre* of any given thinker, perhaps with inverse emphasis, "the work *and the life*." Hannah Arendt understood better than anyone that the *vita activa* is about the *living* that shapes both our thinking and our failures to think or act. As for me, philosophy would have been no more than a minor irritation had I not felt that it had everything to do with *existence*—that is to say, with the living of the one life we are given to live.

An editor with whom I corresponded early on about the project encouraged me to write the memoir—but with the following proviso: "You must show how these anecdotes relate to the *philosophy* of each and how they shaped your own understanding of the philosophers' *thinking*." An entirely reasonable request. University presses publish for serious readers, and for many of those readers, the word "anecdotal" is always preceded by the word "merely." I suppose I am hoping that my anecdotes are not merely anecdotal. Even if one is interested only in the *systems* of philosophers or in their *ideas*, what is *missing* from those systems or what lies *concealed* among the ideas has to be of interest. And what is missing or concealed often touches on the life of the system builder or thinker. One will—in secret, behind closed doors, abashedly—learn everything one can about that life, even if the testimony about it is anecdotal, a vignette or a cameo.

That abashed fascination with the *lives* of Heidegger, Arendt, and Derrida is the sole motivation for the present project. I will therefore set aside for the extended moment of this book all the problems of the genre and search for anecdotes that seem for one reason or another to be telling, even if I do not know exactly what they tell.

*   *   *

A note on my sources. As the COVID-19 pandemic began to remind the mortal world of its mortal condition, I decided to begin work in earnest on the project. And, yes, to let the reader decide about its worth. Because the pandemic closed the libraries, but also because I wanted the book to be based on personal recollections rather than research, I decided to refer to only a very few sources and to avoid footnotes and scholarly apparatus as much as possible. Yet the few books I did read were extremely helpful, either by jogging my memory or by informing me of things I never knew about, or sometimes by arousing my resistance, and I am grateful to have had the chance to study them.

My book consists of alternating chapters of *autobiography*: accounts of my meetings with Heidegger, Arendt, and Derrida; and *biography*: my recent *reading* of accounts of the lives of these three by Rüdiger Safranski, Antonia Grunenberg, Elisabeth Young-Bruehl, and Benoît Peeters.[4] Because Heidegger's and Arendt's lives were so closely intertwined, if complicatedly so, the biographies by Safranski, Grunenberg, and Young-Bruehl often complement one another but sometimes also offer quite different views of people and events. As for Derrida, Benoît Peeters's informative biography stands alone. Not long after Derrida's death, Peeters contacted me to ask for an interview. Not feeling up to it, still stunned by that death, I begged off. I regret that now, and I am very grateful for his book. I have only a few things to add to it.

A different version of chapter 2, on Heidegger translation, appears in *Heidegger and His Anglo-American Reception*, ed. Pietro D'Oriano and John Rogove (Berlin: Springer Nature, 2022). My thanks to Ulrich Halfmann, Kyle Wagner, Samir Haddad, and Marcia Sá Cavalcante Schuback, who read earlier drafts of the book and made numerous improvements. I am grateful to my editor at Indiana, Anna C. Francis, and to the entire staff there, especially David Miller, David Hulsey, and the editorial team at Amnet. Thanks also to Brittan Nanenga of the Special Collections and Archives, DePaul University Library, Chicago, Illinois, for help with the illustrations. I am grateful to Amy Rothblatt for the wonderful Derrida portraits from April 1991 and to Juliana Cárdenas Toro for the cover photo. Thanks also to David Matthew Krell of dmkdesign for help with the

4 Rüdier Safranski, *Ein Meister aus Deutschland: Heidegger und seine Zeit* (Frankfurt am Main: Fischer, 2001 [1994]). The book has appeared in an English translation with an unfortunate rendering of Safranski's title. See Rüdiger Safranski, *Martin Heidegger: Between Good and Evil*, trans. Ewald Osers (Cambridge, MA: Harvard University Press, 1998). I did not have access to the English version until quite recently, and so the translations of passages from Safranski are my own. However, I will cite Safranski as "RS" with the page numbers, first of the German, then of the published English translation, in the body of my text. Antonia Grunenberg, *Hannah Arendt und Martin Heidegger: Geschichte einer Liebe* (Munich and Zurich: Piper, 2006); English translation: Peg Birmingham, Kristina Lebadeva, and Elisabeth von Witzke Birmingham, *Hannah Arendt and Martin Heidegger: History of a Love* (Bloomington: Indiana University Press, 2017); here, too, the fine English translation was unavailable to me at the time of writing, so my translations depart in minor ways from the English edition. I will cite this work as "AG" with the German/English page numbers. Elisabeth Young-Bruehl, *Hannah Arendt: For Love of the World*, 2nd ed. (New Haven, CT: Yale University Press, 2004), cited in my text as "YB" with page number. Benoît Peeters, *Derrida* (Paris: Flammarion, 2010). I will cite this book as "BP" with page number.

design of the cover. My gratitude also goes to Brigitte Bruns and her entire family: their generosity has enabled me to enjoy the solitude and magnificent surroundings of the Strobelhütte in Geiersnest, St. Ulrich, for decades. The book is dedicated to the two people who engendered and raised me and the three who sustain me now.

D.F.K.
Strobelhütte, St. Ulrich

THREE ENCOUNTERS

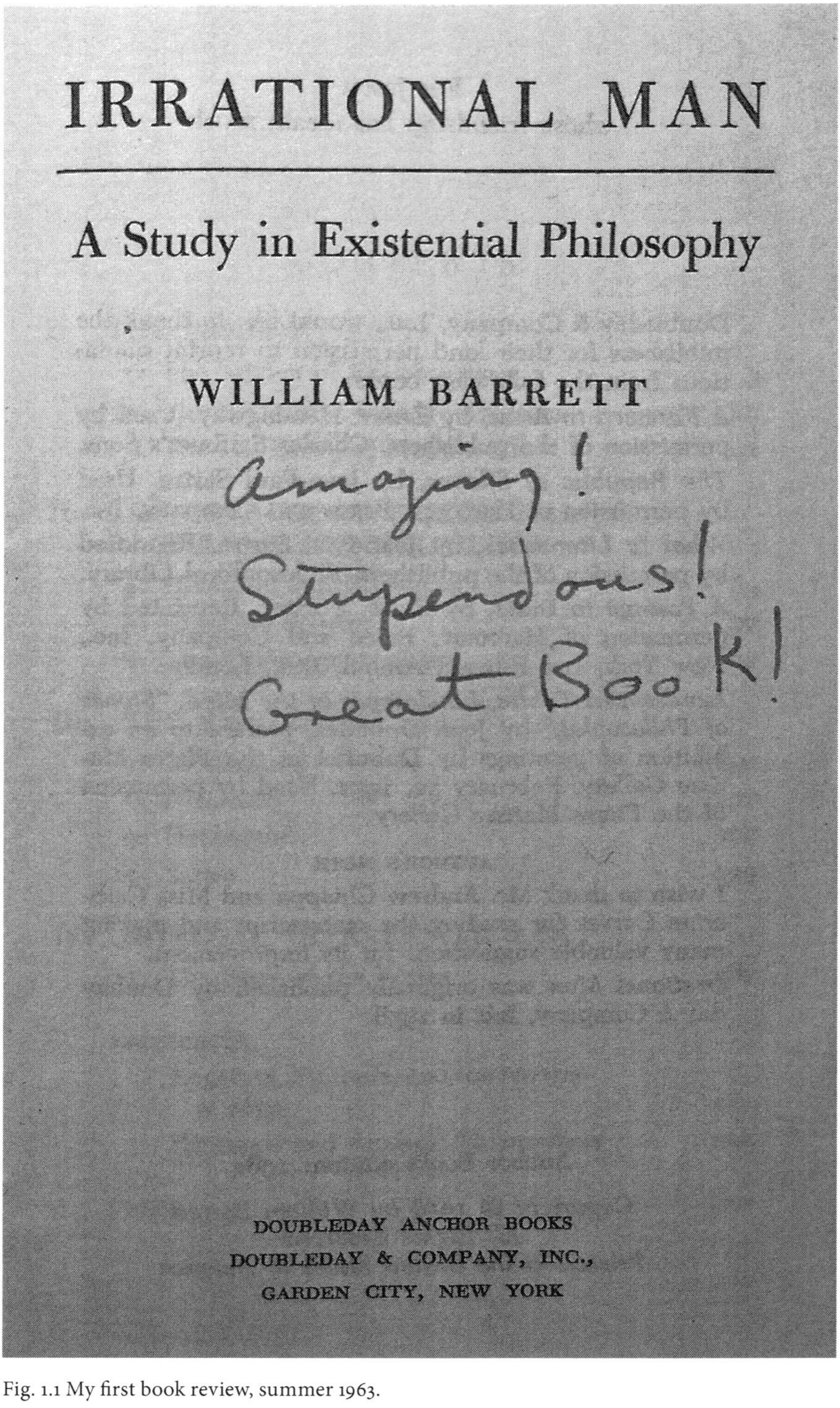

IRRATIONAL MAN

A Study in Existential Philosophy

WILLIAM BARRETT

DOUBLEDAY ANCHOR BOOKS
DOUBLEDAY & COMPANY, INC.,
GARDEN CITY, NEW YORK

Fig. 1.1 My first book review, summer 1963.

1

BEFORE THE BEGINNING

"Amazing! Stupendous! Great Book!" These words, in an oversized, awkward adolescent hand, grace the title page of my copy of William Barrett's *Irrational Man*.[1] The book had been assigned as required reading for the second half of a two-year survey course in world history that I took during my freshman year at Duquesne University in 1963. Barrett's was the first work of philosophy that earned such accolades from me. During my high school years, I had read Aristotle's *Poetics* and Plato's *Symposium*, and a teacher had put a stick of dynamite into my hands—Nietzsche's *Beyond Good and Evil*—but what impact any of these may have had on me, I no longer remember.

The philosophy courses I was required to take at the university, all of them Thomistic apologetics of one sort or another, left me cold. Angry, actually. I jotted into a notebook my verdict: "The philosopher—a bizarre mix of naïveté and arrogance." There were exceptions: I heard Alphonso Lingis deliver a paper on Hiroshima Day entitled "Reflections on Nuclear Death," and I have never forgotten it. By my senior year, as a history major, I was auditing a graduate course on Heidegger's *Being and Time* taught by André Schuwer. I asked my parents to make the Macquarrie–Robinson translation a Christmas gift to me, which they did, bemused though they were by the request. Nevertheless, I remained a history major through my bachelor's and first master's degrees, drawn especially to the history of science and the history of ideas.

---

1 William Barrett, *Irrational Man: A Study in Existential Philosophy* (Garden City, NY: Doubleday Anchor, 1962), originally published in 1958. Hereinafter cited as "WB" with page number.

At the University of Virginia, as a Danforth Fellow in a doctoral program in history, I proposed to write a dissertation with the title *Nietzsche's Insanity: The History of an Idea*. My supervisor, an expert on European fascism, could see that my interest in Nietzsche, whose works occupied much of my spare time, was running too deep, that I was taking it all too seriously.

—You seem to care about whether these ideas are true or not, he observed.

His irritation was showing. I said nothing, puzzled by his objection to truth.

—Why not do something interesting on the French police during the 1930s? he suggested.

I left Virginia and returned to Duquesne University, taking courses in philosophy, principally with André Schuwer and John Sallis. That is when my training in European philosophy began.

When I stumbled onto my worn copy of Barrett's *Irrational Man* a year or two ago, I read through the many passages I had underlined and commented on in the margins during that freshman-year history course. Once again, after sixty years, the book seemed to me amazing, stupendous, great. I was most impressed by Barrett's ability to see threads of "existentialism" running through the enormous tapestry of Western thought and letters, a tapestry that included Aeschylus's *Eumenides* and Shakespeare's *Lear* and *Hamlet*, Pascal's *Pensées* and Swift's *Gulliver*, as well as Barrett's four principal subjects: Kierkegaard, Nietzsche, Heidegger, and Sartre.

Nietzsche and Heidegger had already become the essential ones for me. Six years after reading Barrett, I would sketch out a new dissertation topic, this time accepted by my mentors: *Nietzsche and the Task of Thinking*. The "task" referred to here would involve Heidegger's two-volume commentary on the dynamite that had been too hazardous, or simply too overwhelming, for the high school student. Barrett had not been able to read Heidegger's *Nietzsche*, which did not appear until 1961, so he was not especially relevant for my later absorption in the Nietzsche–Heidegger relation. Yet so many aspects of *Irrational Man*—a title Heidegger would have hated—remained important enough to me that I want to refer to a series of passages from it, if only to indicate how a more or less normal American boy got mixed up in all of this.

From "The Advent of Existentialism," I underlined the remark by Kierkegaard's hero, or antihero, who is so remote from the life he is living "that he hardly knows he exists until, one fine morning, he wakes up to find himself dead" (WB 3). What Barrett calls "the encounter with nothingness" seemed to be not nothing but everything to me by that time, and the two dominant schools of philosophy to which I had meanwhile been exposed—Thomistic apologetics in my own little world and "analytical philosophy" in the larger world—had nothing to say about such an encounter. Analytical philosophers were merely keen to show how cleverly they could argue about nothing, and the Thomists insisted that God had turned the nothing into creation. What would a philosophy that encounters nothingness and the nothing be about? For starters, *life*. "The divorce of mind from life was something that had happened to philosophers simply in the pursuit of their own specialized problems. Since philosophers are only a tiny fraction of the general population, the matter would not be worth laboring were it not that this divorce of mind from life happens also to be taking place, catastrophically, in modern civilization everywhere. It happens too, as we shall see, to be one of the central themes of existential philosophy—for which we may in time owe it no small debt" (WB 9).

Apart from "life," what specifically did this encounter with the nothing entail? Answer: psychology, principally "phenomenological psychology," which became a strong interest of mine during my undergraduate years. Barrett identified Kierkegaard and Nietzsche as "witnesses" who identified the "secret wound" of their time, identified it by suffering from it themselves (WB 13). Their thinking, he wrote, did not construct systems of concepts; rather, it sought self-realization. "No wonder," he concludes, "both are among the greatest of intuitive psychologists" (ibid.).

During my undergraduate years, I read Freud for the first time, beginning with the Clark lectures, *The Interpretation of Dreams*, and *The Psychopathology of Everyday Life*. These works, and, a bit later, *The Future of an Illusion*, made the connection with Nietzsche inevitable. In an undergraduate course taught by Edward Murray, I read Erich Fromm and Viktor Frankl. From my sophomore year through my doctorate, with only a few interruptions, Murray and I met on Wednesday afternoons "to compare notes," as he put it. During those sessions, he taught me more about psychology and my own life—my position in my family, my goals and ambitions, my emotional and nonexistent sexual life—than any human being I have ever met. And the philosophical companions for that sort of learning turned out to be Nietzsche and Heidegger.

Barrett stressed the German sources of existentialism, emphasizing the roles of Karl Jaspers and Martin Heidegger, and these German sources no doubt struck a chord in me. Some of my earliest memories are of singing Christmas hymns for my paternal great-grandmother, *Grossmama*, who steadfastly refused to learn a word of English. My father kept alive the German of his early years, which was the German of the Alsatian *Dialekt*, even though he never used it as we were growing up. Two years before he died, he visited me in the small village near Freiburg where I have lived much of my adult life. When he and my mother walked through the door, my landlady offered them something to eat, and my father replied in perfect Alemannic German.

—Nä, nä, mir sin' müd.

It was a remarkable moment for me: I was struggling to learn a language that was a part of my heritage but that was stubbornly resisting my efforts, and there it came, flowing freely from my father's mouth. What I inherited from *Grossmama*, it seems, was the ability to make some of the strange noises that German requires. Grammar and vocabulary had to be eked out on my own.

I did not visit Europe until I graduated from college in 1966, having just turned twenty-two. I felt strangely at home there, especially in Germany, even though my German was weak. (Years later I was surprised and pleased to learn that I was experiencing—on a much smaller scale, no doubt—what W. E. B. DuBois experienced when he traveled to Berlin as a graduate student.) I was most excited by Paris, even though my French was even weaker than my German. I say this to make it clear that there was nothing predestined about my later work as a translator; these languages were not handed to me at birth, and language learning has always been a struggle for me, even if the languages themselves have always struck me as miraculous.

The first theme discussed in Barrett's second chapter, "The Encounter with Nothingness," is "The Decline of Religion." In red ink, the oversized hand enthused, "Excellent essay!" Barrett understood that there was no path back to the world of *The Divine Comedy*, that the mind or soul "evolves like everything else in nature" (WB 25–26). My contempt for the courses in Thomism that I was being subjected to found its justification here: "We could not expect to produce a St. Thomas Aquinas, any more than a Dante, today. The total psychic condition of man—of which after all thinking is one of the manifestations—has evolved too radically. Which may be why present-day Thomists have on the whole remained singularly unconvincing to their contemporaries" (WB 27). Barrett's analysis of the historical situation was convincing to me, even if as a history student I loved Eileen Powers's *Medieval People* and, later, as a traveler, stood in awe of the cathedrals and basilicas of Europe. That analysis helped me to affirm my own past—as a chorister who was excited by the role of music in church liturgy—but to let the rest go. The dogmas, the authoritarianism, the influence of an absurd clergy all fell away during my early teenage years. Yet the decline of religion left me caught in a dilemma. Barrett explained what I sensed was the case: as long as the Age of Faith endured, the shadow side of humankind could be explained—Mephistopheles had more explanatory power than the Demiurge. But as the modern world became increasingly secularized and human beings were left to account for their own folly, confusion mounted. Luther and the other Reformers offered a scathing account of human nature, but that did not seem to help much. The result of all this was that "Protestant man begins to look more and more like a gaunt skeleton, a sculpture by Giacometti," attenuated and tenuous (WB 28–29).

If religion no longer supplied the binding power that any community (and, presumably, every individual) needs, my own community (and my own self) included, the "rational ordering of society" left its members restive and unsatisfied. I recall my history professor, Donald M. Lowe, who had assigned the Barrett book, repeating several times Max Weber's assessment of Western society as rational in each of its parts and utterly irrational as a whole. Everyone of my generation, I believe, could feel it. And I still feel it. After the assassinations of the Kennedys and Martin Luther King Jr., after the murderous quagmire of Vietnam, the debacles of Nixon and Agnew, the reactionary regimes of Reagan and Cheney, and now the cretinous Age of Trumpery, nothing appears to be countering the American tailspin.

Barrett's third theme under the general rubric of "The Encounter with Nothingness" was that of *finitude,* not as a philosophical concept but as the result of developments in science and technology, and also doubtless as a result of catastrophic wars and genocide. Barrett argued that "the radical feeling of human finitude" was behind the complaints one was hearing everywhere, finitude as a frigid wind to which the entire civilization was now exposed: "Alienation and estrangement; a sense of the basic fragility and contingency of human life; the impotence of reason confronted with the depths of existence; the threat of Nothingness, and the solitary and unsheltered condition of the individual before this threat" (WB 36). Long before I encountered the word "finitude" in Heidegger's fundamental ontology of Dasein (that is, "being-there" in the way that you and I, as existing in the world, *are*), Barrett's analysis of this "radical feeling" struck me with full force. For that frigid wind threatened knowledge itself: if Gödel showed that complete systematicity is impossible even for mathematics, there needed to be a *philosophical* reckoning with that chilling impossibility. The same wind battered my confidence in the work of historians: whereas Hegel's dream of "reason in history" had its allure—it continues to dazzle young philosophers today—someone needed to develop a rigorous and vigilant interpretation of that pipe dream.

Barrett's third chapter, "The Testimony of Modern Art," is not heavily marked up in my copy, which indicates how undeveloped and uninformed I was in matters of art apart from music. I had always loved stories, which were now beginning to be called "literature," but it was only after I visited the great museums of Europe—the Louvre and the former Jeu de Paume of Paris, the Prado of Madrid, the Uffizi of Florence—that painting and sculpture entered into my life. By contrast, a remark by Barrett on Hemingway's "A Clean, Well-Lighted Place" and a long quotation from it struck home. Barrett's "encounter with nothingness" found its most telling formulation. The story, if I remember rightly, had caught my attention during a high school literature course. Many years later, I would learn of Hölderlin's insistence that spirituality can open up a space for the gods only if it goes to meet deity with a word of blasphemy in its mouth. As a young man, I was astonished by Barrett's analysis of these unforgettable words uttered by a waiter in a clean and well-lighted Spanish café:

> It was all a nothing and a man was nothing too. It was only that and light was all it needed and a certain cleanness and order. Some lived in it and never felt it but he knew it all was nada y pues nada y nada y pues nada. Our nada, who are in nada, nada be thy name thy kingdom nada thy will be nada in nada as it is nada. Give us this nada our daily nada and nada us our nada as we nada our nadas and nada us not into nada but deliver us from nada; pues nada.[2]

---

2 Ernest Hemingway, "A Clean Well-Lighted Place," in *The First Forty-Nine Stories* (London: Jonathan Cape, 1972), 310–14, cited by Barrett at 283.

I knew that Nietzsche had experienced this "nothing," which was the reason why every serious modern artist or writer had read him, and I was beginning to suspect that Heidegger was the thinker who was taking this "nothing" to heart.

Why am I recording so much about one piece of assigned reading in an undergraduate history course? What I am trying to understand is how a Pittsburgh boy who had his heroes ("And now, batting right-handed, the right fielder, number 21, Ro-BER-to Cle-MEN-te") arrived at the place where he could meet and work with three philosophic luminaries. It seems to have been a series of accidents, none of which redounds to my credit. And if I were to dig even deeper and push farther back into my personal history, these encounters, I suspect, would become increasingly implausible.

If the strange mix of arrogance and naïveté prevented me from pursuing philosophy as an undergraduate major, William Barrett encouraged the would-be historian to open himself to new influences. He did this by paying attention to the historical roots of existentialism in "Hebraism and Hellenism," in "Christian Sources" ("Very Important!" exclaims a marginal note of mine), and in "The Flight from Laputa," meaning modernity's gradual abandonment of Platonism and Idealism ("Excellent!"). Barrett advances from Jonathan Swift to the Romantics, observing the following about Wordsworth, my favorite poet of those early years: "With the exception of the German poet Hölderlin, Wordsworth was probably the most philosophic poet of Romanticism; and it is to be regretted that no English philosopher has made the kind of commentary on his poems that Heidegger has made on those of Hölderlin" (WB 125). That may have been the first time I read the name "Hölderlin."

From the Romantics, Barrett turns to Russian fiction, to Tolstoy and Dostoevsky, who were already important to me. Dostoevsky, condemned for a time to Siberia, learned from his fellow prisoners the qualities that human beings are so anxious to deny in themselves, "contradiction, ambivalence, irrationality" and, above all, "the will to power—the demoniacal will to power" (WB 136–37). Dostoevsky's Raskolnikov embodied that overpowering will before Nietzsche had a chance to theorize about it. Many years later, I learned that Nietzsche, toward the end of his active life, read Dostoevsky in French translations and was enthusiastic about his discovery of this novelist of *ressentiment*. Barrett noted that the Enlightenment thinkers, "dreaming of a perfect organization of society," failed to see what

Dostoevsky saw as a novelist and what Nietzsche uncovered as a thinker: "as modern society becomes more organized and hence more bureaucratized it piles up at its joints petty figures like that of the Underground Man, who beneath their nondescript surface are monsters of frustration and resentment" (WB 139).

I doubt I had read much Nietzsche, even in translation, by the time I came across Barrett's discussion. Even so, that account encouraged me to read every Walter Kaufmann translation I could locate.[3]

Barrett's *Irrational Man* was not an "elementary" or merely "introductory" study, not simple or superficial, not a book one could safely leave behind. In fact, many of his ideas about Nietzsche have never left me, not even after decades of reading and rereading Nietzsche's own works and letters. Barrett's accounts of Zarathustra's descent from the mountain (WB 188–89), of Nietzsche's *Genealogy of Morals* (WB 191), and of a crucial scene in *Thus Spoke Zarathustra*, "On the Vision and the Riddle" (WB 192–94) have stayed with me. Finally, his image of Heidegger "digging his way patiently and laboriously out of the Nietzschean ruins, like a survivor out of a bombed city" (WB 205) remains striking. I was not surprised to learn that William Barrett, who taught philosophy at Columbia and was a member of the *Partisan Review* group, was also a member of Hannah Arendt's circle of friends in Manhattan during the 1950s.

*   *   *

I must have purchased a second Doubleday-Anchor paperback, Ralph Manheim's translation of Heidegger's *Introduction to Metaphysics*, published in 1961, not long after studying Barrett's *Irrational Man*.[4] My copy of the Heidegger book is even more tattered than the Barrett, worn by weather and rereading. Heidegger's *Einführung in die Metaphysik*, taught in 1935, was an important book for Heidegger. In later editions of his *Sein und Zeit*,

3 I remain grateful for Kaufmann's translations, but his way of constantly interrupting the text—as I am doing now—with footnotes explaining how ineptly former translators rendered Nietzsche's text irked me; in effect, he was announcing over and over again how skilled and otherwise wonderful his own work was. I remember thinking, "Walter Kaufmann—will to power in a footnote." I have tried not to emulate that aspect of his translation work.

4 Martin Heidegger, *An Introduction to Metaphysics*, trans. Ralph Manheim (New York: Doubleday-Anchor, 1961), originally published in 1959. Since I have only now referred to Arendt's connection with Barrett, I should mention that Manheim requested and received help from Hannah Arendt on his translation. I will refer to his translation as "RM," with page number, and Heidegger's German original as "EM."

those printed from 1953 onward, he referred to that 1935 lecture course as an essential "elucidation" of the question of being. My ratty copy of the paperback shows years and years of marginal commentary, some of it more sophisticated, with its scribbled Greek and German. Yet much of it is in that awkward hand I see in the margins of Barrett. It is these early comments that interest me now.

I am embarrassed to confess how much of my earliest reading of Heidegger's *Introduction* took place. My parents were both devout Catholics, and as long as I lived at home, I attended Sunday mass to keep the peace. And to keep a roof over my head. My more courageous contemporaries would have resisted the pressure to attend a liturgy that had long since become meaningless to them, but I was not made of such stuff. I kept my thoughts to myself. Luckily, the hymnals at church were large tomes: my tiny paperback nestled comfortably in the pages of the songbook, and, instead of joining what Henry Miller once described (from his vantage point in the choir loft of Notre-Dame Cathedral) as a hundred heads of wailing cauliflower, I wondered why there were beings at all, and why not far rather nothing?

That first line of the book is underlined: "Why are there essents [what we translate today as "beings"] rather than nothing?" Also underscored is Heidegger's comment: "The question looms in moments of great despair, when things tend to lose all their weight and all meaning becomes obscured" (RM 1). Where Heidegger referred to the "ground" of everything that is, I wrote at the bottom of the page, confusing *Grund* with "soil," "to get at the roots of reality" (RM 2). Later, he cited Nietzsche's "Truth and Lie in an Extra-Moral Sense" to show that among all the things that *are*, the human being is the one that asks questions. I underscored this and added a nota bene to Heidegger's remark, "Still, it is noteworthy that in this questioning *one* kind of essent [one particular being] persists in coming to the fore, namely the men who ask the question" (RM 3). I let the "men" stand uncorrected, not knowing then that *der Mensch* meant everybody. It seemed to me—perhaps I was now making my own contribution to that guild of arrogance and naïveté—that Heidegger was remarkable among the philosophers for actually thinking about what he was doing. Despite Derrida's suspicions about Heidegger's claim that "man," the "questioner," is intimate with "being," whereas no other creature can be, that claim still seems remarkably convincing to me—at least on most days of the week.

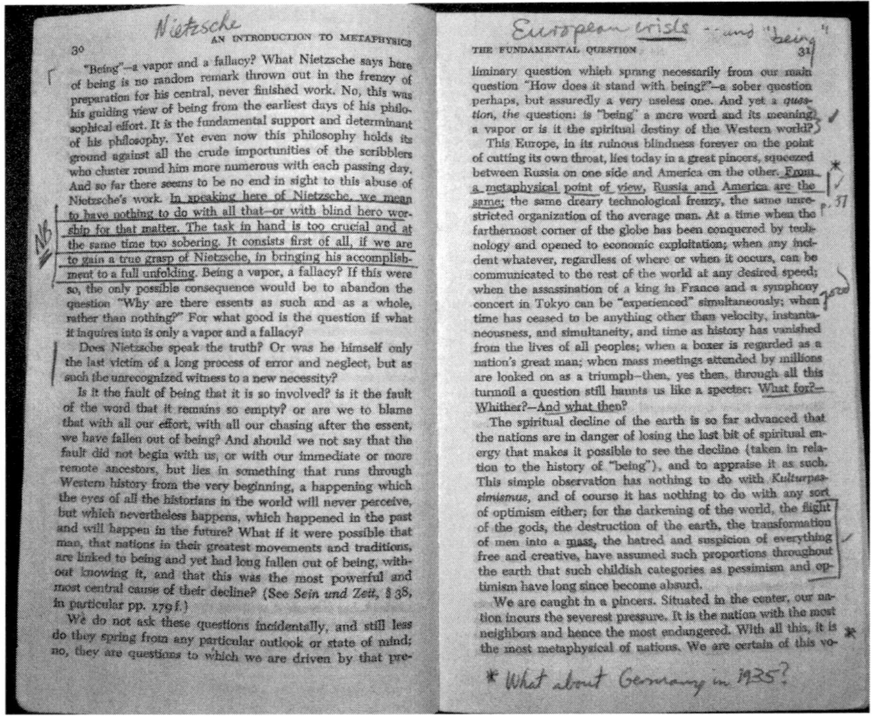

Fig. 1.2 Bringing Nietzsche's accomplishment to a full unfolding, the crisis in Europe's middle, Russian and American pincers—but what about Germany in 1935?

Why are there beings at all? And why the *why*? "Is it moody brooding?" I asked in the top margin of the book, remembering Stephen Dedalus, but then I answered in Heidegger's Kierkegaardian voice, "No: a leap." Heidegger argues that "this privileged question 'why' has its ground in a leap through which the human being thrusts away all the previous security, whether real or imagined, of his or her life" (RM 5). Secreted away in the pages of my hymnal, Heidegger's *Introduction to Metaphysics* declared that "one cannot really question without ceasing to be a believer" and that a so-called Christian philosophy is "a round square and a misunderstanding" (RM 6). Here was a philosopher who took Nietzsche seriously. In fact, Heidegger seemed to acknowledge that his own thought was largely a response to Nietzsche. Underlining this portion of his text and marking it with an underscored *N.B.*, I clearly felt that the following pronouncement was decisive: Heidegger, replying to the "crude importunities of the scribblers who cluster round him [Nietzsche]," insists that in "speaking here of Nietzsche, we mean to have nothing to do with all that—or with blind hero worship for that matter. The task in hand is too crucial and at the same time too sobering. It consists first of all, if we are to gain a true grasp of Nietzsche, in bringing his accomplishment to a full unfolding" (RM 30). Not much later I jotted into my journal the rather melodramatic claim that, after Nietzsche, Heidegger was "the only thinker clean enough for my hands."

For a neophyte historian, such as I was, Heidegger's emphasis on the *history* of the being question was important. Yet I was already troubled by the historical context of these 1935 lectures ("not just any date," as Derrida was later to remark) in which "Russia" and "America" are declared to be threatening the European "center," dominated by Hitler's Germany. In the top margin, I scribbled one of Heidegger's key phrases, "The world is darkening," but I added the date and underscored it: "*1935* lectures" (RM 37). The thinker I was taking up into my hands was evidently not so "clean," and even early on I was not altogether incautious. Yet when in the early 1960s I read Heidegger's 1935 account of this darkening of the world, "the flight of the gods, the destruction of the earth, the standardization of man, the pre-eminence of the mediocre" (ibid.), it seemed that he was rendering an account of my own world. I recalled a then-recent conversation with my advisor in the history department at Duquesne, William G. Storey.

—You are fortunate to have been born in this age of decline, he said.

When I asked him what he meant, he elaborated.

—If you had been born into an empire on the rise, it would have absorbed your entire life, and you'd have had no freedom. Had you been born into an empire whose decline had already advanced too far, you would have been caught up in the chaos and your life may ended all too soon. Decades of gradual decline—that is best.

During the early Kennedy years, his words seemed unduly cynical. But then the Kennedys were killed. To repeat, after the intervening years, and now as the US continues to show the world how defenseless a republic in decline can be, it seems about right. Time for you and time for me, time—altering Eliot—for asking about the destruction of the earth and the darkening of the world. Even as one fears the echoes of Weimar defeatism in such words, which are words of despair, their echo resounds.

I am far from certain whether or not I understood much about the rest of Heidegger's book about being (*Sein*) as opposed to beings (*das Seiende*) or about the importance of the third-person indicative "is" as opposed to the first-person "I am." But clearly, I was moved—my marginal jottings and underlinings show it—by at least two things. First, Heidegger's commitment to historical knowledge: "Only the most radical historical knowledge can make us aware of our extraordinary tasks and preserve us from a new wave of mere restoration and uncreative imitation" (RM 106). Second, and this was bound up with "the discovery of finitude" that Barrett had emphasized in his chapter on Heidegger, it remains true that, even if Western humanity is enthralled by and in thrall to its technological prowess, pursuing all its projects with ever greater avidity and violence, "all violence shatters against *one* thing. That is death" (RM 133).

The final marginal jotting in that adolescent scrawl is the one word that Heidegger's translators will always shy away from translating: Dasein. I accepted Heidegger's judgment that the book *Being and Time* "points in an entirely different direction of inquiry" than that taken by traditional philosophical anthropologies (RM 171). After all these years, and after all the intervening debates and necessary refinements, I still accept that judgment, if tremulously. As far as I can see, Arendt and Derrida accepted it too, even if the two of them had to develop the most stringent criticisms of Heidegger's work, criticisms based on their ideas about the "different direction" philosophical inquiry should take in our time.

I cannot pretend that the present book of personal reminiscences will expatiate much on those different directions for a philosophy of the future. I have begun here by reporting on my jottings "before the beginning," trusting that a range of readers may find traces of their own beginnings in these marginalia of mine. I will continue by emphasizing, principally by way of anecdotes and vignettes but also through journal notes and correspondence, what I remember about the *persons* of Heidegger, Arendt, and Derrida. None of this will halt the destruction of our Earth and the darkening of our world. Yet there is pleasure in remembering and, perhaps, especially in destitute times, a kind of nurture in it.

Fig. 2.1 The first of the two volumes of the paperback edition of Heidegger's *Nietzsche* in English translation, 1991.

2

TRANSLATING HEIDEGGER

My first effort at Heidegger translation was the essay "Logos: Heraclitus B50" from *Vorträge und Aufsätze* (*Lectures and Essays*), presented to a graduate seminar taught by John Sallis at Duquesne University in the late 1960s. For years, I kept a fragrant mimeographed copy of this first effort as a kind of memento mori, but, happily, it has since disappeared. The version that eventually appeared in *Early Greek Thinking* in 1975 was much altered. In the early 1970s, after completing my doctorate from Duquesne in 1971, I sent the translation to J. Glenn Gray at the Colorado College. Glenn was the director of the Harper & Row (now HarperCollins) Heidegger Series. He thought well enough of my effort to ask Joan Stambaugh to meet with me in Pittsburgh—she was a native of Coraopolis, on the Ohio River, not far from my native Pittsburgh—to discuss its publication along with some of Heidegger's other essays on early Greek thinking.

Joan Stambaugh was an ebullient, genial, and generous person, long engaged in Heidegger translation, and she was supportive of both the project and my involvement with the editorial circle in general. Fred D. Wieck, an editor at Harper's who had collaborated with Glenn Gray on the translation of Heidegger's *Was heisst Denken?* ("What Is Called Thinking?") was the official head of the project—although I never met him. The editorial work was done principally by Glenn Gray and his daughter, Sherry Gray Martin, along with Joan Stambaugh. All three, however, would have said that the real leader of the circle was Hannah Arendt, and this was no doubt true, in that she was no mere "helper" (YB 304). It is well known that Arendt played a leading role in the editorship of Karl Jaspers's works; far less well known is the fact that for decades she was every bit as active in overseeing the translation of Heidegger's works. Nothing appeared in the Harper series in those days that did not pass through her hands and under her alert eyes. My meetings with her—among the most privileged events of my life—always had these translation projects at their center. She had approved and even praised my translation of Heidegger's *Der Spruch des Anaximander* ("The Anaximander Fragment"), the first essay of *Early Greek Thinking*, and although she had justified doubts about my youth and the shaky state of my German—I was learning more every day, but life is never long enough— she, too, was nothing but supportive. There were particular passages in the "Anaximander" piece that we spoke about at length, and I will mention at least one of them shortly.

Early Greek Thinking was a collaborative work with a fellow Duquesne graduate, Frank Capuzzi. Because I was already living in Germany by the early 1970s, it was a collaboration by post. The final correction of proofs fell largely to me, if I remember correctly, and the little book that cost the two of us considerable blood, sweat, and tears appeared in 1975. It was later revised and published in paperback in 1984. Today it is out of print.[1]

My letters to my parents and my journals say very little about the work done on *Early Greek Thinking*. A letter dated June 15, 1974, says that the typescript was mailed to Harper & Row on April 15. I was expecting the book to be in print by December of that year (ah, the impatience and inexperience of youth!), but my memory of the process by which the book finally appeared lies too far back to be trustworthy. Two recollections do stand out. One involves a long discussion with Arendt, the other discussions with Reiner Schürmann. Reiner was a young professor at Duquesne, a brilliant man and very generous with his time and expertise. He worked through an early version of my attempt at "The Anaximander Fragment," which should have been rendered as "Anaximander's Saying," of course, but I, like Glenn Gray, was obstinate about reducing as many "Heideggerisms" as possible. Earlier translations had suffered from the tendency to translate Heidegger

---

1 Martin Heidegger, *Early Greek Thinking*, 2nd ed., trans. David Farrell Krell and Frank A. Capuzzi (San Francisco: Harper & Row, 1985 [1975]). At some point in the late 1990s or early 2000s, HarperCollins released the World Rights in English of *Early Greek Thinking* to me, and Indiana University Press immediately attempted to do a reprint; this was blocked by the Klostermann firm, which argued that Heidegger had insisted on the publication of *Holzwege* and *Vorträge und Auf-sätze* as complete entities. HarperCollins took this to mean that he did not approve of *Early Greek Thinking*, which was nonsense. He was happy to have these essays in English and was grateful for the little book, which I handed over to him during one of my visits.

into Pennsylvania Dutch. Anaximander's "Saying" made the ancient pronouncement on "being" and "disorder," ἀδικία, sound too much like an old saw, and so I went with the colorless "fragment." Reiner and I sat at the dining room table in my apartment in the Squirrel Hill section of Pittsburgh and pored over Heidegger's "Anaximander." But therein lies a tale.

TRANSLATION, OR, TRYING ONE'S HAND AT DESTINY

All went as well as it could go until we reached this sentence: *Geschick versucht sich an Geschick.* Readers will find it in the first line of page 311 of the 1950 Klostermann edition of *Holzwege*. What could be simpler? Two identical nouns connected by a reflexive verb and a familiar preposition. Five words. I had done my homework, and so I knew that the verb *sich versuchen* was a relatively rare instance of the familiar verb *versuchen*, "to try or attempt." *Der Versuch* was such a "try" or "effort," or, more formally, an "experiment." What made the noun especially interesting was its close relation to *die Versuchung*, "temptation." Nietzsche had already teased his readers with a play on these words: no "essay" of his, no "attempt" was without its diabolical side, its "temptation." James Joyce would not have hesitated to have Shem the penman translate *Versuch* and *Versuchung* with the single word "attemptation." But *sich versuchen* is less entertaining than all that. It means simply to try one's hand at a thing, to undertake a task, or to pose a question or a thesis to oneself: *ich versuche mich an einem Thema*, says the dictionary: "I shall try my hand at a theme."

What was odd about this use of the verb is that *Geschick* was doing this to itself—in the third-person present indicative. *Geschick* was the "dispensation" or "destining" of being, from the verb *schicken*, "to send." The broader sense of something's being "sent" one's way is one's personal or collective "destiny" or "fate," and that is perhaps the most common sense of *Geschick* as *Schicksal*. But the adjectival past participle *geschickt* also means "skillful," presumably as a result of one's having been "sent" a special gift or talent for something—for singing, dancing, woodwork, and so on, if not for translating. I knew that Heidegger often played with the notion of a "skillful" thinking that would trace the history (for *Geschichte*, "story," or "history," is a near-homonym of *Geschick*) in terms of its destiny or "sending," so that *skill* in thinking requires that one have a sense for what is *fateful* or even *destined* about the history of being. Those were the "parts," but what was the sense of the whole?

Reiner smiled amiably and, in his deep, rather stentorian voice, repeated the German sentence over and over again.

—*Geschick versucht sich an Geschick.* What does it mean?

I sagely reviewed the context for him. Heidegger is talking about errancy (*die Irre*) in Western history at this moment in his "Anaximander" essay. I will cite here the paragraph that culminates in the redoubled *Geschick*, which we were struggling to render in English and which Reiner was making me feel would seal my fate:

> As it reveals itself in beings, Being withdraws. [I was still doing "Big *B* Being" at this point, but, on Glenn Gray's urging, I would soon give it up. In any case: *Das Sein entzieht sich, indem es sich in das Seiende entbirgt.* Paragraph break, and then:]
>
> In this way, by illuminating them, Being sets beings adrift in errancy. Beings come to pass in that errancy by which they circumvent Being and establish the realm of error (in the sense of a prince's realm or the realm of poetry). Error is the space in which history unfolds. In error, what happens in history bypasses what is like Being. Therefore, whatever unfolds historically is necessarily misinterpreted. During the course of this misinterpretation, destiny awaits what will become of its seed. It brings those whom it concerns to the possibilities of the fateful and fatal [*Geschicklichen und Ungeschicklichen*]. (H 310–11; EGT 26)[2]

"Fatal" for *Ungeschicklichen* is, of course, an overtranslation, although Heidegger clearly means something both fateful and dire, something significantly amiss and remiss. Then comes the fateful, fatal sentence that Reiner, still smiling benevolently and handsomely, insisted on repeating.

—What does it mean? he asked smilingly.

Who knows what I initially did with the sentence. I no longer have any of my early drafts. Here are some of the ways the translation could have gone and probably did go in my conversation with Reiner.

—Destiny tries its hand at destining. The sending undertakes to send itself. Skill hones itself on fateful destining.

And so on and on, a different effort for each of Reiner's repetitions. Long after the fact, I realized that he was trying to get me not to crack the riddle but to crack my head. That is to say, he wanted me to wake up and realize that there are aspects of any text, and, certainly, of Heidegger's

---

2 That is, Martin Heidegger, *Holzwege* (Frankfurt am Main: V. Klostermann, 1950), 310–11, and *Early Greek Thinking*, 26.

texts, that will not boil down to a particular sense, a sense that one could confidently render in any language. I did not know at that time Walter Benjamin's insight that translation places infinite demands not merely on the two languages involved but on *language as such*, if one may say such a thing. The risk of overtranslation or undertranslation is therefore in principle never overcome. The primary "skill" of a translator is a finely developed sense of paranoia—not a sense of assuredness or the illusion of mastery.

In any case, I must have noticed that the next sentence of Heidegger's paragraph says something about the *human being's* inability, while in errancy, to recognize itself, an inability that corresponds to the self-concealing clearing of being. The upcoming mention of *der Mensch* in Heidegger's essay either rescued me or drew me into a fatal attemptation, for the English translation of *Geschick versucht sich an Geschick* eventually became:

—Man's destiny gropes toward its fate.

The only thing that is right about this translation is that it "gropes." Whether or not my solution had Reiner's blessing or forbearance I no longer remember, or I have repressed, but it surely came to me only after our long discussion of the line.

In later years, Reiner continued to be kind to me—always full of praise, always encouraging. Some years after our "Anaximander" discussions, he honored me by asking me to translate a newly discovered poem of Hölderlin's. Reiner Schürmann's early death was an enormous personal loss for me, and it continues to be a terrible loss to contemporary philosophy.[3]

Perhaps I may insert another anecdote about Reiner. He attended an early public lecture that I gave in Pittsburgh on Plato's *Timaeus*. Not long after that, he moved to the New School in New York City, becoming a valued colleague of Hannah Arendt, Hans Jonas, and others. A decade intervened, and our paths did not cross until I gave a lecture in New York. It must have been on a related topic because Reiner came up to me after the lecture.

---

3 For the Hölderlin poem, see "Hölderlin's 'Hymn to Serenity': A Newly Discovered Poem," translated, with introduction and commentary, in *The Graduate Faculty Philosophy Journal* (New School for Social Research) XI, no. 1 (1986): 3–15. Reiner Schürmann has left us a number of incomparable books, including two of the most challenging books on Heidegger—and beyond Heidegger—that we possess: *Heidegger on Being and Acting: From Principles to Anarchy*, trans. Christine-Marie Gros (Bloomington: Indiana University Press, 1987), and *Broken Hegemonies*, trans. Reginald Lilly (Bloomington: Indiana University Press, published posthumously in 1996 and reprinted in 2003).

—If I am not mistaken, you were saying precisely the same thing the last time I heard you.

My heart sank. Reiner was so impressive, one of the most beautiful and brilliant human beings I have ever met, someone that no one ever wanted to disappoint. I recall Alphonso Lingis, one of the most original and profound thinkers in the United States, telling me how terrified he was of Reiner! As for me, I suddenly had to wonder: had I made no progress at all over the past ten years? Reiner then smiled.

—How wonderful to find someone at last who is consistent.

My heart returned to its station, even a bit higher than usual.

Many years later, not long before Reiner died, and knowing of his illness, I phoned him and asked if I could come to New York to see him.

—No, he replied, you will remember me the way I was, not the way I am now.

After Reiner's death, philosopher Judith Walz, who cared for him during those final months, sent me two articles of clothing that belonged to him: a Japanese *gi* (the traditional Japanese uniform for practicing martial arts) that his friend Louis Comtois had given him, and a white woolen sweater that Reiner's mother had knitted for him. I have never understood why Judith Walz honored me in this way, but I wear them as often as I can, in gratitude to both Reiner and to Judith and in the hope that some of the genius will rub off. But it is high time to end these tales and return to the "Anaximander" translation.

*　*　*

Hannah Arendt, an enthusiastic admirer of Reiner Schürmann, read the "Anaximander" translation only at a late stage in the preparation of *Early Greek Thinking*, although I am certain that Glenn would have run by her any doubts he may have had about my renderings. In any case, her reception of the translation was very generous; it convinced her that I should continue as a translator and become a member of the informal "editorial board." I remember a conversation with her in the Schlossbergblick Hotel, where she always stayed during her visits to Freiburg, about Heidegger's treatment of the word κατά in the phrase κατὰ τὸ χρεών, usually rendered as "according to necessity." The context in Heidegger's "Anaximander" essay is as follows: "The word κατά precedes τὸ χρεών. It means 'from up there,' or 'from over there.' The κατά refers back to something from which something lower comes to presence, as from something higher and as its consequent. That in reference to which the κατά is pronounced has in itself an incline [*ein Gefälle*] along which other things have fallen out in this or that way" (H 334; EGT 49).

I was no doubt pleased with myself for having found a way to save two senses of *Gefälle*, the "incline" by which things have "fallen out" in this or that way. *Der Fall* is a "case," as in a legal case or the case in a noun's declension, but also a "fall" or "drop." *Eine Falle* is a trap, and *Gefallen* is the verb "to please." Whenever you feel pleased by a translation from the German, you can be certain that you have fallen into a trap. Obviously, not all these senses could or should be retained in a rendering of *Gefälle*. "Incline" was not a bad solution. But Hannah spoke of a stairway, remarking that the *Gefälle* between the steps should be regular so that one does not stumble and fall. *Gefälle* has to do with the rate of fall or descent, for example, of a mountain stream: the Chärstellenbach of the Maderan Valley in the central Swiss Alps has such a steep *Gefälle* that an incredible amount of water flows by at any given interval of space and time and with reckless speed. Hannah would have loved a passage in the fifth of Rilke's *Letters to a Young Poet*, dated Rome, October 29, 1903. Rilke is praising the many beautiful stairways of Rome, which, he says, have as their model a wide stream of water rolling over stones—*breit im Gefäll Stufe aus Stufe gebärend wie Welle aus Welle*, "wide in their regular descent, each step giving birth to the next, like a wave giving birth to a wave." She would also have loved a sentence—a very Heideggerian sentence—I found years later in Musil's *Der Mann ohne Eigenschaften*: "A brook that drives factories loses its *Gefälle*." In Musil's novel, Agathe remembers her brother Ulrich saying this as a metaphor for how "goodness" can exhaust itself in "good deeds."[4]

The stream I mentioned to Arendt, however, is one near my home in the Black Forest, which flows over moss-covered stones down a steep hillside. The hillside's incline is more or less regular, except that each stone or boulder over which the stream pours varies in size and shape. (I later discovered the carpenter's word for what I was calling the "back" or the "instep" of the treads on a stairway: the correct word is "tread riser" or, simply, "riser." The "risers" for a stream in the wild, because of the irregularly shaped rocks over which it flows, are usually wildly uneven and zigzag.) At

---

4 Robert Musil, *Der Mann ohne Eigenschaften*, ed. Adolf Frisé (Reinbek bei Hamburg: Rowohlt Verlag, 1978), 729.

some point, I called the stream a "cascade," *eine Kaskade* (from the Latin *cadere*, "to fall," the source also of our word "cadence"), and I recall that her face lit up with the sound of that word. She repeated it several times, saying, "That's it, that's it!" She did not necessarily mean as a translation of the word *Gefälle* but as part of a context or word-field that would *lead to* a good translation. And I think she simply enjoyed the sound of the word, the beautiful noise that "cascade" makes whether spoken in German or French or English. I recall many other instances when she would repeat a line of verse by Heine or Hölderlin or Goethe, savoring each word, her deep voice—she could have been one of The Whiskeyhill Singers—growling it out between long drags on her cigarette, which was her way of singing. I would not say, as Mary McCarthy does, that there was something of the diva about Arendt at moments like this, but I have to accept McCarthy's description of something "theatrical" about Arendt: "What was theatrical about Hannah was a kind of spontaneous power of being seized by an idea, an emotion, a presentiment, whose vehicle her body then became, like an actor's. And this power of being seized and worked upon, often with a start, widened eyes, 'Ach!' (before a picture, a work of architecture, some deed of infamy), set her apart from the rest of us like a high electrical charge" (YB, quoting McCarthy, 199).

All I would add to this is that a single word, a word like "cascade," could have this remarkable effect on Arendt.

We must also have labored over *Geschick versucht sich an Geschick*, if only because Arendt had more *Geschick* than anyone and in both senses of the word, namely, both "skill" and "destiny." But here my notes and my memory fail me.

Arendt's savoring of words and her love of language sometimes meant trouble for other translators—I was fortunate to have been spared, but others were not so lucky. Glenn, Joan, Hannah, and I met one morning at the Schlossbergblick Hotel to talk about a number of typescripts of proposed translations that Harper's had sent us, one of them a translation of a Heidegger text on a German poet. Each of us had read the script and had our own thoughts about it, but Hannah was the first to speak. That was not usually the case. She was usually quite reticent, a good listener, and quite aware that English was not her native tongue. But she turned to some pages in the typescript that she had earmarked, reading from them nothing of *Heidegger*'s text but only the German and the proposed English of the *poetry* on which Heidegger was commenting. It was painful. She then put the pages back on the table and announced, "This person has wooden ears." She then shunted the typescript aside. In English, we insist that an unmusical person has a tin ear, but in German—and in Hannah's English—the ear was wooden, and it was not the wood of a marimba. We all nodded our assent and went on to the next proposal.

Each of us, and Arendt, too, I am certain, felt a twinge of regret about all that labor on the part of the translator, which was now labor lost, but she knew that the first priority in translation was to protect two languages, the original and the "target" language (horrible expression!). She affirmed something that Glenn used to say on many occasions: translations usually fail because of trouble in one's primary language, the so-called target. The worst mistake a translator can make is to assume that he or she is competent in at least one of the two languages, in his or her *Muttersprache*—or in some cases *Vatersprache*. There is no comfort anywhere. Glenn and I, working hard on the introduction to *Being and Time* for the *Basic Writings* anthology, spent most of our time worrying the English and American language(s) that we had been born into, as we tried to find a way to render the German. We never stopped using every tool we could think of, especially *Roget's Thesaurus*, in our search for words and word fields. And even after we had found a decent alternative to a failed translation of a word or phrase, Glenn would often say, "There will be a third way; let's put it aside for now." That is why he and Hannah Arendt could be such close friends: their love of and respect for language was paramount.

Glenn Gray's correspondence with me—I have sixty-eight letters from him, dating from August 15, 1973, to October 23, 1977, six days before his death in Colorado Springs—tells me much more about the gestation of *Early Greek Thinking*. In that first letter to me, Glenn lists his emendations to the "Logos" essay I had sent him. He refers to Joan Stambaugh's corrections as being more important than his own, but I no longer have a record of hers: they must have been absorbed into my typewritten drafts (no computers back then!) and then discarded after the book appeared. Among the issues noted in this list, Glenn is thinking over the translation of *sich ereignen*, and he suggests the biblical "come to pass," "biblical" in the sense of the King James version—and therefore eloquent. He resisted both "eventuation" and "appropriation," the first for aesthetic reasons, the second for perhaps the same philosophical reasons that caused Derrida to invent "propriation." A second full page and part of a third page, single-spaced, list various typos but also matters of substance: *gleichsam*, "as it were," which I had omitted from a passage; *einen Wink*, not an "insight," as I had it, but a "hint" or a "clue"; *zugleich*, "at the same time," which I had omitted; *bildarm*, not "prosaic," since thinking for Heidegger is essentially poetic, but rather "'nonpictorial' or something similar." And sometimes there were simply words requiring a less Germanic English: *vielmehr*, not "much more" but "rather"; *zusammenfallen*, not "to fall together" but "to coincide."

It will be tiresome for my readers, no doubt, to be dragged through these details, but such details determine whether a translation succeeds or fails. Virtually every translation I sent to Glenn received this kind of detailed scrutiny, line by line, word for word. At the same time, Glenn and I wrote back and forth about the forest that contained all these trees—speculating on what Heidegger might have meant by any given phrase against the backdrop of the whole. From time to time, Glenn would instruct me to ask Heidegger for guidance on my next visit with him, and I always did so.

A further word about the "Logos" essay. I did not know at the time that Jacques Lacan had tried his hand at translating the essay into French—and it is good that I did not know it, for his rendering would have befuddled me. Yet his translation, published in the first issue of *La psychanalyse* (1956, 59–79), is a psychoanalytic tour de force—"force," just one letter away from "farce"—since Lacan takes liberties that only an analyst would dare take. In this case, the liberty in question involves the very meaning of λόγος. Heidegger regularly defines the meaning of λόγος in terms of *sammeln* and *Versammlung*, "to gather," and "gathering together." Lacan translates Heidegger's *Versammlung*, which for Derrida is the bête noire of Heidegger's thought, not as "gathering," however, but as "redistribution," "reapportionment," or even "diffusion," *répartir*. Lacan's outrageous translation of *Versammlung* is no Freudian slip on his part, nor is it even a Lacanian *lapsus*. Rather, it is the mark of a subject that is rent by desire, the so-called barred subject; it is the mark of the phallus as signifier, which works its effects only in and through dispersion and absence. Lacan, as translator, is daring to render the *resistance* within Heidegger's text, understanding his "Logos" as a response to the call of *desire*, not to the call of *being*. Thus my "final word" about the "Logos" essay, at least as Jacques Lacan reads it, is that no element of language, and therefore no translation, is ever final. It waits on the next *redistribution*.[5]

But to return to a more mundane level of translation, which is the level that I occupied as a young translator. From one of these early letters of Glenn's, I note that my former professors at Duquesne, John Sallis and André Schuwer, also read the essays that went into *Early Greek Thinking*. The more I look into the history of these early translations, the more I realize my debts to others, many others. As I have already indicated, the essay that received the most attention was "The Anaximander Fragment." Both Glenn and Sherry Gray—she from a classicist's point of view—worked carefully through my version, as Glenn's letter of March 15, 1974, indicates. (Sherry, Glenn's daughter, was working on her doctorate in classics at Boston University, but she devoted endless time and her great talents to the Heidegger translation project.) His (or their) comments were particularly valuable, and whereas I would like to reproduce them all here, I will cite only a few— they fill two pages of single-spaced type:

> 1. *Das Seiende* we translate usually as beings, τὰ ὄντα. The plural prevents one in class teaching from talking of big *B* and little *b*. I talked this over with Heidegger and he readily agreed that he thought of the plural here, as in τὰ ὄντα. Sometimes it is desirable to use the singular nevertheless and then we insert the word "particular" before "being." I note in this essay a few instances where you properly use the singular without qualification, but usually you should change them to accord with other translations. Okay?
> 2. *Versammeln, Versammlung* is best rendered as "gathering," "to gather," rather than "assembling." When we meet I shall tell you a story about Jean Beaufret, Heidegger, and I discovering that this word goes back to the medieval *gattern*, the union of two, and hence back to ἀγαθόν. We got quite excited about the matter. Beaufret had objected that our translation of *versammeln* as "assemble" or "collect" was too external, and Heidegger

---

5 For further discussion of Lacan's translation, see chap. 5 of David Farrell Krell, *Derrida and Our Animal Others* (Bloomington: Indiana University Press, 2013). Lacan's translation of "gathering" as "redistributing" might have astonished—and pleased—Derrida, who worried a great deal about Heidegger's insistence on *Versammlung* as *gathering*, but I do not know whether he knew of it or ever commented on it. An excellent account of Lacan's translation is Hans-Dieter Gondek, "*Logos* und Übersetzung: Heidegger als Übersetzer Heraklits—Lacan als Übersetzer Heideggers," in *Übersetzung und Dekonstruktion*, ed. Alfred Hirsch (Frankfurt am Main: Suhrkamp, 1997), 263–348. I am grateful to Gerhard Richter of Brown University for sending me Gondek's remarkable essay and to Jeffrey Powell of Marshall University for sending me, many years ago now, Lacan's translation of "Logos."

explained that he thinks of *versammeln* as an ontological word with inner power, not an external bringing together. A good dictionary will tell you, as mine does, that "gather" *is* different from "collect" or "assemble". . . .
7. *lichtend-bergende Versammlung*—"the gathering that lightens and shelters." Heidegger thinks of *Licht* both as making lighter (*leicht*) and as illumination. So [Albert] Hofstadter and I hit on "lighten," which is delightfully ambiguous. *Bergen* seems also to have the sense here of protecting or sheltering. Please think it over and also note whether Joan agrees with us.

It is important to notice that these suggestions were always tentative in at least two senses of that word. First, no translator was ever constrained by them but in the end had to find the way by his or her own lights; second, Glenn, Hannah, Joan, and I changed our minds often enough about which of the many possible solutions was best. The more important the word was for Heidegger, the less certain we all were about how to render it in English. Let us call this inverse ratio of self-assuredness to aptness of translation, at least when it comes to the most important notions in a text, "Gray's Law," in his honor, even if it seems likely that translators have been obeying that law for a long time now.

As for "gathering" being related to *gattern*, "the union of two" in coupling or mating, and thus to "the good," Lacan would have smiled broadly and affirmed that he had known this all along. "The gathering that lightens and shelters" is a problem we will have to come back to in the next chapter.

I received my first copy of *Early Greek Thinking* on July 19, 1975. That I was inordinately proud of it, especially after all the hassles that had occurred during its making, is indicated by the passage from Nietzsche's unpublished notebooks (from 1868 to 1869) that I sketched onto the frontispiece, here in translation: "A small community still lives that takes artistic pleasure in the world of Greek forms and is completely charmed by that world; a still smaller community survives for which the thinkers of antiquity have not yet been thought through to the end—indeed, for which the thinkers of antiquity themselves have not yet ceased thinking."

* * *

That same letter of March 15, 1974, from Glenn Gray also says, "Your division of the *Nietzsche* volumes seems now just right to me, as do your English titles for them." By the time I had moved to Germany, in the summer of 1974, after spending the winter in the Spanish Pyrenees, two translation projects had already been agreed on: a translation of Heidegger's eleven-hundred-page *Nietzsche* and an anthology of his writings for university students. The anthology, eventually called *Basic Writings*, occupied my first three years in Germany. It was an enormous amount of work, and it left me so exhausted that I had to ask for help with the *Nietzsche* translation. Let me discuss the anthology first.[6]

The initial question, of course, was what should go into the anthology. On November 12, 1974, I wrote to my parents, "The Heidegger anthology is shaping up, slowly but surely, as I make plan after plan, changing my mind about what belongs where!" Harper's had given me a very strict page limit, one that caused me to edit down two of the pieces—"The Origin of the Work of Art" and "The Letter on Humanism"—a terrible mistake of judgment that was corrected in the second edition of the anthology in 1993. Heidegger had direct input into the book's contents, and he affirmed the final form that the anthology took. My first proposal to him, however, which I unfortunately no longer have, included much more from *Being and Time* than the introduction. Section 40 on anxiety, for example, and section 53 on the full existential conception of death, were included in the proposal, as were at least parts of section 44, on "Dasein, Disclosedness, and Truth." I note that both Glenn Gray and especially Hannah Arendt desired this fuller presentation of Heidegger's magnum opus. Heidegger took the time to examine the proposal carefully, and the only real objection he had pertained to the treatment of *Being and Time*. He asked me, in that raspy, high-pitched voice of his, and looking at me with those protruding eyes, yet quite calmly and in the friendliest possible way, "What is the *principle of selection* for what you have chosen here?" *Das Prinzip der Auswahl* was his expression, and when I heard it, something like my Dasein drained out of me. An honest answer would have been, "Well, I just sort of *liked* these sections," but luckily honesty was kept in abeyance that day. It was clear to me, and to us both, that there was no such *principle* of selection operative here. After a long discussion, we agreed that it would be best to offer the introduction to *Being and Time* alone.

There was something like a principle of selection for the anthology as a whole, however. Our effort was to offer as many aspects of Heidegger's thought as possible to students, aspects that would speak not only to young philosophers but also to budding architects, artists, mathematicians, natural scientists, poets, and so on. When Harper's granted me a bit more space

---

6 Martin Heidegger, *Basic Writings: From* Being and Time *(1927) to* The Task of Thinking *(1964)*, 2nd ed. (San Francisco: HarperCollins, 1993), referred to in the body of my text as "BW," with page number.

for the second edition, I made certain that "The Origin of the Work of Art" and "The Letter on Humanism" appeared complete and then added an essay on language, one that I felt would be most comprehensible to linguists and students of languages and literatures. On December 15, 1974, I wrote to my parents:

> The anthology is coming along slowly but surely, but the *Nietzsche* translation only slowly. After Christmas I have to get busy on the latter, which I haven't touched in a couple of months. No word from Harper & Row about either project yet, even though Glenn Gray writes them about once a week. He assures me that all is a "go," so far as they are concerned, and that they are just too lazy or disorganized to write. He even says that they are no worse than most other publishers! More's the pity. I may be able to visit Heidegger shortly after the Christmas break to talk about the anthology, if his health and energy hold up. And his interest, of course!

And six months later, on May 17, 1975, the following:

> Dr. Gray is here now and we are working like a couple of old Roman slaves, hoping that the September deadline for the anthology can be met. He is a fine gentleman, and we are enjoying his visit. . . . Our [i.e., Frank Capuzzi's and my] translation of *Early Greek Thinking* should be out soon, that is, by the fall. Frank and I completed our work on the proofs, and so we are sitting around waiting for the book to be printed and bound. . . . I visited with Heidegger—alone—yesterday for a quarter of an hour. The immediate occasion was to pick up some books Glenn and I need for our work on the anthology. But Heidegger invited me in and we had a nice discussion about that project and other matters. I'm astonished by how much he knows about me. You would figure that the greatest living philosopher, at almost 86, would have other things to occupy his mind. He is quite a gentleman, and it is really a shame I could not have gotten to know him earlier and done some studying under him.

Once the selections had been determined for the first edition of the book, Glenn and I settled down to work on the introduction to *Being and Time*. Glenn was able to stay for an entire month in the house where I lived, and we worked every day from dawn till dusk on a draft translation of the introduction by Joan Stambaugh, who was retranslating *Being and Time*. Joan later accepted the results of our work and used our version for her new translation, eventually published by SUNY Press. Therein lies an unhappy tale, however, and I pause now to tell it.

Joan Stambaugh was, as I said, an energetic and effervescent person. I remember her visiting my family at our home in the Black Forest several times, each time disappearing for several hours to head up toward the source of the Möhlinbach, the brook that flows through the valley—or, after a rain and after snowmelt, *surges* through it. She would find a secluded spot and then lie down in the brook for an hour or so. I never saw this, but she reported it to us with a laugh, and her face, red verging on purple, testified to it. Now, I have swum in Lake Michigan at five in the morning in October, and my most recent dip in the Aegean Sea was on January 14, but I would not, could not let the sparkling, frigid waters of the Möhlinbach flow over my body, not even in July. I asked her how she could stand it.

—I'm Scandinavian! she replied.

Joan's German was far superior to mine, and she was a serious philosopher, one who commanded and received everyone's respect. Glenn and Hannah were also very fond of her. However, as I once again read Glenn's letters to me from 1974, I see that he refers to her "not being well" many times. There was obviously a shadow side to her manic, energy-laden states. When she was on the shadow side, her ability to work diminished, sometimes stopping altogether. One of the things that became difficult for her was the repeated refinement and constant polishing that translation requires. Glenn and I both felt that Joan's initial effort to translate *Sein und Zeit* required a major reworking. There were simply too many impossible choices for the key words of *Being and Time*—and almost the entire vocabulary of *Sein und Zeit* is presented in those opening eight sections of the introduction, as one would expect. In a sense, Glenn and I were required to translate all of *Sein und Zeit* in cameo form, *en miniature*.

It was an amazing month of work. And the result of our labors, even after all these years, generally pleases me. What we were unable to do, of course, was to look at the rest of Joan's work. Years later, when I was teaching at the University of Essex in England, Harper & Row wrote to ask me if I would rework the entire manuscript of Joan's translation of *Being and Time*. As it stood, they refused to publish it. I knew that she had given her life's blood to this translation, and I also knew that she had worked with Heidegger on parts of it, but I also recalled the many problems that Glenn and I had encountered in it. In fact, I informed Harper's that they would do better to revise the Macquarrie–Robinson translation: there were many problematic choices in that earlier version as well, but at least those two scholars were remarkably consistent in their renderings of the German, and their notes on the German text were very useful. One could emend some of their choices for a range of key "existentials," and the translation would continue to serve well.[7] Harper's would not follow my advice, however, so I wrote to both Harper's and Joan, asking whether a doctoral student of mine—Will McNeill, who was both a Germanist and a philosopher, and who is now a professor of philosophy at DePaul University and one of the very best scholars and translators of Heidegger at work today—could take on the task of revising Joan's work. I would help as much as I could, but my duties as chair and senior lecturer made it impossible for me to do the required work.

For reasons that I now entirely understand and regret, Joan was furious and hurt by our insistence on a collaborator. Joan's and my friendship ended then and there, I fear, and during the final years of her life, we had no contact at all. Glenn once wrote me to say, in another context altogether, that translation is "bad for the soul," and I think he may be right: it is such hard work and it is so disrespected, or at best so taken for granted, that insult is often added to injury. Furthermore, the responsibility the translator has to assume is too heavy a burden: botch your own text, and only you and your text suffer, and the fault is your own; botch the text of another, a text that you know requires your best effort, and the fault ripples outward and damages what you most wanted to save. It was Joan who had met with me in Coraopolis, encouraged me, and brought me onto the team, as it were; it was also she who had taken me on my first visit to the Heideggers. She surely felt betrayed. For my part, I could never really communicate to her with candor the extent of the problems I saw in her translation. Even today, despite Dennis Schmidt's valiant efforts to improve the SUNY edition of *Being and Time*, it seems to me that Heidegger's magnum opus has to be retranslated from beginning to end. It is, after all, one of the greatest works in the philosophical literature, and it deserves our best efforts. There are translation teams at work today who could do this—Will McNeill and Julia Ireland, whose Heidegger-Hölderlin volumes are brilliantly done (no wooden ears there), or Daniela Vallega-Neu and Richard Rojcevich, who have translated the formidable *Beiträge zur Philosophie* so ably—if only some publisher were willing to release yet another translation of *Sein und Zeit*. But this seems unlikely at least for the present generation, and that is a shame.

---

7 In the chapters on Arendt in this book, there is further discussion of the earliest efforts of Edward Schouten Robinson at translating *Sein und Zeit*.

To return to the anthology. It appeared in the spring of 1977, but not before a whole series of crises, which I want to detail here. Apart from the crises, however, there were delightful discoveries. Most important, I found that the best translators of Heidegger were absolutely dedicated to the originals and not to their own versions, so that by and large they did not object to my effort—essential in my view then as now—to unify the vocabulary of the anthology as much as possible. Albert Hofstadter, the gifted translator of "The Origin of the Work of Art" and "Building Dwelling Thinking," was a model of courtesy, cooperation, and kindness; W. B. Barton Jr., writing also on behalf of Vera Deutsch, was equally as forthcoming about the suggested changes. When I think back on my correspondence with Glenn Gray, who as general editor of the Heidegger Series carried out all these difficult negotiations, I am filled with gratitude: the participating translators, under the gentle yet vigilant guidance of Glenn, showed the generosity of spirit that I have found in every thinker with whom I have had the privilege to work—among them, Heidegger, Arendt, and Derrida.

The crises often came in the form of obstructions introduced by the German publisher of Heidegger's Collected Works, the Klostermann firm of Frankfurt, or by confusion and ineptitude at Harper's. Here I will rely principally on my correspondence with Glenn Gray, for me the most important source of information about the Heidegger translations. And Glenn's letters, if I may add, also have a great deal of philosophy in them.[8] Yet much of our correspondence involves the irascible German publishers of Heidegger's works, above all, the Klostermann firm. Add to this the overworked and underpaid editors at Harper & Row, and you have the makings of a long-standing fight over the world rights in English for Heidegger's works. The first sign of trouble appears in a letter to my parents dated July 24, 1975:

> I found out today that Harper & Row do not have the rights for three of the most important essays in the anthology—the German publisher will sue if we go on with the project. Harper & Row assured me before I began last

8 I discuss these letters in greater detail and on a broader range of topics in "A Smile and a Sense of Tragedy: Letters from J. Glenn Gray," *Philosophy Today* 25, no. 2 (Summer 1981): 95–113. I reread all the letters once again recently, marveling at their wisdom and generosity of spirit. Let me also note here Elisabeth Young-Bruehl's excellent account of Glenn's friendship with Hannah Arendt, especially at YB 440–45. I am also wondering whether Glenn's and Hannah's correspondence will be published; clearly, it would be crucial for understanding her writing of *The Life of the Mind.*

November that all the rights were in their hands and that there would be no problem. So for a year I took their word for it. Now that I am preparing the final manuscript, after all the work is completed, I find out that there is a major legal obstacle. I've written Glenn Gray about it, and am simply going to sit back and wait until they resolve the matter. A year of one person's time is enough to waste. But I don't have much hope for the project. The German publisher is dead set against it, and Harper & Row will let the whole thing fall through if the threat of a suit comes up. But I'm not giving up altogether: as I say, I'll let à few weeks pass to see if anybody else is interested enough to negotiate a settlement with the German publisher. . . . A real shame, though, since all my work was done—the manuscript was to be sent away at the end of August for printing. So, live and learn. The first volume of translations is now out: *Early Greek Thinking* is its title, and I will send you a copy as soon as Harper & Row send me a few. Basically it is well done, most of the printing errors being in the Greek.

I will ignore here the early stages of the publishers' quarrels over the anthology, in which Martin Heidegger eventually intervened. At each phase of this imbroglio over the rights, Heidegger would shake his head and say, "I've *told* Klostermann. . . ." Yet I soon learned that publishers and authors live on two different planets following quite distinct orbits. Add to this two different cultures and languages, and the metaphor inflates to cosmic crisis.

To be fair, the Klostermann firm was only half of the problem. An undated letter from Heidegger—it could have been anytime during 1975, since the rights problem was a perpetual companion of the project, but was probably written in midsummer—says, in translation, "I am extremely sorry that you and Herr Gray are now having difficulties with the publishing of your excellent translation work. But the blame lies squarely with Harper & Row, who have not bothered to secure the translation rights. I've now asked Klostermann to arrange matters in a generous way, but I cannot order him about in such matters. I wrote him immediately to say that I place the highest value on your and Herr Gray's translations. I truly hope that the issue can be resolved to everyone's satisfaction. With friendly greetings and best wishes, etc." A second undated letter, probably from mid-October 1975, from Elfride Heidegger, who often served as Martin's secretary and who actually knew more about rights questions than he did, says, "I'm happy to be finally able to tell you that Klostermann has communicated the following to me: 'The firm Harper & Row has received the rights [*die Lizenz*] for the *Holzwege* volume as well as for all the component publications [*Teilausgaben*] for the planned anthology that they are producing.' With hearty greetings, etc."

I was clearly feeling more confident when I wrote home on September 30, 1975: "If all goes well I can mail it [the printer's manuscript of the anthology] to New York by the end of October. . . . I was at Heidegger's not long ago and he assured me that all would be well with the rights problem, that the German publisher ultimately had to follow his wishes in the matter. So, with Heidegger on our side, I feel as though the team may win after all. I'm anxious to have the book behind me, since it has absorbed all my time and attention, leaving me free for nothing else really."

However, the problem was that three of the anthology texts came from *Wegmarken*, not *Holzwege*, and so the wrangle continued up to the time of the production of the anthology. The final stage in the rights quarrel came in August 1976, as the book was about to be printed. On August 10, 1976, Glenn wrote me to say that both he and Harper's would be grateful for a letter from Elfride—for Martin had died on May 26 of that year—to Harper & Row listing all the texts to be taken up into the anthology and expressing support for their publication. The Klostermann firm was in the process of buying all the rights to Heidegger's works from Günter Neske of Pfullingen and Max Niemeyer of Tübingen, an expensive and diplomatically delicate process for them, so the rights issues (and the economics behind such issues) were more volatile than ever. Whereas Martin had said that he could not order Klostermann about, it was also clear that the publisher could not contravene the wishes of the Heidegger family. I prepared the letter and brought it to Elfride, who signed and dated it by hand on August 25, 1976. I sent it to Harper & Row soon thereafter. That was the end of the first and longest-lasting crisis.

The second crisis falls into two parts, both involving my editorial work. The first was an instance of my over-editing, the second of my under-editing. Each shows how fragile the ethics of translation can become. Glenn and Sherry Gray went over every word of the original translations and also my edited versions. At a certain point, well into the project, I must have felt a greater freedom—Glenn called it "the editorial itch"—to alter already approved and published translations. I did this in the name of a certain unity of vocabulary, but it became clear that I had overstepped that boundary on many occasions. Glenn was furious with me, and rightly so, for he then had to restore many of the original choices, which meant double the workload for him and Sherry. His letters from late December 1975 and early January 1976, already desperately sad because of Hannah's unexpected death in early December, contain the harshest reproofs I ever received from him, for he was the gentlest of souls, never quick to anger.

And then in July of that year, very near the end of the project, something equally distressing occurred. One of the translations that was intended for the anthology was revised (not by me but by the translator) in a way that Glenn could not accept, revised radically, without Glenn's having had a chance to go over it. Meanwhile, I had acquiesced in the new version, throwing in the towel, as it were, and Glenn asked me how I could possibly have done so—I had failed in my duties as editor! I can only suppose that by that time I felt browbeaten by the whole project. In a letter home dated June 27, 1976, I apparently refer to the piece in question:

> I've been correcting galley proofs for the anthology. It has been well printed, so there is not a lot of correcting to be done. Still, it is strenuous and boring work, proofreading, and I'll be happy when it is finished. The book is due to appear in September, but I'm skeptical. Yet another set of proofs has to be gone through, and then comes the printing and binding. In general I'm satisfied with the way it looks, except for one piece, which seems to have been translated into Chinese instead of English. But the other nine look okay, and so do my little introductions. I'll be happy when the book *is* a book, and I'll have H&R mail you a copy.

In the case of the essay latterly transmogrified into what the Germans call *Fachchinesisch*, or what Glenn and I called "Pennsylvania Dutch" or "Engleutsch" or "Dinglish," Glenn replaced it with the earlier version, the one that he and Sherry had checked. He then accepted my last-minute emendations, even though the anthology was already at the page-proof stage, the stage we now call "the second run," in which authors normally dare not change a word, much less an entire chapter, because of printer's costs. In this respect, the editors at Harper's were angels of patience.

The third crisis was a personal one because well after the book was published (the publishing date was April 1977), a young friend and colleague, Reginald Lilly, alerted me to the fact that I had skipped a sentence in my translation of Heidegger's "What Is Metaphysics?"

—Impossible! I cried.

I had checked my English version against the German text several times; at one point I read my translation into a tape recorder, playing it back slowly as I read the German. But Reggie was right. On each occasion when I checked my translation, always as carefully as I could, my eyes and my brain betrayed me. I had skipped a sentence of the original! I was able to restore it in the second edition of the book, published in 1993, but I never got over the shock. It did teach me something about proofreading, namely, that when we leave words out of a sentence, our minds restore them and we "read" blissfully on. In one of my recent books, I skipped the verb "is" in two sentences—enacting the withdrawal of being, as it were—seeing the word when it was not there. I am always incredulous when this happens, but Reggie taught me something about finitude, and I am grateful to him. Glenn once wrote me to say that translations are never truly finished, never adequately corrected and polished, and that colleagues, friends, and strangers can often improve them on the spot and off the cuff, as it were. I recall Ralph Waldo Emerson's remarking in an essay or journal entry that the only demonstration of human finitude we need is correcting our page proofs. This may be part of the reason why translation is bad for the soul: the responsibility is so great and the chances to make mortifying bloopers never end but only multiply. Perpetual humiliation is the lot of the translator, even if, every now and again, the inevitable typos are rare and at least some renderings—veritable trouvailles, as Reiner Schürmann once assured me—exceed our expectations.

At all events, a letter home dated March 30, 1977, announces that the anthology "is finally at the printer's," adding, "I mailed the final proofs in last week. Harper & Row pulled a few dumb stunts right up to the last, however, so I'm afraid when the book does appear (June is my guess) I'll have my red pencil in hand. Anyway, the Fates have it on their desk now, and that's fine with me." I have no idea what those "dumb stunts" may have been, but the phrase reflects my state of mind.

Readers may have smiled over my use of the word "crisis," and even "*cosmic* crisis," in the above paragraphs to describe events that now seem to me no more than tempests in a teapot, and I have to confess my tendency to overreact. Glenn attributed this to my youth, but he was too kind. Things have not gotten any better for me in this regard. J. L. Mehta used to write me from India, repeating Meister Eckhart's admonition, "*Gelassenheit in allen dingen.*" Yet releasement or letting-be has never been my strength. What did help to reassure me was the news contained in what turned out to be Glenn's last letter to me: Harper's had sent him a bound copy of the proofs for the anthology so he could teach it to his undergraduates at Colorado College, and he found that the anthology "worked," that is, that his students could read it and understand it. He praised it and me to the rooftops, and I had to remind him that the three people to whom the book was dedicated—Hannah Arendt, Joan Stambaugh, and J. Glenn Gray—deserved equal credit. Only his modesty prevented him from accepting all three-thirds of the dedication.

That the *Basic Writings* volume, with its bright red cover, has been influential in the reception of Heidegger's work in the English-speaking world is, I think, beyond doubt. About forty thousand copies of the second paperback edition have gone out into the world, if I am right, and I have no idea of the numbers for the first edition (1977–92), probably about the same. The book has been used not only for classroom teaching, however. Decades ago, I traveled to Como to give some lectures to Daniél Libeskind's architecture studio, and he greeted me—we had not met before—on the runway of the tiny Como airport with a big smile.

—So you are the Big Red Book! You should be much older!

I replied that working on the anthology certainly should have made me look older and wearier. But Daniél and his young colleagues—architects Donald Bates, Peter Davidson, and Ben Nicholson—took it as a given that Heidegger was an essential source for contemporary architects and artists, and they knew Heidegger's texts very well. Others' appreciation of the anthology has likewise meant a lot to me over the years, as Glenn predicted it would.

As for my looking much older, which by now I have doubtless achieved, I should mention that I recently wrote to the current editor at Harper-Collins about the possibility of rewriting my general introduction to the anthology, partly in response to revelations of Heidegger's antisemitic remarks in the *Black Notebooks*, but also to update the anthology in general. I also proposed adding the essay "Die Zeit des Weltbildes," which I intended to call "The Age When All the World Becomes an Image." The editor showed no interest in expanding or updating the volume, but he did express his surprise that I was still alive. I wanted to reply, as Mark Twain once did, that the reports of my death were exaggerated, but I suppose it was merely a sign that the big red book had become something of an institution. When HarperCollins issued a paperback edition of the *Nietzsche* translation in 1991, they registered it with the Library of Congress as the work of "David Ferrell Kress," which proves either that I am related on my mother's side to a well-known comedian or, on my father's side, am indeed already dead.

Around the time of our work on the anthology, during the mid-1970s, Heidegger began to prepare the publication of his Collected Works—now over a hundred volumes. It was clear that Harper's would never be interested in bringing these new works into English. It was principally Indiana University Press, in the series edited by John Sallis, that undertook the task. I believe I can say that the Indiana series differs from the Harper series in that it is intended for the specialist, not the young student or general reader. The main goal of the Harper series was readability. This was surely Glenn Gray's understanding, since many of his emendations had to do with avoiding Engleutsch. Whenever my translations were too freighted with neologisms or attempts to play with etymologies, Glenn would say *ugh!* and insist on a more elegant solution.

Interestingly, this was Arendt's desire as well: as much as she loved her mother tongue, she loved the English of Shakespeare and Randall Jarrell and W. H. Auden, and she, too, wanted translations that did not *sound* like translations and prose that did not seem forced and unheard-of. Translators will debate the matter of "precision and soul" forever, I suppose, but I will only observe that achieving the elegant and natural flow of English or of any "target" language—even as language *as such* is being stretched to its limits or even pushed beyond its limits—is the most difficult task of the translator. That is my tiny footnote to Walter Benjamin.

*   *   *

Speaking of readability and elegance of language, allow me to add a brief word about Heidegger's *Nietzsche*. In a letter home dated November 12, 1974, I noted that I had developed a final plan for the *Nietzsche* volumes, one that Harper & Row found acceptable: "There will be four English volumes in all," I wrote, "if I can hold out that long." In a later letter, dated July 21, 1976, I mention that "the first volume of the *Nietzsche* is due (in manuscript) in January. I'm about a fourth of the way through it, so I have a lot of work ahead of me." That is merely an indication of how the work on the *Nietzsche* had been held up by the anthology: I was already working on the first Nietzsche lecture course in 1974, and by July of 1976, only a quarter of it had been completed!

I have no other information regarding the timeline of the *Nietzsche* translation, so I revert to the theme of readability, for Heidegger's lecture courses on Nietzsche have always seemed to me to be instances of his best writing. People often kindly credit my translations for this, but no, it has to do with Heidegger's original, which reflects his desire to communicate clearly—and often elegantly—to his student audience.

Even before the *Early Greek Thinking* volume went to the printer's, I had drawn up an outline of the *Nietzsche* project.[9] Some parts of volume II of the 1961 Neske edition had already been extracted from it and translated by Joan Stambaugh in a volume called *The End of Philosophy*. Harper's called for four separate hardbound volumes (combined into two volumes for the paperback edition in 1991), and I immediately began to work on the 1936–37 lecture course, "Will to Power as Art." That work, to repeat, was interrupted by the anthology, which proved to be so time-consuming and exhausting that I eventually had to call for help with the later *Nietzsche* lecture courses. I translated the first two courses, the second one, "The Eternal Recurrence of the Same" (1937), being in my view the high point of the series. Joan did a first draft of the third lecture course, "Will to Power as Knowledge" (1939); Frank Capuzzi did a first draft of the essay "Nietzsche's Metaphysics"; and I did the two undelivered lectures of 1939, "The Eternal Recurrence of the Same and the Will to Power."[10] Finally, volume four of the Harper hardbound *Nietzsche* contained the 1940 lecture course on "European Nihilism," translated by Frank Capuzzi. I believe it is fair to say that I reworked all the translations, editing them much in the way that Glenn and Joan and Hannah had edited me. I added whatever explanatory notes were necessary, checked Heidegger's many citations from Nietzsche's works against the historical-critical Colli–Montinari edition, retranslating many of the passages, and wrote "Analyses" for each of the four volumes. I did not finish the task until 1982, several years before the "personal computer" arrived on my desk, the tool that would have made the translation work so much easier. Imagine translating all these pages without word search, so that every decision to alter a particular word required endless

9 Martin Heidegger, *Nietzsche*, 2 vols. (Pfullingen: G. Neske, 1961). I will refer to the German *Nietzsche* as "N," with volume and page numbers. These two volumes have been translated into four English-language volumes, published by Harper & Row, now HarperCollins, between 1979 and 1984. I will refer to the second, paperback edition, published by HarperCollins in 1991, as "Ni," with volume and page numbers.

10 A first draft of "Nietzsche's Metaphysics" was also prepared by my colleague at Mannheim University, Bruce Pye. I was uncertain at that time about whether Frank Capuzzi was still working on that essay, and Bruce translated the entire essay for me. He never received credit for it, nor certainly any payment, and I have always felt wretched about that. Clearly, I was stretched beyond my limit, working in Germany and publishing in the United States, casting about for help and desperate to find it. After all these decades have passed, I still must repeat my apology to Bruce Pye.

searching—one became totally *verzettelt*, and it was no dream but *Zettel's Nightmare* instead.

I will not comment on translation difficulties regarding the *Nietzsche*, but I will try to justify my remark about the "high point" of the lecture series. What I really mean to say is that Heidegger's *lecture courses* from 1936 to 1940 strike me as infinitely superior to the *essays* on the history of being that occupy much of volume II of the Neske edition. The later essays tend to reduce Nietzsche's position in the history of metaphysics in a way that the positive readings of Nietzsche's texts (in the earlier lecture courses) resist. Although it is only a phrase, it is perhaps useful to characterize the essays as asserting that Nietzsche is the *last metaphysician* of the West, whereas for the lecture courses he is the *most recent thinker* of the West. The terms "last" and "most recent" translate the same German word, *der letzte*, but for Heidegger, there is all the difference in the world between metaphysics and the thinking of being. My feeling has always been that all the evidence provided by Heidegger's *readings* of Nietzsche's works, especially the reading of *Thus Spoke Zarathustra* in the 1937 course on "The Eternal Recurrence of the Same," refutes Heidegger's efforts to enclose Nietzsche within the house of metaphysics.

On the spine of the German volumes of Heidegger's *Nietzsche*, designed, I believe, by Günter Neske's wife, only two names appeared: "heidegger" and "nietzsche." It was therefore impossible to say which was the author and which was the title of the work, especially because, as Nietzsche said, "some are born posthumously." What became impossible for Heidegger was a decisive and final evaluation of Nietzsche's *Gedankengut*, the "fund" of his thinking—or, as Derrida would say, the multiple *signatures* of Nietzsche's name and the rich variety of Nietzsche's *styles* of thinking. What this really means is that the efforts to reduce Nietzsche's thinking to a mere inversion of Platonistic metaphysics, or to caricature the thought of eternal recurrence as the rotary machine of technology, as Heidegger later does, are bound to fail. The result is that Heidegger's *Nietzsche*, especially in its *readings* of Nietzsche, is not as remote from Georges Bataille's *Sur Nietzsche* or Pierre Klossowski's *Nietzsche et le cercle vicieux* or even Derrida's *Éperons: les styles de Nietzsche* and Gilles Deleuze's *Nietzsche et la philosophie* as one might have thought. And this may be one of the most positive aspects of Heidegger's reception in the Francophone and Anglophone worlds, not a weakness but a strength.

It may well be that, alas, both Heidegger and Nietzsche are falling into abeyance or going into eclipse in the English-speaking world nowadays. Heidegger's antisemitic remarks, in addition to his initial strong support of National Socialism, to be discussed in later chapters of this book, doubtless explain much of the ostensible decline of interest in his thought. The eclipse of Nietzsche is more difficult to understand—perhaps it is simply our inability to withstand the radical recoil of Nietzsche's genealogical critique or to rise to the challenge of "fashioning a new lyre" for philosophizing. However, as Derrida remarks in his 1984–85 seminar, "The Phantom of the Other," thinkers are measured not by their persistent presence and uninterrupted impact but by the number of eclipses they survive and by the changes in the reception they receive when they do come out of eclipse. No eclipse, I believe, will obscure either Heidegger or Nietzsche for long, at least for those readers who, in Glenn Gray's words, think about "the intimate and the ultimate."

* * *

Before this chapter comes to a close, there are two matters to clear up—for myself—as best I can. Both are about the powers and the vulnerabilities of memory. Even though my notes from the time are fairly detailed, I have vivid memories of discussions with Heidegger about translation issues for which I can find no written record. For example, I remember—or firmly *believe* I remember—taking pages of notes from the *Oxford English Dictionary* to Heidegger to discuss this or that English word as a possible rendering. I particularly remember our discussing some older uses of the verb "to brook." Nowadays, we use the word only negatively, as in "I'll brook no refusal on your part." But apparently the word was once used more positively, and so it seemed to me that it would be an excellent translation of the German word *Brauch*, "custom, usage." The verb *brauchen* means "to need" or "to use," and it may be that the connection with "brook" lies there—as in the colloquial "I don't *need* to hear that from you." Indeed, both the German *brauchen* and the English "to brook" go back to the Latin *fruor*, and both have to do with *usufruct*, that is, the right to reap and to enjoy the crops of a parcel of land.

Heidegger makes much of the word *Brauch* in his "Anaximander's Saying," and I labored over that word. What I remember is that Heidegger, having no contemporary English to speak of—indeed, I never heard a single word of English from him—was able to respond to Old and Middle

English quite well. This is not surprising, given the Nordic input into Anglo-Saxon. It is no exaggeration to say that the *Oxford English Dictionary* was as valuable a tool of translation for me as any German or German-English dictionary.

What makes this vivid memory about "to brook" doubtful, however, is that I had completed my work on the Anaximander translation shortly before I met Heidegger, so I cannot imagine what could have occasioned a conversation about it. Heidegger doubtless uses the word *brauchen* in other texts of his, such as *Was heisst Denken?* (at 114-17), and we may have been discussing one of these—I simply cannot remember.

Nor can I remember the precise date of another conversation I had with him, one that I never recorded but that is clear in my memory—and it is one of the most humorous moments in our encounter, so I want to record it here. I was working on that same 1951–52 lecture course, *What Is Called Thinking?* for the anthology, and I came across a sentence I simply could not unravel. I took it to him. He sat there reading the passage several times over, in no hurry to say anything. Then he looked up and slowly shook his head.

—That's really bad. But you know what I *meant*, so translate *that*.

That scene, along with the discussion of "to brook," are crystal clear in my memory, even though no note of mine records them. Yet I ought to be skeptical—so many decades have flown by! And I am reminded of Jean Piaget's study of memory in young children: he was able to demonstrate that children's *conviction* that they are remembering something correctly bears absolutely no relation to the *veracity* of their memories. Things do not get better as we grow older. Hence, as we turn to my meetings with Heidegger, I will rely as much as I can on the written evidence—my notes taken immediately after each meeting.

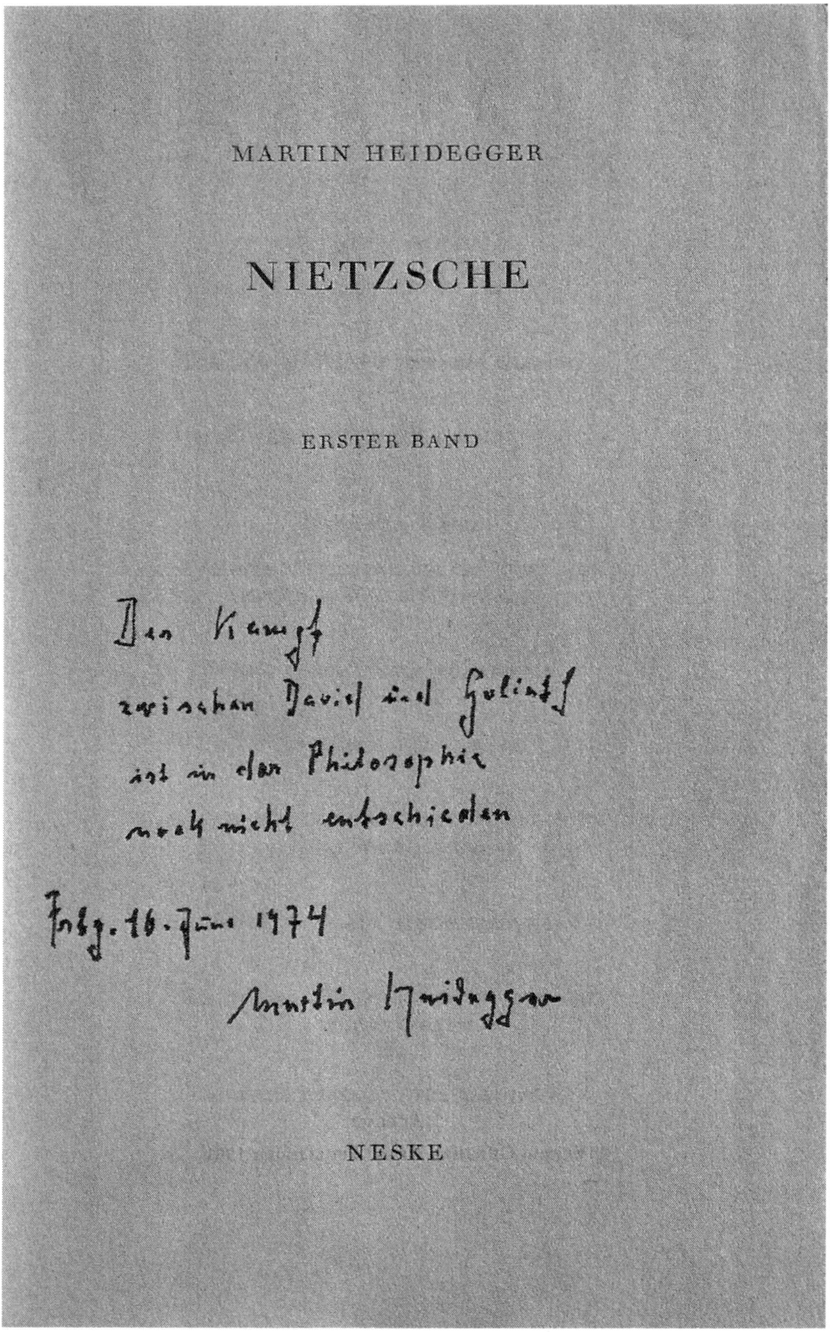

MARTIN HEIDEGGER

NIETZSCHE

ERSTER BAND

Den Kampf
zwischen David und Goliath
ist in der Philosophie
noch nicht entschieden

Frbg. 16. Juni 1974

Martin Heidegger

NESKE

Fig. 3.1 The title page of my copy of the first volume of Heidegger's *Nietzsche*, with Heidegger's "Goliath" inscription, 1974.

3

MEETING MARTIN HEIDEGGER

I will recount my few meetings with Heidegger—four work sessions, with perhaps several other brief meetings; my notes are not clear about the number—by reproducing entire sections of my journals from the time. I will transcribe the notes afresh, even though I published a synopsis of them decades ago, six years after Heidegger's death.[1]

I often have a difficult time with my handwritten notes: they are clearly "blue-eyed and breathless" in tone, and an old man with fading hazel eyes has to take a deep breath and reduce all those doses of adulation and enthusiasm. Nevertheless, these were exciting meetings for a young and not so very well prepared philosopher—I had just turned thirty at the time of our first meeting. After transcribing my journal notes and reproducing them as faithfully as possible, I will provide some comments about the memories that have lasted beyond the note-taking. How I remember these things *now* may be as valuable as those contemporary jottings, no matter what the archivists may insist.

My "Work Sessions" article begins by referring to a story Aristotle reports about Heraclitus. Heidegger recounts it in his "Letter on Humanism." As the story goes, the renowned Ephesian was warming his backside at a stove on a chilly winter morning when some visitors arrived. They were anxious to see a thinker in action and were embarrassed to see Heraclitus in an all-too-human position. He put them at ease by saying, "Come on in; here too the gods are present." According to the "Work Sessions," I did not wish to be one of Heidegger's tourists, but that is only partly true. I had

---

1 "Work Sessions with Martin Heidegger," *Philosophy Today* 26, nos. 2/4 (Summer 1982): 126–38.

spent several years studying and admiring his work, and I was thrilled to meet the man. Yet my good upbringing, if I may say so, made me chary of wasting his time. I am gregarious (some would say garrulous) by nature, at least by half—the Irish half—but the other half is German and terribly responsible and disciplined.

Initially, my contact with Heidegger was indirect, with messages going back and forth through F.-W. von Herrmann, with whom I later quarreled because of the changes he had introduced into Heidegger's *Sein und Zeit* without footnoting them. But at the time, I was following von Herrmann's seminars, and every now and then I prevailed on him to take a translation question to Heidegger. That changed in June 1974 when Joan Stambaugh, urged by Hannah Arendt and Glenn Gray, offered to introduce me to Heidegger. From that point on, I could take my questions directly to him.

If my notes are accurate, there were four extended work sessions that took place between June 1974 and January 1976, along with several brief unrecorded meetings during those years. The four work sessions had to do with the following matters, some of them mentioned in the preceding chapter:

1. Heidegger's lectures on Nietzsche at Freiburg University between 1936 and 1940, which I was beginning to edit and translate into English.

2. Discussions concerning a number of his later essays, with a view to their inclusion in the English-language anthology of his works that I was preparing for Harper & Row.

3. Circumstances surrounding the composition of the "Introduction" to *Being and Time*, and the much-discussed problem of that book's "incompleteness."

4. The significance of the word *bergen* in his later essays. *Bergen* means "to rescue, preserve, safeguard," but, because its negation (*entbergen*) means "to uncover" and "to reveal," there is at least a suggestion in *bergen* of a hiding away or concealing. Because Heidegger defines truth as *Unverborgenheit*, "unconcealment," one has to wonder how *bergen* relates to it—if not by sheer negation. In other words, truth, in Heidegger's view, seems to involve hiddenness, or at least the need to shelter and safeguard whatever reveals itself.

Although I tried to take notes during our sessions, that was usually impossible. The handwritten notes from our first long meeting have gone missing, I do not know how, but those of the other three are preserved. For reasons that escape me, I did not tape-record our conversations, but it was probably because Heidegger would have hated that. In effect, I was not interviewing him, nor was I coming to chat; the purpose of each visit was well defined. After each meeting, I spent hours recording in notebooks the course of our conversations, trying to recall quite precisely the words that passed back and forth. I discovered that my memory for German—Heidegger never spoke English, even though he could read it—was far worse than it was for English. As a result, most of my notes are in English, except when it was important to recall Heidegger's choice of words. He knew how to make himself understood, even if some readers of his works may not credit that claim.

To repeat, the handwritten notes from our first meeting have disappeared, but a typed version is preserved in the Special Collections Department of the DePaul University Library in Chicago. What follows is an edited version—not too heavily edited—of those typed notes. The context of the notes is as follows.

At the time, I was translating the first lecture of the *Nietzsche* series, "Will to Power as Art" and preparing some comments for an "Analysis" at the end of the translation. As I mentioned in the previous chapter, it had struck me that virtually all the commentary on these volumes focused on the *second* volume, which contained lectures and essays in which Heidegger tried to situate Nietzsche in the long and complex history of metaphysics. Most of the material in that second volume circled the question of whether or not Nietzsche was indeed a metaphysician. Did he remain embroiled in Platonistic idealism, or did he merely invert it and so fail to "overcome" it and "escape" it? It seemed that a kind of ambivalence marked Heidegger's reading of Nietzsche. On the one hand, Heidegger insisted that Nietzsche was a fundamental *thinker*, not a clever stylist or an adamant atheist or Clark Kent or anything else, but either the *final* or the *most recent* thinker of Western metaphysics. On the other hand, Heidegger did argue that Nietzsche remained caught up in the traditional "guiding" question of metaphysics, the question concerning the totality of beings, without ever confronting the basic question of being as such.

As I translated the lectures of the *first* volume, especially those on will to power as art and the eternal recurrence of the same, Heidegger's emphasis appeared to fall on Nietzsche *the thinker*. His dedication to Nietzsche's works and to a close reading of a careful selection of his texts was apparent on every page of these published lecture courses. It clearly could not be a matter of either trapping Nietzsche inside the burning building of metaphysics or releasing him entirely from that structure. In short, it seemed to me that Heidegger's contribution to the study of Nietzsche lay in a phrase he used in his 1935 *Introduction to Metaphysics*—we heard it earlier, declaiming between the pages of a church hymnal—to describe the task of his own, Heidegger's, work, namely, "to bring Nietzsche's accomplishment to a full unfolding" (EM 30). That did not seem to me to be a reduction of Nietzsche's importance. Nor did it seem that Heidegger was "refuting" Nietzsche or even that he had a straightforward "interpretation" of him. I had not yet seen Jacques Derrida's confirmation of this: in his *Spurs*, Derrida affirms that the thesis of Heidegger's *grand livre* "is much less simple than people have generally tended to say."[2]

Here, then, are my notes from the initial meeting, with some explanatory additions in square brackets and, on occasion, some interruptions.

> June 10, 1974
>
> 11:00 AM. Will see Heidegger tonight at six. Long talk with Professor von Herrmann this morning concerning the structure of the *Nietzsche* volumes. He advised me to look at Richardson's appendix on the dates of the lectures and gave some good hints concerning the projected English volumes.[3] Tonight may also be my last visit with Heidegger, since von Herrmann has agreed to be my "connection" with Heidegger, and since I will *not* be one of those tourists who come to have their picture taken with Heraclitus. Still . . . I will ask for an inscription!
>
> 11:00 PM. Hail storm and high winds under a black, irritable sky [this afternoon]. I was one hour early: I was supposed to have registered at the local Bürgermeister's office before my appointment with Heidegger, but I was too nervous and feared I might not be able to find Heidegger's house. I found it without any trouble and waited from five until six. Joan had said, "Come at six."

Meanwhile, like a good German, for whom arriving early is a capital crime, I wandered through the Zähringen neighborhood. But to resume.

> "The They" [what Heidegger in *Being and Time* calls *das Man*] are building houses like mad in Zähringen: shortly before he saw us to the

---

2 Jacques Derrida, *Éperons: Les Styles de Nietzsche* (Paris: Flammarion, 1978), 60.

3 The reference is to William J. Richardson, *Heidegger: Through Phenomenology to Thought*, 2nd ed. (The Hague: Martinus Nijhoff, 1967), which contains a valuable appendix listing the courses Heidegger taught during his long career.

door [after our meeting], Heidegger showed me a photo of his garden looking in the direction of the Zähringer Burg ruins, a photo only several years old. But several years ago there were no houses. "Now there are houses everywhere," he said.

At number 25 Fillibachstraße[4] there were two doorbells with name labels. The lower one read:

MARTIN HEIDEGGER

I do not know what I was expecting, but the label astonished me; I did not notice who was occupying the other apartment in the building. I pressed the button and pushed the door just in time, that is, just before the buzzer silenced and the lock took hold again, and entered. White vestibule smelling of new plaster. Far from the ski hut of Todtnauberg. Stairs to the left. Uncertain, I started to climb. Frau Heidegger opened a door on the second floor.[5] She looked older than the photos of her I had seen. She greeted me courteously as "Herr Professor." Joan then appeared [in a different doorway], all in a rush, excited as usual.

"How many times did you ring? Have you been waiting long? We didn't hear a thing!" all in one breath.

She assured Frau Heidegger that we would be leaving soon. Frau Heidegger did not hear at first. Joan repeated her assurance, and Frau Heidegger nodded in concurrence. Joan and Heidegger had been working for two or three hours on her new translation of *Sein und Zeit*. She looked tired.

Heidegger was in the study beyond the dining room. Joan and I chatted by the dining room table. My knee rested on one of the chairs. She had asked Heidegger "to formulate something" for her, and she had left him alone to write. Later I learned that he was formulating an inscription for Joan's copy of *Sein und Zeit*—it was a little birthday gift she had promised herself.

As Joan was telling me about the day's work and showing me her legal tablet covered with hastily sketched notes, Heidegger suddenly appeared in the doorway. He came to me, held out his hand, and smiled.

"Herr Professor Krell, I am pleased to meet you. Joan has told me some things about you and your work."

"Professor Heidegger. . . . I am pleased. . . . I hope they weren't altogether bad things!"

---

4 That is the address of the "garden house" that Heidegger and Elfride occupied during their later years, just behind their large house on the Rötebuckweg.

5 This may be confusion on my part. Rudolf Safranski (RS 471/427) notes that the garden house had only one floor, so the Heideggers no longer had to climb stairs. At any rate, Frau Heidegger emerged from a doorway. . . .

I had forgotten how witty I could be. Probably out of courtesy, Heidegger laughed, inviting the two of us into his study. He appeared to be fragile, but he was surprisingly quick and stable on his feet. Not nearly so stocky as the older photos suggested. He wore a beige suit and a dark tie—a wear-at-home suit and tie—and soft leather shoes, suede, gummy-soled. He was also smaller than I had anticipated, although I knew well from descriptions I had read or heard that he was short, perhaps five foot four inches.[6]

I sat on a straight-backed chair, not very comfortable, Joan to my right. Heidegger sat at the foot of the old brown chaise longue beneath the length of the window. The window looked out over the garden to the hills and the Zähringen fortress ruins—and the multiplying houses. On the wide windowsill lay a copy of the French edition of the first half of *Being and Time*. Books lined the wall opposite the window. There were not enough of them, if the stories I had heard about the hut were true. [The Rötebuckweg house at the top of the property held a much larger library.] There were piles of lecture notes, organized in cardboard folders of various colors: material that quite unconsciously we were already calling the *Nachlaß* (literary remains). All in all, Heidegger's apartment did not look sufficiently lived in, as though there had not been enough time or strength to see to things. . . . Everything but the man was too new.

An unadorned blond pinewood table served as a desk. A few papers and books lay on it, not scattered but neatly aligned along the edges. Small writing pad, a felt-tip pen.

"Do you have my *Schriften*?" Heidegger asked.

I did not know which writings he meant, so I said I had just about everything. At the moment, I did not have the Kant book. He asked which Kant book. The first one. He answered that at the moment, he had no copies of it, but that he would get one for me and deliver it via Professor von Herrmann. He asked if I had a copy of the *Frühe Schriften* ("Early Writings"). No. He rose and left the room. There seemed to be some sort of storage room across the hall. After a moment, he returned with a copy still wrapped in brown paper, walked to the desk, sat down, and began to write in it.

"Pardon me. What is your first name?" His voice slid in and out of several higher registers, the keenest witness to his age.

"David."

He returned to his writing. He held the pen without crooking his index finger; the book he was inscribing also lay at the proper angle.

---

6 Heidegger's "official" height is recorded as having been a fraction over five feet four inches, although he may have lost some height in his old age.

He would have been a perfect model for penmanship classes. Heidegger took a long time to write, although he seemed to write without any difficulty. His script proved to be neat and firm, quite legible. Hands small and delicate, not a peasant's hands, as I had also been given to expect, although they were a rich, healthy color. He handed me the book. The inscription read, in translation, "For Herrn Dr. David Krell, with good wishes for his stay in Freiburg," with date and signature. Not satisfied with one autograph, I gave Heidegger my copy of *Nietzsche*, volume one, and told him a story, a true story, no less.

"When I defended my doctoral dissertation—it was directed by André Schuwer and treated your *Nietzsche* books, which I am now to translate, it seems—Schuwer introduced me to the audience as 'a David who has been challenged by a veritable Goliath, the eleven-hundred-page *Nietzsche* book of Martin Heidegger.'"

Heidegger leaned over his desk toward me; his eyes opened wide and his jaw dropped.

"*So? So!*" Then he laughed freely, eyes still wide.

"He didn't mean that my challenge was to murder the book," I added hastily. But because I was laughing myself, I had difficulty continuing. "In any case," I said, "the translation will surely be a challenge, and I thought maybe you might inscribe a bit of courage into my copy there."

Again he took up the pen and bent over the book. I chatted with Joan, who again advised us not to stay too long. She was quite right to protect the man: I was getting comfortable and would happily have eaten up his time—and he at eighty-five years! But I assured Joan that I had only one question and not a very profound one at that. Heidegger handed me my (or his) book and rose to move to the couch again. As I began to formulate my question, he leaned forward in concentration. He looked into my eyes all the while or would have if I had not occasionally averted mine.

> I have a question, not about any genuine matter in the *Nietzsche* volumes, but about the reception they have had. I've read some reviews and have heard some commentators speak of your Nietzsche interpretation, and it seems to me that the understanding of the work is generally one-sided. People interpret your attempt to locate Nietzsche in the history of metaphysics as a *criticism* of Nietzsche. Perhaps moving too quickly through the textual analyses of the first volume, they hasten to the second in order to learn your conclusions. They assert, "Heidegger says that Nietzsche is just another metaphysician, whereas we know that he is the great anti-metaphysician." What I want to ask is this: Could I . . . it would be fine if I could . . . in *your* name

encourage readers of this translation to work carefully through the lectures of this *first* volume before moving on to the *second*, and before making any judgment about Nietzsche's position in the history of being or about *your* thoughts in that respect?

Heidegger turned to Joan and asked if she could clarify my question—which was really a little speech—and Joan ably condensed it in the following way: "People are often in a hurry to know what you say *about* Nietzsche in your second volume without having first followed the careful working-out of the matter in the first volume; Herr Krell wants to know whether in your name he can suggest that readers work through the first volume before taking up any of the judgments in the second."

Heidegger looked at me again and after a long hesitation answered, "*Aber selbstverständlich. Die Vorlesungen bringen alle Probleme vor. Die muss man zuerst . . .*" ("Well, of course. The *lectures* bring all the problems to the fore. They must first be. . . .")

He did not go on. It was as though nothing further could be said. Far too late, I realized the *Dummheit* of my question: the man gathers together and refines six hundred pages of lecture material as the foundation for his later essays on Nietzsche, and here am I, asking if he would suggest they be read! But I understand Heidegger's *Aber selbstverständlich* to be a rather exasperated affirmation of my doctoral thesis: before one begins to expostulate on Heidegger's *interpretation* of Nietzsche or Nietzsche's place in the history of philosophy, one must first make an effort to *read* the Nietzschean texts brought forward in Heidegger's first volume and to think through Heidegger's reading of them. He must, in other words, engage himself to the problematic elaborated in the lectures on will to power as art and knowledge and the eternal recurrence of the same, which Heidegger describes as matters for *thinking*.

As for the remark "Heidegger argues that Nietzsche is just another metaphysician," Heidegger responded, "*Ja, es gibt viele Menschen, die das Wort 'Metaphysik' nur so verstehen als etwas wie . . .*" ("Yes, many people understand the word *metaphysics* to mean merely something like . . ."). Here Heidegger stopped and rolled his eyes up and about, as though in search of Socrates among the clouds. Joan and I burst into laughter. "*Solch' ein Metaphysiker ist Nietzsche natürlich nicht*" ("Naturally, Nietzsche is not that kind of metaphysician").

Joan asked Heidegger if he was tired. He smiled. "*Ja!*" As we began to gather our things, Heidegger asked Joan, apparently for the second or third time that day, about Glenn Gray and Hannah Arendt. Joan promised to write Glenn and to call Heidegger back to report on Hannah's condition (she had suffered a "mild" heart attack some months before while delivering the Gifford Lectures in Scotland). Heidegger then noted on a pad in a neat hand Joan's and his next appointment. Joan requested the loan of a book; Heidegger handed it to her after examining the cover closely to make certain it was the right one.

He invited me to return for a visit "any time." I told him that Professor von Herrmann had kindly offered to convey to him any messages or questions of mine. Then I offered to aid him during my stay in any way I could. Joan said, "Yes, he's young and strong: let him run to the library for you!" Heidegger laughed and nodded.

He saw us to the door and cautioned Joan to be careful during her jaunts about Freiburg and environs, that is, the world. Warmly, quietly, he shook my hand.

Two hours later, at supper with Joan and other friends, I opened the *Nietzsche* volume Heidegger had inscribed after my Goliath story. There stood a riddle I cannot solve. I cannot even tell who the characters named in the riddle are, or if, as though it were a dream of mine, I must be one [or all] of them. I do not understand it at all. One thing is certain: Heidegger's laughter was so spontaneous and full of delight that there can be nothing in the inscription that should make me afraid. When I first read it, I laughed but then became uneasy. What did it mean? Who did it involve? I still cannot decide, but I can only reproduce it here:

> *Der Kampf zwischen David und Goliath ist in der Philosophie noch nicht entschieden.* (The battle between David and Goliath, in philosophy, is not yet decided.)

> Freiburg, den 10. Juni 1974

> Martin Heidegger

P.S.: August 16, 1974. My understanding of the riddle now, some weeks later, is something like this. The battle of which Heidegger speaks is not a struggle between him and me, or between him and Nietzsche; rather, "Goliath" here means the matter for thinking that has been prepared in the long and infinitely rich history of philosophy. If this is so, then "David" is the alliance of Nietzsche, Heidegger, and all others who in the post-metaphysical age—where nevertheless metaphysics still dominates [as technology]—undertake the task of thinking. Whether the undertaking can make a decisive difference in our thoughtless, thought-provoking time, no one knows. It is . . . *noch nicht entschieden.*

Our discussion of Heidegger's *Nietzsche* volumes did not end with this first visit, however. They were the main topic of my *third* visit with him. But before presenting my notes from our *second* meeting, allow me to return to my first impressions, now with the benefit of several decades of hindsight.

What I remember most about that first meeting with Heidegger was my astonishment at how small he was. Age had no doubt contributed to the slightness and fragility of frame. Yet a thought occurred to me almost immediately that I was never able to shake. The smallness of size and the gentle and almost timid manner of the old man did not square with the image of the young revolutionary in the university—for that is what he was in the 1920s and 1930s, a "young Turk" who despised the complacent conservatism of his older colleagues. Nor did it square with the style of the Marburg writings, which are very often polemical and almost always, in the words of a critic, "hard and heavy."[7] It did not even suit the style of the later writings, which are often Olympian and almost always disdainful of the efforts of his contemporaries. I could not help but think of other minuscule academics I have met in my life, many of them as aggressive as the fyce in Faulkner's "The Bear," and the curbstone psychologist's "Napoleon Complex" became a thought I could not suppress. A taller man, a Cassirer or a Jaspers, could afford to be more tolerant and easygoing. What this first impression leaves out, however, is how deft much of the early polemic is and how much serious thought stands behind the Olympian gesture. Here are two favorite examples of the polemic, the first from the mid-1920s:

> Today we decide about metaphysics and about even more elevated things at philosophy conferences. For everything that is to be done these days we first have a meeting, and here is how it works: people come together, constantly come together, and they all wait for one another to turn up so that the others will tell them how it is, and if it doesn't get said, never mind, everyone has had their say. It may very well be that all the talkers who are having their say have understood little of the matter in question, but still we believe that if we accumulate all of that misunderstanding something like understanding will leap forth at the end of the day. Thus there are people today who travel from one meeting to the next and who are sustained by the confidence that something is really happening, that they've actually done something; whereas, at bottom, they've merely ducked out of work,

---

7 Winfried Franzen, "Die Sehnsucht nach Härte und Schwere," in *Heidegger und die praktische Philosophie*, ed. Annemarie Gethmann-Siefert and Otto Pöggeler (Frankfurt am Main: Suhrkamp, 1988), 78–92.

seeking in chatter a place to build a nest for their helplessness—a helplessness, it is true, that they will never understand. (20:376)[8]

The second example, much more subdued in tone yet quite severe in substance, is from the early 1950s:

> It is no evidence of any readiness to think that people show an interest in philosophy. There is, of course, serious preoccupation everywhere with philosophy and its questions. The learned world is expending commendable efforts in the investigation of the history of philosophy. . . . But even if we have devoted many years to the intensive study of the treatises and writings of the great thinkers, that fact is still no guarantee that we ourselves are thinking, or even are ready to learn thinking. On the contrary—preoccupation with philosophy more than anything else may give us the stubborn illusion that we are thinking just because we are incessantly "philosophizing." (BW 371)

Between these two pronouncements lies the period of Heidegger's entanglement in National Socialism. No amount of curbstone psychology can make Heidegger's leap to the right in the early 1930s clear to us. There, the polemics and the actions are of a more insidious nature. For those who read and study Heidegger's work, this period remains a nightmare, whether or not one has met the man, although the nightmare is perhaps more terrible for those who did. I will devote a separate chapter to it. My models for how to deal with it will be Hannah Arendt and Glenn Gray, both of whom were dedicated to Heidegger's work but critical of and perspicuous about the man and his work. The only thing they were unable to do, and Derrida follows them in this respect, was to light a match to burn either the man or his work. They persisted in the task of trying to understand, learning to live with blatant contradiction.

At any rate, there was the conspicuous shortness of stature, most noticeable when he was standing at the door or near a window, pointing up to the Zähringen fortress, least noticeable when he was sitting at his desk with pen in hand. And there was that high-pitched, raspy voice, perhaps aggravated by the slight stroke he had suffered in 1968, the voice that spoke

---

8 That is, Martin Heidegger, *Prolegomena zur Geschichte des Zeitbegriffs*. Martin Heidegger *Gesamtausgabe* volume 20. Marburg lecture course, Summer Semester 1925 (Frankfurt am Main: V. Klostermann, 1979), 376. I will cite the Heidegger *Gesamtausgabe* throughout simply by volume and page in the body of my text.

in pointed phrases, never waxing eloquent. Karl Jaspers confirms what I experienced: *die eindringliche knappe Weise seines Sprechens*, "the conspicuously succinct way he spoke" (RS 138).

As for David and Goliath, it later seemed to me that he was identifying himself with David in battle against the gigantic history of metaphysics, where decisions concerning any given thinker are difficult. Or perhaps Nietzsche himself was the opponent. Or, yet again, Heidegger may have been aware of my own Nietzschean strain, as intense as his own, if not as learned, such that my struggles with his readings of Nietzsche culminated in a certain ambivalence. Yet my ambivalence perhaps mirrored Heidegger's own. Difficult to decide.

* * *

Let me now present the handwritten notes from our *second* meeting, on May 16, 1975. Glenn Gray, who was visiting me at the time and who wanted me to pick up a number of Heidegger's books that had recently appeared in new editions, had arranged the meeting. Here are my notes, with only a few excisions and minor editorial changes. As always, our conversation was in German.

> Second visit with Heidegger. I dropped Glenn off at the university library and drove out to Zähringen, Fillibachstraße 25, at 10 A.M. Again Frau Heidegger met me at the door. She seemed younger and healthier than the year before, and she was handsomely dressed. I had expected her to hand me the books that I had come for through the door, which had been opened just a crack, but she opened it wide after I said my name, and she led me directly through the hall into the dining room and from there into Heidegger's study. He was reclining on his dowdy brown couch over by the window, reading the newspaper, I think, as mundane as that may seem, but he swung his legs down, stood up, and walked toward me with a quick and sure step. He too seemed somehow younger and more spry than last June, fresher and sharper in appearance, more clean about the edges, his eyes smaller but even brighter brown than I had remembered. Same suit and shoes.
>
> Heidegger shook my hand and turned immediately to get the books. He bent over the still wrapped volumes, making out the titles, printed in small type on the labels. Then he looked up.
>
> "Did you get the . . . ?"
>
> "The Reclam edition by Gadamer? Yes, it arrived in the post yesterday."
>
> The paperback edition of *Der Ursprung des Kunstwerkes* ("The Origin of the Work of Art") prepared by Hans-Georg Gadamer had indeed come one or two days earlier, addressed to me in the "s' Murershus" of St. Ulrich. How the Albert Buchhandlung or Heidegger himself had learned the local

name of my house I cannot imagine. [Clearly, I must have told him at some point: he was interested in the Alemannic dialect—the "s' Murershus" was the stonemason's or *Maurers* house—and in all things involving the villages about Freiburg.] In any case, I thanked him for the book.

As he was getting the books Glenn and I had asked for, I returned the seven photographs Frau Heidegger had sent me several weeks earlier. Heidegger asked his wife if he could see them. He seemed surprised, looking through the set as though he had never seen any of them before. Elfride had probably sent them to me without much ado. He wondered why I was giving them all back, and I explained that copies of them had been made. I did not mention that I had lost one of them outside of Stober's photo shop and that by a stroke of luck a customer had returned it to the shop.[9]

Heidegger now picked up the Kant book from today's pile of books [a new edition of *Kant and the Problem of Metaphysics*], but there was no copy of the Hölderlin book [the new edition of *Erläuterungen zu Hölderlins Dichtung*] in the house. He insisted that I get that book from Albert Buchhandlung and charge it to his account. Then I learned how unsure my German still is: I thought I understood him to say that I should return the volumes to him when I was "done" with them, which struck me as being a bit cheap, but I agreed with alacrity, of course. A few minutes later he looked surprised when I assured him I would return the volumes when our work with them was done.

"But no—hold on to them, keep them!"

So much for my German. I will keep the books.

Heidegger held a second book in his hands as we stood there beside his desk: *Wegmarken* ("Pathmarks"). On the wrapping he had written "Hegel und die Griechen." He pointed to the title of that essay.

"Do you know this piece?"

"Yes, of course. I used it for the introduction to the Greek essays we have just translated."[10]

"I think it would be a good addition to your anthology."

"Yes? Dr. Gray said nothing to me about that essay."

"No, no, we didn't talk about this one. It occurred to me only after he left the other day. This is an important essay. . . ."

His voice broke curiously over the word *wichtiger*, "important." But I had no trouble understanding him this time, that minor misunderstanding mentioned above notwithstanding. He continued.

---

9 I believe that the photographs had been requested by the editors of the journal *boundary* 2, but I cannot be certain of this.

10 That is, *Early Greek Thinking*, published in spring 1975.

"During the past few years there has been a great deal of interest in Hegel generated in the United States, isn't that so?"

"Yes."

"I think it is important not to let Hegel stand in isolation. What I tried to do in this essay was to provide a horizon on which Hegel's relation to the history of philosophy could be seen."

"That becomes clear in the essay."

"It would be a good addition to the anthology, I think."[11]

He offered me the copy of *Wegmarken*, but I said I had the book already. He nodded, then invited me to sit down.

"Well, I don't want to disturb you. . . ."

Heidegger said nothing in reply to this, but he asked how long I intended to stay in Germany.

"Two more years. My wife and I don't have any children yet—although we hope to have some sometime—and so we've decided to have our *Wanderjahre* now in Germany. I do want to improve my German and to continue with . . ."

My hands made an awkward gesture, as though to say "continue with what I have been doing for the past year."

"Besides," I added, "we live in a beautiful village, St. Ulrich. Do you know it?"

"Yes, St. Ulrich, but how do you get your mail? I couldn't find it in the directory."

"Through Bollschweil."

Heidegger opened his eyes wide, a gesture I had seen before, and repeated the name of the village to which St. Ulrich belonged.

"Ah, so! Bollschweil!"

He then turned and made a note of it on a pad on his desk.

"Incidentally," he added after a moment's pause, "let me thank you for the *Arion* piece—it is beautifully done!"

He meant the special printing of *Der Spruch des Anaximander* ("The Anaximander Fragment," literally, "Anaximander's Saying").[12]

"The essay will be coming out again, isn't that right?"

"Yes, the book should be out in just a few weeks."

"Only a few weeks?"

I nodded, being the eternal infernal optimist. "Yes, it contains that piece plus 'Logos,' 'Moira,' and 'Aletheia.'"

He nodded, then added, "And Joan Stambaugh is working on *Being and Time*. But that is a difficult job!" He broke into a grin.

---

11 As it turned out, Glenn Gray and I decided to reserve all the essays devoted to specific figures in the history of philosophy for a second anthology that we hoped Harper & Row would publish.

12 The journal *Arion*, edited by Donald Carne-Ross and cofounded with William Arrowsmith, both at Boston University, had requested advance publication of the Anaximander piece, which

"Yes, Herr Gray and I are going over her translation of the Introduction just now—trying to help as much as we can."

I then mentioned something that I thought would please him—John Sallis's forthcoming volume of essays on Heidegger's and Eugen Fink's *Heraclitus* seminar.[13] He seemed confused by that, wanting to know if it had anything to do with the anthology.

"No, no, it's a different project altogether."

The conversation dwindled. He smiled. I rose to go.

Heidegger accompanied me to the door. I was jabbering like an idiot:

"Well, I'm glad to see that you are in such fine fettle, so *rüstig*, as they say up in the hill country, and I wish you the best of luck and if there's anything you need in town because you know I'm in town a lot and I'd be happy to get it for you. At your service."[14]

I was out the door before I knew it. Too soon. Too late. The morning of this evening.

Allow me to add a note or two to my discussion in the foregoing chapter of the anthology of Heidegger's *Basic Writings*. During our discussions with Heidegger, we referred to it as an English-language *Studienausgabe*—he did not like the word "anthology," despite its Greek roots. What should be included, what excluded? The question was partly decided by extrinsic matters—copyright issues, the status of a particular translation, the recalcitrance of this or that publishing house—but there were many options. For example, the essay "Aletheia," based on a fragment of Heraclitus, was in my original plan. Heidegger did not object to it, but, as we have already heard, he did ask that "Hegel and the Greeks" appear alongside it. He was intrigued by the Hegel-renaissance that was underway in England and the United States, but what he wanted to add to the discussion was Hegel's debt to the tradition. During his seminar on Heraclitus, taught with Eugen Fink in 1967, he had gone so far as to suggest that our every contact with Heraclitus unavoidably passes through Hegel—to be unaware of Hegel's having

was to be the opening essay of *Early Greek Thinking*. The *Arion* group of classicists were deeply interested in Heidegger, a rarity at the time, and both Glenn Gray and I were happy with their presentation of the essay—as was Heidegger. See *Arion: A Journal of Humanities and the Classics*, New Series 1, no. 4 (Winter 1974): 576–626.

13 Martin Heidegger and Eugen Fink, *Heraklit* (Frankfurt am Main: V. Klostermann, 1970). See also David Farrell Krell, "The Heraclitus Seminar: Review of *Heraklit* by Martin Heidegger and Eugen Fink," *Research in Phenomenology* 1 (1971): 137–46. The book of essays I am referring to here is John Sallis and Kenneth Maly, eds., *Heraclitean Fragments* (University: University of Alabama Press, 1980).

14 This, of course, is nothing like what I actually may have said at the time. Yet my notes, downright silly, show how exhilarated I was.

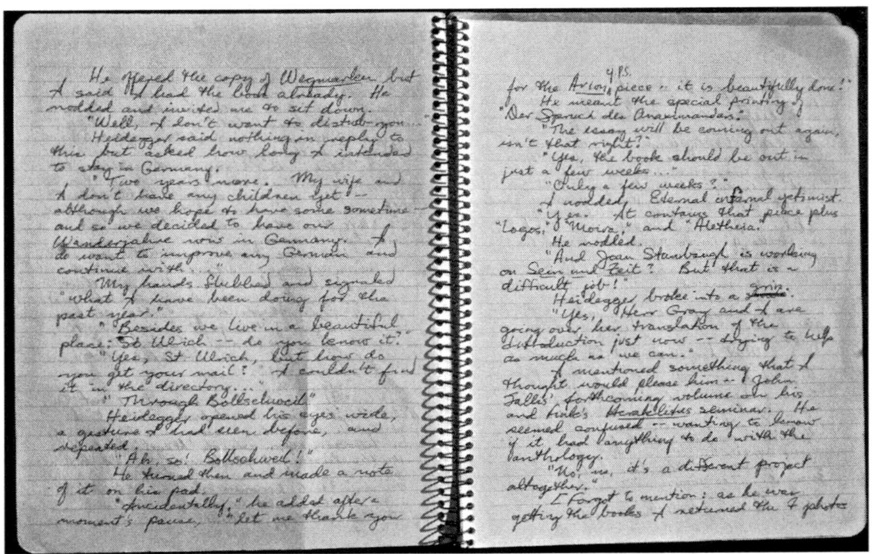

Fig. 3.2 Two pages from my notebook.

shaped contemporary thought would be to overestimate our chances of thinking through any of the fragments that the early Greeks left us.

As I noted earlier, after our ensuing discussion of "Hegel and the Greeks," Glenn and I decided that all essays devoted principally to individual thinkers in Heidegger's "history of being" had to be excluded. No principle of selection seemed possible here, neither to me nor to Heidegger, especially since only one or two essays of that kind, at most, could appear, given the American publisher's firm decision about the size of the book. Such essays would have to wait on a second volume.

Heidegger also wanted to include the essay "Wissenschaft und Besinnung" ("Science and Reflection") in the anthology to stress for the English-language readership his preoccupation with questions of science and technology. The essay ultimately could not appear, primarily for reasons of space. Even though Heidegger often made suggestions for inclusion, however, he occasionally recommended exclusions. For example, we discussed all the essays assembled in the book *On the Way to Language*, and he rejected one after the other. He would shake his head and say, *"Schwierig, zu schwierig"* ("Difficult, too difficult"). He was perfectly aware that these essays, especially the ones that focus on poetry, are so bound up with the particular genius of the German language that they would resist all efforts at translation. Most philosophers would agree with him, among them Derrida, who often called Heidegger's essays on language and poetry the richest and most difficult of his works. Heidegger and I eventually decided on one of his early essays on poetry, but a horrendous copyright problem stymied us. The absence of an essay on language and poetry—despite the remarks in Heidegger's "On the Origin of the Work of Art," which itself was abridged—was the most unfortunate exclusion in the first edition of the *Basic Writings*, published in 1977. The book's most glaring flaw, as I have mentioned, was the abridgement of both the art essay and the "Letter on Humanism." The second edition, published in 1993, added the final essay of Heidegger's *Unterwegs zur Sprache*, namely, "The Way to Language," perhaps the most accessible and most "programmatic" of the language essays, and printed the whole of the art and humanism essays.

Another essay that Heidegger did *not* want to have included, and this was and remains surprising, was "*Zeit und Sein*" ("Time and Being"). This late essay, from the early 1960s, reverses the order of the words in the title of his magnum opus *Sein und Zeit*, so it was assumed by almost everyone to be either the culmination or the reversal or perhaps even the retraction of that earlier work. Even though Heidegger had often admonished his readers that the later essay by no means carried out the "reversal" presaged in *Being and Time* and that it could not be "attached" to the torso of the earlier book as its missing part, commentators felt that the very title of the piece justified their viewing it that way. Whether out of dissatisfaction with the reception of the piece—the Great Expectations that attended its publication—or because of more deep-seated doubts about the essay itself, which is strangely tentative, Heidegger requested that I strike it from the plan. I did not comply with this wish for months, until he convinced me that the proper culmination of his thinking—fittingly, a thoroughly *questioning* culmination, every bit as tentative as its companion piece despite its assertive title—was the essay "The End of Philosophy and the Task of Thinking." Even when I inserted the language essay into the second edition of *Basic Writings*, I made certain to let the "End" essay appear at, and as, the end.

*   *   *

The Introduction to *Being and Time*, which was the book that occupied the third area of our discussions, assumed ever greater importance as the anthology project developed. Eventually, I was to compare those first eight sections of Heidegger's magnum opus to Hegel's preface to the *Phenomenology of Spirit*. That preface, composed while Hegel's manuscript was being set in print, served as an introduction to the entire *System of Science*. It may well be that Heidegger's introduction to *Being and Time* will come to occupy the privileged place that Hegel's preface has generally come to have in Hegel studies.

On September 23, 1975, Heidegger wrote asking me to come to the garden house six days later, on the twenty-ninth, at five in the afternoon. Here are my handwritten notes from the third visit:

September 29, 1975

I visited Heidegger for the third time today between five and six P.M. The man looks younger each time I see him! Perhaps I'm always expecting him to deteriorate—at eighty-six he could fall apart at any instant!—and I am therefore surprised to see him looking fit.

He was reclining on his couch near the window and did not rise as I entered the study. Frau Heidegger showed me in, then retreated, and Heidegger invited me to pull up a chair close to him. He cupped his hand around his left ear as we spoke, complaining about his hearing. Indeed, a couple of times during the meeting he seemed more to surmise than to hear what was being said. He had set out some wine on a silver tray and he asked me if I would serve myself.

"Did you drive over?"

"Yes, I did."

"Then I suppose you shouldn't have any wine?"

"Maybe just a *little*?"

He laughed and I poured myself some—a Côte du Rhône, "St. Joseph" by name—predictably good. There were some stale pretzel sticks on the tray also, what I call "polite pretzels," since they are a useless tidbit but, alas, omnipresent.

Before even sipping the wine I extracted from my briefcase a sheet of paper on which I had sketched some questions the evening before. I first asked him when the lecture course "Nietzsche's Metaphysics," reprinted in the second volume of the *Nietzsche*, was delivered. The date 1940 appears in the Neske *Nietzsche*, whereas the initial *Gesamtausgabe* plan (for volume 52) and the Richardson list cite this title for the Winter Semester 1941–42. Heidegger held to the date 1940, and at first suggested that the other listings were a mistake. Then he said that he might have repeated the course during the 1941–42 Winter Semester and that in 1940 the material had been presented in a seminar. Now that I look, I cannot locate any possible time for its delivery in 1940.

Yet the brevity of the text suggests that it may have been planned for one of those trimesters of 1940; surely volume 52 will have to include a good deal more material than the seventy-five pages of *Nietzsches Metaphysik*. That problem remains unsolved, but, as Heidegger remarked, "It isn't very important, is it?"

"No, I was just trying to get the chronology settled."

Allow me to pause for a moment to clarify if I can the matter of "Nietzsche's Metaphysics," which early plans for the *Gesamtausgabe* placed variously in volumes 52 and 57. As it turns out, "Nietzsche's Metaphysics" now appears in volume 50. It was announced as a lecture course for the winter semester of 1941–42, but it was never held. For reasons that are not entirely clear, Heidegger decided to lecture instead on "Hölderlin's Hymn *Andenken*," the transcript of which now appears in the published volume 52. The editor of volume 50, Petra Jaeger, tells us that Heidegger prepared the lecture course on "Nietzsche's Metaphysics" a year earlier, in August 1940, revising it from October through December of that year. This is a bit odd, and it may be responsible for the confusion. On the front page of Heidegger's detailed notes appears its ostensible topic:

NIETZSCHE'S METAPHYSICS

elucidated in terms of the stanza:

> "Welt-Spiel, das herrische,
> mischt Sein und Schein:—
> das Ewig-Närrische
> mischt *uns*—hinein! . . ."

> ("World-play, all-ruling,
> mixes Seems with To Be:—
> the Eternally-Fooling
> mixes *us*—in the melee! . . .")

Sein und Schein, "Being and Seeming," from the second line of the stanza, was a topic of particular interest to Heidegger, especially regarding Nietzsche. That phrase became the subtitle of an *Übung*, or "workshop" course he had offered in the summer of 1937, now published in volume 87 of the Collected Edition. One of the odd things about the projected lecture course on "Nietzsche's Metaphysics," however, is that this verse, the concluding stanza of Nietzsche's parodic poem "To Goethe," plays no role at all in the transcript, at least as far as I can see.[15]

It took some time for the editors of the *Gesamtausgabe* to discover and set in order all the Nietzsche courses that Heidegger taught, whether lecture courses, advanced seminars, or "workshop" courses. My confusion about all this increased when, eighteen months after Heidegger's death, I paid a visit to Otto Pöggeler at the Hegel Archive in Bochum. My journal contains the following note on my visit with Pöggeler, who was, as always, very gracious and helpful:

> November 18, 1978
>
> Visited Pöggeler this past week. Surprise: he is the author of the *titles* [of all the sections] in the *Nietzsche* volumes! Heidegger rejected only one or two of his proposed titles, adopting all the rest. (Heidegger had asked Pöggeler to read the ms. and to insert titles—since there were *hundreds* of pages without any kind of interruption.) According to Pöggeler, Heidegger taught two "unlisted" courses on Nietzsche. The course on the second *Untimely Meditation* Pöggeler dates from 1928 or 1929, right after the publication of *Sein und Zeit.* The second course was on Nietzsche's poem "To Goethe," concerning *Welt-Spiel* ("world play"). Pöggeler seemed to know less about this course and did not mention a date. Perhaps it was held in conjunction with the course on "Eternal Recurrence of the Same," during the Summer Semester of 1937? I'll have to ask Dr. [Joachim] Storck.[16]

Pöggeler told me that when he tried to jog Heidegger's memory about where these manuscripts or typescript materials might be, Heidegger replied that maybe his brother Fritz, who often typed up Martin's lectures and essays, had them somewhere. As I have already reported, when I pushed Heidegger on the matter of the content and the date of the mysterious typescript of "Nietzsche's Metaphysics" (typed by Fritz?), he wrestled with it but then said with a smile that it really did not matter much.

As for the other unlisted course, it turns out that Heidegger did offer a lecture course under the title "Toward an Interpretation of Nietzsche's Second *Untimely Meditation*, 'On the Use and Disadvantage of the Study of History for Life.'" I knew that the Heidegger-Archive at the Schiller

---

15 The poem "To Goethe" does play an important role in a text from 1944–46 on "Nihilism as Determined by the History of Being." See N 2:380–81; Ni 4:235–37.

16 Dr. Storck was at that time at the Deutsches Literaturarchiv in Marbach, where the Heidegger papers are held.

Nationalmuseum in Marbach possessed a folder marked with that title and dated "W.S. 38/39." To repeat, when I discussed the matter with Pöggeler, he seemed convinced that the date must have been closer to 1928–29, a full decade earlier, mainly because of the analysis of Nietzsche's second *Untimely* in *Being and Time*, section 76. Yet Pöggeler's suggestion would have made more sense if Heidegger had held such a seminar *before* publishing *Being and Time*, since he often based eventually published material on prior lectures and seminars. To be sure, Heidegger was *reading* Nietzsche throughout the 1920s, but I knew of no formal courses at Marburg on Nietzsche's philosophy. The course devoted to Nietzsche's second *Untimely Meditation* was in fact held during the winter semester of 1938–39, fairly late in the series of Nietzsche lectures.[17]

The course is particularly interesting for several reasons. There is a great deal of material on "life," including animal life—readers will recall that Nietzsche begins his treatise with an account of contented cows at pasture, who seem to have little sense of history and are better off for it. History and memory are major themes for Heidegger right from the start. Furthermore, the earliest course Jacques Derrida ever offered on Heidegger at the École Normale Supérieure was on the importance of history for the question of being.[18] In Derrida's course, Nietzsche's second *Untimely* plays a crucial role, so it would be intriguing to read volume 46 of the *Gesamtausgabe* with Derrida's course alongside it. Furthermore, Derrida's *last* course on Heidegger was on the problem of *animality*, so those contented cows we are so prepared to slaughter are never far from Derrida's mind. One final reason for my interest in the 1938–39 course is that its transcript, at least as the *Gesamtausgabe* presents it, is written in a style that is obviously influenced by Nietzsche, a more "aphoristic" style of brief paragraphs, notably different from the style of the other lecture courses. I recall Otto Pöggeler's once remarking that a "Sils-Maria wind"

---

17 Martin Heidegger, *Zur Auslegung von Nietzsches II. Unzeitgemässer Betrachtung, "Vom Nutzen und Nachteil der Historie für das Leben,"* ed. Hans-Joachim Friedrich, *Gesamtausgabe*, vol. 46 (Frankfurt am Main: V. Klostermann, 2003). The course was planned as an *Übung*, or workshop, but it was so heavily visited that Heidegger wound up having to lecture.

18 On the importance for Derrida of Heidegger's reading of Nietzsche's second *Untimely Meditation*, see Jacques Derrida, *Heidegger: la question de l'Être et l'Histoire. Cours de l'ENS-Ulm 1964–1965*, ed. Thomas Dutoit with Marguerite Derrida (Paris: Galilée, 2013), esp. 312–20; Geoffrey Bennington, English trans., *Heidegger: The Question of Being and History* (Chicago: University of Chicago Press, 2019). See also David Farrell Krell, "Three Timely Untimelies: Heidegger and Derrida on Nietzsche's Second *Untimely Meditation*," *Oxford Literary Review* 43, no. 1 (2021): 131–54.

wafts through Heidegger's *Beiträge zur Philosophie*, written from 1936 to 1938, and those same gusts of Zarathustra's Oberengadin wind are felt in Heidegger's *Untimely* course.

Another unlisted seminar or workshop, this one conducted during the winter semester of 1941–42, had the title "Introductory Exercises in Philosophical Thinking." It treated Heraclitus's fragment B7 alongside Nietzsche's aphorism 493 in the compilation *Der Wille zur Macht*. Fragment 7 of Heraclitus, which Heidegger had already cited in the 1935 *Introduction to Metaphysics* (EM 112), says, "If all being went up in smoke, it would be for the nose to grasp and articulate it." Nietzsche's aphorism 493 says, "Truth is the kind of error without which a particular species of living being could not live. The value for *life* ultimately decides."[19]

Perhaps the only thing worth remembering about all this is that Heidegger's largest single publication, the two Neske *Nietzsche* volumes, is by no means complete. Heidegger returned to Nietzsche again and again in a variety of contexts, and the more one looks into the recently published volumes of the Collected Edition, the more one finds topics for research. For example, and I will offer only one example, in a "workshop" accompanying Heidegger's lecture course during the summer of 1937, "The Eternal Recurrence of the Same," which I regard as the high point of Heidegger's entire series of lectures on Nietzsche, we find Heidegger working on an idea that is only barely mentioned in the lecture course, indeed, at the very end of the course. There (N 1:470–71; Ni 2:206–207), he floats the idea that *amor fati*, "love of fate," is not merely a caprice on Nietzsche's part but is his "basic metaphysical position." In fact, the workshop has the title "Nietzsche's Basic Metaphysical Position (Being and Seeming)."[20] Only in the workshop does Heidegger elaborate on this idea of *amor fati*—which is the most interesting and challenging idea in his interpretation of eternal recurrence. The idea that otherwise seems to prevail in Heidegger is that "eternal return" is a mere appendage to "will to power," a derisory aspect that one sees mirrored in the rotary machines or turbines of our technology, endlessly churning. Anyone who reads Nietzsche seriously, of course, takes that interpretation of Nietzsche's "thought of thoughts" to be nonsense. Far more serious, and far more thought-provoking, is the idea

---

19 See Martin Heidegger *Gesamtausgabe*, vol. 88, ed. Alfred Denker (Frankfurt am Main: V. Klostermann, 2008), 149–205.

20 See Martin Heidegger *Gesamtausgabe*, vol. 87, ed. Peter von Ruckteschell (Frankfurt am Main: V. Klostermann, 2004), esp. 161–70.

that *amor fati*, which is closely related to the theme of "the innocence of becoming," is the fundamental metaphysical notion for Nietzsche. I have to add that both Arendt and Derrida, for whom the word and the thing called *amor* had enormous importance, would have been intrigued to see Heidegger—if only this one time—relating "love" to a "fundamental metaphysical position."

I will not go on about this, except to say that even as I write this "memoir," there are topics and themes that pop up and invite me to continue working on heidegger's nietzsche or nietzsche's heidegger. Once Heidegger had "found" Nietzsche, he never really "lost" him, and, as Nietzsche warned, that could cause confusion in the search for one's own identity. The problem waxes exponentially for us, since we have to add the name Heidegger to that of Nietzsche, and once we add that name, it is difficult to know who is writing about whom and to what end. Heideggerietzsche? Niedegger? It is a problem that could make one *kaputt*. A note from my journal tells this story:

> April 7, 1986
>
> From a conversation with Hans-Georg Gadamer at the Goethe-Institut in London. Gadamer had heard a story from Franco Volpi, which he then corroborated in a telephone conversation with Heidegger's son Hermann. The story goes that Heidegger used to repeat quite often—but with what sort of expression? with irony? in despair?—the phrase, *Nietzsche hat mich kaputt gemacht* ("Nietzsche ruined me"). I wish I had known about that, so I could have used it somewhere as an epigraph: "Nietzsche made me *kaputt*!" But, I would add, "he also made me *the* thinker *after* Hegel"!

The sense of my addition to the "epigraph" is that Nietzsche's philosophy made it impossible for Heidegger himself to be the consummate metaphysician. With Nietzsche, in other words, Western thinking introduces metaphysics to the era of its demise, to the beginning of its end. That Heidegger never "lost" Nietzsche or "left him behind" became particularly clear in his course *What Is Called Thinking?* taught in 1951–52, the first course he was allowed to teach after World War II. There, Nietzsche was the first "star witness" in the matter of thinking; the second was Parmenides, older than both Plato and Platonism. The recent publication of the *Black Notebooks* from the 1930s and 1940s confirms that Heidegger variously tried to identify Nietzsche as a failed metaphysician *and* to affirm that no one has risen to the challenge of taking his thought seriously enough. This ambivalence toward Nietzsche permeates everything Heidegger wrote on his extraordinary forbear. Perhaps if one can translate *ambivalence* into what Derrida calls *undecidability*, however, there would be no need to go *kaputt* on account of Nietzsche.

I return to my notes from the meeting of September 29, 1975. "I then asked him about a quotation from Aristotle's *De anima* on page 14 of *Sein und Zeit*, ἡ ψυχὴ τὰ ὄντα. . . . The question was whether the word πάντα should come next, as it does in modern editions—according to Glenn and Sherry Gray. Heidegger had me get his Teubner edition from the shelf, telling me exactly where it would be. We found the passage, *without* the πάντα, which for the Teubner edition is the first word of the *following* sentence. Heidegger suggested that we quote it as it stands in *Sein und Zeit*."

Here again, I have to interrupt and comment. My notes do not record it, but I recall Heidegger's telling me explicitly not to modernize or "correct" the quotation. Since he had used the older Teubner edition and not the more recent Oxford Classical Text (OCT), it was important to retain the version of the Aristotle quotation that is no longer accepted. I recall him saying that if he were writing today, he would use the OCT version, but that I could not simply alter the text of *Being and Time*. I further remember that he instructed me to add a footnote to the *Basic Writings*, explaining the problem. (I followed that instruction: see note 6 on page 56 of the second edition of *Basic Writings*.) The issue is not so important, except for Aristotle scholars, but it shows that Heidegger was actually very careful in his use of texts and that he was not at all averse to entering footnotes or other apparatus to clarify matters of philology. This is actually quite significant because the editors of the *Gesamtausgabe* have always claimed that Heidegger's strict instruction was to avoid all footnotes in their edition and to eschew all introductory material and every bit of philological "apparatus." This is an instruction I have never accepted as authentic, having experienced Heidegger's own care concerning such matters. I can only attribute it to the editors' and publisher's desire to produce as many volumes as quickly as possible. Critical editions take time, and time, as they say, is money.

My notes of the meeting resume as follows.

I then asked about the "Introduction" to *Being and Time*, specifically, *when* it was written, mentioning that von Herrmann had told me that it was composed at the very end. Heidegger said that he had kept the "Introduction" before him at every stage of the work, and that he updated it constantly. Even when the book itself began to be printed, Heidegger continued to make changes in those first eight sections. What was behind my asking was, for example, the detailed description of the "phenomenological destruction of the history of ontology" in section 6, pertaining, extrinsically at least, to the "second half" [i.e., the never-written half] of *Being and Time.*

"Then you did have a clear idea about going on with the work, the Introduction serving both parts, the written and the unwritten?"

Aber natürlich! ("Of course!").

I mentioned his Jaspers review, and commented on the importance of the "destruction" even there, between 1919 and 1921. Heidegger responded that the "destruction" was a constant theme of his lectures between 1919 and 1928, although he never published anything on it. He mentioned that the Winter Semester course of 1924–25, on Plato's *Sophist,* would be particularly enlightening in this respect. (I was not surprised to hear this course cited: it is the one Hannah Arendt is thinking of when she recalls how the rumor spread like wildfire, the rumor that *thinking* was *alive* in Germany once again!)

"When will this course be published in the Gesamtausgabe? Can you say?"

Heidegger shook his head, expressing doubt.

"Difficult to say. Very difficult."[21]

But to return to the problem of the "Introduction" to *Being and Time.* I asked him when he began to have real doubts about working out the second half of *Sein und Zeit.* His answer was slurred a bit, but it seemed to me he said, "1924 or 1925."

Now, this is plainly impossible. He had just insisted that he had had every intention of going ahead with the second half while he was preparing the Introduction for the press in 1927. I wonder if I misheard him, and that he said, "1934 or 1935"? Or perhaps I didn't make my question clear, or *loud* and clear!

Allow me to interrupt. For there is a good possibility that I did not mishear at all. The usual account of Heidegger's "turn" from "being and time" to "time and being" places it in the 1930s, with his turn to the work of art and the poetry of Hölderlin. That same account understands Heidegger to be turning from "the temporalizing of Dasein," *die Zeitlichkeit des Daseins,*

21 See now, first published in 1992, Martin Heidegger, *Platon: Sophistes,* Winter Semester 1924–25. Ingeborg Schüßler, ed., Martin Heidegger *Gesamtausgabe,* vol. 19, rev. ed. (Frankfurt am Main: V. Klostermann, 2018). The English translation of Heidegger's *Plato's Sophist* is by André Schuwer and Richard Rojcewicz (Bloomington: Indiana University Press, 1997).

to "the temporality of being," *die Temporalität des Seins*. Ten years after my discussion with Heidegger, in a chapter of *Intimations of Mortality*, I reported something about my reading of the transcript of Heidegger's lecture course from the summer of 1925, *Prolegomena to the History of the Concept of Time*.[22] Several aspects of that lecture course, which has correctly been called "the first draft" of *Being and Time*, are surprising. First, the key aspect of the temporalizing of Dasein, namely, the interpretation of *ecstatic* temporality, is missing altogether. Second, the theme of the temporality of being as such is already quite clearly important to Heidegger, even though he does not yet use the locution *Temporalität* to refer to it. Let me cite here a bit more of that 1925 lecture course than I did in my *Intimations* chapter, to clarify this admittedly abstruse point.

Near the outset of his lecture course, Heidegger asserts that beings as a whole have always been interpreted on the horizon of time. There are ostensibly extratemporal beings, such as the mathematical (or arithmetical) assertion that $2 + 2 = 4$. Yesterday, today, and tomorrow, this assertion will be taken as being true, provided all the fuss about variable number bases is forgotten. (Yet why the fuss? When did mathematicians first make that fuss? And, once again, why?) There are supposedly supratemporal beings, such as the Virgin Birth and Papal Infallibility, even if it took some time for the popes to announce these things, thus causing ripples of mirth to pass through the nineteenth and twentieth centuries. (Yet why do we laugh now at what earlier generations never dared mock?) And there are of course beings that come to be and pass away in time, some of which formulate a discourse on the regions of being against the backdrop of time. Less obvious than the importance of time for *our* understanding of the regions of being is the fact that the horizon of time is itself *historical*. We are vaguely aware that the early Greek conception of time differs from "our own," even though it takes careful study to elaborate the differences. We are also vaguely aware that different groups of people all over the world have very different ways of thinking about time. (Why are we so vague about all this? Why is it not evident to everyone everywhere that the horizon of both being (*Sein*) and beings (*Seiendes*) is whatever for their own time and place they

---

22 See David Farrell Krell, *Intimations of Mortality: Time, Truth, and Finitude in Heidegger's Thinking of Being*, chap. 3 (University Park, PA: Penn State Press, 1986), 47–48, for this and the following. There I am citing volume 20 of the Heidegger *Gesamtausgabe*, *Prolegomena zur Geschichte des Zeitbegriffs*, 7–10.

take *time* to be?) Heidegger, at the outset of his lecture course, writes two wretchedly long and difficult sentences that speak to all these parenthetical questions. He underlines many of the words in these sentences to stress their importance for him:

> But then *the history of the concept of time* is *the history of the discovery of time* and the *history of its conceptual interpretation*, which is to say that this history is the *history of the question concerning the being of beings*, the question of the attempts to uncover beings in their being, a question borne by the given understanding of time, that is, borne by the given stage of the conceptual elaboration of the phenomenon of time. Thus, to speak more precisely, the history of the concept of time is in the end *the history of the decline* and *the history of the garbling of the basic question* for scientific investigation into the being of beings: the history of the incapacity to pose the question of being in a radically new way and to elaborate that question in its primary fundamentals—an incapacity that has its grounds in the being of Dasein. (20:8)

There is something about *us*, something about our very *existence*, that has made it impossible for us to see time clearly and unmistakably as the horizon of being in general. Yet there is also something about us that makes it possible for us to elaborate such a history, even if it is, as Nietzsche said, the history of an error.

Is it therefore possible that Heidegger, before he was able to work out the detailed analyses of the *ecstatic* temporality of Dasein, analyses that we have in sections 61, 63, and 68 of *Being and Time* but that do not appear in the first draft of that book, had doubts about what seemed so obvious about the history of the concept of time and *Sein*? Doubts about whether he would be able to *return* to that horizon to take up the question of *being* in general? I think it is fair to say that all the lecture courses *after* the publication of *Being and Time* make it clear that such a return was fraught with difficulty. It is possible that Heidegger spent the rest of his life trying to work out what was highly dubious to him by 1924–25. It is possible that I heard him correctly.

I return to the notes of my third visit with Heidegger, on September 29, 1975.

> In retrospect it seems to me that Heidegger might well have repeated that such fixations on chronology are not really very important. What is important is to note how sections 5 and 6 of the Introduction seem to foreshadow or "introduce" *both* projected halves of *Being and Time*, and that

especially toward the close of section 5 there are some essential hints about *die Temporalität des Seins* ("the temporality of being") and therefore about the whole problem of Heidegger's ostensible *Kehre* or "turning."[23] The way section 6 fits the *outline* of the Second Half as described in section 8 suggests to me that the last part of section 5 (SZ 18–19) points toward the projected content of "Time and Being," that is, the third part of the First Half. This is obvious enough. The point is to think about it—by rereading those pages, where, it may be, "Heidegger II" is putting in an unscheduled appearance. Which led me to my last question.

I mentioned to Heidegger my complaint concerning the Richardsonian I-II business, and asked him about a line from the penultimate page of *Sein und Zeit*, which I'll here emphasize (Heidegger had the book on his lap; I came off my chair and read more or less over his shoulder):

> *Das* Ziel *ist die Ausarbeitung der Seinsfrage überhaupt. Die* thematische *Analytik der Existenz bedarf ihrerseits* erst *des Lichtes* aus der zuvor geklärten Idee des Seins überhaupt.
>
> ("The *goal* is the elaboration of the question of being in general. The *thematic* analysis of existence, for its part, requires *first of all* light from the idea of *being in general,* [which must be] *clarified ahead of time.*") (SZ 436)[24]

At that point I stopped and said that this seemed vital to the matter of the unity of his thinking in *Being and Time* and in the later work. He nodded with animation and said, "It is an indication of the *hermeneutical circle*—it *is* the hermeneutical circle!"

I mentioned that I had noted in an article that Heidegger was not a model airplane, and that the I-II would have to go. He smiled and said, "You know, I *told* Pater Richardson, but. . . ." He shrugged his shoulders and raised his eyebrows. We returned to the citation and read down to the formulation of the "principal problem": *läßt sich die Ontologie ontologisch begründen oder bedarf sie auch hierzu eines ontischen Fundamentes . . . ?* ("Does ontology allow itself to be grounded *ontologically,* or does it require for this too an *ontic* fundament . . . ?") (ibid.)

---

23 The point is difficult to make in English. By referring to the *Temporalität* of being, as opposed to the *Zeitlichkeit* of Dasein, Heidegger at least appears to be indicating a shift in his understanding of time in fundamental ontology. As I indicated in the long digression above, however, it is unclear whether the introduction of the word *Temporalität* is decisive here. It may well be that *ecstatic* temporality makes the very notion of *horizon* untenable, leaving the question of time as the horizon of the meaning of being in general in a kind of limbo.

24 Apart from the words *Ziel* and *thematische,* which Heidegger sets in italics, the emphases here are mine.

I stopped reading at that point, even though the "principal problem" continues by asking, "and *which* being is to take over the founding function?" In lecture courses immediately after the publication of *Sein und Zeit*, Heidegger discussed this mysterious matter—perhaps the oxymoron—of an "ontic fundament" in some detail, and he never stopped insisting on it. If it is an oxymoron, it is one that befuddles all the many discussions of the famous "ontological difference" that have taken place over the years.

I recounted the many times in *Sein und Zeit* where "ontic testimony" is taken in an effort to "ground" the designated structures in genuine experiences of Dasein: clearly the analysis of Dasein takes the second option. My voice must have lingered in a questioning way.

"*Ja*," he said.

"But in your later writings there is no talk of an 'ontic fundament'; there are no beings at all in question, but rather being itself?"

I was getting into very deep water now, especially since these formulations (for example, in "Zeit und Sein," 1961) have always troubled me: if we go off to encounter being "itself" without recourse to beings, what happens to the way taken in *Being and Time*?! Unawares, I was Richardsonizing myself!

"You must remember that the attempt to think being without reference to beings is always an *historical* attempt. That is to say, being takes on varied significance in the different epochs of the sending of being. That is what it means to try to think being without beings."

It was clear that this historical inquiry—this expansion of the destruction—did not resort to that first alternative, namely, the "ontological" grounding of ontology without reference to some sort of fundament. But *Temporalität*, rather than *Zeitlichkeit*, was to be the new fundament, one that itself was sent, that endured, and then passed in the history of being. Verily, an utterly concussible fundament!

As we were speaking about Richardson and the I-II cha-cha-cha, or the model airplane, Heidegger also complained about the "psychological" interpretation of *Sein und Zeit* by Ludwig Binswanger and Medard Boss. He nodded when I mentioned Sartre and Camus. We agreed that the customary "American" interpretation would crumble and fall if *Being and Time* were actually *read*—perhaps for the first time! He did seem to lament this state of affairs: "Everyone simply passes right on by that book."

Before I left, Heidegger wrote an inscription on the title page of my copy of *Sein und Zeit* that suggested this lament and the hope that the new anthology would provide a better introduction to the question of being: "For Dr. Krell, with special thanks for his labor in the service of genuine reflection [*Nach-denken*] on the 'question of being' ('*die Seinsfrage*'), which even today remains scarcely understood." Signed and dated "Freiburg-im-Breisgau, September 29, 1975."

Before departing I discussed with Heidegger and Frau Heidegger, who entered at the point when I mentioned Klostermann's name, the problem I was having with the Frankfurt publisher. I showed them Klostermann's letter asking me to support him in getting Harper & Row to fulfill their contract and let *Holzwege* appear as a whole. They were as puzzled as I was, since *my* problem concerns *Wegmarken*. But they promised to write him again. Frau Heidegger asked her husband if Klostermann could disregard his wishes (Heidegger had already written once that our work was to be supported), and he issued a terse negative. I thanked them, much relieved, for this second show of support. Frau Heidegger noted that we were making progress with Klostermann: his letter did not say No!

Incidentally, I mentioned that so far as *Holzwege* was concerned I was all in favor of seeing it appear as a whole, reminding Heidegger that in my introduction to *Early Greek Thinking* I stressed the organization of [the essays contained in] *Holzwege*. He seemed genuinely to remember this, for he elaborated on the point to his wife. I guess I was a little bit proud of that.

Finally, we chatted about the weather—it was a beautiful summer's day, but humid in Freiburg. Heidegger explained to me the meteorology of the Rhine plain! (. . .) I also told him about the time I spoke to my landlord [a forester] about the word *legi*, which Heidegger mentions in the *Logos* article as a weir or dam in a stream. My landlord understood it as a support to hold back the earth, for example in a garden terrace, which was the place where my landlord and I were talking at the time, and Heidegger nodded. When I mentioned [the apparent contradiction between] water and earth, Heidegger said that of course the word could be understood that way, so that both gentlemen, Heidegger and my landlord, agreed.

By this time I was gabbing so much that it was time to go. Either that or make a *real* fool of myself. So, Heidegger took time to write that inscription, while I chatted with Frau Heidegger. I then made a friendly but fast withdrawal. I was surprised at how firm Heidegger's handshake was and how genuinely he thanked me for my work on the anthology, which was a kind of thing, Elfride confided to me, that her husband seldom supported. . . .

I've forgotten [to mention] a thousand details, for example, Heidegger's personal copy of the second volume of the *Nietzsche*, with markings in multicolored inks *everywhere*, even on the inside covers, or his remarks on publishers as businessmen, for example, Gallimard. My forgetting is explained by memory and the collective toll of wombweariness. To bed. I will remember more. And some day I will have to talk about that trout with Hannah Arendt.

There is much to comment on here, but let me mention only one somewhat whimsical matter. When Heidegger took up my copy of *Sein und Zeit* to thank me for my labors in a "genuine reflection" on the being question, he might have noticed that his was not the first inscription. Opposite the title page, I had inscribed a passage from the opening chapter of *Finnegans Wake*, a single sentence in which the word "existentiality" appears. I do not believe I had ever seen the word outside of Heidegger's magnum opus, and I can only imagine that Joyce must have seen it there. The sentence (FW 18) reads: "In the ignorance that implies impression that knits knowledge that finds the nameform that whets the wits that convey contacts that sweeten sensation that drives desire that adheres to attachment that dogs death that bitches birth that entails the ensuance of existentiality."[25] I have always felt that this one sentence is as cogent and succinct an account of the fundamental ontology of Dasein as we have. I took it to be definitive evidence that Joyce had read *Being and Time* and obviously understood it. I am waiting for an invitation from the International Joyce Society to address its members on the matter, but so far the call has not come. On that day years ago in Heidegger's study, however, I was curious—and a bit nervous about—whether Heidegger would read Joyce's sentence and, if he read it, would recognize its source. He did not read it.

The truth is that my "labors" in reflecting on the question of being are not so impressive, neither then nor now. I have always marveled at Heidegger's analysis of "being-there" (*Da-sein*), especially his account of ecstatic temporality, but I have not been so wild about "being" (*Sein*) "as such." Devotion to "being" sometimes seems to me a perverse Platonism, a Platonism ("the babbling pumpt of platinism" [FW 164]) not of anamnesis but of amnesia—given, as Heidegger repeatedly says, that it is not we who have forgotten being but being that has forgotten us. I have therefore always felt vaguely guilty about Heidegger's inscription. By contrast, a sentence that begins with "ignorance" and ends with "existentiality" is much more to my liking, especially with all those delightful alliterations and assonances along the way, dogging the death that indubitably bitches birth.

And yet. As for my not being so wild about "being," the truth is that each time I read *Being and Time*—most recently in a doctoral colloquium

---

25 James Joyce, *Finnegans Wake* (New York: Viking Press, 1959), 18. There is something (or everything) irrepressible about this extraordinary work, and I fear it may be popping up throughout these three encounters. This may be due to the fact that I was teaching seminars in Freiburg on *Ulysses* and *Finnegans Wake* during the years I was meeting with Heidegger and translating his work under the watchful eyes of Glenn Gray and Hannah Arendt. My later meetings with Derrida only reinforced the importance of Joyce's meandertale for me, referred to as "FW" with page numbers.

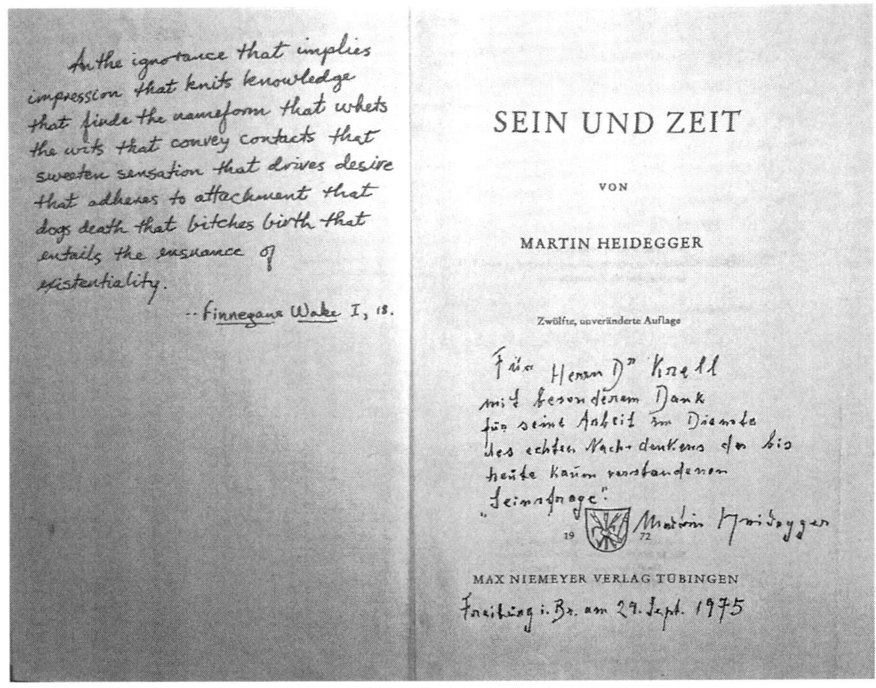

Fig. 3.3 Heidegger's inscription in my copy of *Sein und Zeit*—opposite James Joyce's inscription, as it were.

in Freiburg during the winter semester of 2021–22—Heidegger convinces me utterly that the question of the meaning of being *in general* needs to be posed anew. If I am among the "needless and heedless" whose *Bedürfnislosigkeit* causes them to scratch their heads over Heidegger's impassioned effort, his book, each time I read it, without fail draws me willy-nilly into its orbit.

* * *

My fourth visit took place on the last day of January 1976, some five months before Heidegger's death. Here, I will break the rule that I have set for myself by not reproducing my handwritten notes of the meeting but instead offering a fuller, more discursive account. The reason? The visit occurred because of my desire to discuss two translation problems in several of the essays to appear in the *Basic Writings*. For readers who know German well and who are familiar with Heidegger's work, my account here will be oversimplified; for those who know little or no German, the account will be befuddling. I will aim to explain as clearly as I can what our discussion on that day was all about.

In *Being and Time*, Heidegger offers a theory of *truth*, one of the oldest and most often discussed problems of philosophy. He defines truth as "unconcealment," *Unverborgenheit*. It is as though when something "shows itself" to us in clear light, it comes out of the shadows, comes out of hiding, as it were. I think it is true to say that all his life Heidegger was more interested in this initial and recurrent hiding, this concealment, than in the "truth" we all take for granted. After *Being and Time*, Heidegger continued to press the question of this obscure concealment. He continued to refer to "concealment," *Verborgenheit*, but the sense of that word, along with its negation, *ent-bergen*, "to uncover," began to shift. He became more interested in the active-voice verbs, *bergen* and *ent-bergen*, which have to do with concealing and revealing but which also point toward something else. When miners who are trapped below the surface of the earth or climbers who have slipped into a deep crevasse on a glacier are finally *rescued*, such rescue would be expressed by various forms of *bergen*. "Rescuing," "safeguarding," "protecting," "preserving," and "sheltering" all seem to adumbrate the sense of this German word for "concealment."

Oddly, perhaps, Heidegger felt that *language* is what has to do this sheltering and preserving of whatever shows itself. In *Being and Time*, he had written about the need to "wrest" things out of their concealment, believing that so much of what we say about things tends to cover them over rather than reveal them. In his later work, he was more inclined to think of language as a revealing that does not snatch things out of concealment but protects them from both getting lost in the dark and being drowned out by light. Heidegger's efforts with his own language—notoriously convoluted and difficult to understand—always involve the double task of bringing something to light without tearing it out of concealment.

During our conversation, I complained that the word *bergen* always seems to be taken as something "active," some rescuing action originating in "me," and therefore as being something "subjective," as though I am the captain of the rescue team. Heidegger countered that the word fundamentally has to do with the Greek word we translate as "nature" or "growth," namely, φύσις, *physis*, the root of our "physical" and "physics." *Bergen*—as sheltering and preserving—is the other side, the shadow side, of growth as rising into the light. Whatever rises or surges upward in nature does so by its own power, *von sich her*, as Heidegger says. A seedling or a squirrel or perhaps even a mathematical equation (I am less certain about a Virgin Birth) comes to the fore "on its own" or "under its own steam," as we say. *Bergen* is the part of this *ent-bergen* that reflects the *von sich her*. Actually, he added, the reflexive *sich* should be *ihm*, the dative personal pronoun: *von ihm her*, coming to the fore "all by itself." Hegel, said Heidegger, sometimes uses the personal pronoun when he slips back into the Swabian dialect that was native to him, speaking of a thing *an ihm selbst*. Because the *sich* is reflexive, it seems to relate back to a subject, as though the "doer" were what is important in *bergen*. In Heidegger's view, however, the Greeks understood "nature" as *das von-ihm-selbst her Aufgehende*, whatever grows and rises "on its own." (My notes did not say, as they should have, that the personal pronoun in that case ought to be *ihr*, that is, the *feminine* form of the dative, appropriate to the feminine noun φύσις.) In any case, said Heidegger, this appearing "on its own" or "all by itself" is what the great poet and naturalist Goethe understood by "objectivity," even if the philosopher Kant understood "objectivity" quite differently as something dependent on "the knowing subject."

In any case, to repeat, *bergen* has a strong relation to language. In Heidegger's published writings, if I am right, the word *bergen* first appears in an important essay of the early 1930s, "On the Essence of Truth," in section 9. (True, this section seems to be a later addition to the essay, from the late 1940s, but the philosophical import of the essay's account of *bergen* remains what I want to stress.) There (BW 137), Heidegger uses the expression *das lichtende Bergen*, which is, to say the least, a paradox: "the sheltering that clears" is not immediately comprehensible. The "clearing" or "lighting," better, the *lightening* of being, *die Lichtung*, is an important idea for Heidegger from *Being and Time* onward. The clearing is precisely what a forest ranger would understand it to be: a place in the forest where the trees have been thinned out, so that the density of the forest is "lightened" in such a way that "light" can penetrate. The rich and varied undergrowth of grasses and shrubs characterizes the clearing. Or, altering the metaphor, Walt Whitman tells us of the "lighters" in New York harbor, that is, small vessels perhaps the size of tugboats that would "lighten" ships of their cargo when their midship depth was too great to allow them to dock at the wharf. In both cases, it was not the luminosity of *lichten* that Heidegger wanted to stress but the making less dense or less heavy.

For Heidegger, *das lichtende Bergen*, the sheltering that clears or lightens, is intrinsically related to language: he refers to it as a kind of "saying" or "telling" (*die Sage*) that is not a "pronouncement" or "assertion" (*eine Aussage*) but something far less authoritative. Most theories of truth, especially in the Anglo-American tradition, have to do with assertions or "propositions," and truth is held to be a property of such assertions when they are correct. For Heidegger, *die Sage*, a word that is pronounced like our word "saga," is a more responsive sort of language than the language of proposition. During our conversation, Heidegger related *das lichtende Bergen*, "the sheltering that clears," to "sheer naming," as he discusses it in the last of his essays on the poet Friedrich Hölderlin, "The Poem" (1968).[26] Heidegger emphasized that what he (and Hölderlin!) meant by "naming" was not the usual sort of "designation" described by linguists, and not what the French structuralists meant by the *signifiant-signifié* relation, but something more like "invocation." Language *invokes* or *invites* what comes to the fore all by itself and shows itself, and this invocation implies a safeguarding, not a calculating or commanding.

At this point, I will revert to my final notes on the meeting, which return from the sublime to the mundane:

> Apart from all that, Heidegger seemed to be in good form. He left his couch two or three times to find books, pausing once to tease Elfride, who was there for the whole conversation, merely by bending over her and smiling as he went by. He read without glasses, which in fact he has *never* worn. Heidegger had some trouble finding the right texts, picking up *Der Satz vom Grund* instead of *Vorträge und Aufsätze*, and some difficulty finding the right page [he was looking for page 262 of the latter].
>
> Whenever I ask him a question with regard to a passage he first finds it and reads carefully through it before commenting. Taking proper time.
>
> No wine, no small talk other than to thank me for the Jaspers piece, which the editor of the *Journal of the British Society for Phenomenology* had sent him.[27] At the end of our talk we discussed again the "American

---

26 See Martin Heidegger, *Erläuterung zu Hölderlins Dichtung*, 4th ed. (Frankfurt am Main: V. Klostermann, 1971 [1951]), 187–89.

27 David Farrell Krell, "Toward *Sein und Zeit*: Heidegger's Early Review (1919–1921) of Jaspers' *Psychologie der Weltanschauungen*," *Journal of the British Society for Phenomenology* 6, no. 3 (October 1975): 147–56, later revised as the first chapter of my *Intimations of Mortality*.

interpretation" of *Being and Time*, and he ventured the guess that it would take a century to pass. He seems prepared to wait.

I was not so comfortable yesterday, being somewhat disorganized, and with Elfride interrupting occasionally to clarify philosophical questions (!). It was in any case a hurried meeting, since it came about only because Elfride had written to ask for the *boundary 2* photographs to be returned—photos I had returned last June!

I still have her letter of April 1, 1975, which accompanied a number of photographs of Martin Heidegger, with the request to return "the complete set" sometime soon. She sends her husband's hearty greetings to "Frau Prof Ahrendt [*sic*], Herr Glann Gray [*sic*], and Frau Prof. Stanbaugh [*sic*]." I had access to a darkroom in the university at that time, and so I made new negatives and prints of those photographs, prints that in the intervening years have unfortunately disappeared.

Two or three final notes from my meetings with Heidegger ought to be recorded here, even though Heidegger was absent from them. He died on May 26, 1976. Here is a note recording my learning of his death. As so often, one learns of a death in the most indirect ways, so that one feels as though one should have been better informed, should have been closer to the lives that have mattered to us in a special way. I have learned, sadly, that death often does its work without letting the rest of us know—until it is accomplished, and sometimes long after it is accomplished.

> May 27, 1976
>
> Yesterday afternoon a rumor began to circulate that Heidegger had died. A student among those who came to the Schweighof restaurant for our final Faulkner class told me she had heard a news report of it. At eleven last night the report came over television. My wife and child and I will try to travel to Messkirch for the funeral tomorrow morning.

And then, a month later:

> June 28, 1976
>
> On our way out the door we were stopped by the postman, who carried a telegram informing us of the death of my wife's father. She and our baby daughter have been in Honduras since June 1.
>
> I spoke with von Herrmann this morning about Heidegger's death. Heidegger had suffered several attacks of "weakness" during the three weeks prior to his death, but he had recovered from each of them sufficiently to continue with his work. (He had made an appointment with von Herrmann for the Friday that followed his death. I myself had no appointment for that day, but was merely *intending* to make one.) He

died in the morning while Frau Heidegger was preparing breakfast. She came into the bedroom and noticed that he had changed his position in the bed, his arms akimbo, hands palm upward. She touched him gently. He was warm. She went back to the kitchen. A friend and helper of the Heideggers, a person they trusted, a household helper of some sort, went to get something from the room. As soon as she saw Heidegger she knew: the man lives no more. His hand was cold. She called Elfride into the room.

The burial in Messkirch took place on Friday, May 28, two days after the death. Even so, some four hundred persons were there for the burial at two in the afternoon.

"The quietest death mortals can have," commented von Herrmann, a death without any sort of forewarning, without agony or drama of any kind. At a certain moment his heart "simply stopped beating."

Three final sets of notes from my journal record visits with Frau Elfride Heidegger some months after her husband's death. And not many pages after that are notes on the deaths of Hannah Arendt on December 4, 1975, and J. Glenn Gray on October 29, 1977, and the passing of my father on April 2, 1978. These years, from late 1975 to early 1978, were the first in my life when death struck home, as it were. Hannah's death, then Heidegger's, Glenn's, and my father's: I began to learn the meaning of the word *bereft*.

There continued to be problems with the Klostermann firm and the proposed anthology. Even though I had written Frau Heidegger a condolence letter, I had to continue troubling her with our problems. As for that condolence letter, I had to tell her about the death of my father-in-law, explaining our absence from the funeral in Messkirch. Elfride Heidegger wrote me on August 21, 1976, expressing her condolences in turn. She also said that if troubles with Klostermann persisted, I should call to arrange a visit. "I had hoped," she wrote, "that everything was in the clear." Here is my record of the two visits with Elfride Heidegger after Martin's death.

August 26, 1976

Visited Frau H yesterday, mainly on account of the Klostermann mess. "What's the problem?" was the way she began our conversation. She was in black, but with a handsome beige blouse. Sharp, clear-witted.

While she searched through her files for the Klostermann letters—they all begin with lamentations about regrettable misunderstandings, "Oh, yes, with Klostermann it's always about a 'misunderstanding,'" she muttered wryly—I had a chance to look around the empty office. Yes, it was more an office now than a study. A photo of the Todtnauberg hut, a sketch of the pine-filled countryside. A tiny graphite sketch of "the Three Holy Kings," that is, the children who march through the village every January 6 singing their hymns. Above the left side of the work table, two portraits of Hölderlin, the first a silhouette of the handsome twenty-year-old, "Hölderlin as a Master's Student," the second a sketch of the decrepit seventy-two-year-old by Louise Keller.

The faded brown velvet chaise longue, worn and now empty until Elfride sat at the foot of it, I in a chair near by. Heidegger's library still intact—but no folders on the table or on the window sill, no projects, no agenda for the day.

Our discussion was mostly business, although I gave her a photo of our five-month-old daughter in an undershirt but with a philosophical expression, and I invited her several times to our home in St. Ulrich. She explained with evident pride that she is the *Universalerbin* ("the sole literary executor"), that all the rights to her husband's writings are now hers, and that even the translation contracts that Klostermann makes must be approved by her. "I won't be holding the rights for long, of course." I thought or feared that she meant she was planning to sell them. She smiled at my puzzlement and added, "I'm eighty-three." After her death the rights will be in the hands of their younger son, the second son, not Jörg but Hermann.[28]

I must have written once again to Elfride Heidegger asking if I might visit. There was an issue about my reproducing a manuscript page from the first volume of Heidegger's *Nietzsche*. She sent me a card on March 26, 1977: "You will find me at home every morning, from 10 o'clock on). Whether I can help you is questionable. Friendly greetings and best wishes to you and yours, etc."

March 30, 1977

A second visit with Frau Heidegger, in order to get permission to print a photo of one of the manuscript pages of the *Nietzsche*, which was granted. Frau Heidegger took me over to the main house on the Rötebuckweg and up to Heidegger's study. The whole house is paneled in pine, with wooden floors and ceilings. The study looks out onto the Zähringer Burg. A mammoth desk, probably oak. A simple, warm room, with all the walls covered with bookshelves. Heidegger worked in that study for thirty-seven years, said Frau Heidegger.

She gave me a few more details about his death and the funeral, and she showed me the sheet of paper on which, a week before his death, he chose some lines from Hölderlin to be read over his grave. I could not

---

28 Elfride died in 1992. The rights passed to Hermann Heidegger and are now, as I write, in the hands of Hermann's son Dr. Arnulf Heidegger.

make out the citations, but I noticed his arrangement and rearrangement of their order, from one to five.

Before I left I proposed writing a biography. She quoted the Aristotle-lecture epigram to me ["Aristotle was born, worked, and died"] and said she concurred with her husband's view. Project dropped.

She recollected Heidegger's relations with students, saying that many distraught young folks came to him for advice and counsel—*labil*, she called them, "unsteady," "delicate," "sickly." They seemed to be soothed by the steadiness and sturdiness that radiated from him. And Heidegger would give them assignments in tune with their own interests, encouraging them to sink into their work, into something "entirely neutral, impersonal." Heideggerian logotherapy.

I am certain that the reference to "logotherapy" was ironic on my part. I, like almost everyone of my generation, had studied Viktor Frankl's *From Death Camp to Existentialism*, where "logotherapy" has its origin. And my discussions with Hannah Arendt kept Heidegger's support of National Socialism at the front of my mind while I was joining her in the effort to translate Heidegger's work as ably as possible. Clearly, I owed an enormous debt to Heidegger's work, whatever the increasing distance from it in later years.

It was not only a debt to Heidegger's work, however, that I owed, and I should not allow this chapter to end without saying that I felt respect and even affection for the man I met. My relation to Heidegger was not simply about philosophy or the academy. I clearly was drawn to this man who was more like a grandfather than a father to me, a grandfather who had the history of philosophy at his fingertips. No doubt, the expressions of that affection remained stiff and stodgy on both our parts. After all, he was a German professor and a thinker of worldwide renown. Yet there were some personal exchanges in addition to the conversations I have mentioned. I recall the handmade card he and Elfride sent welcoming our first child into the world. I also recall sending him a letter congratulating him on what turned out to be his last birthday. I still have a faded photocopy of the letter, written in German, which I'll put into English here, especially because it cites Yeats:

Dear Professor Heidegger!

In the year of your birth, a poem appeared by the Irish poet William Butler Yeats, which contains the following stanza:

The wandering earth herself may be
Only a sudden flaming word,

> In clanging space a moment heard,
> Troubling the endless reverie.[29]

I then attempted a translation of the stanza into German, one that reveals why I no longer make such attempts, and closed with "hearty congratulations for September 26, 1975."

---

29 These are the final lines of the first stanza of "The Song of the Happy Shepherd," from *Crossways*, in William Butler Yeats, *The Collected Poems* (New York: Macmillan, 1956), 7.

Fig. 4.1 and 4.2 Two views of Heidegger's *Hütte* at Todtnauberg, the top photo approaching from the path above the cabin, the second taken from below its southwest corner.

4

THE DEBT AND THE DISTANCE

In her article for *The New York Review of Books*, "Martin Heidegger at Eighty," Hannah Arendt writes about the first seminar of Heidegger's she attended. It was during the winter semester of 1924 at Marburg University, where Heidegger had recently joined the philosophy faculty. The subject of the seminar was Plato's *Sophist*, one of the "late" dialogues, famous for its complexity and the uncertainty of its conclusions or even of Plato's intentions. Arendt was struck most by the fact that Heidegger spent the entire semester on this one dialogue, although he preceded it with a long look at Aristotle, and that he did not make general remarks about "Plato as a whole," as though Plato could ever be a whole. An entire course on *one* dialogue? "Today this sounds quite familiar, because nowadays so many proceed in this way; but no one did so before Heidegger."[1]

Arendt's comment reminds me of a similar observation by Jacques Derrida in a seminar on Heidegger's reading of the Austrian poet Georg Trakl. Derrida tells his students that before Heidegger, no one would have had the temerity to devote an entire lecture course to a poet, much less to the *single* poem of *one* poet—he is thinking of Heidegger's lecture courses on Hölderlin's *Der Ister* and *Andenken*, taught during the 1930s and early 1940s. Nowadays, courses on "philosophy and literature" abound, of course, but can one imagine a "philosophy and literature" course on *one* poem?

---

1 Hannah Arendt, "Martin Heidegger at Eighty," in *New York Review of Books*, October 21, 1971, 51, for this and the later quotation; see also BW 14–15. For the original form of this famous text, see Ursula Ludz, ed., *Hannah Arendt-Martin Heidegger, Briefe 1925–1975 und andere Zeugnisse*, 3rd ed. (Frankfurt am Main: V. Klostermann, 2002 [1998]), 179–92. I will cite the Arendt-Heidegger letters as "AHB" with page number throughout my text.

Teaching experts in the dean's office would object, "But what if a student doesn't feel *comfortable* with that one poem?"

Arendt records the way students from all over Germany came to Marburg with the express purpose of studying with Heidegger—the presence there of theologian Rudolf Bultmann was also an important draw—even though Heidegger had not yet published a book and therefore could not have been known through publications. He was achieving renown as a teacher, and his fame spread by word of mouth among students who were serious about philosophy. "Thinking has come to life again; the cultural treasures of the past, believed to be dead, are being made to speak, in the course of which it turns out that they propose things altogether different from the familiar, worn-out trivialities they had been presumed to say. There exists a teacher; one can perhaps learn to think" (AHB 182; YB 49). Rüdiger Safranski gently ironizes Arendt's account, remarking that it sounds like a eulogy (RS 461/417). Yet Arendt is not alone in her adulation of Heidegger-the-teacher. Antonia Grunenberg cites Hans Jonas's *Erkenntnis und Verantwortung* (1991), which offers some "first impressions" of Heidegger as a teacher:

> My first impression, right from the beginning, was that Heidegger was much, much more difficult than Husserl. . . . One immediately had the sense, without really understanding anything yet, that here there was something new, here novel perspectives were being opened up and new linguistic tools were being developed. I know that in this semester [i.e., the summer semester of 1921], without understanding much at all, I was completely convinced that significant, essential philosophizing was at work. Here was a man who was thinking in front of his students, not lecturing on thoughts he'd already had, as was the case with Husserl, but someone who was carrying out the act of thinking itself in the presence of his pupils. And that was earth-shattering, even, for instance, when it came to externals: it often happened that he turned away from his audience, turned aside and gazed out the window, or rather looked inside himself and thought aloud. One had the feeling that here one was accompanying the originating action of an entirely original, unique, new thinking, discovering, and disclosing. At the same time, he was an excellent pedagogue. I still remember today a seminar on Aristotle's *De anima*, his treatise on the soul. I don't think we got any farther than the first three or four chapters of the entire book. The text was interpreted sentence by sentence—naturally, we were reading it in Greek, that was automatic back then—and we didn't relent until we had penetrated the innermost chambers of Aristotle's thinking and seeing. And many times it happened—and this is something I learned

from Heidegger for my whole life—that someone would say something, using technical philosophical terminology. Then Heidegger would say, "Much too learned, much too learned; please express yourself a little less learnedly." He wanted to be liberated from the firmly established terminology in the philosophical field, to get back to the original phenomena. He wanted us simply to be able to *see*. That did not mean that it was easy, because for him the simple insights lay in the depths, not on the surface. (AG 90–91/56, quoting Jonas.)

I did not have Heidegger as a teacher, at least not in the straightforward sense. Yet tributes from his students, even those who had every reason to take infinite distance from their former teacher, tempt me into making an extended personal remark. I often find myself taking distance from Heidegger's interpretations of those "cultural treasures of the past," whether thinkers or poets, and I find many agitated cries of "No, no!" scribbled into the margins of my copies of his books. Heidegger often seems to me now to have little to do with *my* Plato, *my* Nietzsche, *my* Schelling, *my* Hölderlin, *my* Trakl, until I realize that "my" discovery of these figures was almost entirely due to Heidegger. He introduced me to them; he made me take them seriously. Richard Rorty once remarked that Heidegger's readings of various figures in the history of philosophy would be what he will be remembered for, and although I believe there is much more about Heidegger to remember, Rorty is right. And even if one resists the results each time Heidegger interprets a text, that resistance itself shows us on whose shoulders we are standing, hoping to maintain balance as we make our "own" way forward. The distance and the debt, never the one without the other. Hannah Arendt is the very embodiment of this principle for me.

In the following pages, I will read and comment on Rüdiger Safranski's biography of Heidegger. My reflections on Heidegger's life are most often in accord with his, but occasionally not. Safranski begins with a critical observation: in a brief prefatory remark, he observes that Heidegger loved "the grand gesture," and one often does not know whether he is talking about the fate of the Western world or about himself. Safranski also identifies Heidegger's tendency to "self-mythologize," especially regarding the time and place of his birth and his childhood (RS 15–17/1–3). I am reminded of two of the most absurd examples of this mythologizing that I have seen, both of them in the *Black Notebooks*, and I will mention them shortly. Safranski is also right when he says that a certain "luster," or *Glanz*, is reflected in every one of Heidegger's references to his youth and the village of his youth.

Messkirch is the seedbed of his nostalgia for the "homeland," a nostalgia in which his mother plays an important role. Indeed, she *embodies* the homeland for her son (RS 21–22/7–8).

Safranski adds an aspect to Heidegger's small size, even as a boy, an aspect that seems to be merely metaphorical but that may be quite significant (RS 36/20). In terms of social standing, Heidegger's birth family belongs among what the Germans call *die kleinen Leute*, "the simple people," hoi polloi, the many-too-many. Heidegger's invective against the cult of personality that is so rampant in his and our time reflects something of the *ressentiment* that adheres to someone who has suffered the rebuffs of the high and mighty. Even as a professor in Marburg, where he is idolized by his students, Heidegger is often mistaken for the janitor by colleagues who do not know him. Heidegger takes stubborn pride in his nonacademic attire and appearance, both when teaching at the university and when attending other functions. At Davos in 1929, he was pleased when the conference participants were startled by his showing up in his ski outfit.

Beyond such nostalgia for—and pride taken in—his rural origins, however, Heidegger often stylizes his childhood in Messkirch. He sometimes paints it as the bucolic background to his later heroic struggle with *beyng*— as though in Messkirch he was in fact the child Achilles on the slopes of Mount Pelion preparing for Troy under the tutelage of Chiron the centaur (95:290). In an earlier *Notebook*, he stylizes the date of his birth in a way that causes me to gasp: in 1806, Hölderlin is interned in a psychiatric clinic; in 1813, Wagner is born at the zenith of German power and influence; in 1843, Hölderlin dies, and one year later Nietzsche is born; during the years 1870 to 1876, the German *Gründerjahre*, its "Gilded Age," a complacent Germany is challenged by the publication of Nietzsche's *Untimely Meditations*; in 1883, Wagner dies and the first part of *Thus Spoke Zarathustra* is published; in December 1888, Nietzsche's "euphoria" in Turin leads to his collapse in January 1889. After staging this elaborate tableau, Heidegger enters two dashes into his notebook and then, in the lower-right-hand corner of the page, he writes "September 26, 1889," the date of his birth (94:223). True, numbers and dates fascinate the unconscious of us all: recall Freud's uncanny experiences with them; recall also Derrida's often whimsical play with dates—he pledges absolute sincerity and total transparency in one text, then signs it "April 1." I have always noticed that my birth year follows Nietzsche's by exactly one hundred years. Yet Heidegger's stylization or lionization of his birth year strikes me as nothing short of megalomania, a grand gesture indeed, and perhaps an astonishing overcompensation for the small size of the boy who dwells among the simple people. Decades ago, at the time I was meeting with Heidegger, I was told—I believe by both Joan Stambaugh and Hannah Arendt (YB 306)—that his brother Fritz was the only one who could mock Martin's grand self-stylizations, and that for this reason Elfride hated her brother-in-law.

Safranski tells us a lot about the shadows that haunted Heidegger's bucolic childhood in Messkirch. He identifies perhaps the most baneful characteristic of the "populism" of small villages such as Messkirch during the period of Heidegger's youth, namely, their antisemitism: pious and true to the Roman Catholic Church, while hateful toward "Prussia," nationalistic only in the sense of a "regional" Swabian-Alemannic nationalism, the villagers were closely tied to a sense of "homeland," a homeland that was agrarian, anticapitalistic, wary of the city, and antisemitic (RS 18/5). The poorer among the villagers—and that would include Heidegger's family—regarded the more liberal and generally wealthier "Old Catholics" as enemies. Indeed, the *Altkatholiker*, members of the higher end of the middle class, despised the poorer farmers. Martin and Fritz Heidegger suffered under this contempt, such that in his later youth, Martin became an opponent of the Old Catholics and a zealous proponent of the Roman Catholic "anti-modernist," "anti-liberal" movement (RS 20–21/6–7). Because his parents could not afford to pay the fees charged by the better schools in the region, they (and he) came to depend on scholarships offered by the Church to boys who showed promise for the priesthood. For the thirteen years of his middle school, high school, and university education, Heidegger was dependent on these scholarships. He was thus trapped in what he later called "the system of Catholicism," even as his faith faded away (RS 24–27/9–13). This led to a lifelong resentment against all the Christian churches, whether Catholic or Protestant. "Only with difficulty can one forgive those from whom one has had to beg," remarks Safranski (RS 63/47).

Safranski takes such resentment to be a major factor in Heidegger's sympathy for the anticlericalism of the Nazi movement. I would add that it is certainly true that this anticlericalism becomes a major theme of Heidegger's *Black Notebooks* from the 1930s and 1940s, which rail against the Christian churches much more than against "world Jewry." Inasmuch as the National Socialist Party had its own priesthood, as it were, anticlericalism also seems to underlie Heidegger's contumely vis-à-vis the party in the *Notebooks.*

Even though Heidegger was housed in a seminary during his high school years in Constance, 1903–06, the school he attended was a public school. According to Safranski, the curriculum there, along with the general atmosphere of the school, reflected the "Baden liberalism" of the southwestern region, famous for its resistance to Prussian domination during the 1848 Revolution. At the cultural center of the town, the Insel Hotel, students attended not only concerts but also public lectures that reflected a certain liberalism and modernism. Among the themes of these lectures were Nietzsche's philosophy, Ibsen's plays, Eduard von Hartmann's *Philosophy of the Unconscious*, Hans Vaihinger's *Philosophy of the As-If*, psychoanalysis, dream interpretation, and "atheism." Whereas the leaders of the seminary tried to counteract and even suppress these influences, the public high school teachers encouraged them. Piety at home, skepticism at school.

In 1906, at age seventeen, Heidegger transferred to the *Berthold Gymnasium* in Freiburg, where a less liberal curriculum awaited him. True, he read widely, especially in German literature—a bit too widely, laments his final report card in 1909—but never in the modernist modes. Nothing of the naturalist, symbolist, or *Jugendstil* authors belonged on his shelves. Safranski notes the tension in Heidegger's early education between the liberal bourgeois-urban environment in the towns where he studied and the antimodernist conservative Catholic institutions that housed him and paid for his education. The ideology of these institutions seems to have prevailed at least until Heidegger was in his early twenties, at which point he broke with the "system of Catholicism."

Yet something of the intense discipline and rigor of these early years remains. Safranski speculates that the opposition between what Heidegger in *Being and Time* calls *the proper* or *authentic* and the mundane public world of the "they," *das Man*, reflects this tension: on the one side, we find rigor, seriousness, submission to duty, persistence, and patience; on the opposing side, speed, superficiality, caprice, and the craving for novelty. Earnest effort confronts mere busyness; rootedness in a tradition confronts rootlessness. Some take everything to heart and are true to what is their "own," while others live free and easy in distraction and dispersion. Heidegger's *rigorism* will never allow him to abide the free and easy. According to Safranski, that rigor will remain steadfast even as its manifestations change: "The young Heidegger depends on tradition and discipline. Later it is a matter of resoluteness, decisionism. Later still it is *Gelassenheit* ('letting-be') on which he relies" (RS 37/23). One might wonder how iron discipline comports with letting-be, heavy metal with either Paul McCartney or Meister Eckhart.

Heidegger's early enthusiasm for seventeenth-century reformist monk Johann Ulrich Megerle, alias Abraham a Sancta Clara, born not far from Messkirch, reflects Heidegger's early antimodernist rigor. He accepts and adopts in his own early essays the Augustinian's polemics against the pleasure-seekers of the corrupt cities, the proud who resist the Church's teachings and authority, the profligate rich, the greedy—and the "so-called 'usurious Jew'" (RS 33/18). Antonia Grunenberg also recounts in a thought-provoking way Heidegger's devotion as a fervent young Catholic to Abraham a Sancta Clara. It was principally Megerle's connection to the regional homeland that drew Heidegger to him, but the rigor and the readiness to engage in polemic also surely captivated him. Grunenberg comments, "Today one would call Abraham a Sancta Clara a talented populist" (AG 28/14). Not a Trump; rather, a *talented* populist. Unfortunately, Megerle's regionalism and his reformist zeal were infected by a strong strain of antisemitism, one that was bound up with suspicion toward and even hatred of city dwellers, endemic among country folk—resentment toward the wealthy bankers and the merchants that cheated them and enjoyed an easy life, fear of the new technologies that invaded and complicated their space, suspicion aimed at every form of "liberalism" and "modernism," which their priests were loudly condemning every Sunday morning.

Heidegger resisted and feared the urban environment all his life. "Urbanity" and "cosmopolitanism" are among the things he despised most, for they were things he was never able to achieve. Even in his dress, he affected the style of the peasant, craftsman, or man of the countryside. The cities where he spent most of his life, Marburg and Freiburg, were anything but metropolitan, but even so, Heidegger preferred to be at his cabin in Todtnauberg. Even after he was able to shake free of the conservative Catholic inheritance of this south-German country life, something of the antisemitic and antiurban strain no doubt persisted. He was able to shed the dogmas of the Catholic faith by his early twenties, but there were strains and stains that he was never able to remove, not entirely. Grunenberg cites an early article by Heidegger in a conservative Catholic journal in which he speaks of the need for "renewal" and for a "healing of the folk soul." She asks, "How does the young Heidegger know that the folk was ill? People said so, the pastor was preaching it, the archbishop said so, it was in the newspapers" (AG 31/15). Already in his early adulthood, a sense of "the darkening of the world" (*Weltverdunkelung, Weltverdüsterung*) haunted Heidegger: the world was sinking into chaos and confusion, alien forces were menacing the spirit of the people, and only rigorous faith and discipline would offer rescue.

In short, Catholic antimodernism was both *heimatverbunden*, "bound up with the homeland," and *antisemitisch* (RS 33/19). And yet, Safranski emphasizes that this notorious antisemitism, promulgated by the influential mayor of Vienna, Karl Lueger, is entirely absent from Heidegger's early "Catholic" writings (RS 34/20). Instead, the young university student inveighs against the modernist cult of personality: Oscar Wilde, "the dandy," Paul Verlaine, "the ingenious drunkard," Maxim Gorky, "the great vagabond," and "Nietzsche the Superman" (RS 35/21).

Even though it may be an anachronism, I want to introduce here a much later judgment concerning Heidegger's internal struggles with Catholicism. In 1947, Max Müller, a Catholic philosopher at Freiburg, was asked by Church leaders there to prepare a report about Heidegger's relation to the Church. Even though the report comes almost three decades after Heidegger began to pull away from the Church, I find it worth citing. There seems to be a genuine insight here, no matter how drastic the language:

> Heidegger is a vastly deep but internally tortured and lacerated human being, one whom God's fish hooks, which were cast at him in baptism and throughout a very pious education, can never again be removed from his flesh, even though these hooks often prove to be instruments of torture that he ought to extract. On this basis one may perhaps understand why he hates the Church as much and as often as he loves it. This entire torture and inner laceration make him wholly unclear as a figure; they allow us no decision to which we might come. But one thing is certain: the religious problem and the Christian problem are major problems for him, and he is relentlessly circling about the question of the Absolute. (AG 292/212, citing Müller)

Heidegger as Ahab, complete with harpoon and hempen hawsers, toiling in the coilings of the faith that will be his doom. Or as the stricken whale, circling to face the setting sun of the Absolute. No doubt overdrawn, this portrait, and yet there is something, perhaps a great deal, to it.

*   *   *

One of the ways Safranski's biography helps me is that he offers a careful account of at least some of the way stations on Heidegger's path of thought. For example, his account of *Being and Time* in his ninth chapter, while quite positive in tone, also pinpoints some of the most problematic issues of that masterwork. In chapter 11, he treats in detail the first half of the lecture course that Heidegger offered in 1929–30, and his treatment is perspicuous. At a certain point, however, Safranski throws in the towel. Heidegger's work of the 1930s and 1950s he simply cannot take seriously, and so he caricatures it. Here, too, for me, it has to be a matter of both the debt and the distance. For I believe I understand why Safranski cannot abide the products of Heidegger's "inner emigration" of the 1930s and 1940s, nor even the postwar essays and lectures of the 1950s. Heidegger the phenomenologist Safranski can read and understand. Heidegger the "thinker of being" represents a radically different sort of challenge.

Perhaps the central work of the 1930s, Heidegger's *Contributions to Philosophy: On* Ereignis (1936–38) offers the best example. Safranski, in his eighteenth chapter, calls this massive collection of aphorisms "a laboratory for inventing a new way to talk about God" (RS 345/308). He is clearly reacting to two small sections of the book—which some call Heidegger's second magnum opus—which admittedly do speculate on what Heidegger calls "the last god." These sections distill Heidegger's absorption of Schelling, Hölderlin, and Nietzsche, and the result is a heady elixir. If *Being and Time* pledges to "radically extrude" all theological speculations, those speculations return in force toward the end of the 1930s. The language is exceedingly strange. Heidegger's proclamation, *Das Seyn ist die Erzitterung des Götterns* (65:239: "Beyng is the shivering of a god at birth"), seems nothing short of necromantic. Safranski comments, disdainfully, "Words. Can Heidegger be thinking of something with them? He tries to, for several hundred pages" (RS 345/308). Safranski tries to define the strange word *Göttern* as "a happening that causes us to tremble" (ibid.), and Heidegger is indeed offering us his version or vision of the medieval *tremendum*, the final version, since this is indeed the *last* god. The word *Göttern* seems to imply the *accouchement* of deity, the birth or coming-to-be of gods. One thinks of the disastrous first birth of Dionysos, born of a Semele blasted by lightning.

Safranski thinks more in terms of the medieval: he calls the *Beiträge* Heidegger's "litany" or "rosary," or, taking a desperate leap into modernity, "an entirely metaphysical Dadaism" (RS 346/310). It is fortunate that Safranski did not have the opportunity to read Heidegger's *Black Notebooks* before writing his biography, since the litany and the Dadaism there become even more pronounced, with the god or dog of *beyng* endlessly chasing its tale, as it were.

Only once did I dare to write about the *Beiträge*.[2] I tried to develop the idea that this very odd book is *paranoetic,* a condition that is more devastating than *paranoia.* The paranoiac has at least some sense that a *particular being* is threatening him; the threat to Heidegger, however, is precisely one that comes from being itself, being *without* beings, hence from *beyng.* I interwove in my chapter on the *Beiträge* a number of passages from Freud's account of the Schreber case to show that paranoid schizophrenia provides at least a thought-provoking parallel to Heidegger's *Contributions.* Not many Heideggerians have forgiven me for that, and I sympathize with them. Perhaps I, like Safranski, should have simply thrown in the towel. Yet "The Last God" and "The Futural Ones" have not lost their perverse attraction for me—as a speculative goety for our darkening world—at least when they are read in the rich contexts offered by Schelling and Hölderlin.

As for Safranski's treatment of Heidegger's essays and lectures of the 1950s, the twenty-third chapter of Safranski's biography is his weakest. Despite his later warning not to mock when Heidegger's language becomes most convoluted and his thinking most obscure, this chapter merely ironizes Heidegger's thought of the 1950s. Safranski sees it all as nebulous fluff about being, or *beyng,* which is, as Hegel says, equivalent to nothing, nothing but what the Germans call *Frömmelei* or *Frömmlerei,* "pious prattle." However, while much of the work of the 1950s is doubtless what Merleau-Ponty and Sartre eschewed as "high-altitude thinking," there is much more that remains remarkable: Heidegger's essay on technology has been and will be remembered long after all the texts by others to which Safranski compares it have been forgotten. It is no accident that architect Daniél Libeskind has long been drawn to the essay "Building Dwelling Thinking"; no accident that Ute Guzzoni, occupying a space somewhere

---

2 David Farrell Krell, "Paranoetic Thinking: 'Life' in the 1936–1938 *Contributions to Philosophy (Of Propriation),*" in *Daimon Life: Heidegger and Life-Philosophy* (Bloomington: Indiana University Press, 1992).

between the study of Adorno's work and an admiration of Eastern thought, prizes these later essays of Heidegger's even more than *Being and Time*; no accident that René Char valued "The Thing" so highly; no accident that Arendt felt that *What Is Called Thinking?* marked Heidegger's return to and expansion of what was best about his thinking; no accident that Derrida regarded Heidegger's essays on language, published in 1959, especially the essay called "Language in the Poem," as his richest and most challenging philosophical work. Even if "the fourfold," "the granting," "the event," and other constructs of this period seem ethereal, we still find in them Heidegger's persistent emphasis on the mortals, who never fly as high as they might wish:

> Mortals are human beings. They are called mortals because they can die. To die means to make death *as* death possible. Only human being dies, and indeed it dies continuously as long as it remains on the earth, under the sky, and in the face of the deities. If we name the mortals, then we think the other three along with them, although we do not reflect upon the unity of the four.
>
> We call this unity *the fourfold*. Mortals *are* in the fourfold insofar as they *dwell*. Yet the fundamental trait of dwelling is safeguarding. Mortals dwell in a way that safeguards the fourfold in its presencing. ("Building Dwelling Thinking"; BW 352)

After Levinas and Blanchot, we may wonder whether mortals really do make death *as* death possible, or whether they simply have to *wait* for the *impossible* to arrive. After Derrida, we are more likely to expand the notion of mortality to all the living, to everything that comes to be and passes away. All the living, admittedly, requires safeguarding. And if nowadays the faces of deity seem to have withdrawn for every rational and sober person, it may well be that deity has always worn a thousand masks. This seems to be tepid paganism to monotheists, who love the stony authority of their particular monolith. Yet monotheism has not done much to safeguard earth and sky, much less to shelter the mortals. In any case, earth and sky are raging now, and mortals might do well to think about building for the sake of dwelling. It is easy to be snide about all this and to call it fluff. But as Yeats said, "Mock mockers after that."[3] For it is hard to believe that the way we are thinking and acting now will enable us and our Earth to survive and flourish. At his worst, Heidegger succumbed to the seductions of power,

---

3 Yeats, *The Collected Poems*, 207.

destructive power, authoritarian power; at his best, he searched for the origins of that destructive power and tried, without authority, to promulgate a different sort of thinking. I am unable to mock the effort.

*   *   *

Safranski does have many excellent chapters on Heidegger's work, especially the early work, and I do him a disservice to leave these chapters without comment. Yet I want to take up now that aspect of Heidegger's biography that is most troubling. After *Being and Time* was published in 1927, critics were quick to find fault with Heidegger's account of being-with-others in the social and political worlds. Georg Misch and Helmuth Plessner, for example, argued that Heidegger failed to develop a radical sense of historicality as *decision*; he offered no prescriptions for the political consequences of "authenticity" for "the nation" (RS 239/209). Of course, that was not Heidegger's intention, but still, the critique stung. Safranski believes that such criticisms helped to push Heidegger in a "decisionist" direction—not that Misch or Plessner was responsible for Heidegger's imbroglio with National Socialism, but that Heidegger allowed himself to be tempted by the search for power and political influence.[4] At all events, Safranski, at the end of an exhaustive analysis, writes the remarkable sentence, "The fact, not that he was apolitical, but that he did not notice he was not political, and the fact that he confused his historical *gnosis* [i.e., his notion of a history of *beyng*] for political thinking—this is what makes his political activity during these months so treacherous" (RS 300–301/267).

It all begins modestly enough. On May 10, 1930, Heidegger writes to Elisabeth Blochmann that an enduring philosophy must be one that "is equal to its times" or that "rises to the challenge of its times," *ihrer Zeit mächtig ist* (RS 241/211). For Heidegger, rising to the challenge most often means learning how to read the Greeks: "Every time I advance a bit farther in my own work the more certain I feel compelled to return to the grand beginning with the Greeks. And often I have to wonder whether it isn't more

---

4 A student of mine at the University of Freiburg, Julian Pfitzer, who knows Plessner's work quite well, assures me that Safranski's account misconstrues Plessner's critique of Heidegger. Plessner's criticism is not that Heidegger needs a more "decisive" politics, but that Heidegger's analysis of *Eigentlichkeit* (appropriateness, authenticity) in his fundamental ontology of Dasein is essentialist: it underestimates in a fatal way the quite varied societal underpinnings that every philosophical anthropology has to take into account. The "essence" of human existence cannot be "grounded" or "founded" in such a supposed authenticity.

essential that I drop all my own efforts and work in such a way that their world is not merely transmitted to us but stands before our eyes as a model in its revolutionary grandeur" (RS 245/215, citing the December 19, 1932, letter to Blochmann). Yet Heidegger at least for a time leaves his Greeks in abeyance and turns to politics.

Initially, *university* politics, not *national* politics, are his focus. In a 1925 letter to Arendt, he laments, "But it may be that stagnation permeates our universities" (AHB 17). Yet by the winter of 1931–32, Heidegger is openly declaring his support for the National Socialist German Workers' Party . His students are "completely surprised," as is his friend and fellow "revolutionary" (at least where the academy is concerned) Karl Jaspers (RS 258–59/227–28). By February 1933, Heidegger is prepared to act—by way of plunging into academic politics at the university. In March, he tells Jaspers that "one has to engage" (ibid.). There can be no doubt that by this time, Heidegger is caught in a revolutionary fervor and furor. He has always been desperate to reform the university, to purge it of its stodgy, narrow-minded specialists and replace them with something philosophically profound, something charismatic. Now is the time to renovate. He will be able to "use" the National Socialist revolution to that end.

Heidegger regards the party's antisemitism as a passing phase—as do even some members of the Jewish population who are sympathetic to the need for a "national" revolution (RS 261/230). Disgusted by the political wrangling of the Weimar Republic, Heidegger and others want to have done with pluralism. They are determined to have the unique, the single and the singular, in Safranski's words, "the German, the member of the *Volk*, the worker of fist and brow, the spirit" (ibid.). As for the "passing phase" of antisemitism, there turn out to be many such phases during the 1930s, each phase ceding to a more disastrous one. Yet Heidegger seems to be immured against any recognition of them: "political repression, mob vandalism, antisemitic attacks, all seem to him to be epiphenomena that one has to accept as the price to pay" for the revolution (RS 266/234). In June 1933, Heidegger visits Jaspers for the last time before the war. Jaspers notices immediately that his friend has changed (RS 264/232).

—How is such an uneducated man, a man like Hitler, to govern Germany? asks Jaspers.

—Education is entirely indifferent, replies Heidegger. Just look at his wonderful hands!

Safranski now raises the controversial question about the relation between Heidegger's "political error" and the *philosophical* or *theoretical* work that might have paved the way for it. He writes:

> Thus we see a Heidegger cocooned within his dream of a history of being, and his actions on the political stage are those of a philosophical dreamer. In a letter to Jaspers on April 8, 1950, he will admit that he was *politically* dreaming and that he was therefore deceived. But that he was politically deceived because he was dreaming *philosophically* he will never be able to concede. For as a philosopher who wanted to ground historical time, he had to defend—also to himself—his competency to judge philosophically what was happening historico-politically. . . . Something philosophical occurred to him with regard to Hitler; Heidegger brought philosophical themes into play; he set the stage, an entirely imaginary philosophical stage for historical deeds. . . . True, he will later transform his "mistake" into a philosophical story, one in which he reserves a grandiose role for himself: it was being itself that had erred in and through him. He had carried the banner of the "errancy of being," *Irrnis des Seins*. (RS 266/234–35)

Safranski's judgment, apparently harsh, seems to me essentially correct. Heidegger's militancy, decisionism, and national fixation—especially his confusion of the Swabian-Alemannic *regional* with the German *national*—were rooted in his confidence that a certain *authenticity* and *resoluteness* must be the object of our striving. When authenticity is taken to be rooted in the *soil* of the region of his childhood, a phantasmatic nostalgia comes to surround it like an aura. Moreover, the confidence with which he expatiates on the *epochs* of *beyng*—with the Greek as the grand beginning, the Roman as the vulgar translation of the Greek, the medieval Christian as the mania for security in sanctity, and modernity as the egocentric and willful machination of Roman vulgarity and Christian mania—seems to have convinced him that being, or *beyng*, finally has to be purged.

It does seem to me essential when reading Heidegger to be aware of the dangers of such confidence, such militancy, such decisionism, and such nostalgia. Yet to devote oneself solely to "unmasking" Heidegger's texts, avidly and even gleefully searching out the National Socialist strain and stain in everything Heidegger wrote and thought, seems to me to partake of that selfsame noxious militancy and decisionism. By contrast, my model here is Derrida, who formulates his suspicions and worries about Heidegger as clearly and forthrightly as he can, but who always allows these doubts to ricochet onto his and our thinking and writing. Derrida is forever firing warning shots across his own bow. He shows us that *worry* has to be a partner to thinking, a steady and persistent partner, and that worry dares not settle itself comfortably into the seat of judgment. And worry is never gleeful.

Chapters 13–16 of Safranski's biography focus on Heidegger's role in support of Hitler and his own active role in *Gleichschaltung*, the "streamlining" or "synchronizing" or "meshing" of the German university with the National Socialist regime. His analysis is well researched and fair, it seems to me, and I commend it to my readers. Yet I want to focus on two matters, namely, (1) those aspects of Heidegger's life that pushed him in the fatal direction he took, and (2) the particular aspect of his callousness.regarding his students, especially his Jewish students. Concerning the first, Safranski argues, correctly, I believe, that in addition to those childhood influences already mentioned, Heidegger's limited engagement in World War I (as a censor of the mail in the Freiburg post office, then at a weather station in the Ardennes) was what made him later want to embody a "soldierly spirit" in the university. When as rector he signed off on a proposal (not formulated by him) to rid the faculty of "unworthy elements" and to prevent future "degeneracy," however, he knew that what was meant was not his and Jaspers's militant opposition to incompetent colleagues but Jews and political opponents of the regime (RS 286/253). And so the first aspect leads us immediately to the second.

Particularly uncanny to me are Heidegger's letters to Elisabeth Blochmann during the 1930s. Blochmann, half-Jewish, was astonished and chagrined by Heidegger's efforts to explain to her his enthusiasm for the "revolution" (RS 268/236). To Hannah Arendt, he did not even try to explain. Not only students but also colleagues came to suffer. Husserl, Heidegger's *Doktorvater* and staunch supporter, is surely the most famous case. When Husserl was forced into early retirement, Heidegger had Elfride send a bouquet of flowers to his home. Frau Husserl promptly returned them (RS 287/254). After the flowers incident, Husserl wrote to a student that he had seen Heidegger's antisemitism "coming to ever-stronger expression" in recent years "in the faculty and also toward the group of his enthusiastic Jewish students" (ibid.).

Safranski now poses the question "Heidegger—an anti-Semite?" and his detailed answer (RS 287–89/254–57) will serve as the basis for my response. He argues that Heidegger "was not an anti-Semite in the sense of the insane ideological system of the National Socialists." It is noteworthy, Safranski insists, that antisemitic and racist remarks are not found "either in the lectures and philosophical writings or in the political speeches and pamphlets" (RS 287/254). Heidegger's National Socialism, rather, "was decisionist." This means that one's political decision to support the regime or not is what set the standard for Heidegger, not ethnic background. "To use his terminology, a human being is to be judged not by his or her thrownness but by their project" (ibid.). Heidegger intervened with the Culture Ministry to resist the firing of a number of Jewish colleagues (Eduard Fraenkel, Georg von Hevesey, Werner Brock), sometimes successfully, sometimes not. As he declared in his defense after the war, he resisted a student group's effort to hang an antisemitic poster ("Against the Un-German Spirit") in the university. These acts, says Safranski, "show Heidegger's reserve when it came to a vulgar ideological antisemitism" (RS 288/255). Against this, it is clear that Heidegger participated in a kind of "competition-oriented antisemitism," expressing his regret for "'the growing Jewification of our *German* spiritual life'" (RS 289/255–56). At bottom, he appeared to view the presence of Jewish culture in Germany as a foreign influence—in strong contrast to Nietzsche's insistence that German culture, at least its high culture, was *essentially* Jewish. Yet Heidegger's apparent resistance to Jewish culture is contradicted, says Safranski, by remarks in lecture courses that reject, for example, the vulgar allusions of others to Spinoza's Jewishness. And in his notes to a Nietzsche seminar, Heidegger counters the party's claim that Nietzsche is an antisemite by writing, correctly, that Nietzsche was in fact "an anti-anti-Semite" (43:276).

In short, the picture is confusing—except for one remarkable fact: even if it was not antisemitism that motivated Heidegger to support the National Socialist revolution, the brutality against Jews that became evident early on did not cause him to reject it. "Heidegger covered for the mob," writes Safranski, "he believed he owed that to the revolution" (RS 290).[5] Even when his students (Arendt, Blochmann, Jonas, Löwith, and Marcuse, among many others) were forced to flee Germany, he remained committed to Hitler and the party. Once he became rector of Freiburg University, in the spring of 1933, he stopped seeing his Jewish colleagues, including Husserl, and he sent

---

5 This sentence, which Safranski may have added to the 2001 printing of his book, does not appear in the English translation (cf. 256–57).

his doctoral students who were Jewish to other faculty members, principally to Max Müller, for supervision (RS 291/257). As for those who had already been forced to flee, there is a shocking passage in one of the *Black Notebooks* (96:262) that I feel compelled to cite, even though it expresses either utter cynicism or complete benightedness on Heidegger's part. Heidegger complains that "the world Jewish order" has been "stirred up" by those German Jews "who have been allowed to emigrate" from Germany.

Two further comments. First, the recent publication of the *Black Notebooks* reveals—for the first time—a kind of antisemitism that I, like Safranski, have always denied, a kind of "intellectualized" or "cultural-spiritual" antisemitism that appears to run deep in Heidegger, perhaps all the way back to his childhood. Second, to repeat, the personal betrayal of many of his best students and of people that he loved leaves me speechless and defeated. I have written elsewhere in detail about this "intellectualized" or "cultural-spiritual" antisemitism of the *Schwarze Hefte*—"intellectualized" in the sense that Heidegger absurdly claims that "world Jewry" is responsible for the "calculative thinking" or "reckoning" that he takes to be a threat to the thinking of being, "cultural-spiritual" in the sense that Heidegger takes the German *Geist* to be threatened by Jewish culture.[6]

It remains for me to reflect further on the betrayal of his students. I want to be careful not to confuse 1933–35 with 1943–45. Even so, it is impossible to imagine that Heidegger could not foresee that his Jewish students were in danger—if not yet of their lives, then certainly of their livelihoods and their careers as scholars in the academy. True, not for another five years did the Freiburg synagogue burn, but the street violence and the organized vandalism against Jews had begun before Heidegger assumed the rectorship. What could Heidegger have done to resist it? I am not sure. I only hope that what is now being called "Trumpism" does not advance to the point where I am plunged into Heidegger's situation. Yet what troubles me is that I see no signs of Heidegger's *suffering* on account of the dangers to which his best students were exposed from 1933 onward, and even before 1933—no signs of suffering or worry in his letters, no signs in any second-hand accounts of conversations I have seen, not a trace of alarm or concern. Add to this something that troubled Glenn Gray so strongly, as I recall, namely,

---

6 See David Farrell Krell, *Ecstasy, Catastrophe: Heidegger from* Being and Time *to the* Black Notebooks, part 2 (Albany: State University of New York Press, 2015), for a more detailed account.

Heidegger's encouraging the German students to sacrifice all to their fatherland, an encouraging he undertook not only in official addresses but also in the "campfire" meetings that he organized in Freiburg-Schauinsland and in Todtnauberg. All of this cannot be encapsulated in the phrase "political error." Nor can it be a thorn that allows itself to be neatly extracted, leaving no painfully suppurating wound. If the causes of such suffering among Heidegger's best students are not, to say the very least, "thought-provoking," indeed, the most thought-provoking thing in Heidegger's thought-provoking time, then what are they?

Later we will hear Arendt say that "shame" is not enough. What is called for, she will say, is "responsibility," in the sense, the minimal sense, that one *respond*. This will seem woefully inadequate to some, if not all, but I want to put it in a way that Heidegger would have understood, a way that would have hurt him most: such disregard and even callousness toward one's students— do not such failures call on us to *think*, even if we are not certain *what* to think about them, how to *deal* with them, how to *respond* to them?

*   *   *

One has to concede that Heidegger's desire to be the "spiritual" *Führer* of the *Führer* did not ingratiate him with the party. More fully committed and subservient Nazis like Ernst Krieck and Erich Jaensch argued that Heidegger was merely "playing" at being a National Socialist, and their skepticism carried weight with the authorities in Berlin. Jaensch, a psychologist, even diagnosed Heidegger as "a dangerous schizophrenic," one whose writings were "Talmudic and rabble-rousing" (RS 302–303/268–69). Rosenberg's office, alerted by Krieck and Jaensch, and learning that Heidegger had been lecturing at the Beuron Monastery, suspected that Heidegger was engaged in "Jesuitical intrigues." One has to wonder (although Safranski does not say so) whether this sort of "denunciation" fueled Heidegger's hatred of the Church and all churches (RS 359/322). A pro-Nazi professor of philosophy in Karlsruhe, Arthur Drews, knowing that Heidegger was lecturing on Nietzsche in Freiburg, complained that all the attention to Nietzsche was counterproductive: Nietzsche was "an enemy of every German," Drews realized, insofar as he prided himself on being "the 'good European'" (RS 336–37/300). In 1936–37, the Security Office of the Reich ordered Heidegger's lectures (on Nietzsche) to be "observed." Heidegger learned of this observation but still continued to attack the racism of the regime. Even so, he preserved the Hitler salute. As always, the message was mixed (RS 360/323).

Heidegger did not hesitate to use the regime's antisemitism when he wanted to denounce a colleague (the Baumgarten case) or decry a colleague's lack of patriotism (Staudinger). Yet often these denunciations, including the two just mentioned, boomeranged. Heidegger became increasingly suspect to the authorities. By 1938, the official party organs were publishing articles critical of Heidegger—a philosopher "whom no one will ever understand and who teaches nothingness" (RS 309/275).

In general, the Freiburg faculty felt that Rector Heidegger had run amok, and they hoped that he would step down. Heidegger became convinced that the most influential party members were not revolutionary enough. After one year of intense engagement, on April 23, 1934, he resigned from the rectorate. A protracted period of inner emigration, with no public resistance, followed (RS 304–305/271–72). His companions now would be Schelling and Nietzsche, but above all Hölderlin and the Greeks. And even though the lectures and seminars on these figures are inspired and inspiring, doubtless among the best of Heidegger's offerings, it is still true to say, as Safranski does, that what characterizes them is his inability "to reflect in a self-critical way on his own engagement" with Nazism (RS 332/296).

Allow me to add a word about Hölderlin among all the thinkers just mentioned, a word about the distance that my reading of the great poet has taken from Heidegger. It is fair to say, as Safranski does (RS 317–22/282–87), that Heidegger appeals to Hölderlin as a "test" for the German people and as the avatar of Heidegger's "other beginning," his own interior revolution for thinking. In light of the times from which Heidegger himself is in flight, this talk of a test may be understandable. Yet my response to Hölderlin has increasingly stressed the importance for his poetry, not of the "fatherland" or even "the flight of the gods" but of his travels through and admiration of France, his specific experience of the "foreign," and his abiding love for Susette Gontard, his "Diotima."[7] Heidegger never deigns to make much of Diotima, at least not for the task of his own thinking. For him, poetry has to be about the fate of nations, especially his own, the destiny of the Occident and the Orient, and the shivering of gods. Eros is viewed by some—and Heidegger appears to be among them—as a minor god, the mere infant

---

7 Allow me to mention my "novel," if that is what it is, based on Susette Gontard's love letters to Hölderlin: David Farrell Krell, *The Recalcitrant Art: Diotima's Letters to Hölderlin and Related Missives* (Albany: State University of New York Press, 2000), which tries to show how thought-provoking love can be.

of Aphrodite, the goddess that Homer is quick to ridicule. Others, such as Hölderlin's friend Schelling, avow that Eros may be, as Hesiod said, the primordial god and the very "beginning" of the epoch that so dazzled Heidegger, the grand epoch of the Greeks.

Yet where and when does the grand epoch of the Greeks begin or end? My most recent response to Hölderlin has to do with the poet's journey to Bordeaux and back, not with his "homecoming," not with his desire for a "return" to the homeland that was so problematic for him but with his enduring love of and fascination with what he found in the South of France. What he found there, it seems to me, has more to with his love for Diotima and his love of both the French language and of "southerly humanity" than with Heidegger's grandiose philosophemes. Heidegger's rare travels, by contrast, result in something far less profound than Hölderlin's journeys: even after three trips to Greece and multiple journeys to southern France, both quite late in his life, what Heidegger admires about ancient Greece is its battle against "the Asiatic" (RS 362–63/326). By contrast, Hölderlin and Schelling knew that Greece owed an enormous debt to "Asia," meaning preeminently the Near East and the Levant, and they devoted much of their time and efforts to demonstrating that debt. I will return to the theme of Eros for Heidegger—which I take to be intimately bound up with his political debacle—in my two chapters on Hannah Arendt and at the end of the book.

*   *   *

The suspicion that undergirds much of the discussion about Heidegger today is expressed well by Safranski in his chapter on the *Beiträge*: "When Heidegger dreams that with his philosophy he is 'standing like a mountain between other mountains,' when he wills to 'erect something essential,' so that people down in the plains will be able to orient themselves, it is manifest that Heidegger's mad rush for power is undergirded by ideas of power" (RS 350/313). Critics who comb Heidegger's texts, searching for parallels to the National Socialist ideologies that are more nakedly expounded by Rosenberg, Krieck, Jaensch, Baeumler, and others, are driven by that suspicion. Two things prevent me from joining these critics wholeheartedly: first, the conviction that there are more affirming and affirmative thoughts in the philosophers, including Heidegger, thoughts more deserving of our time and effort; second, to repeat, my suspicion that the rush to expose and denounce feeds on the identical lust for power, the identical "decisionism" that one claims to be condemning in Heidegger.

Concerning Heidegger's efforts to justify his engagement in 1933–34, Safranski is surely right when he says that Heidegger never engaged in the "self-testing" that under the rubric "examination of conscience" was once held in high repute by philosophy (RS 350–51/314). Critical self-observation does not occur either in Heidegger's *Black Notebooks* of the 1930s and early 1940s or in his statements to the denazification committees of 1945–47. These committees were astonished by the fact that Heidegger failed to express any sort of remorse about his active support of the regime before, during, and even after his rectorship. He confessed his "mistake," but he did not feel in any way responsible for the crimes of the regime. Heidegger did not admit to having any remorse, comments Safranski, "because in fact he felt none" (RS 376/337).

Accusations abound in the *Black Notebooks*, but all of them are directed outward toward others—Christians, Jews, Nazis, contemporary philosophers, and anyone else who might cross Heidegger's mind. Safranski is close to the mark—if there is a "mark," a clear standard of measure here—when he writes that Heidegger's incapacity for self-critique is more than a "moral" problem (RS 352/315). If one takes seriously Heidegger's constant talk about mortals as *finite*, then it is a *philosophical* problem. What Heidegger's *thinking* often seems to lack is the kind of meditative or reflective quality, the very thought-fulness that he most wanted to achieve. For Safranski, the German word that says all this is *Besonnenheit*. It is the word that Nietzsche uses to describe the more serene and perspicuous moments of the Dionysian philosophy—admittedly more famous for its capacity for ecstasy, but very much in need of that calmer, more reflective quality. King Pentheus, in Euripides's *The Bacchae*, lacks *Besonnenheit*: he cannot admit to himself that he is wild to see the women at their worship in the mountains, with the result that he is passionate to curb them and confident that he can do so. These errors destroy him. *Besinnung*, which would be the very activity of *Besonnenheit*, is a word that appears everywhere in Heidegger's writings from the 1930s through the 1950s; it is precisely what Heidegger proposes as an alternative to the calculative and power-oriented thinking that dominates our technologies and politics more than ever today. "Science and *Besinnung*" is one of the essays that Heidegger wanted to include in his *Basic Writings*. Yet nowhere in Heidegger's polemics and plaidoyers in his own defense is that quality palpable. Safranski: "Heidegger's infamous silence is also an inner silencing, almost an obduracy [*fast eine*

Verstocktheit] with regard to himself. Also a contribution to the oblivion of being" (RS 352/315).

Herbert Marcuse, a former student of Heidegger's at Marburg and a brilliant theoretician, writes to him on August 28, 1947, asking for "a word" that would declare his abjuration of National Socialism. Heidegger replies that he has already spoken that word during his Nietzsche lectures, which criticize all biologism and racism. Furthermore, says Heidegger, his silence results from his unwillingness to join those who loudly repudiate their earlier convictions and "announce their change of heart in the most disgusting way" (RS 465/421, quoting Heidegger). When critics demand that he take distance from the murder of millions of Jews, Heidegger takes this to be a monstrous affront, and Safranski feels compelled, at least in part, to agree with him. It is true that in the *Black Notebooks*, one finds Heidegger condemning the Reich for its "crimes," but there is no admission that those crimes have anything to do with his own early support of the party—even though, to repeat, violence against Jews and others began even before Heidegger assumed the rectorship of the university. Can he really have believed that these crimes would abate? One wants to avoid retrospective illusion, but can there really have been no intimation on his part? (The destruction of the Jewish synagogue in Freiburg in 1938 occurred just outside the windows of his classroom; perhaps by that time he began to realize what was happening.) Heidegger expects his silence after the war to quash every accusation of complicity, but that silence in fact opens the door to doubts of the most terrifying kind. And it makes a mockery of his question, six years after the "liberation" of the camps, "What calls for thinking?"

Safranski argues that Heidegger does "think Auschwitz," precisely when he analyzes it as a part of the machinations of modernity, which reduce even human beings to mere stockpiles. Yet Philippe Lacoue-Labarthe and many others find that analysis too sweeping, too amorphous and bloodless when it comes to the Shoah. Did not that "event" call on Heidegger, the thinker of "the event," to think? In his first lecture course at Freiburg after the teaching ban has been lifted, Heidegger urges his students to attend an exhibition on the suffering of German soldiers, "Prisoners of War Speak." Why does he not add that there are many other sites of human suffering and death to be visited in Germany? "Thinking is remembering," says Heidegger. Yet partial remembrance is selective perception.

Fig. 4.3 The roof of the cabin slopes to meet the hill on the north side; to the left, the "star fountain" and water trough, which Paul Celan could not have failed to notice. Photo by Stephanie Richter.

I have written in greater detail about this recently, and so I will not dwell on it here.[8]

In the final pages of his chapter, Safranski tells the agonizing story of Paul Celan's visits to Heidegger and his hope for "a word" from him (RS 466–69/421–25). Celan had been studying Heidegger's works assiduously for years. His copy of *Being and Time* was heavily marked with underlinings and notes. He had also found his way to the later work, and even

8 See Krell, *Ecstasy, Catastrophe*, 187–89. Safranski devotes a number of pages more to this most difficult aspect of Heidegger's political engagement, namely, the silence that he wraps around it, silence even about the horrors of the Shoah (RS 465–66/420–21). That silence disquieted me from the start, and even now I cannot account for it. I remember talking to Glenn Gray about it during the 1970s, and he could offer no explanation. Heidegger had admitted his "error," but he had nothing to say about the deeds of the party he had supported, as though his "error" were but an oversight, a slight miscalculation. I remember Glenn saying that at least Heidegger had confessed his enthusiasm for Hitler, whereas it was rare to find anyone during the denazification period who admitted to having had anything to do with the movement. They saw, heard, spoke, and *did* no evil. I know that I am repeating myself in all this, but that is because the problem is so irascible, so unrelenting. Surely, one expects more from Heidegger, a great deal more, and one is left wanting.

Heidegger's most difficult themes and formulations concerning the history of *beyng* attracted him. For his part, Heidegger had been reading Celan's poetry since the 1950s. Yet Heidegger's support of the Nazi regime made it impossible for Celan to embrace Heidegger's thought wholeheartedly. When Gerhart Baumann, a Freiburg professor of German studies, invited Celan to give a reading in Freiburg during the summer of 1967, Baumann let Heidegger know about the event. Heidegger visited the various bookstores in Freiburg, asking each one to place Celan's books of poetry in their shop windows. They complied. On July 24, in a packed auditorium, with Heidegger in the front row, Celan gave his reading. A group of guests, including Heidegger, had a glass of wine with Celan after the reading. Celan refused to be photographed with Heidegger, however, and he left the room for a moment, apparently in some consternation. Heidegger urged Baumann to drop the idea of the photograph. When Celan returned, he said that he now had no objection to the photo, but it was never taken.

Heidegger invited Celan to Todtnauberg, and Celan agreed. After Heidegger's departure, however, Celan said that he could not forget Heidegger's past support of the regime and that he wanted to cancel the proposed excursion. He admitted to admiring Heidegger's work, and even liking the man, but even so, no, it was too much. Safranski comments, "He [Celan] sought nearness and he forbade himself the nearness" (RS 468/423). The next morning, however, he relented and agreed to the trip. He and Heidegger spent the morning hiking and talking—about what we do not know. Into Heidegger's guest book at the cabin Celan wrote the following: "Into the cabin's guest book, with a view to the star on the fountain, with a hope in my heart for a word that will come" (ibid.).

Despite the way in which virtually everyone interprets that hope for a coming word, Baumann reports that Celan was elated with the visit and in an elevated mood after it. On August 1, Celan wrote the poem "Todtnauberg," in which he reformulates his inscription into the guest book, remembering his line about hope, hope for a "word / to come / in the heart," the word of a thinker, *eines Denkenden, im Herzen.* There was an exchange of letters and a few more meetings. Heidegger proposed that he guide Celan through the landscape of Hölderlin's upper Danube, but that trip did not take place. Their last meeting, shortly before Easter in 1970, did not go well. In the course of their conversation, Celan accused Heidegger of not listening to him. Heidegger was nonplussed. Later that evening, Heidegger remarked to Baumann that Celan was clearly "ill, hopelessly ill." Not long after that, in Paris, Celan ended his life.

"What did Celan expect from Heidegger? Probably Celan himself did not know," writes Safranski (RS 469/425). He may be right. But what does a man know of his own wanting to know about anything—when both of his parents have perished in a death camp, whereas he and Heidegger both live on? And could such a man be anything other than hopelessly ill, ill with hopelessness?

Let me add a word, if I may leap far ahead, about *Derrida's* meetings with Celan. For years, Celan and Derrida were colleagues at the École Normale Supérieure—without knowing one another. Indeed, the director of the school was astonished when a Germanist informed him that the greatest living German-speaking poet was employed as a lector at the school. After Peter Szondi introduced Derrida to Celan, the two of them would meet on occasion. Yet those meetings were experiences of silence. The presence of the poet, his behavior, Derrida noted, "with all its gestures and in its very being was of an extreme discretion, elliptical, effaced" (BP 239). The two men exchanged publications, with dedications to one another, but scarcely exchanged a word. I recall Derrida's telling me about these uncanny meetings or nonmeetings with Celan, and he never spoke of Celan without visible expressions of grief. Celan's death by drowning on April 20, 1970, followed by Peter Szondi's death a year later, also by drowning, left indelible marks on Derrida. And Celan's death, I cannot help but think, left its mark on Heidegger as well.

On one of my visits to Heidegger, I pointed to a book lying on his windowsill. I do not know why it caught my eye. It was by a French author, I believe, and I asked Heidegger about it. We were both standing, so I imagine that I was about to depart. The book probably had nothing to do with Celan, so I am not sure why the memory of the incident comes to me only now.

—*Er denkt, ich bin ein Nazi*, said Heidegger. "He thinks I am a Nazi."

What I recall was the sound of his voice, which was very quiet. There was no truculence, no irony, no haughtiness, not even any defensiveness. Nothing but sadness.

My chapter ought to end here. How does one continue after the Celan catastrophe? Perhaps only by remembering that Celan *read* Heidegger, over years and years, even if, after meeting the man, the catastrophic questions remained unanswered.

* * *

It is strange for me to read Safranski's twenty-fifth and final chapter, since at this latest stage of the Heidegger biography I find myself realizing, as I turn each page, "Here is where I enter the story—at the end." Heidegger working on the plans for his *Gesamtausgabe*, Arendt arriving for visits during the summers after 1967. I am especially moved when in the final pages of his book Safranski introduces Melville's Queequeg; yes, that is where I come in, at the tail end, at the tale's end, hurrying to the station to pick up Hannah Arendt. And thus in a way introducing my own next chapter.

Arendt begins to visit Heidegger regularly every summer after 1967, after a fifteen-year hiatus. Safranski imagines that the pause occurs because of Heidegger's jealousy over Arendt's books and their (and her) success in both Europe and the United States, but I cannot help but feel that Elfride must have had something to do with the distance after the attempted reconciliation in the early 1950s. Even so, beginning in 1967, Hannah and Elfride are on first-name terms. In August 1969, Hannah brings her husband, Heinrich Blücher, with her. The atmosphere is relaxed—apart from Hannah's chain-smoking. Future visits are planned. But at the end of October 1970, Blücher dies. Safranski writes:

> Hannah Arendt devotes her final years to her great never-completed work, *The Life of the Mind: Thinking, Willing, Judging*. In the thoughts she develops there, Heidegger is closer than ever before. In short, Heidegger has won back for philosophy "a thinking that expresses gratitude for the fact that it has been granted access to the 'naked that-it-*is*' in general." In all other ways too her connection with Heidegger is no longer torn. She visits him every year and involves herself energetically in the editing and translating of his works in America. Heidegger acknowledges her help gratefully; once again, as he writes her, she proves to be the one who understands his thoughts better than anyone. (RS 471/427)

By this time, remarks Safranski, Heidegger was "a highly respected old man" (RS 472/428). That was the old man I, too, respected, admired, worked with, and even liked.

Safranski, perhaps regretting his own inability to write in a thoughtful way about Heidegger's work of the 1950s, to say nothing of the late 1930s, urges his readers in the final pages of his book not to mock what they cannot comprehend (RS 475–76/431). Avoid piety and fake profundity, avoid poll-parroting, yes, but do not mock. Instead, he says, think of Heidegger's later formulations as the tattoos on Queequeg's body.

Everyone knew, including Queequeg, that these tattooed mysteries would die with him, and so, having grown desperately ill but then mysteriously recovering, he copied the tattoos he could see on his body onto the lid of the coffin that the ship's carpenter had fashioned for him. To be sure, that coffin lid could not have contained all the mysteries inscribed on Queequeg's back—no matter how many mirrors he had wielded and how many contortions he had made to decipher the book of himself. The final lines of chapter 110 of *Moby-Dick*, "Queequeg in His Coffin":

> And this tattooing, had been the work of a departed prophet and seer of his island, who, by those hieroglyphic marks, had written out on his body a complete theory of the heavens and the earth, and a mystical treatise on the art of attaining truth; so that Queequeg in his own proper person was a riddle to unfold; a wondrous work in one volume; but whose mysteries not even himself could read, though his own live heart beat against them; and these mysteries were therefore destined in the end to moulder away with the living parchment whereon they were inscribed, and so be unsolved to the last. And this thought it must have been which suggested to Ahab that wild exclamation of his, when one morning turning away from surveying poor Queequeg—"Oh, devilish tantalization of the gods!"[9]

Safranski comments, quite aptly, "Many mysterious passages in Heidegger's immense production have to be read as though they were inscriptions on the sarcophagus of a savage from the South Seas" (RS 476/431). Heidegger, no longer as Ahab quarreling with the last god but as another of Melville's characters, riddling on the riddle of himself. Safranski does not mention—for he cannot have known—that Heidegger read a German translation of *Moby-Dick* with rapt attention during the 1930s. Nor does Safranski mention—although this he surely knew from his own reading of the novel—that after the *Pequod* founders and sinks with all hands, including Queequeg, the narrator of the entire tale (call him Ishmael) is rescued on the inscribed lid of that buoyant coffin.

---

9 Herman Melville, *Moby-Dick, or The Whale*, ed. Harrison Hayford et al. (Evanston and Chicago: Northwestern University Press and The Newberry Library, 1988), 480–81.

5

MEETING HANNAH ARENDT

After seeing Margarethe von Trotta's film *Hannah Arendt,* and after read-ing Elisabeth Young-Bruehl's monumental biography of Arendt and An-tonia Grunenberg's excellent study of Arendt and Heidegger, I became more acutely aware of how much of Arendt's life I had missed by the time I met her, aware of how much already lay behind her. How much more, I felt, would Jerry Kohn or Joan Stambaugh and others have been able to tell us about her than I. As a student of European history, I had studied her *Origins of Totalitarianism* with something akin to devotion. There were, of course, things I did not understand, among them, why and how anti-semitism could be a constituent of *every* form of totalitarianism. Decades after her death, when I saw film clips of white supremacists marching on Charlottesville, I suddenly understood: the white racists, who had recently been organized to hate the Iranian, Iraqi, Pakistani, Arab, and Palestinian peoples, to hate them as viscerally as they hated African Americans and Latinos, were chanting antisemitic slogans. Wherever hate flourishes, the Jew is hated. It is time for me to read Arendt's *Totalitarianism* again, if only to understand better what is happening in the United States today—in the neo-Nazis' Charlottesville, for example, or at every right-wing "rally."

Arendt's *On Revolution,* which I read for a seminar offered at the Uni-versity of Virginia in 1967, in that same Charlottesville, did not garner the same devotion. Those were the years of the Vietnam War, the "War on Pov-erty," and the fight for civil rights, when "the public space" seemed to be mere superstructure and socioeconomic issues the genuine *Unterbau.* The perversion of the public space into a theater of chauvinism and warmonger-ing was especially severe in those days at the University of Virginia, "the Hahvahd of the South," "Mistah Jeffahson's university," or so it seemed to me in 1966–67, and it was important not to be fooled. Those were the years during which I studied Marx with particular fervor, so I naturally (albeit unwittingly) sided with Heinrich Blücher, Hannah's husband and main disputant in their arguments over class warfare and political struggle. I studied other works of hers diligently, including *On Violence* and *Men in Dark Times* and, of course, *The Human Condition*, but the essay that moved me most—I remember hearing it on October 30, 1970, as the keynote address at the Society for Phenomenology and Existentialism meeting at the New School in New York—was her remarkable account of "thoughtfulness" in "Thinking and Moral Considerations," an early form of the first volume of her *Life of the Mind*, an essay on *thinking* that was good for those times "when," as she concluded her lecture, "the chips are down."[1]

My meetings with her years later, as I have said, were always in the context of Heidegger translation. I knew nothing of their early relationship, nor did she ever speak of it. Why should she, to me? I was surprised when I learned about it after her death, surprised and struck by a kind of awe, while others immediately started wagging their heads and their tongues. So many mindless things have been said and written about that relationship that I suspect I ought to stay altogether clear of the field. Except to say that almost all of those tedious and moralizing things that people have expressed, whether in book form or on stage and screen, whereas they have the intention of protecting or "rescuing" the young Arendt from the clutches of The Monster, wind up belittling and insulting her. She would have been horrified by all that presumptuous "rescue." Even von Trotta's otherwise admirable film, by confusing things Heidegger taught in the 1950s with the 1920s, thus botching what the young Arendt heard from him, and by portraying both Hans Jonas and Heidegger as pathetic fops and bumblers, does itself and its main subject a disservice. As far as I have seen, one of the few book-length studies that does not engage in such presumption and disrespect is Antonia Grunenberg's insightful book, which is wonderfully researched and written—and always respectful of its theme and its subjects.

As far as I could see back then when I knew her, Arendt's interest in Heidegger had to do with his philosophical teaching and his publications—and

---

1 Hannah Arendt, "Thinking and Moral Considerations: A Lecture," *Social Research* 38, no. 3 (Autumn 1971): 417–46. "When the chips are down" are the final words of the lecture, which should still be on every American's reading list.

I believe I saw correctly. To be sure, she was acutely critical and perceptive, and she both publicly and privately condemned his involvement in National Socialism. I cannot imagine that she was ever fully blinded by love, even though the person I knew was anything but unfeeling. Nor, remarkably, was she blinded by hate. What remains incomprehensible to most of us, I suppose, was her capacity to make distinctions and her incapacity to condemn anyone universally. Even in the case of Eichmann, she had to conduct an intense debate with herself. In the case of Heidegger, she recognized the originality and brilliance of the work. Already during her lifetime, but even moreso after her death, the Heidegger scandal industry has called for the banning of Heidegger's books. And that industry has been productive and lucrative: prestigious American university presses gobble up anything in that vein that is offered to them, since they have to pay their way nowadays, and scandal sells so much better than philosophy. It is thus an attractive career path for academics: Heidegger's books are maddeningly difficult to read and understand, so one does much better publishing exhortations not to read him. Over and over again. Arendt was not fooled by that industry, and she would still not be fooled if she were alive today.

What I remember about Arendt's work during those last years of her life, as she was giving the Gifford Lectures in Aberdeen and working on *The Life of the Mind*, was that she treated Heidegger's texts with the respect she felt for Plato, Kant, and Nietzsche. (She often cited such poets and thinkers from memory, and of course I would have to ask after the source.) Heidegger was part and parcel of her love of German literature and philosophy, of Lessing, Hölderlin, Rilke, Kafka, and Benjamin. I recall, years after her death, seeing extensive notes on Arendt in a seminar Derrida taught in Paris on "philosophical nationality and nationalism"; part of that seminar was devoted to Jewish philosophers in exile, philosophers for whom German was still the mother tongue even after the mother had gone homicidal. And I recall Arendt talking to me many times about the great German poets and writers, encouraging me to read them. For these were a large part of her heritage and inheritance; these things belonged to her, she to them. She was unwilling and unable to part with them, no matter how much the German language had been irreparably damaged during the National Socialist years, and no matter how important the American and English language(s) had become for her. Elisabeth Young-Bruehl is entirely right when she says that Hannah Arendt thought of herself "not as a German but as a speaker of German" (YB 199).[2]

However, Young-Bruehl is mistaken when she goes on to say that Arendt's intention with the Gifford Lectures was "a critique of Heidegger's work" (YB 460, 465–66). What Arendt consistently practiced was what Heidegger called an *Auseinander-setzung*, a confrontation or, better, a going-to-encounter. Whatever Heidegger had done or had failed to do, and whether one interpreted it as the result of stupidity or malevolence, Arendt would not let herself be deprived of the thought-provoking texts he had produced: *Sein und Zeit, Der Spruch des Anaximander, Brief über den Humanismus,* and *Was heisst Denken?* were the texts she mentioned to me most often and most positively.

As for the "Letter on Humanism," she regarded it, at least later in her life, as his *Prachtstück*, as she said, his most splendid effort, his "gem," as it were. And each time she said this, it did not fail to irritate me. There were—and still are—many aspects of the "Letter" that trouble me, above all, a certain inflation of the language, a certain manneredness, and a tone that betrays an odd self-inflation, an odd puffing up of this creature called *Mensch* and of the thinker who makes claims about this creature's "essence." A more subdued manner, it seemed to me, would have been fitting after the recent catastrophes of war and genocide. Glenn Gray and I went back and forth about this in our letters. But Arendt would have none of that, not from me. For her, it was a masterpiece of thought and writing. And, to be sure, there are many places in it where I bow to her judgment, especially when Heidegger talks of being as dwelling in the house that language provides (BW 217), or when he says that thinking is a kind of action (ibid.). His words on "the dictatorship of the public realm" (BW 221), words she had heard from him in the 1920s and that had endured in her memory for a very long time, urged her to conceive of a "public space" that would not succumb

---

2 For a discussion of Arendt's relation to the *Muttersprache,* or "mother tongue," see the final chapter of Barbara Cassin, *Nostalgia: When Are We Ever at Home?* trans. Pascale-Anne Brault (New York: Fordham University Press, 2016), esp. 41–52. Cassin's chapter title, "Arendt: To Have One's Language for a Homeland," says it all, as the chapter contrasts in a sensitive and thought-provoking way Arendt's and Heidegger's very different relations to the German language. One small correction: Cassin mishears Arendt's answer to Günter Gaus's question as to whether Arendt feels any nostalgia for pre-Hitler Europe. Cassin understands the response to be "I can't say that I don't have any nostalgia for it," whereas Arendt's response actually supports Cassin's thesis more strongly: "I cannot say that I feel such nostalgia," says Arendt, so that, when it comes to feelings for the homeland, "what remains is the mother tongue."

to empty talk. In these respects, I could accept her enthusiasm for the piece. Yet when Heidegger went on to assert confidently that the house of being was strictly for *human* beings, and that other "living creatures," the silent ones, were exiled from the house, cut off from it "by an abyss" (BW 230), he began to sound like the preachers I had been forced to listen to for far too long. Arendt and I agreed to disagree about the "Letter."[3]

· We had several meetings at the Schlossbergblick Hotel in Freiburg, which is where she always stayed after traveling north from her summer residence in Ticino, Switzerland. We had one long conversation on my translation of "Der Spruch des Anaximander," which had already appeared in print and which she had found acceptable, and perhaps even better than that. Had she not found it acceptable, it is certain that we never would have met. In general, she worried that my German was not up to the task of Heidegger translation, and she was right. Perhaps she had more confidence in my English. She and Glenn Gray convinced me early on, as I mentioned earlier, that bad translations have more to do with incompetence in one's "own" language, the "target" language, than with difficulties in the tongue one is translating.

Arendt was infinitely patient at these sessions on Heidegger translation, even though patience did not seem to be her strong suit. I have already told that sad story about the man with wooden ears. What I want to emphasize, however, is the gratitude she generally showed every young and inexperienced scholar who was at least trying, doggedly, to render a text with care. In such cases, her strong suits were generosity and gratitude.

I was in touch with Arendt by letter from the summer of 1974 until her death in December 1975. Her letters were typed and usually in German, "because it's good for you," as she wrote. Mine were sometimes in German, sometimes in English. I notice that my first letters to her addressed her very formally, but by the summer of 1975, I was writing "Dear

---

3 Actually, as I later learned, Arendt had her own misgivings about Heidegger's "Letter on Humanism" when it first appeared in 1947. They were not as severe as those of Rüdiger Safranski, who argues that in terms of politics or political thinking "this text is dull-witted [*stumpf*]" (RS 404/364). (The English translation says "blunt," but I suspect that "dull-witted" is closer to Safranski's sense.) On September 29, 1949, Arendt wrote to Jaspers from New York about Heidegger's postwar statements and the 1946–47 "Letter": "The way he twists things is unbearable, and the sole fact that he now interprets everything that happened as an interpretation of *Being and Time* shows that everything will once again turn out to be twisted. I read his letter against humanism, which is also highly questionable and in many ways ambiguous, but it is still the only piece in which he achieves once again the level of his older works" (Arendt, cited at RS 411/370).

Hannah!" On June 15, 1974, on the urging of Joan Stambaugh, I wrote to Arendt in Ticino suggesting that I meet her at the station on her forthcoming trip to Freiburg, planned for July 9. On June 19, she wrote from Ticino that she would be very happy to meet me—up to that point our contact had been by letter—and she thanked me for my offer to pick her up at the Freiburg train station. "I am arriving on the express train at 3:18 in the afternoon on July 9. I presume that we will recognize one another somehow; not too many people will be disembarking there. Till then, with friendly greetings, etc."

Arendt was in Freiburg from June 9 to 11, 1974, and on the thirtieth of that month, I wrote her, thanking her for "our conversations and the lunches!" Our conversations mostly had to do with translation projects; by that time, I was hard at work on the first volume of Heidegger's *Nietzsche*. My letter also mentions a book of my own that I was beginning to sketch out, which my letter calls an *Erinnerungsversuch*, an "essay" in memory or, more literally, an "attempt to remember." I was interested in "long-term memory," and what fascinated me was the way in which *writing* is often able—perhaps as a form of self-hypnosis—to gain access to memories long buried. But I was also struck by the fact that when we try *willfully* to remember, we usually chase the memories away or bury them even deeper in the gloom. I began to use the expression "on the verge" of remembering, no doubt recalling Poe's "Ligeia."[4] I can almost hear Arendt suggesting a number of things for me to read on the topic, among them Hölderlin on memory as a gift of the sea, Novalis on memory as "indirect calculus," as "with music." What stands out in my memory of her now was how intrigued she was by every project we discussed, her enthusiasm for ideas and for the life of writing, whether hers, Heidegger's, or mine. I know full well that Arendt is chiefly prized as a proponent of the *vita activa*, but I also knew her as a person who loved above all else the *vita contemplativa*. Yet it is true to say

---

4 The book was eventually called *Of Memory, Reminiscence, and Writing: On the Verge* (Bloomington: Indiana University Press, 1990). The editors at the press decided that my main title, *On the Verge*, should become the subtitle. (I recall a conversation with Arendt in which she said that one can know one has "made it" as an author when publishers can no longer overrule what an author wants to call his or her book.) The passage from Poe's "Ligeia" that served as my motto for the book is as follows: "There is no point, among the many incomprehensible anomalies of mind, more thrillingly exciting than the fact—never, I believe, noticed in the schools—that in our endeavors to recall to memory something long forgotten, we often find ourselves *upon the very verge* of remembrance, without being able, in the end, to remember."

that for her, *thinking* was never untroubled, tranquil contemplation. Rather, thinking had to wrestle with the problems of the world and with the ways in which we either rise to the occasion or falter and fumble when responding to those problems.

Our next exchange involved my request that she help me with some grant applications. At that time, I was teaching part-time at the university, but only as an adjunct, not earning much of an income. Both Glenn Gray and Arendt were more than generous in supporting these applications, none of which succeeded, however. "Something ought to happen," Arendt wrote me on October 24, 1974, after having written several letters of recommendation. My favorite rejection came a year later from the distinguished Alexander von Humboldt-Stiftung, which said that they would be happy to give me a grant to come to Germany, but that they could not, because I was already there. Which was indeed the case. Luckily, with the support of the head of the *Amerikanistik* department at the university, Franz Link, and especially through the help of Ulrich Halfmann, I became a *Lektor* in the department and so was able to continue working on the Heidegger projects and also survive. That post not only allowed for survival, however. My colleagues in Freiburg and later in Mannheim, Ulrich Halfmann, Helmbrecht Breinig, Jochen Barkhausen, and Joseph Schöpp enriched my life in several ways: first, by introducing me for the first time in depth to American literature, my heritage; second, by helping me to understand and translate some of Heidegger's most obstreperous phrases; and third, not least, by becoming generous and supportive lifelong friends.

At the end of my letter to Arendt on October 8, 1974, I mention that I am already working on the anthology of Heidegger's writings—clearly, that is one of the projects we had discussed at length during her visit that past summer. Although there has already been a lot of discussion about the *Basic Writings*, I want to present here my exchanges with Arendt during the winter of 1974–75, if only because they reveal the level of her involvement in the project. On November 12, 1974, writing from Geiersnest, in the hills above St. Ulrich, I wrote:

Dear Dr. Arendt!

Joan communicated to me your suggestions concerning the anthology—the inclusion of the "Foreword" and the "Afterword" [to Heidegger's lecture "What Is Metaphysics?"]—which jogged my memory [that] I had not yet sent you a "plan" of the work.

Forgive my delay, and that opening sentence, both too long!

I have sent copies of the enclosed proposal to Glenn and Joan, and also to Clay Carlson and John Shopp at Harper & Row. Would you do me the kindness of taking a careful look at it and giving me your critical judgment?

If I may respond to your first suggestion—as I understand it from Joan's note: "What Is Metaphysics?" itself appears as the second selection. Heidegger himself requested its inclusion, which pleased me, because at least for me it has always been one of his most powerful pieces. The "Introduction" to that piece appears as number 6 in the current plan. (Originally I had placed the piece quite late in the volume, to serve as a requestioning of *Being and Time*, but Werner Marx, who was kind enough to offer his critical views, was sharply critical of this, so I relocated it to follow the piece on "modern metaphysics.") Although it has been some time since I studied the "Afterword," that piece did not make as powerful an impression on me as did the essay itself and the *Einleitung*. But on your suggestion I will take another good look at the *Nachwort*. It seems to me you are surely right about the excellence of these pieces, which offer a sort of "micro-cosmic" view of Heidegger's path of thought, his development of the question of *Being and Time*.

May I ask your opinion on an important matter? John Sallis suggested to me the two "options" concerning *Being and Time*. Because of the importance of that work, and because of its structural "solidity," I am shy about trying to "adequately represent" it. Professor von Herrmann tells me that Heidegger himself is dubious about anthologizing it. If Joan's and your work on the new translation appears in the not too distant future, especially in a paperbound edition, the necessity of including it in the anthology is greatly reduced. Am I right about that? Is it planned to bring out *B&T* in an edition students can afford? If so, couldn't the anthology reproduce just enough to provide its "basis," and then provide more of the later pieces—thus serving as a kind of companion to *Being and Time*? A difficult question, about which I need advice.

All other comments are welcome! I am sure Joan and Glenn would be willing to write them up and send them on to me, although naturally I would be delighted to have them from your hand! Thank you for your help! Best wishes, etc.

I did not hear back from Arendt until March, and in the meantime, I had written her again. I ought to have been reluctant to do so. She was preparing her Gifford Lectures, which, as I mentioned, turned out to be the first draft of her final book, *The Life of the Mind*, published posthumously. And especially because her health, unbeknownst to me, was fragile, I should have left her alone. On February 19, 1975, I wrote:

Dear Dr. Arendt!

Glenn Gray has been writing in a state of great excitement over your Gifford Lectures text, and he says he considers himself a "privileged character" to be able to read them in manuscript form. I am jealous, since your theme is close to those things that brought me into philosophy—for example, Heidegger/Nietzsche, willing, thinking, and judging! So I hope it won't be too long a time before the book is available. I recall some remarks you made during our first lunch on the difference of "will" in the first and second volumes of Heidegger's *Nietzsche*. As I am deeply involved in the translation of these lectures, I am particularly anxious to follow your thought in these matters. Years ago you were my first teacher in the problem of totalitarianism, you and [Carl] Friedrich and Zbigniew Brzezinski, whose name continues to baffle me! The point is that I am happy to continue as a student of yours in these Heidegger/Nietzsche matters. Glenn also mentioned an article on Auden that he much admired. I am on my way to our library to get it!

After mentioning the status of my grant applications, the letter continues:

You have admirers here in Freiburg! Every copy of *Merkur* in which your "Martin Heidegger at Eighty" appears has been stolen! So I asked Sherry Gray to see if she could somehow get a copy to me. And I hope you don't mind if I cite something from it that I like very much in the Heidegger anthology.

Speaking of which! The selection from *Being and Time* remains the greatest single stumbling block. If sometime you could send me your ideas on the matter (maybe even a plan!), I'd be more than grateful.

I have been teaching as an adjunct in the English Seminar, apparently with some success, since I've been asked to continue. This past semester I taught a course called "Herman Melville and the Absurd," for which we read *Moby-Dick* and *Le mythe de Sisyphe*. During the summer semester I will teach [two courses, one on] Mark Twain's travel books and [the other on] James Joyce's *Ulysses*. A rather crazy compound! But the contact with students is important to me, and gives me some sort of stimulus to work harder on my own research, translating, and editing.

If my teaching schedule allows, I'd like to come up to Düsseldorf in May to hear the lecture Glenn mentions you'll be giving. And is there some chance you may be here in Freiburg? It was important for me to meet you: you somehow made me entirely comfortable in your presence, although I kept my ears wide open so as not to miss a word! Important for those inside reasons that don't so easily reveal themselves.

But it is too early in the morning for my misty (or fuzzy!) recollections. It is drizzling now—but it has been a glorious, sunny winter. "Funny business!" says the farmer with whom I live! It would be fine to see you again, especially if I can be of any service to you. Best regards, etc.

Before I cite Arendt's response to this effusive note, I ought to mention something about the teaching. She and I clearly had spoken about the teaching profession. I remember her dedication to it. And even though I had not been a student of hers at the New School, she treated me with the generosity that I know she showed her own students—the fact that she was so willing to write letters of recommendation for me illustrates that generosity. Clearly, I felt free to talk about my teaching in Freiburg, not fearing for an instant that she might not be interested. I did not know at the time that she had met Albert Camus during a visit to Paris in 1952, and that she came to admire him greatly (AG 318/228), so my course on Melville and Camus would have struck a chord with her in any case.

As for the importance of students, I have to mention the odd coincidence that as I was writing these words, I received an email from one of my early Freiburg students, Michael Walter. Michael is one of the most distinguished translators of English and American literature into German (among his authors are Melville, Henry James, Lewis Carroll, Laurence Sterne, and Edward Gibbon), and virtually all these translations have been awarded prestigious prizes. On one of these prize-awarding occasions to which Michael invited me, at the Frankfurt Book Fair, I spent an entire evening talking with Toni Morrison, who was there to receive an award— but that unforgettable conversation would need a chapter of its own. I have remained friends with Michael Walter and with two other exceptional students from that time, Ashraf Noor and the late Ursula Willaredt. Noor later did his doctoral work in philosophy with Françoise Dastur and became a distinguished scholar in Husserl studies. Ursula Willaredt and I remained in close touch even after she moved to Seattle and began to work in the translation department of Microsoft. Her last email to me read: *Werde next week operiert am Kopf, alles halb so schlimm. Lese sehr viel Camus, der tut gut* ("I'll be operated on next week, brain surgery, not all that terrifying. Reading a lot of Camus, he does me good"). When I think that almost half a century has passed since I read Melville (together with Camus) with these three friends, then, later on, Yeats, Dickinson, and Joyce (both *Ulysses* and *Finnegans Wake*), and that they have remained in close touch ever since, I become aware what a blessing the teaching profession is. These days, however, as young teachers are being squeezed in the olive press that professional administrators mistake for higher education, teaching so many courses that they cannot really notice who is there and how they are faring, the blessing is perhaps becoming a curse. But I digress, even if Arendt, a passionate and dedicated teacher, would approve of the digression.

On March 10, 1975, Arendt replied to my letters and cards from the past winter. Her letter is in English.

> I finally come around to answering your letters. I enclose a copy of my Heidegger article. You certainly will need it in English and this English translation has been checked by myself. Now to your real problem, the selection from *Being and Time*. I know that Glenn Gray suggested something on care, anxiety, etc., and these are of course the best known parts of the book. I had a look the other day and I think I understand why Heidegger would prefer simply the first chapters [i.e., the Introduction, §§1–8]. Only in this way could the fundamental-ontological idea of the book be adequately presented.
>
> Don't come to Düsseldorf to hear me. It's a symposium where I shall be together with several other people; it's certainly not worth coming for. I doubt that I shall come to Freiburg but I shall be in Europe again and it would be nice to see you then. Let's keep in contact. All the best, Yours, etc.

By this time, Heidegger himself had impressed on me the fact that no "principle of selection" for the sections from *Being and Time* seemed possible. With Arendt agreeing, the anthology took its final shape, the shape it still has today, barring a few corrections and additions.

On August 6, 1975, Heidegger wrote me:

> Dear Herr Krell!
>
> Frau Hannah Arendt is coming to Freiburg on the 12th of August and would very much like to see you. She asks me to tell you this, along with her wish that you telephone her:
>
> > Casa Barbatè
> > 6652 Tegna, Ti[cino, Switzerland]
> > Telephone: 093–81.14.30.
>
> Unfortunately, she did not tell me at what *time* you could reach her by phone.
>
> Meanwhile, I'd like to thank you heartily for all your efforts with the translation of my essays on early Greek philosophy.
>
> > With friendly greetings,
> > Martin Heidegger

On July 6, 1975, Heidegger had written Arendt to say that he had learned from Glenn Gray that she was in Marbach at the archive. "I thought you were in Scotland," he says, alluding to the Gifford Lectures. He apologizes for the long gap between letters, saying that the preparation of the Collected Edition of his works is creating more work than he had anticipated. He hopes that she can travel down to Freiburg, perhaps between June 10 and 15, for a visit. "There is much to talk about and even more to think about" (AHB 253). He mentions an honor that she has received in Denmark, the Sonning Prize, in recognition of her account of the exceptional resistance of the Danish people to the persecution of the Jews during World War II, and he promises to raise a glass in recognition of the prize when she comes. Indeed, much to talk about and even more to think about (YB 463).

Heidegger promises it will be a good wine he offers her, testifying that Glenn has pronounced it so during two recent visits. "It seems to me that he—together with Dr. Krell—have once again done some excellent translation work" (AHB 254). He is apparently referring to the *Basic Writings* volume and, presumably, as Ursula Ludz surmises (AHB 164), to the editing that Glenn and I had done on Joan's translation of the Introduction to *Being and Time*.

On July 27, 1975, Arendt, writing from the Casa Barbatè in Tegna, not far from Locarno on Lago Maggiore, replies to Heidegger's letter. She says nothing about the Sonning Prize, even though it must have been on her mind. But there is a brief reference to me in it, both a critical and complimentary one, and so I shall reproduce it in full (AHB 254):

Dear Martin,

It is by now almost August, and I'd like to know soon about how it would be with a visit to Freiburg. Here it is a splendid summer, not too hot, the air quite clear, with warm evenings. After Marbach, where every day was cold and rainy, it is lovely and refreshing.

The second part of my lectures in Scotland I will write in October. Here I am slowly getting back into the work. Whether I can finish it by October—Judgment—is questionable, but I'm not worried, since I have the lecture for Scotland well-nigh finished.

Was [Bernhard] Zeller [that is, the director of the *Deutsches Literatur-archiv*, where Heidegger's papers are held] able to offer some help for the Collected Edition? The index [to *Sein und Zeit*] by Frau [Hildegard] Feick is excellent and a big help. Can Krell help? If his German is okay in the meantime, that should be possible. Glenn was quite satisfied with him.

I hope you are well and that the two of you won't be plagued by too many visits.

Hearty greetings to you both, etc.

The embarrassing part for me is that even after three decades in Germany, my German is not so okay. Praise me for consistency. The compliment is the very idea that Arendt seems to have that I might be able to help with the planning of Heidegger's *Gesamtausgabe*, which would have required better-than-okay German and an excellent grasp of *Sütterlinschrift*, which is the script in which Heidegger's lectures were written. I have always needed to run to others for help when deciphering that script—and Heidegger's minuscule handwriting did not help.

At all events, Heidegger writes Arendt on July 30, 1975, asking her to come on August 12 between three and four in the afternoon and to stay for supper. He complains about his and Elfride's having had "the sniffles" and coughs during July, the result of a flu that was making the rounds. He mentions the recent death of Eugen Fink, who was his assistant for many years in Freiburg and a considerable philosopher in his own right, and he comments on her work on "judging," slated to be the final part of *The Life of the Mind*: "Everything else we will talk about in person; but for now—judgment is a difficult matter" (AHB 255). This letter of July 30 is Heidegger's last letter to Arendt.

Arendt wrote me from Tegna in the first days of August (the letter is not dated), thanking me for having sent her an offprint of the *Arion* "Anaximander Fragment," adding, "first rate—congratulations." She continues:

> I'll come next week and shall be very glad to see you. I intend to arrive on Monday the 11th at 8:07 in the evening from Locarno via Basel. I've booked a room at the Schlossbergblick. Could you be free for the evening and come and pick me up at the station? We could then have a little supper together and talk. I'll see Heidegger on Tuesday and I'll have to leave Wednesday to meet a friend in Darmstadt. In case you are not free on Monday night we could also meet on Tuesday night late—around 9 o'clock. You can't be reached by phone. Perhaps you could call me here some time during the weekend. Most cordially, etc.

I am surprised to read that we did not have a telephone in our Geiersnest apartment, but now that I think back, I remember having to walk about twenty minutes down the road to a neighboring farmhouse to make calls. Another indication of how half a century makes a huge difference is that everyone, including even me, is now geared up with a "smartphone," available for chats and messages every minute of the day. I must have written a quick reply saying that I would be at the station on Monday night. Arendt responded, in German, on August 8, repeating her arrival time. "Our letters crossed," she began. "I wrote you yesterday—but the only address I had was 'St. Ulrich.'" The letter arrived promptly, however, the local postmaster being well apprised of every dweller in the village—another indication of how things have changed! Once again, she suggested that we have supper together on Monday evening, *und dann schwätzen* ("and then we can chitchat"). Arendt loved the vernacular, and *schwätzen* and *quatschen* were words she used often. If she had to give a lecture, she called it *vorsingen*, "an audition," as though she were applying for an academic post.

My second set of meetings with Arendt therefore occurred on August 11, 1975, and the days following. On September 11, I wrote her—presumably to her Ticino address—requesting that recommendation to the Alexander von Humboldt-Stiftung. But my letter begins with "Dear Hannah!" and its tone is far warmer and less formal than that of the earlier letters. It is clear that she had invited my wife, Marta, and me to Ticino for a visit before her departure for Aberdeen and the next set of Gifford Lectures, since my letter tells of my wife's pregnancy, saying that this may make our visit impossible. "May they have the rooms well heated for you," I wrote, concerning Aberdeen, "and may your hearers cease their sniffling!" The letter closes, "Best wishes from your Freiburger 'meschugge,' who greatly enjoyed your visit and is grateful for your kind help." Why I should have been *meschuggeneh* I no longer know, but it sounds plausible; there could be countless reasons.

By September 21, 1975, Arendt was staying for a few days in the Pont-Royal-Hotel in Paris on her way to an international seminar in Jouy-en-Josas, near Versailles, then back to New York. She wrote:

> Your letter reached me here in Paris where I shall stay a few days before I fly home. Of course, I'll recommend you to the Humboldt-Stiftung and I hope your notion about the "tremendous weight" of such a recommendation will not turn out to be an illusion. I cannot do it here because I have nothing with me, not even proper stationery. Even this typewriter is a loan. Is there any time limit?
>
> I enjoyed our talks in Freiburg very much. The anthology business is probably properly taken care of. I'll call Glenn from New York and discuss with him our other concerns. Did you hear from Joan? Incidentally, I think we forgot to discuss the table of contents for the anthology in detail. Do

you still have a copy? Could you let me have a look? I could not do it [before this] anyhow, separated as I was so long from my books. *Herzliche Grüsse,* Yours, Hannah.

Four days later I replied, teasing her about being a "jet-setter," albeit a "distinguished" one. I provided the proposed table of contents but also asked her to help with the Klostermann problem:

On the reverse side of this note is a photocopied letter from Klostermann. Hannah, it confuses me greatly, because the problem with the anthology surrounds not *Holzwege* but *Wegmarken*. So I don't know how to answer Herr K. I've written Glenn about it, and hope that you two wiser heads can figure out what I might reply. I fear it spells disaster for the anthology, however, and I'm in a perpetual state of worry over it. I'm young and foolish, and worry over things I shouldn't! The anthology (if it survives) so far includes the following:

1. Being and Time: The Introduction (complete §§1–8).
2. What Is Metaphysics? (complete original lecture).
3. On the Essence of Truth (complete).
4. The Origin of the Work of Art (abridged).
5. Letter on "Humanism" (complete).[5]
6. What Is a Thing? (the section on modern science, the mathematical, and Descartes, abridged).
7. The Question Concerning Technology (complete).
8. Building Dwelling Thinking (complete).
9. What Calls for Thinking? (abridged).
10. The End of Philosophy and the Task of Thinking (complete).

By the end of September 1975, then, the contents of the first edition of the anthology were fairly settled, apart from having to abridge Arendt's much-admired "Humanism." I closed the letter by thanking her for her letter of recommendation and, notably, sending her *un abrazo fuerte*! Arendt answered on October 6, 1975, with a typed letter containing several handwritten corrections. It is my last letter from her:

Lieber Dave,

I will write in German, first of all because it is good for you, and secondly, because just now I have a German secretary here. I have finished the Humboldt-Stiftung letter and have sent it off. Besides this, I received

---

5 As I have mentioned, it was my intention to print the "Letter" in its entirety, but this did not happen until the second, "expanded" edition.

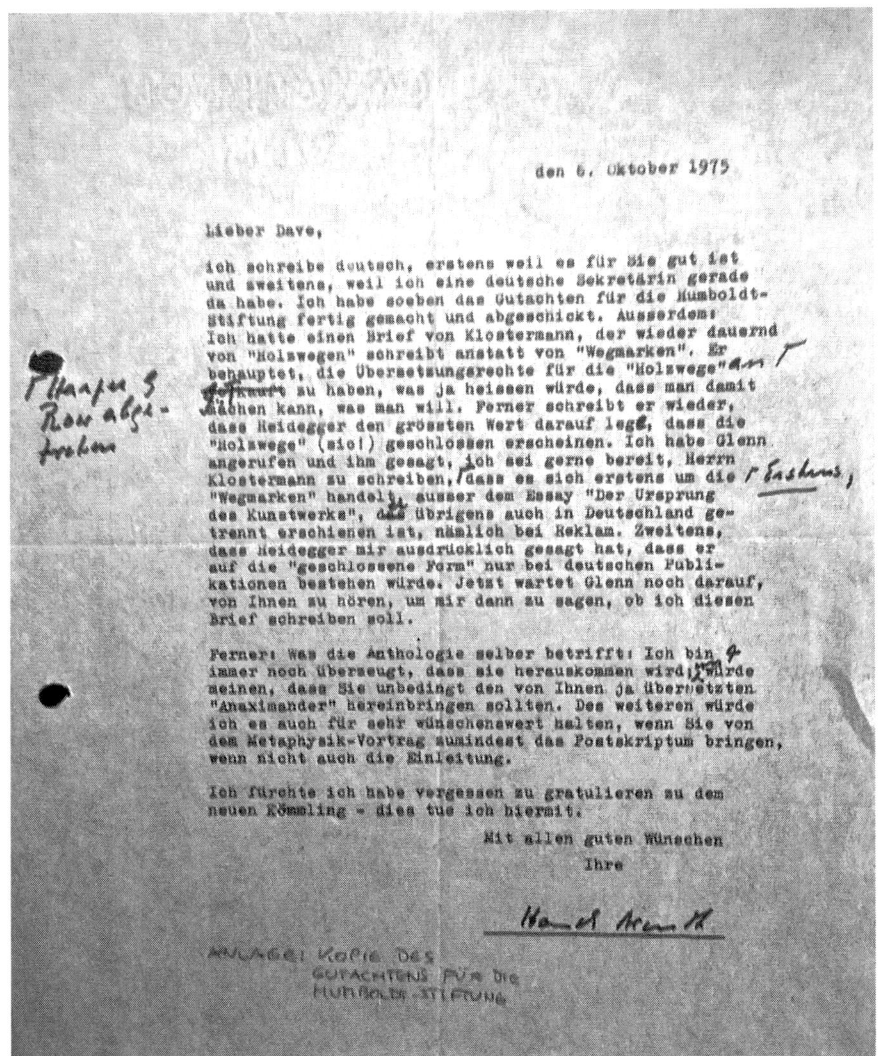

den 6. Oktober 1975

Lieber Dave,

ich schreibe deutsch, erstens weil es für Sie gut ist
und zweitens, weil ich eine deutsche Sekretärin gerade
da habe. Ich habe soeben das Gutachten für die Humboldt-
Stiftung fertig gemacht und abgeschickt. Ausserdem:
Ich hatte einen Brief von Klostermann, der wieder dauernd
von "Holzwegen" schreibt anstatt von "Wegmarken". Er
behauptet, die Übersetzungsrechte für die "Holzwege"
zu haben, was ja heissen würde, dass man damit
machen kann, was man will. Ferner schreibt er wieder,
dass Heidegger den grössten Wert darauf legt, dass die
"Holzwege" (sic!) geschlossen erscheinen. Ich habe Glenn
angerufen und ihm gesagt, ich sei gerne bereit, Herrn
Klostermann zu schreiben, dass es sich erstens um die
"Wegmarken" handelt, ausser dem Essay "Der Ursprung
des Kunstwerks", der übrigens auch in Deutschland ge-
trennt erschienen ist, nämlich bei Reklam. Zweitens,
dass Heidegger mir ausdrücklich gesagt hat, dass er
auf die "geschlossene Form" nur bei deutschen Publi-
kationen bestehen würde. Jetzt wartet Glenn noch darauf,
von Ihnen zu hören, um mir dann zu sagen, ob ich diesen
Brief schreiben soll.

Ferner: Was die Anthologie selber betrifft: Ich bin
immer noch überzeugt, dass sie herauskommen wird. Ich würde
meinen, dass Sie unbedingt den von Ihnen ja übersetzten
"Anaximander" hereinbringen sollten. Des weiteren würde
ich es auch für sehr wünschenswert halten, wenn Sie von
dem Metaphysik-Vortrag zumindest das Postskriptum bringen,
wenn nicht auch die Einleitung.

Ich fürchte ich habe vergessen zu gratulieren zu dem
neuen Kömmling - dies tue ich hiermit.

Mit allen guten Wünschen
Ihre

Hannah Arendt

ANLAGE: Kopie des
Gutachtens für die
Humboldt-Stiftung

Fig. 5.1 Arendt's letter to me of October 6, 1975, in which she writes once again about Heidegger's "Anaximander Fragment."

a letter from Klostermann, who constantly writes about *Holzwege* rather than *Wegmarken*. He claims to have turned over the translation rights for *Holzwege* to Harper & Row, which of course would mean that we can do with it what we will. He goes on to say that Heidegger sets the greatest value on having the *Holzwege* (sic!) appear as a whole. I called Glenn and told him I am more than ready to write Herr Klostermann to say, first, that it is a matter of the *Wegmarken*, except for the essay "Origin of the Work of Art," which in any case has appeared separately in Germany too, namely, with Reclam; second, that Heidegger told me expressly that he would insist on "complete editions" only for publication in Germany. Now Glenn is waiting to hear from you, at which point he will tell me to write the letter.

Furthermore, as far as the anthology itself goes, I am still convinced that it will appear. And in my opinion it should beyond all doubt contain the "Anaximander" that you have translated. And I would find it very desirable if you could add to the "Metaphysics" lecture at least the Postscript, if not also the Introduction.

I fear I have forgotten to send congratulations for the new addition to the family—I hereby do exactly that. With all good wishes, Yours, etc.

There appear to be two replies to this letter. Or, rather, the first letter seems to anticipate Arendt's last letter to me—Glenn Gray had clearly passed on to me Hannah's suggestions. In any case, here is the first of these three last letters to her, this one, which crossed hers, dated October 10, 1975.

Dear Hannah!

Good news: as you predicted, Klostermann accepted Harper & Row's proposal, supported by Heidegger, so that the anthology *will* appear.

More good news: I had a good visit with Heidegger last week for over an hour and found him in good shape. His left ear hears very badly, but he had me sit right next to him, and we had no trouble. He also got up from the couch and moved around a bit, and seemed as fit as ever. Spirits excellent. And we had a *good* conversation about his Introduction to *Sein und Zeit* and the circumstances of its composition.

So, if you have had qualms about Heidegger's health, I'd say to put them aside. To me he seemed fine! As ever, he sent lots of greetings to yourself and Glenn.

Glenn passed on to me your suggestions for the anthology. I'd love to put the "Anaximander" in, but I am already a hundred pages over the ceiling established by [John] Shopp: 375 pages. Besides, between you, me, and Glenn, I have hopes of someday editing a second volume of Heidegger's essays on the history of being: if the first volume "moves" well (is that the right jargon?!) then I think H&R will support the idea.

As for the Introduction and Afterword to "What Is Metaphysics?" the first is in my view a classic, one of Heidegger's supreme efforts. But I don't see how we can get around W.K.[6] The Afterword is not nearly so valuable,

---

6 "W.K." refers to Walter Kaufmann, who had translated the introduction to Heidegger's inaugural lecture. It is no longer clear to me why this would have posed a problem, but I suspect we feared that Kaufmann would not allow the piece to be reprinted.

in my opinion, for it is highly repetitive of the original lecture and of too "apologetic" a character. Besides, the "Humanism Letter" (which will appear entire[7]) seems to do better what the little Afterword attempts to do. . . . Yours, etc.

"To me he seemed fine!" I wrote, even though Heidegger had but six months left to live. And I would have exclaimed the same thing to Heidegger about Arendt, who had but two months: she seemed fine, and I was confident that I would see her soon and we would pick up where we left off. A young man has no sense of this coming and going of people, and an old man has only a slightly better sense, if the truth be told.

On the theme of comings and goings, I should pause a moment over Arendt's admiration of Heidegger's "Anaximander Fragment," written in 1946, the final essay of his *Holzwege* or *Woodpaths*. It is impossible, of course, to read with another person's eyes, particularly if that person be Hannah Arendt, but she felt so certain about the essay's excellence that I am driven to ask why it stood out to her. There are certainly aspects of it that might have displeased her—the grand narrative of a "history of being" or even "eschatology of being" that commences with Anaximander and ends with Nietzsche, and the often incantatory style of the piece with its Olympian pronouncements. Yet it was probably the sweep of Heidegger's essay that impressed her, as though philosophy has to be about beginnings and ends. Arendt might also have been displeased by Heidegger's dispensing with so much of the commentary of the classical philologists, even if he did accept John Burnet's judgment that the first and final phrases of the fragment were either Stoic or Aristotelian in origin, appearing only long after what Nietzsche had called "the tragic age of the Greeks," so that these phrases had to be set aside. It was probably Heidegger's claim that what Anaximander puts into words was essentially *tragic* that most impressed her, along with Heidegger's use of Homer and of poetry in general to demonstrate the tragic sense that all genuine *thinking* has to respect. Ultimately, it was Heidegger's very "translation" of the Anaximander fragment that must have startled her and then gripped her.

The standard translations go something like this: "But that from which things arise also gives rise to their passing away, according to necessity;

---

7 That was at least my intention, although, to repeat, it did not get carried out until the second, expanded edition.

for things render justice [δίκη] and pay penalty [τίσις] to one another for their injustice [ἀδικία], according to the ordinance of time." One would expect Arendt to take umbrage over Heidegger's high-handed dismissal of the entire vocabulary of justice, injustice, and penalty—had she not spent her entire adult life thinking and acting on the basis of such things, or at least searching desperately for them? Yet I suspect that what was most audacious about Heidegger's rendering was what Arendt in fact most admired: ἀδικία, usually rendered as "injustice," means that the world is "out of joint"; δίκη is thus the hope that a "jointure of order" might be established for the world of being; τίσις, however, would not be "penalty" but "mutual esteem," such that beings honor one another by not insisting on their own presence, not persisting in their own drive to prevail always and everywhere, not recklessly claiming sovereignty over the *being* of beings. I would not be surprised if Heidegger's odd positive references to "reck" and "brook" touched on what she was looking for in the phrase *amor mundi* and in the Augustinian (and Heideggerian) *volo ut sis*, "I will that you *be*." Above all, Arendt must have loved Anaximander's thought that being, ἐόν, is both "presencing" and "absencing," if one may utter such strange verbs. Beings "linger awhile" in presencing, but precisely because they will—under the ordinance of time—withdraw from the world scene they must be considerate of one another, even esteem one another. Beings, among them *human* beings, διδόναι . . . τίσιν ἀλλήλοις, which Heidegger translates this way: "beings that linger awhile in presence let belong, one to the other—consideration with regard to one another" (EGT 46).

How much of these Anaximandrian matters the two of us actually talked about I cannot be sure, but I am heartened by Young-Bruehl's revelation in the final lines of her biography that Arendt wanted to end her days by thinking about Heidegger's Anaximander (YB 474). But let me return to the documents of our correspondence and then take up my recorded notes from Arendt's visits to Freiburg.

The penultimate letter to Arendt, dated October 31, 1975, thanks her for her von Humboldt-Stiftung recommendation. It refers to the letter from Elfride Heidegger, which informed me that the Klostermann problem had been resolved. I repeat my intention to include the "Anaximander" piece in a proposed *second* anthology, and I argue for the superiority of the "Humanism Letter" over the afterword to "What Is Metaphysics?" The final paragraph surprises me—referring to something I had forgotten about. The head of the Carl-Schurz-Haus, which is the "Amerika-Haus" of Freiburg, had asked me whether Arendt might be willing to be part of a bicentennial celebration during the summer of 1976. My letter ends with this, not knowing, of course, that Hannah would not live to see the year 1976:

> Finally, I want to mention that the Carl-Schurz-Haus in Freiburg is planning a big symposium—big in terms of its drawing power throughout Germany—on the Bicentennial and our present perilous condition.[8] They are hoping mightily that you will agree to be the key speaker, and so am I. Marta and I will do everything to make your stay here in Freiburg comfortable, and perhaps you can combine this symposium with visits to Heidegger and other friends here, including us!
>
> Sorry for this brusque and business-like letter. Next time I will be more typically *meshugge*. Hearty greetings, etc.

My very last letter to her, more a brief note than a letter, thanks her for having sent me the new edition of her *Origins of Totalitarianism*, in German, published by the Ullstein Verlag. I remark how handsome the three-volume edition is, and I wish her a good visit with Glenn, who I knew was on his way to New York. This last letter is in German, and it ends with this: "You see I am writing you now in German—without shame, without worries, and perhaps still without success! In any case, my heartiest greetings, and once again many thanks, Yours, etc."

* * *

My correspondence with Arendt will be unremarkable to anyone else but me. But it does show something of a growing warmth in our relationship, and it certainly does show her devotion to all the minutiae of the Heidegger translation projects. The few notes that I took after our second visit in the summer of 1975 reflect that warmth. This would be our last visit. I do not seem to have any written record of our meeting before a note jotted down on September 30, 1975. That is the date entered just above the first part of the following handwritten note. The note continues during the first or second week of December 1975, after I learned of Hannah's death. I have edited these remarks a bit—but not much.

---

8 Gerald Ford, who had pardoned Nixon a year earlier, was the lame-duck president; he would be defeated by Jimmy Carter a few days after my letter. It is, of course, odd to see those days described as "perilous," seeing where we are now. Hannah herself, had she been able to witness the fate of the Presidency and of presidential elections in our own time, would have been flabbergasted—and profoundly distressed.

Hannah was here in July and I picked her up again at the station and took her to the Schlossbergblick Hotel. That evening we had supper together at the Oberkirch restaurant on the Münsterplatz. We gossiped about Joan [Stambaugh], Reiner [Schürmann], of whom she said *ich bin sicher, dass er défroqué ist!* ("I'm certain he's been defrocked!" [her tone here was enthusiastic, not critical, clearly approving of the defrocking as a liberation for Reiner]), and she spoke about forming a "Heidegger Collective" to be in charge of the translations. ("Sounds Communist to me," commented Glenn [Gray] by letter.) Some young university people joined us at our table. One fellow was explaining to the younger ones his difficulties in arranging a seminar. Hannah had been tuning in to their conversation for quite a while and finally she interjected, *Ja, das ist immer schwierig!* ("Yes, that's always difficult"). They did not mind, of course, although they clearly did not recognize her, and we chatted in common for a while. Then it was time for us to go. The next day we discussed the anthology in detail up in her rooms at the Schlossbergblick. Then I raised the question of Heidegger's Nazi involvement.

She spoke at some length about it, especially about the origins of the ill-will between Heidegger and Husserl, which she insisted was—however much a philosophical difference raged between the two men—really the matter of a hatred between the wives. Not long after *Sein und Zeit* was published, according to Hannah, Frau Husserl remarked to Elfride that her husband needed to sit back down in Husserl's "workshop" and learn what phenomenology was all about. Frau Heidegger was not the kind to take such a remonstrance without umbrage, and the breach between the two families became irreparable. Hannah also commented sharply on the reasons for Heidegger's resignation from rectorship early in 1934. It was not so much because of Heidegger's anger over the firing of his friends, nor even any genuine enlightenment on Heidegger's part; it was that Heidegger was a "lousy administrator" and the *Kultusministerium* was glad to be shut of him. The ski lodge up on Schauinsland, she said, was his greatest accomplishment as rector. (It seemed to me that this was an impression of Hannah's, perhaps a myopic one—she did not claim to be genuinely well-informed concerning the reasons for the resignation.) As for the recurrent rumors of his antisemitism, Hannah gestured with impatience, as she always does at senseless things. Probably for a mixture of reasons, Heidegger avoided Husserl throughout the 1930s; he also apparently avoided the entire issue of the persecution of the Jews. Was it after the *Kristallnacht* events—no, it was after Husserl's death—that Heidegger sent flowers to Frau Husserl.[9] Hannah winced as she told me about it, in the way you

9 My notes are incorrect here. On April 14, 1933, Husserl was forced to "retire" after the *Reichskomissar* had ordered the firing of all Jewish members of the university faculties. In her remarks to me, Arendt was referring to Heidegger's having had Elfride send flowers to Husserl on the occasion of his forced "retirement."

wince when a thirteen-year-old stumbles gracelessly and falls. The flowers were promptly returned. With Heidegger it was not a matter of malevolence or even ill-will toward Husserl, but something more like fear and awkwardness and powerlessness.

I could not be convinced that Hannah had resolved this question in her own mind, although it could easily have been my own doubts obtruding, but it might be that it was one more aspect of that prevalent banality she had pinpointed. Heidegger was no god for her. Yet he was the one to whom she turned more and more in these last years—perhaps because of Jaspers' death?—and she wanted to grapple with Heidegger's thought, and no suspicion of this sort stood in her way.

If my memory serves me right, Arendt did not comment in detail on Heidegger's active participation in the *Gleichschaltung* of the university, nor did she talk about the colleagues (unwanted by the Nazi-dominated ministry) that Heidegger fired. Yet I myself was not yet well-informed about these things, and wouldn't be until years later when I read Bernd Martin and Hugo Ott's articles and books, so I can no longer be sure whether Hannah talked about these things in detail and they simply went over my head or in one ear and out the other, or whether she said little about them. The one thing I do remember her insisting on, and my notes corroborate this, is that Heidegger's resignation from the rectorate had nothing to do with national politics, was no sort of "statement," and was certainly not an act of "resistance." As for the "lousy administrator" remark, *lousy* was her word, one of those American street words that she relished. Regarding "the only good thing he did as rector," namely, that ski lodge up on Schauinsland, I knew it well, since it was only an hour's walk from my residence in Geiersnest, St. Ulrich. I remember both wincing and laughing at her remark about the ski lodge. Yet the wince was more enduring than the laugh.

A constant thorn in eye, mind, and heart, especially during these conversations with Hannah Arendt, was the repeated accusation from many quarters concerning Heidegger's antisemitism. I was well aware of Heidegger's militant nationalism, always denied by him but ubiquitous in his lectures and essays. I was also aware of his insistence on the hard and heavy rhetoric of "decision," but, apart from accounts by Jaspers and others, it was not until the *Black Notebooks* appeared that I had to confront the evidence of it. The senselessness of Heidegger's antisemitism, which I have tried to characterize in the foregoing chapter and, in greater detail, in *Ecstasy, Catastrophe*, is aggravated by the fact that a great number of Heidegger's best students during the Marburg years were Jewish—so this impatient gesture of hers may have meant something quite different from what I took it to mean. I saw it as an impatient rejection of the accusation. But I now think it may have been a sign of something far more painful and confounding than impatience. However, let me continue with my note on Arendt, which is now interrupted by the terrible news of her death.

> [December 1975]
>
> Hannah Arendt died this past Friday, 5 December 1975 [actually, December 4] in New York City, after a heart attack. So report the German newspapers on the Feuilleton page, together with untrue photographs and with testimonials and reminiscences. Still, I take this death rather personally, one of Melville's "jolly hits," far out of proportion to my acquaintance with Hannah. There is a letter of mine on the way to New York, *auf Deutsch, weil es gut für mich ist,* a letter to her, and one to Glenn too who was to meet her starting today for a four-day stay in the Big City. I wonder if he is there now? Confusion. . . . I'll try to go on with my notes before it all passes and leaves the unremitting fact of her passing.

So many people were disconsolate over this death. Glenn wrote to say that he had comforted many mourners at the memorial service, even though he felt like an orphan himself. Glenn admired a remark by Pope John XXIII that Hannah loved and had repeated to Glenn: "Every day is a good day to be born, every day is a good day to die" (YB 335–36). Uwe Johnson's eulogy of her ended with the sentence, "Thus she had reached an agreement with her death, as all of us should be in agreement with our own death, while refusing to accept the death of the other."[10]

My notes on the August 1975 meeting between Arendt and Heidegger, their last, now continue:

> I drove her to Heidegger's house, and on the way looked madly for a pharmacy so she could buy some pocket tissues, since she didn't want to have a runny nose over supper. [I remember her saying, whether in German or English I'm no longer sure, "One doesn't go to visit the greatest thinker of the twentieth century with a runny nose." I also remember her complaining when she had to give the Gifford Lectures that everyone in Scotland had the coughs and sniffles.] The day after her visit with Heidegger she

---

10 Uwe Johnson, "Ich habe zu danken," *Frankfurter Allgemeine Zeitung,* Feuilleton, Monday, December 8, 1975.

took me out to lunch at the *Zur Traube*. I remember having talked about Nixon over coffee in the Schlossbergblick the year before and her succinct recapitulation of Nixon's "Message to the People."

—*Allereinfältigster* QUATSCH! said she, "Totally simple-minded non-sense!" and I should have had a tape recorder with me to get that gravelly-voiced disgust.

Hannah had made a bet with me—she took joy in wagering—that Nixon would never be impeached, or that, if impeached, he would be clever enough to wriggle out of it. The bet was for a free lunch, and I did not have to remind Hannah that she had lost the bet, at least arguably so, even though Nixon had resigned before he could be impeached. But she did not argue the point, and the trout was excellent. As for that favorite exclamation of hers, the one I heard so many times, "*Quatsch!*" I had not at that point noticed that Joyce also loved the word and offered it a prominent place in his meandertale (FW 520).

After our long discussion of the anthology and the Heidegger-Nazi involvement, I shifted the conversation toward politics and political philosophy in general.

This time I asked her about the chances of her working one more time on a synthesis of modern political life, on the Hegelian model. I explained my confusions, my need for such an "answer" to Hegel. [I recall saying, as we walked from the Münster square up to *Zur Traube*, that if Hegel's theme had been "reason in history," hers would have to be the "unreason" (*Unvernunft*) of our own time.] She demurred. "I'm too old. Let me be. They say you're only as old as you feel. Nonsense. Do you want to know how old you are? Count the candles, that's how!" As for my frustrated need to find sense where there is only waxing nonsense, she offered a curious comfort. "My boy, you picked a miserable century to be born in." But she made me less miserable by buying me a fine dinner of trout and a very dry Markgräflerland Gutedel. . . .

That deep voice of hers, whispering confidentially, amused, ironic, sometimes very forceful, gulping her breaths, then pausing to squint and to wolf a long drag on the ever-present cigarette. That's when the cutting remark would come, coiled in smoke. Or that voice would recite poetry—a waterfall somewhere, or the State erupting like a festering sore, *wie ein Pestgeschwür*, a phrase she repeated two or three times. . . . The voice would sometimes sink so low that it left my hearing-register hopelessly behind, especially when she muttered something *auf Deutsch* and I had to rely on her eyes and eyebrows to catch her meaning.

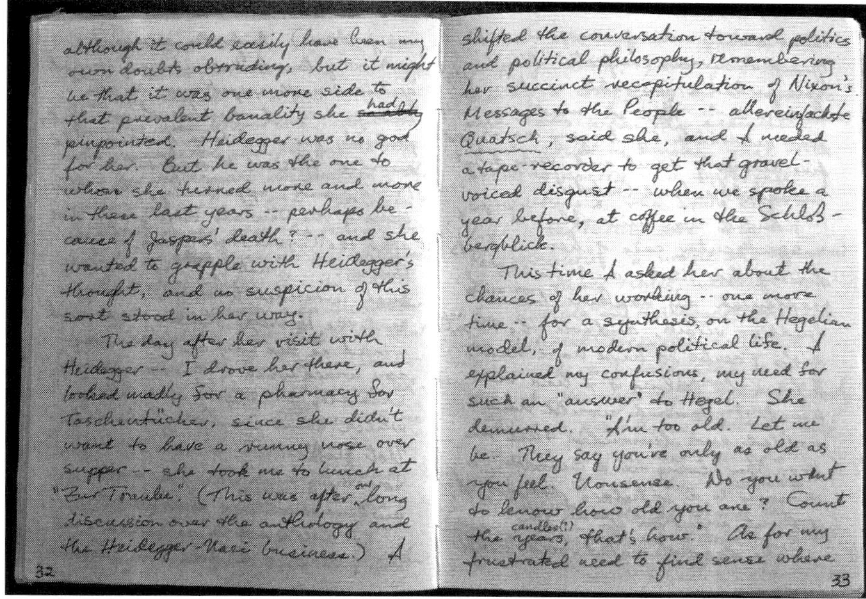

Fig. 5.2 Notes in another of my journals on Hannah Arendt's second visit in summer 1975.

Those eyebrows! Their inner ends, near the bridge of the nose, were much higher on her brow than the outer ends, lending her look a skeptical and ironic aspect, perhaps a bemused and quizzical aspect. I do not need photographs to remember them. As for her recitation of poems, she had been doing that since she was twelve: "She knows everything by heart" said her proud mother of her (YB 32).

> She had doubts about my *Deutsch*, and rightly so, of course; she was therefore hesitant to see me take up Glenn Gray's role [as general editor of the translation series], again rightly so. Naturally, my German was never worse than when I was with her. So I was well aware that she could judge, judge hard and keen. From Glenn I knew that she liked me and from her I could tell that this made absolutely no difference as far as the judgment was concerned. Yet, while anxious for her support for my various projects and grant applications, I did not feel pressed to plead or to please. That was good, because it wouldn't have worked. I was terribly pleased to be treated to suppers and lunches and long conversations with the renowned Hannah Arendt, but during this last visit the fame and the bright lights— as bright as a philosopher gets—faded and I enjoyed the human reality

deeply somehow, even if I am all superficies, watching her wander a bit as we walked toward the car, having the feeling that she did not quite know where she was, rapt in conversation, drifting down the sidewalk, negotiating electric poles and curbs, climbing into my Beetle not like an elderly woman but like Thales approaching the well, only more stubborn and self-assertive than he.

This time when she arrived at the station and I went toward her, she did not recognize me. This annoyed her. "Did you just grow that beard?" "About ten years ago." "Funny…," she grumbled. But when she left Freiburg this last time I was sure—though I thought about it only afterwards—that she would remember me next time. And when I gave her a philosopher's hug on the train and promised to travel to Ticino to visit her at the end of September, then had to run to get off the train in time, standing on the platform and waving a handkerchief like a German as the train pulled out, I felt an invigorating affection for this woman. And I felt a milder affection, perhaps a bit surprised at itself, coming from her. I was certain that she would return the next spring or summer and that our third visit would be longer, more relaxed, and even richer than this last one—which will be the last one.

On the event of her first visit I bore to the station little-old-lady violets, for which she was grateful, and which she kept in a little-old-lady vase in her hotel room. For her second visit I gathered from the garden flaming dragons and carnations [and even peppery lupins!], anything I could find with color and vibrant life, and I think she liked these much better.

* * *

As I have mentioned more than once, I have always been reluctant to say anything about Arendt's and Heidegger's love for one another, about which I knew nothing at the time, except to say that it seems to have been incredibly resilient. As for all the speculation about it—and condemnation of it—in the literature, it seems to me an eminent instance of projection, of what Heidegger observes as the disturbing side of the hermeneutical circle: "When interpretation, in the sense of the exact interpretation of texts, is happy in particular concrete cases to appeal to 'what stands there' [right on the page], what for the most part 'stands there' is nothing other than the obvious and never discussed preconception of the interpreter" (SZ 150). The same seems to be true of interpretations of other people's lives, and especially their loves. The view from the outside is most often a projection of personal ressentiments and feelings of shame and inexpugnable envy, which Lacan in his *Ethics of Psychoanalysis* calls *Lebensneid*, "life envy." Lacan's psychoanalytic account of "life envy," which is more democratic and, if a layman may say so, far more devastating than the famous "penis envy," may be viewed as an expansion of Nietzsche's account of ressentiment in his *Genealogy of Morals*. Lacan writes,

> *Lebensneid* is not an ordinary jealousy, it is the jealousy borne in a subject in its relation to an other, insofar as this other is held to enjoy a certain form of *jouissance* or superabundant vitality that the subject perceives as something that it cannot apprehend by means of even the most elementary of affective movements. Isn't it strange, isn't it very odd, that a being admits to being jealous of something in the other to the point of hatred and the need to destroy, jealous of something that it is incapable of apprehending in any way, by any intuitive path?[11]

For some reason, Lacan's words put me in mind of something that happened during one of my conversations with Arendt. I cannot remember the context, but in our talk we must have touched on the question of evil, radical evil, because at one point she fixed me with a look and startled me with a question, her voice quiet but tense.

—Iago, she said. Iago. . . . What does he *want*?

Of course, I had no answer. Perhaps Lacan, with his notion of "life envy," was pointing toward Iago's "wanting." It was clearly a mystery that had preoccupied her for some time. Shakespeare's villain could not be called *banal*, but *inscrutable* he certainly was. Years later, while reading Elisabeth Young-Bruehl's *For Love of the World*, I had to write the name "Iago" in the margins of her book at the point where she cites the following, on the radical evil of the extermination, from Arendt's *Origins of Totalitarianism*: "When the impossible was made possible it became the unpunishable, unforgivable absolute evil which could no longer be understood and explained by the evil motives of self-interest, greed, covetousness, resentment, thirst for power, and cowardice: and therefore which anger could not revenge, love could not endure, friendship could not forgive" (YB 205, citing Arendt).

We do not seem to be better prepared to account for love—in this case, the love of Arendt and Heidegger for one another. It may be unwise to be too inquisitive about it. I admire the psychological acuity of a fictional narrator by the name of Sabine Menner-Bettscheid, who scolds a fellow scholar

---

11 Jacques Lacan, *Le séminaire, livre VII: L'éthique de la psychanalyse* (Paris: Seuil, 1986), 277–78.

who is editing the love letters of Susette Gontard to Friedrich Hölderlin. Menner-Bettscheid chides her fellow editor, a man whom she knows quite well, for being so anxious to uncover every titillating detail of the relationship between Gontard and her lover. Her collaborator claims it is his scholarly rigor that drives him, but Menner-Bettscheid replies that he is merely hiding behind the demands made by a scholarly biography: "You are being dishonest about your motives. Why does this project interest you? What are you getting out of it? (. . .) You protested your innocence, you blamed it on whatever could be safely located back in the eighteenth century in order to leave you shiny white and scholarly bright, but no one will be fooled, my friend, no one you want to fool will be fooled. Listen to me. Read me several times over, make an effort to understand, and then burn these letters. All of them."[12]

I would never say that the letters from Heidegger to Arendt should be burned. Quite the contrary. I carried them through the Freiburg railway station on the occasion of Arendt's second visit. She had two suitcases with her, one a modern one, the other the sort of suitcase one sees in old movies: solidly made—presumably of wood—and with a beige cloth covering, the corners and edges reinforced with caramel-colored leather. As I was carrying it from the train platform to the parking garage, Arendt explained to me what was in it, namely, her entire stock of letters from Heidegger. She was donating them to the Heidegger Archive at the *Deutsches Literaturarchiv* in Marbach. I had no idea that many of them were love letters. And even now I do not feel comfortable reading them, not even after they have been published in book form. Not out lack of interest, but out of something like respect for things neither I nor anyone else is given to understand. That anyone would use them as weapons against either Arendt or Heidegger strikes me as that user's declaration of personal bankruptcy. "Why does this project interest you?" Menner-Bettscheid demands of her fellow editor, and I find myself unable to reply, even though my mind is teeming.

That suitcase. The one with all his letters. I remember that it was to be turned over to Dr. Joachim Storck, who was in charge of the Heidegger papers at the Archive for German Literature. Dr. Storck, rightly praised and thanked by the editor of the Arendt–Heidegger correspondence, was also very generous toward me, responding in detail to all my queries during

12 See *The Recalcitrant Art: Diotima's Letters to Hölderlin and Related Missives*, 3.

those years. He was later a colleague at the University of Mannheim, where he taught in the German department. Sometime during the 1990s, I met with him in Chicago, and we enjoyed a supper together with Erich Heller, the renowned Nietzsche scholar. There were so many benefits from my having been engaged in this translation and editing work—I seldom pause to be mindful of them and thankful for them. I often complained about that work, but it was a beige and caramel-colored cornucopia.

Again, that suitcase. I can still hear Arendt asking me if I can imagine what is in it. Of course I cannot. Every letter she had received from Heidegger, she told me matter-of-factly, but—if my memory does not betray me—with a strong resonance of pride. Perhaps even awe.

"Burn these letters, burn them all," cries yet another figure, namely, the writer of the *Envois* in Derrida's *The Postcard*. But of course the letters are not burned; they are ligatured and bound up in a book, open to the gaze of · every letter carrier. To be sure, Derrida's "letters" and "postcards" may be entirely fictional, even if they fail to shift from the first-person singular to the third, as Blanchot requires. Yet love may be the place where truth and fiction meet and mate.

It hurts me to think that Heidegger destroyed the letters from Arendt. Clearly, they were dangerous to him. What does Molly say about Poldy's mild flirtations? Not a million pockets can hide his secrets from me, she says, or words to that effect. Yet I cannot help but think of Hölderlin's holding on to the letters from Susette Gontard—his Diotima—during the thirty-five years of his illness. Such beautiful, powerful letters! One dreams of receiving such agonizingly passionate letters! What would Nietzsche not have sacrificed to receive such letters! I do understand the need for discretion and safety. I can imagine the anxiety that such glad tidings produce, I can understand the urge to hide, to conceal what is too good to be true— precisely because the others will say it is too wicked to be allowed to be true. Hölderlin was not married, there was no vigilant Molly for him, but something far worse happened: his mother found those letters, written by a married woman to her son—he had hidden them beneath the false bottom of his trunk, but like any pious mother she had rifled through his things quite thoroughly—and then she gave her boy hell to pay, never letting him forget his "sin," the sin that he surely felt was the holiest event of his life, the sin overseen by a goddess. Not even Hölderlin's mother dared destroy such letters, and so he was able to keep them throughout the long night of his incapacitation and incarceration in the Tübingen tower. Why could not Heidegger emulate his hero in all things, the important things, the holiest of things?

Because Arendt kept Heidegger's letters, we have a good sense of his love for her, and despite all the usual *gefloofle* of love letters, that love proves, no matter how flawed, to be genuine—perhaps especially when it occasions Heidegger's consistently regrettable poetry. We have very little sense of what Arendt's letters to Heidegger must have been like. But there is a draft of a letter from 1929 that closes with this: "I kiss your brow and your eyes" (AHB 67). That is not the sort of thing one discards. No matter what has been agreed to, and no matter what the danger. Not that it is mine to judge. But it is mine to regret.

6

ARENDT WITH AND WITHOUT HEIDEGGER

One of the first things that caught my eye in Antonia Grunenberg's account of Heidegger's life was his attachment to his mother. Perhaps I was recalling Goethe's account of mother love in *Dichtung und Wahrheit*, mother love as crucial for the later productions of the person of genius. Be that as it may, we find in Heidegger a strong attachment to a mother whose overwhelming desire was that her son become a priest. There is no doubt a parallel to Hölderlin here, although Heidegger's mother seems to have been a far more genial and generous person than the parsimonious Frau Gok. There is also a parallel to Hannah Arendt, who had a strong attachment to a forceful and impressive mother—albeit a secularized, liberal, and emancipated one (AG 32–33/16–17; YB 9, 24–26). Perhaps I was also recalling that freshly published copy of *Sein und Zeit* that its author laid on his mother's deathbed. This by way of prelude.

Grunenberg sets the stage for the love story quite dramatically:

Martin Heidegger: an introverted, learned man, with his five feet four inches rather small and of a lithe but athletic build. Hannah Arendt: a young student eager to learn, slender, with a face of even features, radiant eyes, and lightning intelligence.

Heidegger united contradictions in himself. The man was ascetic yet he could burst into sudden expressions of joy. He was a thinker *par excellence*, and yet in his clothing and mannerisms he had the style of a farmer or a craftsman. He could be quite haughty and fiery, yet what was typical of him was an astonishing modesty. His language was a mix of Platonic gestures and lyrical purity. His way of talking was quiet, with an almost delicate, high-pitched voice. It is therefore not surprising how different and even contrary the descriptions of his appearance and the effect he had on people are. (AG 83/52)

"The First Encounter" (AG 95–110/58–67) tells the story of Arendt's and Heidegger's love with great sensitivity and respect—a rarity in the literature, which is too busy tsk-tsk-ing to pay much attention to the particulars. And, truth to tell, the particulars are as concealed here as they are in any love story. It is clear that Heidegger is overwhelmed by love, and that Arendt is and remains, as Heidegger later confesses to his wife, "the passion of his life" (RS 159/136). And yet right from the start, he worries about the possible self-deception in that passion. I am startled by the skepticism of his letter to Arendt on February 10, 1925: "We will not want to imagine that we are sharing something like a friendship between souls, which is the sort of thing that does not exist among human beings" (AHB 12; AG 97/59). Grunenberg notes that the same could also be said of Heidegger's and Jaspers's friendship: there is little doubt that Jaspers believed in such sharing and that he was crushed by Heidegger's irremediable remoteness, the insurmountable emotional distance that Heidegger seems to have had with all his fellows.

Grunenberg observes that Heidegger was clearly interested in Hannah's family origins. Yet how much would she have discussed with him, how much would she have shared with him? It is impossible to say, since Heidegger did not dare preserve her letters to him (AG 104/64). The text titled "Shadow" is really all we have from her during those early years of their relationship, except for some poems and two drafts of letters from 1929. And yet the two never let more than several days pass without writing back and forth.

As for Arendt's "Shadow," written in April 1925, the text is too long for me to reproduce here (see AHB 21–25). Let me indicate one or two aspects that strike me most forcefully. The narrator is designated as "she," and the first-person pronoun is avoided throughout. Arendt's text thereby takes the step—or feigns to take the step—from confession to fiction. More than once "she" betrays the nature of "her" posture in the world at large as a "diffident and palpating tenderness toward the things of the world," *scheue und tastende Zärtlichkeit zu den Dingen der Welt*. By tenderness, she means "a shy, reticent inclination, not giving itself over," an initially reluctant but then more joyous marveling "at strange forms." If there was a longing that characterized her early life, it was not for anything in particular; it was "a kind of longing that fills an entire life and can be constitutive of it." "She" develops in her childhood a passion for peculiarities, for what others take to be familiar everyday items. "A radicality that always went to extremes made it impossible for her to protect herself, and it deprived her of weapons." Yet she experienced no bitterness on account of this defenselessness, even if her sensitivity and vulnerability were developed to a point that was almost "grotesque." Once again fall the words *a diffident and palpating tenderness.*

Her deepest anxiety? The image a mirror returns to her. "Anxiety struck her, as earlier longing had struck her, not some sort of definable anxiety, but anxiety in the face of existence in general." The radicality that enabled her to go to extremes soon seemed to dissolve, she says, so that things began to drift by, "pallid and colorless and with the concealed uncanniness of a shadow scurrying across one's path." The fiction ends with the narrator wondering whether "she" will continue to fritter away her time with pointless experiments and mere curiosities until some "arbitrary goal" puts a stop to it all.

Heidegger replies to "Shadow" by reassuring its narrator that "she" has freed herself from all the twists and turns that her earlier life may have taken. His own youth, he confesses, offered him fewer choices and made "diligence" and "a sober matter-of-factness" easier to achieve (AHB 27). One is driven to speculate that perhaps Heidegger's youth merely delayed— if it did not stunt the growth of—a palpating tenderness toward the things of the world, since this sounds very much like what his later thought of *Gelassenheit,* or "letting-be," had long been seeking. As for Arendt's own later thought, after the *Origins* book, we are reminded of her "palpating tenderness" when we learn that the first title she chose for what became *The Human Condition* (in German, *Vita activa*), was *amor mundi,* "love of the world" (AG 364/262). And long before the *Origins,* it was Augustine's concept of love that captivated Arendt the doctoral candidate.

In one of his letters, dated May 13, 1925, allowing the hiatuses to say it all, Heidegger writes, "This time all words fail me—I can only weep and weep—and the *why* receives no answer—and it sinks—vainly waiting—into thanking and believing" (AHB 30; AG 105/65). Several weeks later, on June 22, he theorizes about love a bit more generously than he had earlier: "Love is being able to take only the singular 'you' as actual. When I say that my joy in you is great and is growing, that means that I also believe in everything that belongs to your history. I am not fabricating some ideal—even less could I ever be tempted into trying to shape you in terms of that ideal— the way you are and the way you will remain with your history—that is how I love you" (AHB 36). He then adds a remark that in retrospect has something fateful and even fatal about it: "Only then is love also strong enough for the future, not a lightheaded enjoyment of an opportunity—only then is the possibility of the other equally taken up and made viable against the crises and struggles [*gegen Krisen und Kämpfe*] that will never fail to come" (ibid.).

Grunenberg observes that Heidegger seems to be preoccupied with the experience of the otherness of the other when boundaries are crossed or have to be newly drawn. Some three years later, he will reveal his impatience with romantic love and his exhaustion with the struggle over boundaries. In his lecture course, *Introduction to Philosophy*, taught in 1928–29, the very years in which his love of Arendt has tipped into crisis and separation, he says that the original power or might of Dasein is "broken" or "refracted" by human embodiment and sexual difference. This leads him to express scorn for the "coarse materialism" of a Feuerbach, a materialism that Heidegger takes to be inherited by psychoanalysis and psychology in general, all of which misconstrue the "essential neutrality" of a puissant Dasein. The polemic against coarse materialism leads Heidegger to contrast sexual love with "genuine and grand" friendship. Friends, such as Goethe and Schiller, are comrades in the good fight, two friends "going together," as Homer says, passionate for whatever the object of that fight may be for the two individuals. Fraternal friends, presumably unlike lovers, do not "exchange sentimental gazes [*einander rührselig anschauen*]," and they do not "entertain" one another with "the insignificant neediness of their souls [*ihren belanglosen Seelennöten*]" (27:147). A bit later in the course, he feels constrained to defend his use of the word *Sorge* ("care" or "concern"), which seems so laden with emotion, to designate the very being of Dasein:

> It has nothing to do with Schopenhauer or Christian asceticism or the doctrine of original sin, nor is it at all about the concept of "care" thrusting us in the direction of death and conscience, something that sounds harsh to our ears nowadays.—One has understood very little of these things when one puts in a plea for the cheerful worldview of Goethe, hoping to preserve a general respectability and pleasantness for Dasein, going so far as to proclaim the wisdom that life also offers us something like love. Who ever wanted to deny that? Yet I doubt whether what the respectable philosophers secretly take love to be grasps the metaphysical essence of said love. Ultimately, the petty feelings that one expresses under this rubric are way off the mark. One would have to ask whether or not every great love—and it is great love alone that tells us something about love's essence—is at

bottom a struggle [*Kampf*], not merely or preeminently a struggle to win over the other, but a struggle *for* the other. One would also have to ask whether or not it grows in inverse proportion to sentimentality and the coziness of feelings. But enough of this! (27:327)[1]

If Heidegger confesses that early on he was struck by the lightning (*Blitz*) of Arendt's gaze (*Blick*), he does his best—as a theorist of being and of human being—to avoid the squalls of romantic love. Or, if not to avoid them, at least to denigrate them in the distance and retrospect provided by theory. As a Dasein that in addition to *questioning* also *lives*, however, he is often not smart enough to come in out of the rain.

Unfortunately, the Arendt-Heidegger correspondence, as I mentioned, contains very little material from Arendt. And yet I cannot help but imagine how different Arendt's letters must have been! The two of them had agreed to destroy their letters, and Heidegger held to the agreement, whereas—fortunately, if I may say so again—Arendt did not. What strikes me about Heidegger's letters is their struggle to remain formal, reserved, sage, reflective, and sovereign, elevated above all sentimentality and even sentiment. They are full of paternal and even grandfatherly admonitions about how girls are to develop into women, even though Heidegger's lack of experience in such matters is painfully clear on every page. In his very first letter to her, he hopes that everything between them will be "straightforward and clear and pure," whereas everything is already curvilinear, turbid, and hybrid (AHB 11). It is clear that he is resisting every step of the way, even if the steps taken are his. For that first letter also says, "That we were allowed to meet one another we will want to preserve deep within us as a gift. We will not distort it in its pure vitality by any sort of self-delusion" (AHB 12). We have already heard about the principal delusion Heidegger wishes to avoid, namely, that something like a friendship of the soul, *eine Seelenfreundschaft*, is possible for human beings.

Soulful or not, impossible or not, the friendship deepens into something like love, or the love deepens into friendship, and Heidegger is soon enough overwhelmed. Struck by lightning, coup de foudre, he is caught in the storm. In the next letter to her, he writes, "That the presence of the other invades our life is something that no power of the mind [*kein Gemüt*]

1 I have discussed this passage more fully in *Phantoms of the Other: Four Generations of Derrida's* Geschlecht (Albany: State University of New York Press, 2015), 34. My enduring thanks to Will McNeill, who is now translating volume 27 of the *Gesamtausgabe* into English, for these references.

can master" (AHB 13). And in the next, he confesses, "I have been struck by the daimonic [*das Dämonische*]" (AHB 14). By that, he means not the diabolical but the Greek sense of *daimon*, the spirit that communicates between mortals and deities and that is itself divine. Three years later, he will invoke the daimonic realm itself (τό δαιμόνιον) as the crucial site of his thinking, invoking it, to be sure, in parentheses within a footnote, as though practicing a double apotropaism: "(It remains for us to consider: being and the δαιμόνιον, or the understanding of being and the δαιμόνιον. Being as ground! Being and Nothing—anxiety" (26:211). When the deity intervenes—perhaps in the shape of Eros, or in the equally compelling figure of the mother of Eros, Aphrodite—any supposed "ground" drops away, and one is left with nothing to hold on to except the nothing. This *is* the experience of anxiety, which is the experience human beings must attain and sustain, in Heidegger's view, if they are to come into their own. When Narcissus feels the boundaries of his self dissolving or becoming frighteningly porous, such that the other—the Echo of the self, as it were—enters and exits at will, the result may be a life-threatening anxiety. Even for the young Heidegger, however, such anxiety is what enables thinking.

On April 24, 1925, Heidegger exposes a telling aspect of this anxiety. Referring to his first vision of her on her return to Marburg for the summer semester, he writes, "And I was benumbed by the splendor of this human being, to whom I, in you, am allowed to be close" (AHB 27). The word *benommen*, "struck dumb, addled, benumbed," will soon be his word for the essence of nonhuman animals, animals that have no language and only a "poor" world. Before that, in *Being and Time*, the word had a double sense: it is said of all the distractions and inanities of our daily lives, which, almost anesthetizing us, allow us no time for reflection; but then "benumbment" is also said of the fundamentally humanizing experience of *anxiety* (SZ 344). When the mood of anxiety steals over us, we are suddenly struck by the bare facticity of our mortality, our finitude, our being thrown toward death; we are struck dumb, benumbed, rattled by what we now realize we *are*. We are the creature that is not only open to but also defenseless against *being*. The splendor of the beloved other evokes a third form of benumbment, perhaps, somewhere between stupefaction and anxiety.

Antonia Grunenberg now notes a "disturbing" characteristic of Heidegger's, namely, his ability to become so absorbed in his work that he forgets everyone around him. She cites a letter of his from January 10, 1926, apparently in reply to letters from Arendt that express the hope that he has not forgotten her. In these letters, Arendt evidently floats the idea that she should leave Marburg for another university—not that they should break off their relationship, but that the greater distance between them will protect them both. He replies, "I *have* forgotten you—not out of indifference, not because external circumstances imposed themselves, but because I had to forget you and will forget you as often as I get under way on the final concentrated stages of my work" (AHB 54; AG 107/66). He is referring to his work on *Being and Time*, work that is occupying his days and nights and causing him to neglect everything else. He calls this capacity of his to forget everything and everyone by dint of absorption in his work the most "grandiose" of his life experiences, but he also confesses that it lacerates his heart (ibid.). One has to wonder: is it grandiose cruelty toward a lover, cruelty toward himself, or the sign of a genuine vocation to work? All three, perhaps.

Not long after receiving that letter, Arendt packs her things and leaves for Heidelberg. She will pursue her doctoral work there with Jaspers. The contact with Heidegger from then on is intermittent. They exchange letters six or seven times, not angry letters, but missives without hope. Three years after leaving Marburg, Arendt marries Günther Stern.

Allow me an afterthought about this capacity to forget everything and everyone in one's work. I never would have claimed for myself—or confessed as a fault—this tendency to disappear entirely into my work, although friends and colleagues have occasionally expressed astonishment over my ability to submerge myself. And I never thought that anyone else was forced to pay a price for my submersion—until I had a conversation recently with my now-grown children. I must have made a remark about having always wanted to be there for them as they were growing up, because the three of them laughed a bit ruefully and told me this story: each time they had to interrupt the work I was doing in my study, they would knock quietly on the door, and, having been granted permission to enter, they would tell me about their problem. I always listened carefully and sympathetically, they assured me, but they were disconcerted by the fact that I always placed an index finger on the page I happened to be reading. I kept that finger there until they left the study. My index finger was the minute hand on the clock—no, the sweep hand, ticking away the seconds until they would finally leave and I could get back to my page. I therefore have to doubt whether I have always been so attentive to those I have loved, or whether I am able to keep my work and my life in equilibrium. Heidegger probably had greater reason to doubt. Whether or not he ever did so, I do not know.

＊　＊　＊

At this point, I want to interrupt Antonia Grunenberg's account to supplement it with Rüdiger Safranski's report and several observations of my own. When the eighteen-year-old Hannah Arendt arrived in Marburg to study with Rudolf Bultmann and Martin Heidegger, writes Safranski, she did not have to rely on her fashionable clothing and short haircut to draw attention (RS 160/137). Safranski cites a number of those who knew her then. They report that "one submerged in her eyes and had to fear that one would never resurface again," that her "intensity, steadiness of purpose, her eye for quality, her search for the essential, her depth" made for a certain magic (ibid.). When she said something to her friends at their table in the student cafeteria, people at the next table stopped to listen. Something like this, I might add, is what I witnessed at the Oberkirch restaurant in Freiburg a half century later, even if the roles appear to have been reversed.

Regarding the love between Arendt and Heidegger, Safranski occasionally falls into the trap that almost everyone leaps into, succumbing to the obligation to express his or her disapproval. There seems to be little doubt that it was Heidegger—married and with two sons—who insisted that their relationship remain secret. Nor can one doubt that Arendt began to suffer from the lack of shared space in the public world. Safranski cites *The Human Condition*: "In passion, where love merely grasps the Who of the other, the worldly space between us [*der weltliche Zwischenraum*], in which we are bound up with others and at the same time separated from them, more or less goes up in flames. What separates the lovers from the shared world is that they are worldless, that the world between the lovers has been consumed" (RS 162/139, citing *Vita activa*, 237). If they do share a world, it is something like the world created by a novel, say, a novel about Alpine seclusion on a magic mountain. Safranski reports that during the summer of 1924, Arendt and Heidegger read aloud to one another Thomas Mann's *Zauberberg* (RS 213/185). One can almost imagine eavesdropping on the debates between them—Arendt's sympathy for the humanist Settembrini and Heidegger's self-recognition in the caustic and ascetic radical Naphta.

Safranski risks summarizing the eventual *philosophical* relation between the two in the following way: "She would provide the complement to his philosophy, responding as lovers do, and she would provide the worldliness that was missing in that philosophy. She would reply to Heidegger's *running ahead into death* with a philosophy of natality; to his existential solipsism of the *in each case mine* she would respond with a philosophy of plurality; to his critique of our *falling prey* to the world of the *they*, she would answer with *amor mundi*. To Heidegger's *clearing* she would respond by elevating in a philosophical way 'the public world'" (RS 163/140). Later in his book, Safranski elaborates on the "complement" (RS 422–25/381–84). He tries to show how Arendt shifts from Heidegger's "appropriateness" or "authenticity," which singularizes Dasein, to what she calls "the virtuosity of acting together with others"; such a shift, argues Safranski, would achieve the "openness to being" that Heidegger himself is seeking. Safranski refers to the second volume of *The Life of the Mind*, on willing, as the place where Arendt develops her critique of Heidegger's *Seinsgeschichte*, or history of being. Once again, he notes Arendt's emphasis on initiative and commencement—signified by the sheer fact of birth. Hers, to repeat, is a "philosophy of natality," of a "running ahead toward the beginning," not toward the end (RS 425/383). Important themes for her are the possibilities of *promise* (achieving the future) and of *forgiveness* (while accepting responsibility for the past). These, I may add, are principal themes of Derrida's seminars in the 1990s.

While there is much to this sense of Arendt's "complementing" Heidegger, she herself, I believe, would be scornful of the notion. She would defer to the pages of *Sein und Zeit* on natality that in fact inspired her. Long after he has seemed to secure his interpretation of the entire being of human being as finite, as being toward death, *Sein zum Tode*, Heidegger is struck by "a serious reservation" (SZ 372). For death, as the "end" of Dasein, "formally considered, is only the *one* end" (SZ 373). The *other* end, he observes, the end that stands at the beginning, is "birth." The entirety of Dasein can be grasped only when we take *both* ends into account, understanding Dasein as the stretch or, better, as the *self-stretching* between these two ends. It would take many pages to discuss the importance of Heidegger's "serious reservation," and I have tried to do that elsewhere.[2] Yet the most telling point is this: precisely in the way that one's own death is not some future event that has no reality here and

2 See Krell, *Ecstasy, Catastrophe*, chap. 3, "Ecstasy at the 'Other End' of Dasein."

now, so is one's birth not something past, an event that is soon over and done with. "Understood existentially, birth is not, not ever, something past in the sense of being no longer at hand. . . . Factical Dasein exists natally, and natally [or, translating the German *gebürtig* more naturally, "by birth and nationality" or, rendering it more literally, "birthingly"] it is already dying in the sense of being toward death" (SZ 374). Human existence stretches between these two ends, ends that accompany it every step of the way.

A foolish music critic once posed a challenging question to the pianist Hélène Grimaud, regarding one of her programs of Chopin and Rachmaninoff. She claimed that each piece was a reflection on human mortality. The critic objected that the penultimate piece, Chopin's "Berceuse," opus 57, surely had nothing to do with death, since a *Berceuse* is a cradle song, a lullaby. As I remember, Grimaud was very gentle with her answer. She did not say, at least not so directly that it would have alarmed the critic, "Dasein natal is Dasein fatal."

These thoughts of Heidegger's on "the other end" of Dasein clearly struck Arendt with great force, and if she did give them a more positive resonance— each new birth promising enhanced possibilities for humankind— she had no illusions about the finitude impacted in each new birth. Heidegger's *Being and Time* had reminded her of the Bohemian peasant, or "plowman," who berates Death for taking his young wife, whereupon Death, aggrieved by the accusation of cruelty, offers an irrefutable reply. The plowman curses:

> *Grimmiger tilger aller leute, schedelicher echter aller werlte, freissamer morder aller menschen, ir Tot, euch sei verfluchet!*

> Malevolent destroyer of all the people, malignant enemy of all the world, murderous devourer of all humankind, thou Death, my curse on you!

Death, offended by the peasant's vituperation, replies:

> *Weistu des nicht, so wisse es nu: als balde ein mensche geboren wird, als balde hat es den leikauf getrunken, das es sterben sol. Anefanges geswisterde ist das ende. . . . [A]ls schiere ein mensche lebendig wird, als schiere ist es alt genug zu sterben.*

> If you knew it not before, then know it now: as soon as a human being is born it has drunk from the proffered chalice, and so it is to die. The end

is akin to the beginning. . . . The instant a human being comes to be alive it is old enough to die.[3]

"The end is akin to the beginning." Dasein natal *is* Dasein fatal. In addition to Chopin's "Berceuse" and the *Ackermann aus Böhmen*, Arendt may well have known of the remarkable *Midraschim* published by Otto Rank in 1924, which was the same year that she went to Marburg to study with Bultmann and Heidegger. In his classic study *The Trauma of Birth*, in a chapter on "Religious Sublimation," Otto Rank cites "The Book of the Creation of the Child":

> And as soon as the time arrives that it should go out, the angel comes and says to it: "Go out, for the time has come for you to go out into the world." And the spirit of the child answers: "I have already said to the One who when He spoke the Word the world was created that I was perfectly satisfied to remain in the world in which I have been dwelling." And the angel replies: "The world to which I will introduce you is beautiful. Furthermore, you were formed in your mother's body against your will, and against your will you will be born in order to go out into the world." Whereupon the child weeps. And why does it weep? It weeps for the world that was and that it now must leave. And as it is going out, the angel strikes it under its nose and extinguishes the light above its head. It brings the child out against the child's will, and the child forgets everything that it has seen. And as soon as it comes out, it weeps.[4]

The infant, struck by the angel between upper lip and nose, receives the philtrum, that narrow scar that marks, mars, or graces every human face. Note that the infant weeps at least twice, and probably three times, first at the news that it must leave the wombworld; second, presumably, when the angel strikes it, and then once again as it feels the chilly world it has been compelled to enter. The question, of course, is whether the child "forgets everything" about its first home. Are there not, as Rank firmly believes, both fetal and natal memories that remain—fetal, natal, fatal memories?

---

3 Johannes von Tepl, *Der Ackermann aus Böhmen*, written in Middle High German in 1401. I use the edition by Alois Bernt and Konrad Burdach (Berlin: Weidmannsche Buchhandlung, 1917), 3, 45–46, which Heidegger cites in *Being and Time*. Heidegger refers to lines 19 and 20 of chapter 20 of *Der Ackermann* at SZ 245. See now the fine article by Peter Atterton, "'As soon as a man comes to life, he is at once old enough to die': Heidegger and Chapter 20 of *Der Ackermann aus Böhmen*," forthcoming in *Research in Phenomenology*.

4 Otto Rank, *Das Trauma der Geburt und seine Bedeutung für die Psychoanalyse* (Giessen, Germany: Psychosozial-Verlag, 2007 [1924]), 118–19, n. 3.

As for "the public world," Arendt would, I believe, concede that no amount of love of the world can save the public space from its worst enemies. I remember on several occasions her almost snarling the words *wie ein Pestgeschwür* ("like an ulcerated sore of plague," a phrase from the poet, satirist, and cabaret lyricist Robert Gilbert, a friend of Blücher's) and *Gassenmenschen* or *Gassenpöbel* ("alley rats," "guttersnipes") as she recalled the sorts of people who rallied to the Nazi cause. Safranski recalls a phrase from her *Origins of Totalitarianism* that must have wounded Heidegger: she writes of the union of alley rats and intellectuals as "an alliance between the mob and the elite" (RS 263/231).

Regarding life in the United States, Arendt lived long enough and perspicuously enough to see the public space all but entirely mediatized—and that means diminished to a point of almost complete shrinkage, almost to the vanishing point. Already in March of 1967, she observed that "the four walls that are there to shield us from the light of publicity now serve to stave off the darkness," such that we "flee into the private realm."[5] The dismal proof of this in our day is that virtually half the nation she had come to love and to which she was infinitely grateful, half the nation now ensconced in the privacy of its four walls, had been so bamboozled by an inane "reality TV" show that it elevated an unscrupulous incompetent to the Presidency. And she would have worried whether the public space that had been opened so remarkably in the United States centuries ago could survive the two onslaughts of plague, namely, the pandemic of COVID-19 and the epidemic of Trumpery: she had been through this rise of mediocrity, racism, and rancor before, and she would have stood appalled to see it happening again—this time as farce, Marx would have insisted, but a farce with all the trappings of tragedy nonetheless. She might well have feared that a virus could become the Reichstag fire that enabled the fascist seizure of total power. She would of course have railed against the takeover. But for all her love of the world, she had no illusions. Evil could be clownish as well as banal.

* * *

Allow me a final note on natality, but not a mere footnote. For it seems to me that I have only scratched the surface of what is a profound philosophical problem. First of all, there can be no doubt that birth was a focal point

---

5 Hannah Arendt, *Denktagebuch 1950–1973*, 2nd ed., ed. Ursula Ludz and Ingeborg Nordmann (Munich and Berlin: Piper, 2022), 664; hereinafter cited as D with page number.

of Arendt's thought from the time of her doctoral work on Augustine until the end of her life. A glance at her *Denktagebuch 1950–1973* shows us how complex the problem is. A note first sketched out in November 1953, a note that would become important for *The Human Condition*, aligns "mortality" with the "singularity" Arendt was always suspicious of and "natality" with the "plurality" on which political life in her view was based (D 461). Whereas it may be too much to say that she regarded each human birth as messianic in its promise, she did note the following after hearing a performance of Händel's *Messiah*:

> The hallelujah chorus can be understood only on the basis of the verse, *A child is born unto us*. The profound truth of this part of the Christ legend is that every beginning is hale [*heil*], that God put human beings into the world for the sake of a beginning, for the sake of this haleness. Every new birth is like a guarantee of haleness in the world, like a promise of redemption for those who are no longer a beginning. (D 208)

The pathos of beginning, whether of a republic or of a family, is the pathos of *Gründung*, "grounding" or "founding" (D 342). Arendt accepts Montaigne's judgment—later we will see Derrida affirming the same judgment—that "with every birth a world begins, with every death a world dies" (D 353). Every grounding is grounded in the finitude of both natality and mortality, even if Arendt deliberately chooses to emphasize birth:

> It is as though human beings since Plato were unable to take seriously the fact of our being born, but only the fact of our dying. In our being born the human condition is established as an earthly realm to which everyone comes into relation, a realm in which he or she seeks and finds a place, without a thought to the fact that one day he or she will depart from it. This relation is his or her responsibility, his or her chance, etc. Presupposed in this is the eternal duration of humankind. As soon as one thinks of the very possibility of the death of humankind, as Christianity and all eschatology do, the entire earthly-political realm becomes senseless. (D463)

Looking back to *The Human Condition*, however, Arendt notes in April 1968 that if the condition of *action* is natality or *Gebürtlichkeit*, then the condition of *thinking* is mortality, *Sterblichkeit*; yet if thinking is related to the active life, as surely it must be, then it will "elaborate the conditions on the basis of which I prefer life to death" (D 681). Eighteen months later she elaborates on this thought, which is becoming increasingly paradoxical: "If acting is the answer to natality, such that birth is the condition of possibility of freedom, then thinking is the 'answer' to mortality, namely, the discovery, always after the fact, of what death is good for: it is good for enabling births—the negative condition of freedom" (D 746). Perhaps Heidegger's meditation on Anaximander lies behind this strange elaboration of Arendt's: thoughtful acknowledgment of death may be the way we bestow esteem on others, allowing them—by way of birth—their place and time on Earth. A month earlier she had penned this thought: "The wish for earthly immortality is blasphemous, not because it wants to eliminate death but because it negates birth" (D 744). In the end, Arendt refuses to play off natality against mortality, as if it were possible to choose one instead of the other. Existence is "process," a word that is at least reminiscent of Heidegger's "self-stretching stretch" or Dilthey's "coherence of life," a development in the direction of the world of appearances and the eventual "disappearance" or retreat from that world (D 780–81).

A colleague and friend, Peg Birmingham, has entered much more deeply into this matter than I have. In her work on the "predicament of common responsibility," Birmingham considers both the brighter and the darker sides of human natality.[6] If Arendt focuses on birth as *initium*, the new beginning and new possibilities for freedom in the public space that occur with each new birth and the arrival of each new participant, Julia Kristeva, following Melanie Klein and perhaps Otto Rank as well, analyzes birth as trauma. Birmingham agrees that the *givenness* of birth—what Heidegger calls *facticity* and *thrownness*—involves the dramatic and even traumatic event of abrupt separation from the mother. Whatever will become of the public space, that space will never rid itself of the negative and destructive forces that both cause and perpetuate trauma, whether we call these forces "fear of the alien," recoil from the "foreign," "Hobbesian grief," or "the sadomasochistic desire at the very heart of natality" (PB 113–14). In short, the right to have rights has to confront the predicament of birth as not mere possibility but also hazard, a hazard so deeply enmeshed in existence that one is tempted to call it not only "anthropological" but also "ontological" (PB 12). Birth is the "archaic event," an *embodied* event," and one is tempted

---

6 See Peg Birmingham, *Hannah Arendt and Human Rights: The Predicament of Common Responsibility* (Bloomington and Indianapolis: Indiana University Press, 2006), throughout, but especially chap. 4. I will cite the text as PB with page number.

to hear these expressions in the way Heidegger hears the word *Ereignis*, to wit, as *Ent-eignis*, that is, the event of both appropriation and expropriation.

I am unable here to enter in any detailed way into Birmingham's analysis of the psychoanalytic, anthropological, and ontological aspects of *givenness*, an analysis that is both intricate and overwhelming. Yet it is clear that if we continue to think about birth in terms of "the origins of totalitarianism," we cannot avoid all those competing theories that are desperate to account for "our desire to dominate and inspire fear in those to whom we bring nothing but grief" (PB 115). If an "immemorial violence" lies behind or is effected by our birth, which is not only a sleep and a forgetting but also an abiding *abjection* (Kristeva); if there are indeed forces that merit the monstrous title "the destruction and death drives" (Freud); if there is some deep trait or scar that may be fittingly described as "life envy" (Lacan); then we have to accept something that sounds abstract but in fact is philosophically devastating, namely, "the heterogeneity that exists at the very heart of the self" (PB 119).

Such a conclusion does not dash Arendt's hopes for positive action in the public world, nor does it weaken either Birmingham's commitment to Arendt's thinking or the engagement of the two of them in political action. Even if Arendt writes very little about this darker side of our natality, like Birmingham I suspect that it never stopped haunting her, and I believe I am also right in saying that I heard it come to word in every single conversation we had. Perhaps I should have asked her to write not a reply to Hegel's *Vernunft* but a treatise on that *Pestgeschwür*, the plague sore that never gave her peace; either that or a treatise on the birth of Iago.

✶ ✶ ✶

The story about Heidegger's ability to lose himself—and abandon everyone else—in his work now takes on an even more disturbing quality, however. In the twenties and thirties, Heidegger, along with others such as Paul Tillich and (less avidly) Karl Jaspers, began to urge that there be two separate sets of institutions for higher learning in Germany, the first devoted to training specialists for a particular technical skill, the second dedicated to the education of an elite. The elite would have to be highly intelligent, but the students should not be entirely "in their heads," they should not be mere *Kopfmenschen* (AG 145/94–95). Rather, they should pay attention to "the other side" of life, the life of the human body. But by this, Heidegger means sports, as though athleticism were enough, athleticism and a certain "campfire" romanticism.

Yet not everyone will be invited to sit around the campfire. In a remark, almost an aside, concerning Heidegger's enthusiasm for transforming the German university into something like a Platonic Academy, Grunenberg says something remarkable about the type of student Heidegger desires. The students should of course be bright, and they should be interested in something more than mere professional training. Yet they should not be merely clever. Grunenberg remarks that "this was the objection that Heidegger and others made to Jewish intelligence," namely, that Jews tended to ignore "the other side of life: the body, destiny, labor" (ibid.). By the "body," I again assert, Heidegger clearly means the *athletic* body, or the *worker*'s body, not the erotic body; by "destiny," he means a *national* calling; by "labor," he means precisely what in his rectorate address he calls "labor service" to the nation. All these things, writes Grunenberg, pertain to the "campfire romanticism" that was celebrated at the Todtnauberg *Hütte*.

Even though Heidegger's most brilliant students at both Marburg and Freiburg, with only a handful of exceptions, were Jewish, Heidegger harbors prejudices that come to light in the *Black Notebooks* published thus far. Jewish intelligence is calculative rather than speculative, highly proficient rather than adventurously imaginative, urban rather than pastoral, tribal or clannish rather than national, social democratic—or social revolutionary, even Bolshevik—rather than conservative. "In the air" of the times, if not explicitly in Heidegger's writings, was the illusion that the defeat of the German nation in World War I could be blamed on the calculating and self-serving "international Jewish conspiracy" (AG 149/97).

At this point, we are far beyond matters of student life and university reform, and light-years remote from love of the world. As soon as Grunenberg broaches the theme of antisemitism, however, she complicates the subject of Heidegger's brand of antisemitism in a surprising way—surprising, at least, for me. As if matters were not convoluted and baffling enough, Grunenberg takes considerable trouble to show how "racial theories" were widespread during the Weimar years in Germany—and not merely among the National Socialists. Indeed, she reports, "racial doctrines" were common among Zionist youth groups. She refers to a number of Zionists who invoked the need to "purify" the Jewish nation; there was talk of "selection"; only "the strong" should be sent to the new Zion—in Grunenberg's words, "young athletic men, blond and blue-eyed, as models for the pioneers of Palestine" (AG 151–52/99). One of the most disturbing utterances by Heidegger in the

Black Notebooks of 1931–41 places the blame for racist doctrines on Jews themselves, not merely the Zionists but Jews universally:

> The fact that in the age of machination race is elevated to the position of being the exceptional and expressly instituted "principle" of the historic (or of mere history) is not an arbitrary invention of those who are "doctrinaire." Rather, it is a *consequence* of the might of machination, which has to subject every single region of beings to a planned reckoning. By means of the thought of race, "life" is subsumed under the form of breeding, which itself represents a kind of reckoning. The Jews, *with their emphatic gift for reckoning,* have for the longest time "lived" in accord with the principle of race, which is why they are erecting the most vigorous defense against its unrestricted application. (96:56)[7]

"Unrestricted application"? That is an allusion to the Shoah, if only prospectively, an allusion equivalent to the claims of the most virulent revisionist historians. Arendt would have cried, "Foul!" as one no doubt must. It is impossible to think of her affirming *any* principle of racial selection *anywhere.* And yet I remember her telling me how contemptuous she and other German Jews tended to be toward their Eastern European counterparts, the "shtetl" Jews, a contempt of the urban sophisticate for the country bumpkin. Such contempt was also showered on politics in general, at least in those early Weimar years, if Hans Jonas is right. Jonas notes that the small group of Jewish students who came from Königsberg to study with Heidegger in 1924, and that group included Arendt, shared Jonas's contempt for Weimar politics (AG 93/57). Jonas was deeply involved with Zionist groups, but German politics as such meant little to him and to the entire group. They were "above" that sort of thing: even if Aristotle had declared that the human being is a political animal, the pettiness and corruption of day-to-day politics held no interest for them. For Aristotle had also said that the contemplative life, the life of theory, was the life worth living. The arc of Arendt's intellectual life, which begins and ends with the *vita contemplativa,* passes through the most intense political engagement, but only after Germany has exiled her and so condemned her to action. And even during the political years, her engagement is very much her own,

---

7 I have commented on this remark in Krell, *Ecstasy, Catastrophe,* 149–51. If Grunenberg's analysis of Zionism in Weimar Germany is correct, however, then Heidegger's remark is not mere "nonsense," as I claim there, even if it is "half-baked." In any case, I would affirm once again that Heidegger's outrageous remark concerning "unrestricted application" is murderous (150).

always the result of her critical thinking, so that she is often a stinging nettle to her comrades.

At all events, the Nazi persecution of Jews across the Continent surely caused that youthful contempt for both politics and the peasantry to dissolve. Arendt's engagement in the Jewish and Zionist causes from 1933 onward was forced on her by events especially in Berlin, but that engagement absorbed her almost totally. Her family upbringing had made her sensitive early on to the need to defend oneself against antisemitism (AG 156/102; YB 10–12). It is fair to wonder whether the ethnic or nationalist undertones of at least some forms of Zionism, however, caused her work on behalf of Jews to be consistently critical, to the point where it became offensive to avid Zionists. That said, her contributions to the welfare of exiled Jews over decades of time—no matter where they came from—were ambitious and efficacious (AG 163/106).

Yet let me back up a bit, to the fateful winter of 1932–33. We do not have the troubled letter that Arendt wrote to Heidegger from Berlin, but we do have his response. It is their last exchange until 1950, seventeen fraught years later. Even though I have commented on Heidegger's letter elsewhere,[8] I want to reproduce it here:

Dear Hannah!

The rumors that are upsetting you are slanders that are perfect matches of other experiences I have had to endure over the last few years.

I cannot very well exclude Jews from invitations to my seminars, if only because I have not had *a single* seminar to invite anyone to during the last four semesters. That I supposedly do not greet Jews is such a malicious piece of gossip that in any case I will have to take note of it for the future.

To clarify how I behave toward Jews, simply the following facts:

I am on sabbatical this Winter Semester and so in the summer I announced well in advance that I wanted to be left alone and would not be accepting student papers and the like.

The person who in spite of this comes and urgently needs to complete his doctorate, and who is very well able to do so, is a Jew. The person who comes to see me every month to report on a large work in progress (neither a dissertation nor a habilitation project) is once again a Jew. The person who a few weeks ago sent me a substantial text for my urgent reading is a Jew.

---

8 Krell, *Ecstasy, Catastrophe*, 176–78.

The two who received fellowships from the *Notgemeinschaft*, whom I helped get accepted during the past three semesters, are Jews. The person who, with my help, is getting a stipend to go to Rome is a Jew.[9]

Whoever wants to call that "raging antisemitism" is welcome to do so.

For the rest, I am now precisely as much an anti-Semite in university questions as I was ten years ago in Marburg, where, because of this anti-semitism, I found myself supported even by Jacobsthal and Friendländer.[10]

All this has nothing to do with my personal relationships with Jews (e.g., Husserl, Misch, Cassirer, and others).[11]

And *a fortiori* it cannot touch my relationship to you.

The fact that for a long time now I have been in general quite with-drawn has as one of its causes my work's meeting with hopeless incom-prehension, along with some less-than-pleasant personal experiences having to do with my teaching. To be sure, I have long since given up expecting any sort of gratitude or even mere respect from so-called "pupils."

For the rest, I am contentedly at work, although the work gets more and more difficult, and I greet you heartily. [Signed:] M. (AHB 68–69; AG 165–66/107–108)

The letter's aggressive defensiveness—let the oxymoron stand—and the complete lack of sympathy or empathy for Arendt's situation and her wor-ries are abundantly clear. If Heidegger's response is not cynical, its naïveté and narcissism are disturbing enough. And this is the tone that Heidegger will retain always and everywhere, even after the war, in statements made in his defense: it is always Heidegger who is the victim of misunderstanding,

---

9 Meant is Karl Löwith. Arendt is one of the two *Notgemeinschaft* fellows—he does not need to remind her.

10 The two scholars cited here were members of the "Graeca" reading group at Marburg. Paul Jacobsthal (1880–1957), an archaeologist, was forced to retire in 1935 and emigrated to England, where he received a post in Oxford at Christ Church College. Paul Friedländer (1882–1968), whose three-volume *Plato* was a mainstay for anyone studying the Platonic dialogues during the 1960s and 1970s, was likewise forced to retire in 1935. In 1938, he was arrested and sent to the concentra-tion camp at Sachsenhausen. Miraculously, for reasons I do not know, he managed to be released from the camp in 1939. He then emigrated to the United States, where he taught at Johns Hopkins and UCLA.

11 Edmund Husserl is of course well known, and Heidegger's relation to him and more than dubious treatment of him is often discussed and debated. Georg Misch (1878–1965) was a fellow philosopher at Göttingen University; in 1939, he escaped to Great Britain. Ernst Cassirer (1874–1945), the distinguished neo-Kantian, whom Heidegger met several times during the 1920s, left Germany in 1933, first to England, then to Sweden, and finally to the United States.

slander, and ingratitude. He is the one who suffers slights at the hands of others. I can do no more than repeat my chagrin that in Heidegger's private jottings of the 1930s and early 1940s, to say nothing of his public statements, not a trace of concern for his former students and colleagues appears, nor for the loves that he has lost. It is not so much cowardice, I believe, as a certain callousness or blindness, a self-induced anesthesia, a *Benommenheit* that does not arise from love.

Antonia Grunenberg's judgment is nevertheless generous: Arendt's and Heidegger's twenty-year separation is caused by "an external world that acted inimically towards them, forcing them onto the opposite ends of the political landscape" (AG 167/109). The *external* world alone? Surely not. "And *a fortiori* it cannot touch my relationship to you," Heidegger writes, with a confidence that seems both naive and monstrous. For it was not simply the outside world that touched Arendt with a brutal touch—with what might call a cudgel. The inexplicable thing, the miracle, is that where Heidegger was concerned, Arendt was able to hold on and hold out during those disastrous decades. Perhaps he was right in spite of himself: their love could only have been the work of a *daimon*.

* * *

Earlier, I mentioned the importance of Arendt's love of the German language and German literature. A letter to Jaspers written on New Year's Day 1933 confirms this. She is responding to Jaspers's worries about the fate of Germany, of what he calls "German coming-to-be," *das Deutsche Werden*, which is a preoccupation that separates them: "For me," writes Hannah, "Germany is the mother tongue, philosophy, and poetry" (AG 167/109). This she says on the eve of her departure—her *forced* departure. By this time, even her relation to Jaspers has become attenuated or at least stressed. For, like so many others, Jaspers is slow to see what is coming. Arendt, for her part, is the first in her circle of endangered friends to see that timely flight is the only option. Before she *can* flee in March of that year, however, she and her mother are arrested. After several days, they are released, and they escape by way of Prague to Paris.

In her interview with Günter Gaus, Arendt emphasizes her shock at the almost universal "coordination" of the Germans with the Nazis, the *Gleichschaltung* that was proceeding rapidly during the opening months of 1933. She remarks that the real problem was not what her enemies were doing but what her "friends" were doing—so hasty were they to advance the "movement" or to advance their role within the party at all costs (AG 172/112; YB 108). Heidegger confesses to Jaspers that in 1933, after taking on the rectorship, he was caught up in a "power frenzy," *Machtrausch*. Oddly, Elfride seems to have been the one who coined the term, perhaps the most fitting formulation of the charge in the cases of both Martin and Elfride. The denazification committee in 1945 certainly agreed: "Herr Heidegger was titillated by power. . . . What drew him in was the prospect of exercising strong influence" (AG 174/113). Grunenberg makes an astute observation concerning this power frenzy, observing that Heidegger slipped into a pseudo-Hegelian position, identifying the culmination of Western philosophy, in this case, the history of *beyng*, with the Prussian (now the *völkisch*) state, thus enthusiastically occupying a philosophical position that he had always despised and had regarded as overcome (AG 176/114). In May 1933, that baffling conversation with Jaspers occurs, in which Heidegger insists that there is a "dangerous international confederation of Jews"; he replies to Jaspers' lament concerning Hitler's ignorance and brutality by praising the man's hands (AG 178/116).

What, in the end, is Grunenberg's judgment of Heidegger's involvement in National Socialism and his antisemitism? She cites the protocol of Freiburg University's denazification committee, which confirms Heidegger's commitment to the *Gleichschaltung* and his mixed relation to antisemitism: fundamentally, he is not an antisemite, at least not of the most vulgar sort, but for the most part, he acts expediently (AG 184/120). For the rest, the university senate concludes that his actions as rector were so aggressive that he made enemies in all the faculties. His advice to "the German students" was the advice that he himself followed: "Be hard and genuine in your demands. Remain clear and sure about what you are rejecting" (AG 188/122). The denazification process, with contributions from both university and French-occupation committees, lasted six years for Heidegger, from 1945 to 1951 (AG 191/124). Only in 1951 was the emeritus status granted, along with the right to offer courses once again at the university. Grunenberg's judgments concerning Heidegger are generous, although, in the end, they are the judgments that convince me: "Manifestly, he believed that his fundamental ontology could culminate in a collective education for true Dasein" (AG 202/131). And then, regarding Heidegger's philosophical production as a whole, "Heidegger's turn to National Socialism lay in the realm of the possible, not of the necessary" (ibid.).

On occasion, Arendt's view of Heidegger's involvement seems to be much more severe than Grunenberg's. Heidegger's letters to Jaspers after the war, letters that Jaspers had shown to Arendt, displeased her: she described them as "the same old mix of genuineness and prevarication, or better, cowardice" (RS 416/375). Yet she was not consistently harsh in her judgment of him. Arendt's reported remark that Heidegger "lacked character," his *Charakterlosigkeit*, is often cited in literature critical of Heidegger, but usually it is cited in a way that misses what she wanted to say (RS 351–52/314–15). When Jaspers complains that Heidegger possesses "an impure soul," Arendt replies that *Charakterlosigkeit* would be a better expression— "but in the sense that he literally does not have a character, and certainly not a particularly bad one" (ibid.). Lack of character excludes both a good and a bad character: that could be a sentence on which Kafka might have mused. Arendt does not spell out all the forces in Heidegger's life that may have contributed to this absence of character—they would be too many and too disparate to gather into a confident judgment. Instead, she writes the following immediately after the statement about the absence of character: "Yet for all that, he lives in a depth and with a passion that one cannot easily forget" (ibid.; letter of September 29, 1949).

*   *   *

I will not detail here Arendt's engagements in Paris and later in the United States, engagements equally divided between relief work for Jews in exile and intellectual pursuits. These engagements take up one hundred and fifty pages of Young-Bruehl's *For Love of the World*. Arendt declares that her life in the academy has come to a close, and yet in Paris she meets and befriends Alexandre Kojève, Alexandre Koyré, Jean Wahl, and Walter Benjamin (AG 212/137). Later, in New York City, she befriends Hermann Broch, fascinated by his charm and by his *Tod des Vergil*, which "follows the traces of Heidegger's philosophy of being" (AG 240/175). As rich as those lives in Paris and Manhattan must have been in the 1930s, 1940s, and 1950s, there are real losses. Arendt notes with chagrin that the moment she left Germany, her German began to suffer: before she could become proficient in French, Spanish, or English, time began to eat away at her mother tongue (AG 217/161). By way of corroboration, I remember realizing that in my own life, my German began to deteriorate as soon as my airplane, bound for the US and A, gunned its engines on the Frankfurt tarmac.

Grunenberg points out in detail why Arendt's engagement in the Jewish causes was always a source of conflict for Arendt. She befriended the leading Zionists of her time, but almost invariably quarreled with them. Some of her views they found nothing short of disloyal, even scandalous. Already in the 1940s, long before *Eichmann in Jerusalem*, Arendt was arguing that the Jews themselves had played a role in the "origins of the plague," the Nazi persecution in the face of which "the Jewish world collapsed so helplessly" (AG 235/172). Her friends were confused by her strong support of a "Jewish army" on the one hand, but her opposition to a nation-state in Palestine on the other (AG 242–43/176–77). She enthusiastically supported Judah Magnes's plan for a two-state solution, an Israeli-Palestinian federation. Her opposition to the Zionist project of David Ben Gurion and Golda Meir was relentless and acerbic, as was her allergic reaction to any attempt to mix theology or religion with politics (AG 247/180; see also AG 249–55/181–84 and YB 224–330).

The more I read about these disputes in the 1930s and 1940s, the more I am reminded of Derrida's strong support of a two-state solution: like Daniel Barenboim and others, Derrida stubbornly refused to deliver lectures (in Barenboim's case, to give recitals or conduct an orchestra) in Israel unless arrangements were made for him to do the same in Palestine. Arendt's position is all the more striking—others would say baffling—because of her insistence that human rights cannot be protected outside of the nation-state structure. No doubt her Zionist friends reminded her of this concession constantly.

However, the point that Grunenberg stresses most is Arendt's fervent desire that these strong differences of opinion between her and her friends not destroy the friendship, and her devastation over the many times that the friendship suffered and eventually collapsed (AG 254/184). Arendt's ability to argue and disagree without sacrificing friendship turns out to be one of her principal qualities, and it is a rare one. To Kurt Blumenfeld, whom she loves deeply and with whom she is forever arguing, she writes in desperation, "Oh, children, what fools you are!" She adds, "Friendship is rare enough, and it is scarcely possible to have it except on the razor's edge" (ibid.). In a sense, this is her motto for friendship. Strikingly, it is the phrase that Tiresias uses when he tells the tyrant Creon where his condemnation of Antigone has led him, namely, onto the "razor's edge of chance" (l. 906: ἐπὶ ξυροῦ τύχης). Hölderlin translates Tiresias's counsel in a strange way: "Think, even now, in this delicate moment [l. 1053: *im zarten Augenblike*]."

I suppose this could have been the motto for the Arendt–Heidegger love story and also for Arendt's deepest friendships: "in this delicate moment, on the razor's edge."

Arendt's controversial political views do not end with the war. Her resistance to the "guilt question" and Germany's *collective* guilt," to which she knows Karl Jaspers is contributing significant efforts, is quite striking. She takes the whole discussion in postwar Germany to be nothing more than "Christian pious prattle" and "ethical purification babble," a kind of narcissistic self-preoccupation designed to annihilate responsibility rather than establish it and confront it (AG 262–63/189, quoting Arendt). She seems to have absorbed the lessons of Nietzsche's second treatise in the *Genealogy of Morals*: responsibility is not guilt, *Schuld*, which is a notion derived from business affairs. Responsibility is what has to happen when, whether one wills it or not, one's own society or community commits crimes. There is no quick cleansing either of oneself or of the collective for these crimes.

One cannot help but notice that a quick cleansing is what so many in the United States are seeking today. I am thinking of all the pundits and newscasters who boast about their recent past as loyal Republicans and then loudly bemoan the horror that their party has become. There is little discussion of the fact that for decades now the Republican Party has been massaging its "base," which is as base as any base can get, and has for years profited from the very evils that empower it: racism, xenophobia, and the relentless expansion of the gap between rich and poor, "Impovernment of the booble by the bauble for the bubble" (FW 273). Children in cages? Blacks murdered by the police? The chastened pundits find it in bad taste. But what would it mean to take *responsibility* for these crimes? Perhaps no one, whether on the "right" or the "left," has an inkling of what that would mean for the American polity, if such an expression is still fitting. Arendt, if I am correct, is haunted by that call to responsibility rather than to guilt or shame. Yet how does one rise to the occasion of responding to horror? How does one begin to repair the damage that for particular human beings, the caged, the murdered, is irreparable? Not by jubilating each time a right-wing populist drops a few points in the polls or even loses an election, not by expressing relief and satisfaction when *only* 45 percent of the nation approves of these crimes. Arendt? She would drill us with a look.

On her first trip back to Germany in 1950, she described what Grunenberg calls "a collective mentality of simplemindedness"; the Germans, writes Arendt, "are in love with swooning" (AG 276–77/201–202). Swooning in "collective guilt" but quick to point the finger elsewhere as they faint. Arendt is disturbed by the fact that postwar Germany is as full of denunciations and enemy camps as it was during the Third Reich (AG 281/205). I have already mentioned Glenn Gray's remark to me that after the war, you could not find a solitary soul who had supported Hitler.

Astonishingly, on that first trip back to Germany, Arendt contacted Heidegger. A friend had asked her in late 1949 whether she planned to "enjoy Freiburg" on her upcoming trip to Europe, whereupon Arendt replied, "Darling, in order for me to 'enjoy' Freiburg, I would need to have the courage of a wild animal—a courage that does not lie at my disposal" (RS 415; YB 246). Even though her critique of Heidegger's self-serving prevarications and cowardice was relentless, she found that she could not sever the relation, could not erase what had been friendship and gratitude. In the case of Heidegger, it was something more than friendship, of course. In any case, as Grunenberg puts it, "Friends were home and they could not be replaced. The old love sheltered reminiscences of a destroyed spiritual household" (AG 280–81/204–205). Arendt contacted him, and he responded. To Blücher, she wrote, "At bottom, I'm happy simply about the confirmation that I was right not to have forgotten" (RS 166; YB 247).

After a gap of seventeen years—and what years! as Derrida would exclaim—she saw Heidegger in February 1950. After all those years in which contact was entirely impossible, she wrote Blücher of her evening and morning visits with Heidegger at the Schlossbergblick and at his home as "confirmation of an entire life," meaning, presumably, her own (RS 412). In May 1949, the Freiburg University senate, by a slim majority, had voted to restore Heidegger's right to teach at the university (RS 414/373; AG 286/208). Yet the red tape involved was not cleared away until the fall of 1951, whereupon Heidegger taught one of his best-known courses, *Was heisst Denken?* ("What Is Called Thinking?"). Arendt spent some hours alone with Heidegger as he read to her from the notes for his lecture course. She was gripped by the work—and it was perhaps this enthusiasm of hers that caused Margarethe von Trotta to place these words of the later Heidegger into the mouth of the young philosopher of 1924.

Safranski cites Arendt's letter to Blücher, which tells of her "certainty concerning a fundamentally benign attitude" on Heidegger's part toward her, an overwhelming sense of familiarity or closeness (*Zutraulichkeit*) between the two of them, "the complete absence, as soon as he is with me, of all the things that otherwise would surely thrust their way to the fore, his genuine helplessness and defenselessness" (RS 420/379, quoting Arendt). She goes so far as to assume a protective, almost motherly, role, the role, as Safranski says, of "a guardian angel": "As long as he remains productive, there is no danger; what makes me anxious are the bouts of depression that he suffers again and again. I am trying now to ward these off. Perhaps he will remember when I am no longer here" (ibid.). Heidegger was wont to make light of the breakdown he suffered in the spring of 1946—Safranski offers an account of it in his twentieth chapter—and the literature on him generally treats it as a harmless curiosity. Arendt, even four years later, took it seriously.

By February 1950, Heidegger's exclusion from the university has not yet ended. He is aggrieved and confused. He believes that his inward migration will suffice for the others to excuse him, and he is shocked by the university senate's fury over his apparent self-righteousness. Once again, Heidegger sees himself as the victim, not as one of those who were "responsible." The renewed contact with Arendt, who is struck by the high quality of the upcoming lecture course, is therefore of enormous importance to him. He tries to negotiate a peace between Elfride and Hannah, an impossible project, but he tries nonetheless. Heidegger's attempt to woo both Arendt and Elfride simultaneously, seeking "openness" and "trust," is nothing short of astonishing. Up to that time, Elfride has not known anything concrete about the early relationship. Her anger at the news is a mix of private and political resentments, no doubt with an intense antisemitic flair (AG 307–309/221–23). Arendt, for her part, is both passionate and pragmatic. Her feelings are strong, even ecstatic, and yet her perspicuity keeps her sober. She is torn between these two states. Grunenberg speaks, entirely correctly, I believe, of Arendt's loyalty to Heidegger as "a fidelity so radical that it was scarcely sustainable by life" (AG 310/223).

Regarding Heidegger's other love affairs—for Arendt was not the last, and Heidegger proceeded as though there were but "one son of Sorge for all daughters of Anguish" (FW 189)—Grunenberg makes it clear that Heidegger made a genuine contribution to *La Comédie Humaine*, something no reader of his works would ever have expected. On the more serious side, Grunenberg relates that Heidegger's involvements were always connected with his thinking, since his partners were always also partners in conversation. "They replace conversations with his students, assistants, and colleagues" (AG 311/223). Not to mention conversations with his wife.

The direct confrontation between Elfride and Hannah compels Heidegger to try to explain himself. On Valentine's Day 1950, of all the days in the year, he writes to Elfride:

> It is difficult to speak of the other matter, the other to my love for you, which is inseparable from my thinking. I call it Eros, the oldest of the gods according to Parmenides' word. With that I am not telling you anything that you yourself do not know; nevertheless I cannot find the right dimension that will enable me to explain it appropriately. It easily sounds slick, assuming a form that awakens the impression that something evil, something untoward, is being justified. The wingbeat of that god touches me every time I take an essential step in my thinking and dare to enter into unfamiliar territory. It touches me perhaps more strongly and more uncannily than it does others, especially when something I have long sensed glides into the region of what is sayable, and whenever what is said has to be left in solitude for a long time. To be purely in accord with *that*, and still to preserve what belongs to us; to follow the flight and yet return safely; to achieve both of these equally essential things appropriately;—that is where I readily fail, either by straying into sheer sensuality or by trying to force what cannot be compelled by mere labor. My inherited disposition, along with the kind of upbringing I had, my instability and my cowardice when it comes to trust, and then again my disregard, my own abusing of trust, those are the poles between which I oscillate. In that way I all too easily mistake the proper measure, failing to achieve it with respect to Hera and Eros. (AG 311–12/224, quoting Heidegger.)

Heidegger's identification of Elfride with the queen of the gods, the consort of Zeus, was as unlikely to have assuaged her as it did Hera. Nor would the appeal to the authority of Father Parmenides have convinced her of the legitimacy of Heidegger's predicament. Once again, Antonia Grunenberg's judgment is anodyne: Heidegger's "states of excitement," his *Erregungszustände*, both intellectual and erotic, are, as he claims in his letter to Elfride, inextricable. "Out of such excitability," writes Grunenberg, "both emerged: ecstatic thinking and openness toward erotic experiences" (AG 201/131).

As much as I admire Grunenberg's forbearance, however, and as astonished as I am by Heidegger's effort to explain himself, I have to say that his apologia, which he repeats to Elfride four years later (AG 344/249), is hardly original. He seems to have borrowed it from John Steinbeck's *Grapes of Wrath*, although it is almost certain that he never read that novel—Melville, yes, Steinbeck, no. But in the fourth chapter of that very

American work, Tom Joad meets a retired or perhaps defrocked preacher who confesses to him:

> "I use ta get the people jumpin' an' talkin' in tongues and glory-shoutin' till they just fell down an' passed out. An' some I'd baptize to bring 'em to. An' then you know what I'd do? I'd take one of them girls out in the grass, an' I'd lay with her. Done it ever' time. Then I'd feel bad, an' I'd pray an' pray, but it didn't do no good. Come the next time, them an' me was full of the sperit, I'd do it again. I figgered there just wan't no hope for me, an' I was a damned ol' hypocrite. But I didn't mean to be. . . . An' I got to thinkin' how in hell, s'cuse me, how can the devil get in when a girl is so full of the Holy Sperit that it's spoutin' out of her nose an' ears. You'd think that'd be one time when the devil didn't stand a snowball's chance in hell. But there it was."

The claim of a perfect parallel between Hegel's "sperit" and Heidegger's "being" is obviously faulty: as Hegel demonstrated in so many places, spirit is entirely promiscuous and will go with anyone; *der Geist* will be intimate, right up close to anyone, *ganz bei sich*. Try the same with *being* or even *beyng*, and it simply withdraws and hides. Even so, as Derrida was expert at showing, Heidegger often enough betrays *Sein* or *Seyn* for *Geist*, slipping back into that quasi-Hegelian position that he ought to have eschewed.

It is no doubt unfair and disingenuous of me to make a comedy (with help from Steinbeck) out of other people's misery, even if that is precisely what comedy is. There are grounds for admiring the effort that Heidegger makes to confront the two poles of his life, while the rest of us stumble on in silence and embarrassment. Yet that these sidesteps of Heidegger's should be attributed to the uncharted regions and not yet articulated spaces of his "thinking," that their purpose is to grant the thinker "words for being," whereby sensuality is merely the mire into which he occasionally slips—all of that seems as deceptive and self-deceiving as the political defense. That it all arises from his "disposition" and "upbringing" is undoubtedly true. But the upbringing is more St. Paul than Parmenides. And in any case, Heidegger ought to have invoked Empedocles, the hero of both Hölderlin and Nietzsche, in addition to Parmenides. If not Aristophanes.

There are at least two places in Heidegger's corpus where Eros is invoked in a thought-provoking way. In his 1936–38 *Contributions to Philosophy: On Ereignis*, he interprets Plato's notion of "the good," τὸ ἀγαθόν, in terms of the German words *gatten* and *Gattung*, that is, to clusters of beings that are "*gathered* together," perhaps as *genres*, but perhaps also as man and wife, *Gatte, Gattin*. Such "gatherings," he says, are productive of human well-being or εὐδαιμονία (65:210–11). Readers may recall Glenn Gray's discussion with Jean Beaufret and Heidegger, reported back in chapter 2, on the origins of the verb *gattern*. The Greek word εὐδαιμονία, referring to the *daimonion* that is both divine and anxiety-producing, leads him in the *Beiträge* to invoke ἔρως—which, however, he leaves without comment or further development. At about the same time, in his Nietzsche lectures, he defines Plato's understanding of beauty (in *Phaedrus*) as the most radiant and most erotic of beings. These two passages have always led me to hope that somewhere in Heidegger's vast oeuvre, one might find a history of *eros* or of *life* that would advance beyond a history of *beyng*. As far as I can see, Heidegger, who was allergic to life-philosophy, if not to life itself, never rose to that challenge.[12]

Karl Jaspers would have agreed. One of his last "Notes on Heidegger" begins: "He does not touch on the big questions: sexuality, friendship, marriage—life praxis—profession—the state, politics—education, and so on" (AG 396/283, quoting Jaspers). If he ever did so, it is in that astonishing Valentine's Day letter to Elfride, which tries in vain to explain to Hera the formidable power of Aphrodite.

Yet this is not the end of the Arendt–Heidegger love story. There is one more complication, one further fold.

*   *   *

From 1953 to 1967, Arendt avoids Freiburg, even though visits to Jaspers in nearby Basel are frequent (AG 316/227). There seem to be several reasons for this avoidance. One may be Heidegger's inability to recognize Arendt as an equal in philosophy. In 1961, when she is on tour in Germany on behalf of her *Vita activa*, Arendt notices that Heidegger is unable to accept her as an author, thinker, and public intellectual (RS 427/385). She tells Jaspers that with Heidegger she has always had to pretend that she cannot count to three, unless it is a matter of interpreting Heidegger's texts (YB 307). Furthermore, even though both she and Blücher recognize the greatness of Heidegger's thought, both are discouraged and at times disgusted by his self-serving statements, and both are dismayed by his deafening silence concerning the extermination of the Jews, a silence that endures

---

12 See Krell, *Daimon Life: Heidegger and Life-Philosophy*, 199–200.

throughout the 1950s and 1960s. Arendt, following Jaspers in this respect, faults Heidegger for never advancing beyond feelings of "personal shame" to what Arendt calls "political responsibility." The Shoah is something so unheard of, so unprecedented that it leaves both shame culture and guilt culture in tatters. She is of course aware of Heidegger's very specific senses of "guilt" and "conscience" as developed in *Being and Time*. Yet these analyses, too, are unequal to the catastrophe (AG 393/280). They seem to be vague reflections of what Heidegger criticized as a "factical ideal," an inherited ideal that should not be granted ontological significance (SZ 310). As for the "German nation," she shares Blücher's wish that Heidegger could have followed Nietzsche's example, becoming less "German" and more "the good European" (AG 316/227).

Arendt also complains about the "mannerisms" that slip so readily into Heidegger's late style. In 1957, for instance, after reading *Identity and Difference*, she objects to Heidegger's endless self-interpretation and self-quotation, as though his were "a text from the Bible" (AG 323/231, quoting Arendt). The most discouraging reason for the distance from Heidegger, however, is, to repeat, that even after their reconnecting in 1950, Heidegger is never able to accept Arendt as an independent thinker and published author. Much of what she writes—for example, her reference to "the temporary alliance between the mob and the elite" in Germany during the 1930s—can only nettle him. Furthermore, it is always difficult for him, as it is for many professors, to see a former student, to say nothing of a lover, going their own way, going so bravely and with such public acclaim. Arendt finds Heidegger to be in so many ways caught in his own snares, traps that he has set for others but has stumbled into himself. On more than one occasion, Arendt refers to Heidegger as being trapped in his own silence, cornered by his own inability to confront responsibility—not guilt, but responsibility, understood quite literally as the ability to respond. In July 1953, she enters a remarkable parable into her *Denktagebuch*, a parable very much after the manner of Kafka's "The Burrow." It merits reprinting in full:

> Heidegger says, quite proudly: "People say that Heidegger is a fox." Here is the true story of Heidegger the fox.
>
> Once upon a time there was a fox that was so lacking in slyness that he not only stumbled into traps constantly but also failed to perceive the difference between a trap and a nontrap. This fox had another weakness: something about his fur was not in order, so he was entirely missing the

natural protection against all the slings and arrows that a fox comes to encounter in his life.

After this fox had strayed from one trap to another during his youth, traps set by others, so that he did not have a single patch of healthy fur left, as it were, he determined to withdraw altogether from the foxy world and to construct his own fox den. In his hair-raising ignorance concerning traps and nontraps, and yet in his incredible experiences with traps, he came up with an idea that was unheard of and utterly new among foxes: he built himself a trap in the form of a den, entered it, pretended that it was a normal den (not out of slyness, but because he had always taken the traps set by others to be their dens); but then he decided, as though sly in his own way, to shape his own trap, into which he alone could fit himself, as a trap for others. Once again this testified to his complete ignorance of the essence of a trap: no one could really enter into his trap, since he himself was sitting in it. This irritated him. After all, everybody knows that foxes, despite their slyness, occasionally walk into traps. Why should not a fox trap, set after all by the most experienced of foxes, not be able to compete with traps set by human beings and hunters? Obviously, because the trap could not be clearly recognized as such. Thus our fox brainstormed and determined that his trap would be the most elaborately decorated trap. He attached signs to it everywhere that announced quite clearly, "Come one, come all, here is a trap, the loveliest in the world!" From that point on it was perfectly clear that no fox would ever unintentionally stumble into the trap. Nevertheless, many came. For this trap served as our fox's den. If one wanted to enter the den in which he was at home, one had to walk into his trap. To be sure, everyone who wanted to could leave the trap, except for him. For the trap was tailor-made for him, quite literally. But the trap-dwelling fox said quite proudly, "So many walk into my trap, I have become the best of all foxes." And there was something true about what he said: no one knows the essence of a trap better than one who sits in a trap all his life.[13]

I will not riddle on the riddle of the trap, except to say that Arendt herself walked into and out of the trap again and again, the trap that Heidegger

13 AH 382–83; AG 348–49/252. "Heidegger the Fox" is formulated in July 1953 (D 403–404). Yet the preliminary form of the fable, first written after two visits with Heidegger, the first in February and March 1950 and the second in May 1952, appears in a notebook for November 1952, at 266 of the *Denktagebuch*, in the following succinct, droll, and riddlesome form: "Whatever way you look at it, it remains beyond question that in Freiburg I walked into (and did *not* stumble into) a trap. But it is also beyond question that Martin, whether he knows it or not, sits in the trap, is at home in it, has built his house around the trap; so that you can visit him only if you visit him in the trap, walk into the trap. And so I went to visit him in the trap. The result is that he is now sitting alone again in his trap."

himself could never quit. If his silence, his failure to respond to what had happened to him and to others, not only in 1933–34 but through the end of the war, was a trap, then he occupied it in such a way that there was no room for her or anyone else. Safranski would say that *being* was that trap, especially when it camouflaged itself as a *history of beyng* or draped itself with the net of *Ereignis*. Yet if Heidegger's *thinking* was a trap, Arendt was compelled to frequent it—always wary, always choosing her own way in and out, entering surreptitiously by hidden entrances, then exiting again. For she understood that Heidegger was trapped in a philosophical language that he had to use in order to think something that could no longer be thought, since the thread had been broken, the connection to the tradition undone. She never doubted the profundity of Heidegger's problematic, even if much about it seemed to be self-defeating (AG 320–21/229).

But I am reluctant to riddle any further. I can still hear Derrida saying, when one position or assertion seemed as dangerous as another, "Traps on all sides." His favorite example was Robinson Crusoe, who, fearful of being swallowed up by cannibals or by the earth itself, buries himself in a fortress that resembles nothing more than a trap. And the truth is that even if Arendt clearly sees how Heidegger is his own captive, she does not scorn him. Far from it. To those friends and colleagues who simply want to drop "metaphysics" and embrace "common sense," Arendt counters that Heidegger is the thinker who more than any other understands that the lifeline that binds us to our philosophical tradition has frayed and cannot be repaired: Heidegger, she says, "unquestionably gets on our nerves, but that does not make him any less a philosopher" (AG 320/229). Those are Arendt's words, but I can hear Derrida too saying them. For if philosophers turn their fortresses into traps that will trap themselves, that is because they are babes in the woods. "Not a sound, falling. Lispn! No wind no word. Only a leaf, just a leaf and then leaves. The woods are fond always. As were we their babes in. And robins in crews so" (FW 619).

One last word, perhaps, on Heidegger's being caught in snares of his own making. It is something that both Hannah Arendt and Joan Stambaugh mentioned to me on several occasions, namely, the fact that Heidegger for the most part remained trapped by both the adulation and the condemnation of the contending circles around him. As for the adulation, only his brother Fritz could break through it; only he could tease his brother and make him laugh. The pious adulation of so many of Heidegger's followers

is notorious. Perhaps as a young man I too succumbed to it, even though a
bath of caustic in Nietzsche's philosophy had burned away most of my piety
by that time. There can be no doubt that Heidegger's self-stylizations—the
entire mythology of the solitary thinker contemplating *beyng* while hiding
away in the forest—contributed mightily to that adulation. Nor is it deni-
able that for Heidegger such adulation seemed to be the only possible buffer
against the contumely that his politics had earned him.

✳　✳　✳

The German edition of Arendt's *The Human Condition*, which bears the far
more Arendtian title *Vita activa*, immediately celebrated in the German
intellectual world after its publication in 1960, may have particularly nettled
Heidegger, if only because he could see so much of himself in it. Arendt
saw the same—she wanted to dedicate the book to him, as she was later to
dedicate the first volume of *The Life of the Mind*, "Thinking." Her letter to
Heidegger on October 28, 1960, however, is quite reticent:

> Dear Martin,
>
> I have instructed the publisher to send you a book by me. Concerning it, I
> want to mention something to you.
>
> You will see that the book bears no dedication. If things had been
> well with us—I mean the things *between* us, not with you or with me
> as such—I would have asked you whether I might dedicate it to you. It
> originates directly from the first Freiburg years and in every respect it
> owes just about everything to you. The way things are, the dedication
> seemed impossible to me; but in some way I wanted at least to tell you
> the way things stand without cloaking them. All good things, etc. (AHB
> 149; AG 341/247)

Far more moving, far more telling is a loose sheet found among Arendt's
papers that sketches such a dedication, presumably one she never sent
(AHB 319; AG 343/248):

WITH REGARD TO VITA ACTIVA:

The dedication of this book is left open.
How could I dedicate it to you,
My confidant,
To whom I have remained faithful
And not remained faithful,
And both in love.

Perhaps in the entire history of dedications, in the vast archive of inscribed tomes, there is none so painful and so tender as this one.

One of the most famous theses of *The Human Condition*, discussed earlier, is that the birth of each human being holds the promise of new initiatives. Heidegger had been musing over decades about the vague and uncertain "other beginning" of philosophy; Arendt countered that each birth promises as much. Antonia Grunenberg, too, sets Arendt's thought of *birth* as an increment of world possibilities in opposition to Heidegger's emphasis on being-toward-the-end that is death (AG 356/257). To repeat what I have said earlier, however, Heidegger does take up the "other end" of Dasein, namely, its birth. He, too, stresses that birth is not simply behind us, lost in time, but accompanies us during the entire "stretch" of our life. The difference between Heidegger and Arendt is that she emphasizes, in Grunenberg's words, "the enabling of a plural world" (ibid.). Heidegger, too, had stressed that Dasein is *Mitsein*, "being-with," and that existence is shared with others even in solitude. The difference is that Heidegger tended to depict the more disastrous characteristics of the plural world. I recall the transcriptions of his lectures from 1921–22, which stress competition and rivalry, the need for distance, the playing of roles and donning of masks, the tendency to lock oneself away and bolt the door to *fundamental* possibilities. Ironically, Arendt knew at least as much about these tendencies as Heidegger did; her friendships and relationships were always conflicted and fraught. It is not as though she found the plural world either easygoing or easy going. Yet she knew that locking oneself away and bolting the door so that one can think without disturbance will not banish the threats.

Grunenberg argues, correctly, I think, that the key to *The Human Condition* is the reference to Augustine that Arendt makes at the end of *The Origins of Totalitarianism* (AG 352/254): "The human being was made so that there might be a beginning." *Initium ut esset, creatus homo.* Arendt's doctoral thesis on Augustine's concept of *amor* continued to play a role throughout her life. Ironically, that thesis continued to haunt Heidegger as well. Back in chapter 3, I mentioned those striking notes that Heidegger makes in 1937 on Nietzsche's "basic metaphysical position" as *amor fati*, "love of fate," or "love of necessity." Clearly, *amor fati* is not *amor mundi*, and yet *amor* is common to both. Among those notes by Heidegger on Nietzsche are some that refer to Augustine: "*Amor—vgl. Augustin: amo = volo ut sis*" ("Love—compare Augustine: I love = I will that you be," 87:168). Heidegger asks what this means and whom it involves. What sort of necessity or fate is it to love and be loved? Does *fatum* refer to God, to what Nietzsche calls "the vicious circle of God"? Does it refer to "the human being," *der Mensch*? Who or what is the *amatum*? These questions are at least related to Heidegger's truncated effort to think "the good" as "gathering," ἀγαθόν, human "well-being," εὐδαιμονία, and Eros together. Arendt was always prepared to be more specific than Heidegger with both question and answer.

And yet. So much has been written about Heidegger's lack of a positive sense of "community" and "sociality," and so many have confidently pointed to Arendt as an obvious alternative or "complement" to Heidegger that I feel I have to unsettle everyone's certainty on this point. I recall an incident that occurred recently in my life. I was engaged in a weekly seminar several years ago with a number of my colleagues and my daughter Salomé. She, an actor living in Manhattan, had requested a seminar on *Being and Time*, about which she had heard so much but which she had not yet read, and so Walter and Harold Brogan, Kevin Miles, and I spent a year guiding her through Heidegger's masterwork—four professors for one student, as she quipped. As we approached the sections on *das Man*, the "they," the sections that social-minded and communitarian readers abhor, we encouraged Salomé not to shy away from criticism. As a theater actor, she knew better than most how vital the entire *company* is for every successful performance. At the outset of our next session, we asked her whether she felt that Heidegger's analysis of human interaction was too harsh, too skeptical or even cynical, too negative about the possibilities for community. A long pause ensued, and then she said, "Welcome to my world."

That is precisely, I believe, what Arendt would have said, at least many times during her life. She would merely have added that when you have to run for your life, you are forced to strive for a better community and, above all, to seek a political space that does not revert to murder. And the truth is that Arendt's critique of the "they" is even more relentless than Heidegger's. Whereas, according to *Being and Time*, the "call of conscience" can retrieve a forlorn Dasein from its lostness in the public world, Arendt notes the following in her *Denktagebuch*: "Heidegger made a mistake in *Being and Time*: the voice of conscience is precisely 'the they,' indeed, at the very peak of its hegemony" (D 118). And whereas Heidegger holds out the hope that an authentic or appropriate "self" can be salvaged for Dasein despite all the allures of publicity, Arendt seems to deny that such a pristine "self" is retrievable:

> The elementary error of Heidegger's "they"-analysis, which as such is extraordinarily accurate, is that it sees the "they" in the oppositional relation "they—self." The opposite of the "they," however, which is the "nobody" of *Being and Time* (253), is *Everyman* (and not the self), the Everyman that we too always are insofar as we are bound to the ἀναγκαῖα [the necessities of the human condition]. It is never the self that stands in opposition to the they, but Everyman. (D 218)

And the "self" proper, the "authentic" self? Where would that be? Perhaps it is to be found only in the struggle to resist the blandishments of the "they" without succumbing to the false consciousness and the deluded morality of Everyman.

As for that public space and Arendt's more positive hopes for it, Grunenberg is surely right when she emphasizes that Arendt advances beyond the traditional thought of *toleration,* by which one merely puts up with people or thoughts and practices that are alien to one's own, to what Oliver Wendell Holmes recognized as *shared* thinking, thinking itself as *a social activity* (AG 360–62/259–60). Not that the marks of finitude would vanish from such shared thought: the "givenness" of natality does not evaporate when groups join forces. But perhaps thinking needs something more than the private sphere. Even though Arendt is equally committed to retaining respect for the private sphere—a respect that has vanished from American life precisely at the moment when fascism is on the rise—the act of *thinking* and the virtue of *thoughtfulness* are for her crucial aspects of an *active, public* life. That idea would have startled Heidegger, I believe, and I have to wonder whether the two of them talked about it, if not in the 1950s, then after 1967, when again they made contact. In my own experience, something very much like a *shared* thinking, thinking as a social activity, characterized the discussions of the informal "Heidegger Collective" that Glenn joked about but wholeheartedly affirmed and practiced.

* * *

The final and lasting positive shift in Arendt's relation to Heidegger occurs during the summer of 1967 and endures until her death in December 1975 (AG 395/282). Yet before reporting on this final period, the only period with which I am personally familiar, I need to expand my horizons once again. A reader of an earlier form of this book suggested that I drop the word "without" from my chapter title, since I had so little to say about other aspects of Arendt's life, especially her life of love. Arendt never spoke to me about Günther Stern (who later wrote under the name Günther Anders), and I can say nothing about her first marriage, from 1929 to 1937. I know only that their love had run its course by 1933, long before their divorce, that Stern nevertheless later helped Arendt, her new husband, and her mother to receive American emergency visas, and that he survived to enjoy a long career as a writer and political activist in Europe. But Hannah often spoke to me of Blücher, if only in a strange way, a way that aroused my curiosity. His name usually came up in discussions and arguments about politics and Marxian political theory, and it always came up in that form: "Blücher," she would call him, never "Heinrich," as though he were some sort of institution. Blücher thinks this, Blücher says that. . . . It was evident that she was more than fond of the institution, but still, he seemed to be an institution rather than a partner. For better insight into this institution—in effect, into her many years of marriage to Heinrich Blücher—I turn to Elisabeth Young-Bruehl's *For Love of the World.*

In the preface to the second edition of her biography, published in 2004, Young-Bruehl introduces Blücher as Arendt's "Berlin-born, working class, self-educated, intellectually charismatic husband" (YB xi). The correspondence between the two, over thirty-five years, she describes as "a model of loving conversation sustained over a lifetime of intimacy, emigration, acculturation, struggle for success, illness, loss, and wonder at the new world" (ibid.). Late in her book, reporting Blücher's death in 1970, Young-Bruehl makes an observation that rings true to me, one that accords with my sense of the institution: "One characteristic of Blücher's dominated all the others in the memories of those who knew him as companions or students, in his youth or his old age: his argumentativeness, his passion for debate, his willingness to follow an idea to the edge of its reasonableness and even beyond" (YB 431). Blücher, not Jewish, but early on a Spartacist and later a Trotskyite, was as *pariah* as Arendt was to the National Socialists, and this no doubt cemented their partnership early on. The greatest obstacle to that partnership was Arendt's mother, who by force of circumstance had to live with the couple, or quite close by, both in Paris and in New York, and who felt that her son-in-law did not contribute sufficiently to the household. It was only after Martha Arendt moved to England, where she soon died, that Blücher came into his own—it was as though he had been released from a burden.

Blücher and Arendt had met at a public lecture in Paris in 1936, when he was thirty-seven. She and Günther Anders had not been together for some three years by that time. Young-Bruehl offers a striking portrait of Blücher, raised by his mother under the most trying circumstances:

> Blücher's stories are not easy to reconstruct: he was hesitant to tell them, particularly after arriving in America without admitting on his immigration documents that he had been a Communist, and he was given to exaggerating and embroidering what he did tell. In Heinrich Blücher, the combination of cautiousness and hyperbole was always an astonishment. Those members of the Arendt-Blücher tribe who had known him since his youth understood his storytelling for what it was—a way of finding meaning in a chaotic world. His devotees were unskeptical, and his detractors charged him with mythomania. In truth, had he had a gift for writing equal to his gift for talking, he would have made a fine novelist. (YB 125)

Blücher had no interest in schooling, but he read voraciously, especially in political theory (Marx and Engels) and in the history of art, both lifelong passions. He became a close friend of the poet and composer Robert Gilbert, to whom Hannah also became close and whose lines she often recited. Blücher was a capable orator, but one with no proper political stage, especially as an émigré in Paris and New York. Young-Bruehl describes him as "a man on an unwanted leave of absence" (YB 136). While Hannah became increasingly absorbed in her work for various Jewish émigré organizations in Paris, Blücher appeared to be adrift. The late 1930s grew increasingly dark for the couple, as it did for all outsiders; after the *Kristallnacht* terrors, Arendt's mother joined the couple in Paris, meeting Blücher for the first time. When war was declared, the French government ordered all male émigrés to be interned in refugee camps. Blücher spent two months in the camp at Villemalard in the central Loire Valley. Arendt was able to write him and even to visit him on several occasions. In January 1940, the couple, having received their respective divorce papers, were able to marry. That May, they were ordered to go to separate internment camps, Hannah in Gurs, in the Pyrenees region of France. By June, with the German occupation of Paris and the establishment of the Vichy regime, Hannah's "internment" camp had become a concentration camp. Thanks to the chaos in the nonoccupied portions of France, however, Blücher and Arendt were able to rejoin one another in Montauban, north of Toulouse. Her mother joined them from Paris, and together, once again with the help of Günther Stern in America, they "began their quest for visas to America" (YB 158). In January 1941, they received exit visas from the Vichy government, made their way by train to Portugal, and thence by ship to New York.

Many of their friends were less fortunate, among them Walter Benjamin. A particularly dramatic part of the Blücher–Arendt escape involves their last encounter with Benjamin in Marseilles. He gave them a collection of his manuscripts, asking them to deliver these to friends at the Institute for Social Research in New York. Among them was the text of his "Theses on the Philosophy of History," one of the most remarkable and most mysterious of his writings. "While they waited for their ship in Lisbon, the Blüchers read Benjamin's 'Theses' aloud to each other and to the refugees who gathered around them. They discussed and debated the meaning of his moment-to-moment messianic hope" (YB 162).

Whereas Arendt was able to find work with various Jewish agencies involved with resettlement, Blücher was even more adrift in Manhattan than he had been in Paris. He found American English difficult to learn, and schooling had never been his strength, even though, like Hannah, he loved American street talk. It was difficult for him to give up the dream of a quick return to Europe. It was also difficult not to feel the pressure emanating from his mother-in-law, and even Hannah had to tease him a bit about his not-very-energetic efforts to learn the American language. Young-Bruehl cites a letter from Hannah to him from Massachusetts, where she is learning the language and also discovering how socially constrained and conservative Americans are: *"Und, pardon Monsieur, lernst Du noch ein bisschen Englisch?"* (YB 165). After a year of complete disorientation, Blücher managed to get some odd jobs, until he finally managed to land a number of part-time teaching positions; by 1943, he was settled enough to help Arendt with the first outlines of the book that became *The Origins of Totalitarianism* (YB 184). Meanwhile, through her new editorial post at Schocken Books, Arendt was developing friendships with Randall Jarrell, W. H. Auden, Werner Broch, and Mary McCarthy.

It can hardly be an accident that Blücher's transformation began soon after the death of his mother-in-law. The transformation culminated in his teaching philosophy, and with great success, first at the New School (yet again with the help of Günther Stern) and then, from 1952 to 1968, devising and teaching the "Common Course" at Bard College. Kant and Nietzsche remained Blücher's two "titans" (YB 237). One recalls that during his two-month internment at Villemalard, Blücher had read Kant's *Critique of Pure Reason* (YB 151).

If I end this account of Blücher's life long before his death in 1970, it is only to confirm that Arendt *without* Heidegger is also very much Arendt *with* Blücher. Even though they were either on the run or were too poor to have children, they nevertheless found a belated security within their own household. Blücher was the mainstay of Arendt's life not only during the seventeen years in which she did not see Heidegger but also during those years when she did see him again. And she was every bit as much Blücher's mainstay, whatever the ups and downs. Young-Bruehl quotes Hannah as saying, "It is so seldom that people are able to help each other, mutually; but in our case I think it really is true that both of us would, without the other, scarcely have survived" (YB 250). If love of the world was Hannah's prime commitment, Blücher's was "erotics," that is, the arts of friendship, love, and "politics" (YB 433). As I contemplated the Arendt-Blücher partnership, I could not help but think of one of Derrida's most wonderful books, written ten years before his death, *The Politics of Friendship*.

* * *

Arendt and Blücher together visited Heidegger in the summer of 1969, not long after Jaspers's death (AG 399/284; YB 422). Heidegger and Blücher engaged in a long discussion about Heidegger's *Nietzsche*, which both Blücher and Arendt had read and greatly admired since its appearance in 1961. (For *that* conversation, among many others, I wish I had been a proverbial fly on the wall.[14]) Nietzsche had always been in Blücher's view "the good European" that Heidegger failed to become (YB 301–302). Heidegger turned eighty that September, and Arendt carefully prepared a balanced—that is, both critical and adulatory—article, "Martin Heidegger at Eighty." In April 1970 Heidegger suffered a mild stroke, but he recuperated quickly.[15] She visited him again in July and August. On the last day of October, Blücher died of a heart attack. Jaspers had passed the year before. Now that she had lost

---

14 See Arendt's *Denktagebuch* for notebook 26, from September 1969, which offers a detailed reading of Heidegger's *Nietzsche*, especially volume I, on will to power as art and knowledge and the eternal recurrence of the same.

15 Safranski says that the stroke occurred in 1968. There was only one such mild cerebral event, however, and it took place on April 10, 1970 (see D 774, 1146). One of its most serious consequences for Heidegger was that his visits to Todtnauberg, because of the strenuous climb to the *Hütte*, were curtailed. My own visits to the *Hütte* were never in his company, but always in the company of friends who wanted to see where Heidegger had written so many of his books and essays.

two cornerstones of her life in these two years—she describes it as a process of defoliation or deforestation (YB 440)—she began to be preoccupied with Heidegger's health (AG 402/286). She asked Heidegger whether she might dedicate *The Life of the Mind* to him. He gratefully accepted (AG 403/287).

With Grunenberg's discussion of Arendt's visit to Freiburg in summer 1975, I find myself modestly and quite tardily entering the story—unnamed, as I entirely deserve to be, I who am simply carrying a woman's suitcase along a train station platform (AG 404/287). Arendt has been visiting the Jaspers Archive for several weeks. Before his death, Jaspers asked her to take charge of his papers—including her letters to him. I have to ask myself about that suitcase: did it contain Jaspers's letters rather than Heidegger's? Did it contain *both*? I remember its weight, but I never saw the contents, not until the letters were published in book form. My memory tells me—at least on certain days of the week—that her letters from *both* Jaspers *and* Heidegger were in that suitcase.

Grunenberg mentions a three-day visit to Heidegger in mid-August, a visit that is "traumatic" for her because she finds Heidegger so weakened. He seems tired and distant, as she reports to Glenn Gray. The word "traumatic" seems too strong to me, although she may have mentioned to me her impression that his health was failing. There is no doubt that Arendt, having lost Jaspers and Blücher, was worried about losing yet another mainstay of her life. On October 30, 1975, Glenn wrote me to say, "Hannah told me on the phone last evening that you had written her of Heidegger's good health. I am very glad for she is distressed about his state of health. I shall see her in early December on a bypass from Washington where I shall be judging NEH applications." That visit never took place, or rather, it was one-sided. In his letter of December 13, written from Colorado Springs after his return from Arendt's funeral, Glenn wrote:

> Somewhere on the trip the lines of a favorite poem comforted me, because I had taught it to Hannah, who liked it as much as I. It describes exactly my feelings.

> They told me, Heraclitus, they told me you were dead.
> They brought me bitter news to hear and bitter tears to shed.
> I wept, as I remembered how often you and I
> Had tired the sun with talking and sent him down the sky.
> And now that thou art lying, my dear old Carian guest,
> A handful of grey ashes, long, long ago at rest,
> Still are thy pleasant voices, thy Nightingales, awake,
> For death, he taketh all away, but them he cannot take.
> —Callimachus, 260 BC

Hannah's and my friendship was pure, an illustration of Aristotle's third and highest kind where the friend is "another self." So I shall feel lonelier from now on, though grateful for the favor of knowing her so long and intimately. She and I had an intellectual (better, *geistige*) affinity that she once spoke of before an audience, an affinity that was apparently rare for her as it was unique for me. Enough.

Glenn's death on October 29, 1977, affected me in a similar way, if I dare to make comparisons with the incomparable, what a later chapter will call the "each time unique." Before that, Arendt's death, along with Heidegger's death six months after hers, had an effect on me that was much stronger than our brief contact had made likely. Six months after Glenn died, my father died, and that completed the cycle of drastic abandonments—at least for the moment. I recall my mother's saying, when she had reached the age that I now have reached, "My entire social life consists of funerals." Since the 1970s, I have come to appreciate Derrida's insistence—joining Glenn Gray's insistence—that mourning the deaths of others is more powerful than anxiety in the face of one's own death. Indeed, as Derrida also said, one may find oneself in the uncanny position of mourning one's own death—not being anxious about it, but mourning it—and weeping the tears that are in the eyes of one's children.

Near the end of her wonderful book, Antonia Grunenberg reproduces Rhoda Nathan's beautiful photograph of Hannah Arendt, apparently one of a series taken "shortly before her death" (AG 405/158). The unruly shock of hair, neat across the brow but flaring out on the right side, obstreperous as always, the eyebrows with their melancholy, quizzical, inquisitive slant, the mouth refusing to smile, bemused perhaps by all the fuss the photographer is making; the lips firmly set, perhaps against the tic that often accompanies her speech, visible in the interview with Günter Gaus, the tic of lips in desperate search of a cigarette; the dark eyes commanding respect with their look but showing the tenderness that always accompanied the brilliance. She is sitting straight, perfect posture, her head turned to the left, her look contacting the camera lens directly, candidly, almost confidently. Then the reader looks back to the photograph of the eighteen-year-old (AG 84/150): the shy look gazing askance, perhaps toward the Shadow, the dark eyes not engaging the camera lens, the beautiful mouth smiling vaguely, dreamily, the body bending forward, the head turning to the right in three-quarters profile. The same tenderness, the same brilliance, albeit well on the hither side of all or most of the experiences of her adult life, the same Hannah Arendt.

* * *

The chapter has to end here; it has already done so. And yet I have to append one last note on Arendt's role in Heidegger translation, which is where my own story begins and now must close. I recently discovered something quite surprising in the third, expanded edition of the Arendt–Heidegger correspondence (AHB 140–47, 429–31), to wit, a recently recovered letter (no. 83a) from Arendt to Heidegger that shows us how far back Arendt was involved in Heidegger translation issues. On April 6, 1954, she informed Heidegger that the translation of *Sein und Zeit* by Edward Schouten Robinson had arrived on her desk, and that she had gone over it with some care. Robinson (1904–1968), a graduate of Harvard and a professor at the University of Kansas, had already recommended himself to Heidegger by showing him translations he had done of works by the classicist Werner Jäger (not to be confused with the Germanist Hans Jäger), the quality of which Heidegger was unable to determine. He asked Arendt for help. Arendt found Robinson's translations of Jäger to be quite good, but she also remarked that Jäger himself might have made the necessary corrections and that, in any case, Jäger's scholarly German would not pose the sorts of problems that Heidegger's innovative German poses. She praised Robinson's hard work on *Being and Time* and affirmed that he deserved assistance. Such assistance was needed, she went on to say, since the English text, without the German right alongside it, "is as good as incomprehensible" (AHB 430). Ouch. Arendt then went into detail about the terminology, syntax, critical apparatus, the inelegance of many renderings, and the downright mistranslations. Sometimes when Heidegger was criticizing a given interpretation of the history of philosophy, his polemic was turned into praise. Arendt promised to write a detailed letter to Robinson, which she then did: five typed, single-spaced pages.

She asked Heidegger whether he knew of anyone in *England* who was working on a translation of *Sein und Zeit*. When and how Edward Robinson and John Macquarrie, the latter a Scots theologian, came into contact with one another and then completed their joint translation, I do not know, although I assume that it began during Macquarrie's residence in New York during the late 1950s and early 1960s. Nor do I know whether Arendt met and worked with John Macquarrie—it would have intrigued me to know.

Finally, even though Arendt and Joan Stambaugh were close, I do not know whether Arendt actually worked on any early drafts of Joan's translation of *Being and Time*, as Glenn Gray and I did; in any case, Arendt died twenty years before that second translation appeared in print. The important point is that Arendt may well have played a supportive and encouraging yet critical role in *both* of the currently available translations of *Being and Time*, the book that had absorbed so much of Heidegger's energy—at the expense of their relationship.

Heidegger's reply to Arendt's April 6 letter, on April 21, 1954, is also intriguing to me. First of all, he thanks her profusely for her labors over the Robinson attempt, noting that she has both the language skills and, "above all, knowledge of the matter itself and the paths of my thinking" (AHB 140). He confesses that he is "in a desperate quandary" and that he cannot judge the quality of translations that come to him from the United States, even though he would like to see his work introduced there. Yet he fears the sorts of errors that, once made, cannot be altered, citing the French translation of "*être* pour *la mort*" instead of the correct "*être* vers *la mort*." And he emphasizes that he does not "dare" ask her to spend the sort of time and energy on these tasks that would be needed—one of the few times, one must say, that he acknowledges Arendt as a thinker who has her own work to do: "I would have been glad to hear how you are doing and what you are working on," he adds (AHB 141).

As it turns out, after her return from Europe in 1950, Arendt also met and worked with Ralph Manheim, the translator of Heidegger's *Introduction to Metaphysics*, the work that was so important to me as a young man, and not only because of its convenient size. Manheim apparently asked Arendt to write a foreword to his translation, which, as far as I know, was never written (AG 317/227). In 1961, when the two-volume *Nietzsche* appeared, Arendt wrote to the publisher Kurt Wolff, urging him to read the volumes, clearly with a view to having them translated into English. Antonia Grunenberg remarks, as I reported earlier, that both Arendt and Blücher were "deeply impressed" with these volumes (AG 318/227). I am not surprised.

Fig. 7.1 Derrida in the summer of 1987 at the Collegium Phaenomenologicum in Perugia, Italy.

7

MEETING JACQUES DERRIDA

The *Geschlecht* Project

When I first heard the name *Derrida* I am not sure. I believe it was in August 1972 when I went to visit Hélène Cixous to talk about James Joyce. I had not met Cixous before, so that when Queen Nefertiti opened the door and invited me in, I was stunned. I still have the list of books and journals she encouraged me to read, seminars by Lacan and monographs by Georges Bataille, Roman Jakobson, Roland Barthes, and Gilles Deleuze. Her most emphatic recommendation, however, went to three recent books by Jacques Derrida, namely, *Of Grammatology, Writing and Difference*, and *Dissemination.*

Even though this Nefertiti—her blue eye shadow was applied almost as far back as the ears—was a brilliant mentor, I was not a good pupil: it was years before I read anything by Derrida. Indeed, my English and Welsh friends, Robert Bernasconi, David Wood, and John Llewelyn, assure me that when we first met and worked together at the Warwick Workshops during the 1970s, I resisted "the Derrideans" quite vociferously, especially when it came to the Derridean reading of Heidegger. There was one particular "Derridean," as I recall, who seemed to me to be what the Germans not-so-fondly call a *Windbeutel,* our own "windbag," a philosopher who was innocent of all knowledge of Heidegger but who expatiated nonetheless on Derrida's "critique" of the philosopher who, after Nietzsche, meant the most to me. In short, I knew nothing about Derrida's work—except that I wanted no part of it. However, in June 1979, John Sallis put Derrida's *Éperons: les styles de Nietzsche* ("Spurs: Nietzsche's Styles") into my hands with the remark "I think you'd better read this." A day or two later, I took that little book into the garden and read it all the way through in one sitting. From that day on, I read as much of Derrida's work as I could and as quickly as I could. Too quickly, no doubt. Derrida was not only a well-trained and voracious reader of philosophy; he was also a master of rhetoric, linguistics, literature, and literary criticism. It was too much to absorb all at once—and even over decades. Whether Derrida is in or out of fashion today, it is certain that we have not yet caught up with him. I, at least, certainly have not, and not for want of trying.

A brief word about *Spurs* and the aftermath of my reading. That small book spurred me to write my first book, a book about Nietzsche that owed almost everything to Derrida's monograph, except for my digging into Nietzsche's unpublished notebooks. Yet the most important passage for my book was a published one, and it played a central role for Derrida as well. It appears as aphorism 60 in *The Gay Science* and is titled "Women and Their Action at a Distance" (KSA 3:424–25).[1] Nietzsche compares that "action at a distance" to what happens when one sees, at some distance from the shore and its surging surf, a magnificent sailing ship gliding by. Derrida's book is all about ships, their canvas sails and projecting bowsprits, spars, or spurs, and I knew that the book had become important for me when I entered another passage from Joyce onto the title page of Derrida's book, namely, the concluding words to the "Telemacheia" of Joyce's *Ulysses*: "He turned his face over a shoulder, rere regardant. Moving through the air high spars of a threemaster, her sails brailed up on the crosstrees, homing, upstream, silently moving, a silent ship."[2]

The second half of Derrida's book deals with Heidegger's *Nietzsche*, and the effect of that second half on me was initially disturbing. For Derrida noticed some very important things about Heidegger's reading of Nietzsche that had escaped me. After years of laboring over the translation and analysis of Heidegger's book, there were notable items I had missed. I may have felt as though Derrida had intruded on the space that I alone shared with Heidegger's *Nietzsche*. But it was no intrusion. He had blown that space wide open. And that is the feeling I began to have with every text of Derrida's I encountered after that. Everything changed, even and especially if I "knew my way around" the area under discussion, whether it involved Plato, Kant, Rousseau, Hegel, Nietzsche, or Heidegger.

---

1 That is, Friedrich Nietzsche, vol. 3 of *Kritische Studienausgabe der Werke*, ed. Giorgio Colli and Mazzino Montinari (Berlin and Munich: W. de Gruyter and Deutscher Taschenbuch Verlag, 1980), 424–25. I will cite these volumes as "KSA" with volume and page in the body of my text.

2 James Joyce, *Ulysses* (London: Bodley Head, 1969), 64.

Something like a friendship began to develop between us in the early 1980s when Derrida started to publish a series of remarkable essays on Heidegger under the title *Geschlecht*. That word means "sex," "generation," "tribe," "lineage," and even "the human race," *das Menschengeschlecht*. Of course, it was startling to see such a word flowing from Heidegger's pen; sexuality did not seem to be a major preoccupation of his work. Yet Derrida identified the two quite remarkable texts, one from 1928, the other from 1953, in which Heidegger devotes himself to the unlikely topic—unlikely for *Heidegger*, at any rate—of human sexuality. I will not go into detail about Derrida's *Geschlecht* project here, but it did form the core of our exchanges in the 1980s and 1990s and culminated in my book *Phantoms of the Other*. Here, I want to focus on other aspects of what I believe I can call our friendship.

Perhaps I should hesitate to use that word. So many other friends and associates of his and mine knew him better than I did and spent more time with him. Yet during the decades of the 1980s and 1990s, I managed to visit with him at least three or four times a year, sometimes with my wife and children (the children referred to him as "Monsieur Jacques" as they were growing up), so it became much more than a work relationship. Without claiming any special privilege or knowledge of him, I want to record my sense of the friend. Starting, perhaps, at the end.

October 15 is usually the day when I celebrate Nietzsche's birthday, but on October 15, 2004, I recorded something very different in my journal: "I returned from Santorini only to learn that Jacques has died. Friday night, October 8 [actually, Saturday morning, October 9, 2004]. I feel close to death. Never anything like this before, never so deep. Unable even to take walks." The note seems hyperbolic to me now. After all, I had lost both of my parents by that time, and the deaths of Heidegger and Arendt, and then Glenn Gray, were blows I also should have been ready for but was not. And I knew that Jacques had been ill with pancreatic cancer for two years. Yet when I read the blue print at the top of the front page of the *Süddeutsche Zeitung* that he had died—I was on an airplane flying from Santorini to Frankfurt on October 11—I went into a kind of shock. As soon as we landed, I placed a call to Michael Naas in Chicago, who had already learned of Jacques' death. We talked about whether we should fly to Paris, but he advised me that Marguerite Derrida had discouraged this, wanting a small service, one restricted to family and only the closest friends. Michael and I consoled one another as best we could. We are still doing that. Some deaths endure; some deaths just keep happening.

* * *

Apparently, I wrote to Derrida in late 1982, asking John Sallis to pass along the letter and a publication to him. I have no copy of that letter or note, but the article was called "The Mole/*Der Maulwurf,*" and I can only imagine that the important role of Nietzsche and Hegel in the article was what encouraged me to send it to him. It seems a bit nervy, but I could do nervy. The first letter that I sent directly to him involved another favorite author of mine, the Austrian poet Georg Trakl. It was uncanny to me that Derrida would be writing about both Nietzsche and Trakl, two of my principal interests, although "interests" is too weak a word. I had just published an article on Trakl and Heidegger's reading of Trakl, and I must have sent him a copy of that too. My letter mentions that I have read the typescript of his first "Geschlecht" article and have taken the liberty (spell that *chutzpah*) to suggest some changes.

I will not transcribe my entire correspondence with Derrida here, but allow me to cite this "first" letter, since it sets the tone for our early connection. It appears on stationery from the "Anglistisches Seminar der Universität Mannheim," where I was teaching as a lector, and it is dated January 4, 1983:

> Dear Jacques Derrida!
>
> I do not like to receive mail from persons I do not know—and here I am for the second time intruding on you! John Sallis was kind enough to pass on to you my "Maulwurf" some weeks ago, and he was here over Christmas and gave me a copy of "Geschlecht" to read. I was very excited by the piece. (How should I react to *Geschlecht* if not with the greatest excitement?)
>
> Two summers ago I taught a course at the Collegium Phaenomenologicum in Perugia based on your *Spurs.* The course was entitled "Aesthetics Male and Female: Derrida on Heidegger on Nietzsche on Kant on the Beautiful." As an introduction to *Spurs* I selected—of all things—those passages from Heidegger's *Anfangsgründe* which your "Geschlecht" treats. (I enclose two sheets containing English translations of the passages I referred to; they were sheets that I gave to the students during the course.)
>
> I am delighted by the first of your two *Geschlechter,* and I am looking forward to the second.[3] I have taken the liberty of noting on the other side

---

3 The "second" here meant for me Derrida's interpretation of Heidegger's Trakl essay. It turned out to be the missing "third" *Geschlecht* article.

of this sheet four minor suggestions. The final chapter of a book I have just completed (*Intimations of Mortality in the Thought of Martin Heidegger*)[4] involves the theme of *Schlag/Geschlecht* in Heidegger's Trakl study. I take the unpardonable liberty of sending it to you. My piece is undisciplined and ultimately not very critical. It is a first response to Trakl and to Heidegger's Trakl—reason enough to be blown by every wind. Yet it is one of my deepest interests and I'm hoping to develop the depth to be worthy of it.

I'd be delighted if "Strokes of Love and Death" were of any help to you during your preparation of the coming *Geschlecht*.

Forgive my intrusion. I hope we have the chance to meet some day—your work is very important to me, more so with each passing day.

With warm wishes, etc.[5]

Fortunately for me, Derrida balanced the brashness against the obsequiousness and forgave it all. Before he had a chance to reply, I sent him a general notice about a change of address, due to my move to Essex, England, on April 30, 1983. He replied on May 12, 1983, writing in French, by hand, on letterhead from the École Normale Supérieure:

Cher David Krell,

Pardon, a thousand pardons, for the tardiness of this reply. I thank you for your letter and for the very valuable enclosures. The past few months have been terrible for me, depriving me of energy, freedom, and time! I will take into account your necessary and pertinent suggestions and, when the time comes, that is, when I am finishing the second part of my article, I will read you and re-read you once again.

Again my thanks, and pardon me.

Very cordially, with all best wishes, and with the hope of meeting you some day, J. Derrida.

There are certain constants reflected in this very first letter. First, Derrida's double career in France and in the United States was by this time in full swing. One may say that Derrida was serving two masters on two different continents and that his workload was at least double that of the normal academic. References to lack of time, depletion of energy, delays in replying to correspondence—these became mainstays of his letters, and not only to me. But also, a second constant, the expressions of gratitude for the engagement of others in his work, the generosity and gratitude never failing.

---

4 The subtitle became "Time, Truth, and Finitude in Heidegger's Thinking of Being."

5 As far as I can tell, Derrida accepted my four minor suggestions for this first "Geschlecht" ms. For a more detailed treatment, see the first chapter of Krell, *Phantoms of the Other*.

At the end of the month, I responded to his letter with a note expressing again the desire to meet, and in October, enclosing some literature on the program in Continental philosophy that I was helping to organize at Essex with Robert Bernasconi, I wrote him again, "hoping that *Geschlecht* continues to propagate." The year 1984 seems to show no correspondence, but this is very strange. Perhaps by that time, we were telephoning back and forth, but I cannot remember, and that seems unlikely. It seems more likely that some letters have gone missing. At all events, 1984 was the year when John Sallis was preparing a conference at Loyola University of Chicago, which took place in March 1985. I also cannot remember what I talked about there, although I know that it touched on the "theoretical matrix" of Derrida's *Grammatology*. I do remember quite vividly the paper that Derrida delivered in Chicago, "Heidegger's Hand (Geschlecht II)." It was the most powerful presentation I had ever heard—until Derrida's next presentation. I will not go into any detail about it, but I will merely recount what happened after the meeting, when the two of us had to travel to Yale, he to teach a course, I to deliver an invited lecture there.

However, before we leave Chicago, let me tell an absurd yet true little story. It is a story about how Derrida had a special gift for responding to questions. This was my first experience of that special gift of his.

The Story of a Box and Four Hands

As soon as Derrida had concluded his remarks on "the hand of Heidegger," with the large audience still in a state of astonishment, the first hand, not Heidegger's, went up. Looking back to the rear of the auditorium, I observed that the hand belonged to the *Windbeutel* who had confirmed my judgment in the early 1970s that Derrida was not worth reading. I sank deep into my seat. I believe I even prayed, "Oh, dear Baby Jesus, please don't let this happen, please!" But it did happen. The man began, and after he began, he went on beginning and then beginning again, beginning interminably.

—Let's imagine that there is a box in front of me, and I pick it up with my two hands. Now, I can turn the box this way and that way, because a box has six sides, and. . . ."

After about five minutes of multiple hands turning that unaccountable box, Baby Jesus having failed yet again to answer my plea, Derrida gently held up his right hand as though to interrupt the unending story. He spoke quietly, calmly, and in a friendly tone of voice.

—You raised your hand. You have a question. What is it?

The *Windbeutel* suddenly lost his train of thought. And so he needed to gather it again, from the beginning and with as many hands as he could muster.

—Let's say there is a box in front of you, and you pick it up, but you need two hands to do that. You can turn it this way and that way, because a box has six sides, and. . . ."

Can this have gone on for even longer than five minutes? Can it have gone on for ten minutes? Surely not. Yet it seemed an eternity. Not quite in hell, but in some sort of purgatory. Everyone by now was sinking lower into their seats, praying to all the deities that have ever visited the earth that this might pass. Derrida, sensing the growing distress, interrupted again, every bit as gently as the first time.

—You raised your hand. You have a question. What is it?

The would-be questioner, disarmed by the word-for-word repetition of the request to him, grew silent for an instant. Then he spoke.

—I was just wondering if your paper has any connection with Merleau-Ponty.

Without letting an instant pass, Derrida replied.

—That is an excellent question, he said.

The narrator of this little story cannot remember anything that was said after that, whether about the marvelous Merleau-Ponty or the box with six sides and four hands, even though Derrida surely responded brilliantly, as he always did. I cannot remember because the entire room exploded with laughter, heaps and howls of laughter, guffaws, and roars eventually dying down to chuckles. If you give him time, Baby Jesus always comes through.

* * *

I cannot remember the first time I saw Derrida, but it must have been at O'Hare Airport when he arrived for that first Loyola conference. I was in the company of John Sallis, the conference planner and host of the event. I remember knowing that Derrida had experienced some health problems; indeed, that he had undergone gallbladder surgery some nine months earlier. I also remember offering to carry his suitcase, which is apparently something I do a lot, an offer that he energetically refused. I did not know that the previous year, 1984, had been particularly stressful for him both in his personal life and because of the death of his friend Paul de Man (BP 446). Yet I certainly saw no signs of weariness or weakness. The vitality and energy of the man impressed me from the start, which was at the baggage carousel.

After the conference ended, the two of us happened to be heading for Yale University by way of New York City. I recall being irritated at the check-in counter when the airline representative questioned Derrida quite closely about his visa. "Does he not know who this man is?" I asked myself indignantly—and absurdly. It was one of those times when one realizes how minuscule the world of philosophy is; even a giant in Lilliputia has little or no stature in the eyes of the rest of the world.

My first journal note on Derrida, edited only slightly here, with additions in square brackets and with an occasional interruption, says this:

> March 25, 1985
>
> It would have been one of the most exciting flights of my life—had he not been so calm, so gentle, so easy to be with. It was like "everyday." But it was not without headaches: United Airlines had canceled our 7 AM O'Hare to LaGuardia flight and we had to hustle about with baggage and tickets in hand from line to line until we finally arranged another flight.

This was clearly on the day following the Loyola conference. J. Hillis Miller had invited me to give a lecture at Yale (on Nietzsche's *Zarathustra*, as I remember), and Derrida was returning to Yale to teach several weeks of classes, his usual stint for the past few years. I did not know at the time that Derrida's Yale period was about to end and that he and Hillis Miller were soon to leave the Yale comparative literature department for Irvine, California (BP 455). I was aware of the trouble being instigated at Yale, some of it by certain members of the philosophy department, the sort of trouble that analytical philosophers always make when confronting something or someone interesting.

The following notes translate our dialogue into English, but I remember always trying at least to speak French with him—he had a way of correcting my mistakes without interrupting the flow of the conversation.

> After checking our bags we had time for a coffee and a disastrous breakfast roll packed in plastic. Impenetrable and *unappetitlich*! Sitting there face-to-face with him at a tiny table, I decided to put to him the question that Robert Bernasconi had asked me to pose, but not without prefacing it by saying that he should imagine for a moment that I was *un innocent*. He smiled broadly.

—M. Derrida, I said, suddenly formal, when are you going to write an ethics?

Derrida laughed out loud and exclaimed, in English,

—You already know the answer!

I laughed—but waited. He continued, back now in French.

—You don't have to *write* an ethics. *Here* is the ethics already.

He gestured lightly, with both up-turned hands over the white plastic table top.

—You don't have to write it. The ethics is *toujours déjà là*. Even Levinas doesn't want to *write* an ethics. That is what I would say to you. And to Robert!

I told him about my own reluctance, my own fears about the discourse of ethics—its suppressed violence. Impotence to power. He nodded, comprehending, serious and noncommittal, neither agreeing nor disagreeing. Yet what gentleness and wit in one face!

Once we were in the airplane they served us "French toast." I made a joke about it and he assured me that whatever it was it was not "French" toast.

—There is no French toast in France. Only in America.

After a while, he rested, almost dozing off a bit.

These trips to the United States were exhausting for him. Especially the conferences, since he had the custom of attending the papers of every speaker, no matter how many there were, and he generally acknowledged each speaker by asking a nonaggressive but serious question, trying to engage each participant in conversation. Over the years, I noticed what a toll these conferences took on him. In my own case, even as a young man I have never been able to listen to more than three papers in a row without needing a break—perhaps for the rest of the day. I never understood how he found the stamina to sit through two or three days of papers from dawn to dusk. But to return to my account of the flight to LaGuardia. "His head was inclined lightly toward the window and I took the occasion to look at him: the wonderful, fully white, backswept hair, the dark teint of the forehead, cheeks, and hands, branded long ago by the Algerian sun. His mother, brother, and sister live now in Nice, where he visits at least once a year. His own residence is some twenty minutes outside of Paris." Twenty minutes, it has to be said, the way Derrida drove. For me, Ris-Orangis was about an hour southeast of the city, as I remember, depending on how long it took you to escape the tentacles of the Paris *Périphérique.*

At this moment he seemed less a man of the city than I had thought him to be. His stature and the deep color of his small squarish hands reminded me of Heidegger—*la main de l'homme.*

In the coffee shop of the airport I had explained to him about that Op Art painting or poster I had seen years before: "Fly United," it said, as it showed a pair of geese or swans or ducks conjugating in flight. He seemed to enjoy the image. From now on I will sign my letters to him *toujours encore flying United*!

We did not chat much more on the plane. I'm grateful that he made me less compulsively gabby than I usually am. We worked on the lectures we had to give that day, I at 4 in the afternoon, he at 8 in the evening. As we were about to land I looked out at the New York City skyline and the burning blue sky.

—You know, if this plane goes down, *se tombe*! then I will gain immortality for having been on it with you. That notwithstanding, I prefer to live.

—*Moi aussi!* he laughed. I'm sorry if that ruins your plans!

—No, no, I insisted, we are agreed: we shall live on!

And so the plane landed safely.

Another topic of conversation occurs to me: he encouraged me to contact Hélène Cixous again, saying that she was developing increasing interest in Heidegger.

As we walked down the concourse behind a handsome black flight attendant with the tiniest ringlets of hair worked into a sculpture on her head, I gestured toward the hair, and he smiled.

—Lots of work, he said.

It is strange that my journal notes say nothing of Hillis Miller's meeting us at LaGuardia and driving us to New Haven. Miller was elated to see Derrida, that was plain, and it reminds me of something important: Derrida never went anywhere to give a lecture or attend a conference unless there was either a political or a personal motivation. I do not believe he cared a bit for the normal academic parade of conferences. He would fly to South America or South Africa or to Israel *and* Palestine to support a cause. His political engagements were—despite the nonsense one hears—intense and long-standing. Or, if it was not a political engagement, then it was a matter of seeing and being with friends. Basically, he presented his work to friends, and he needed the friendship of those friends, but always with a desire for serious and *challenging* conversation. One thing that never interested him was money. Whether I was at the University of Essex in Maggie Thatcher's England or at DePaul in Chicago, where resources were not what they would have been at Harvard or Yale, we never spoke about money. As for travel arrangements, he would say, "Don't worry, I'll take care of it." If Derrida went to Yale, it was because of the intense exchanges with friends and students there. Never in all my experience have I met a man so generous, so undemanding when it came to "honoraria." For him, the honor was to be among friends.

A day after our lectures at Yale, my journal entry continues: "It is now March 26, 1985. Last night I heard Derrida's first Yale lecture on 'Philosophical Nationality and Nationalism,' which is the context of 'Geschlecht II.' His Wednesday night seminar will analyze closely Heidegger's 'Language in the Poem,' as an essential supplement (!) to these lectures."

I have to interrupt to mention something that seems incredible to me. For years, I was searching for the "missing" part of the four-part "Geschlecht" series by Derrida. But it was right there in front of my nose, or ears. Derrida was teaching a seminar during that very winter semester at Paris, a seminar precisely on Heidegger's Trakl essay, "Language in the Poem," and that is the material he was presenting now at Yale. Yet even though I talked with him about all this during our earliest days together, I soon forgot about it and then later had to do a lot of detective work to find the "missing" *Geschlecht III*. The transcript of his Paris lecture course was in the IMEC Archive (that is, *L'Institut mémoires de l'édition contemporaine*) near Caen, neatly boxed and in the proper chronological order of the seminars, waiting for me to "discover" it. All I would have had to do, however, was remember the Yale lectures.

Now comes a surprising remark in my journal. It must have been based on what I experienced at Yale in those few days there. My journal records: "Yale works him too hard, and although there seem to be lots of bright young people here, I wonder whether it is worth his time and exhaustion." Again, it was his generosity that struck me, his liberality not only with money but with his time and energy. Derrida's biographer, Benoît Peeters, cites an early acquaintance of Derrida's who, in my view, finds exactly the right words to explain his popularity in the United States: "I was quite struck by the combination of rigor and gentleness [*de rigueur et de douceur*]," "the extreme openness to all things," "this *mélange* of gentleness and firmness, of rigor and of the everyday" (BP 233). Gérard Genette finds a humorous way to say the same thing. He reports how impressed everyone at Johns Hopkins was with Derrida in 1966, not only because of the originality and périence interne et la seconde à l'expérience externe » (Jakobson, *op. cit.* p. 112). La différence entre l'invariance et la variabilité ne sépare pas les deux domaines entre eux, elle les partage l'un et l'autre en eux-mêmes. Cela indique assez que l'essence de la *phonè* ne saurait être lue directement et d'abord dans le texte d'une science mondaine, d'une psycho-physio-phonétique.

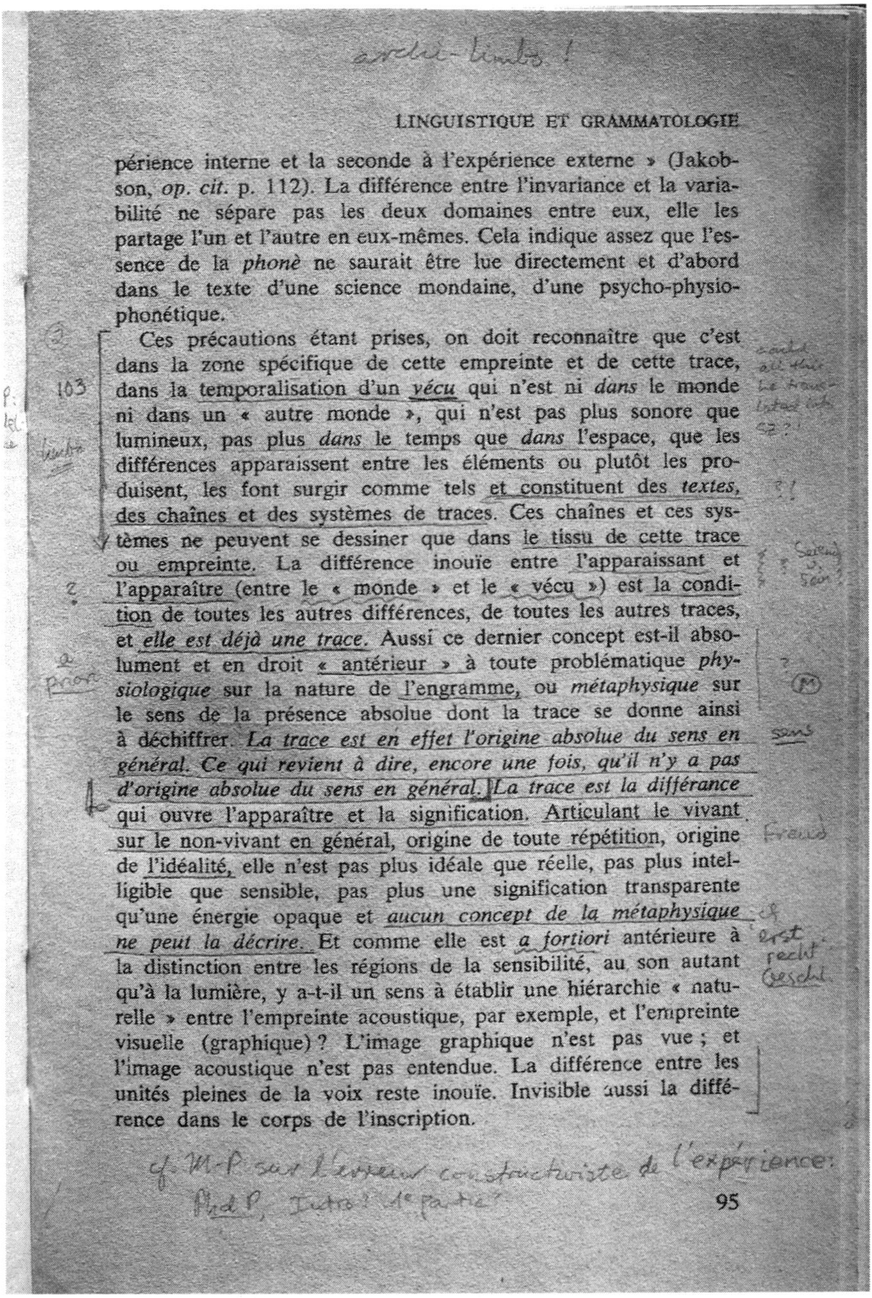

Ces précautions étant prises, on doit reconnaître que c'est dans la zone spécifique de cette empreinte et de cette trace, dans la temporalisation d'un *vécu* qui n'est ni *dans* le monde ni dans un « autre monde », qui n'est pas plus sonore que lumineux, pas plus *dans* le temps que *dans* l'espace, que les différences apparaissent entre les éléments ou plutôt les produisent, les font surgir comme tels et constituent des *textes*, des chaînes et des systèmes de traces. Ces chaînes et ces systèmes ne peuvent se dessiner que dans le tissu de cette trace ou empreinte. La différence inouïe entre l'apparaissant et l'apparaître (entre le « monde » et le « vécu ») est la condition de toutes les autres différences, de toutes les autres traces, et *elle est déjà une trace*. Aussi ce dernier concept est-il absolument et en droit « antérieur » à toute problématique *physiologique* sur la nature de l'engramme, ou *métaphysique* sur le sens de la présence absolue dont la trace se donne ainsi à déchiffrer. *La trace est en effet l'origine absolue du sens en général. Ce qui revient à dire, encore une fois, qu'il n'y a pas d'origine absolue du sens en général.* La trace est la *différance* qui ouvre l'apparaître et la signification. Articulant le vivant sur le non-vivant en général, origine de toute répétition, origine de l'idéalité, elle n'est pas plus idéale que réelle, pas plus intelligible que sensible, pas plus une signification transparente qu'une énergie opaque et *aucun concept de la métaphysique ne peut la décrire.* Et comme elle est *a fortiori* antérieure à la distinction entre les régions de la sensibilité, au son autant qu'à la lumière, y a-t-il un sens à établir une hiérarchie « naturelle » entre l'empreinte acoustique, par exemple, et l'empreinte visuelle (graphique) ? L'image graphique n'est pas vue ; et l'image acoustique n'est pas entendue. La différence entre les unités pleines de la voix reste inouïe. Invisible aussi la différence dans le corps de l'inscription.

95

Fig. 7.2 One of the most difficult passages in the *Grammatology*, with a marginal note on "limbo."

radicality of his thinking but also on account of his unassuming, modest manner: "The only sympathetic Frenchman since Lafayette—all the others are arrogant" (BP 254). As for those who took advantage of the gentleness, I had no idea while at Yale that I myself would soon be plaguing him with requests that would demand his time and exacerbate his exhaustion. My journal note now continues:

> I also learned the difference between the two of us while we were at Yale: at his lecture last evening were some ninety people, at mine during the afternoon there were perhaps ten. However, among them were Hillis Miller and Derrida. After I finished, all Derrida said was, "I want to read your book." I promised to send him a copy. It is now being printed, after a hair-raising set of galleys and pages![6] Last night Derrida learned of Robert Bernasconi's book—a young faculty member was singing its praises—and when he said he would like to read it I promised him that Robert would send him a copy.[7]
>
> During the plane trip I extracted my copy of *De la grammatologie,* opening it to pages 95–96, the pages I had referred to critically in my Chicago paper. On the top of page 95, above the running-head, I had written the word *archi-limbo!* By that I meant the place where Derrida's deconstruction of Husserlian time-consciousness leaves us—on the threshold of transcendence. Derrida didn't know what the word *limbo* meant, and so I gave him an ex-Roman Catholic's childish account.

What gave me the feeling that the *Grammatology* had left me in limbo had to do with what Derrida calls the *brisure,* or "joint, jointure, crack, break, or perhaps hinge." I had been teaching the *Grammatology* with Gabriel Pearson at the University of Essex, and the section on the *brisure* unhinged us both. I cannot reconstitute here either the complicated argument of the text or what it was that troubled me, except to say that by the time I had worked through the second section of "Linguistics and Grammatology," the section titled "The Outside Is the Inside," with the "Is" crossed through after the manner of Heidegger in some of his late essays, I was beside myself. Having pursued the "trace" of an "arche-transcendental" structure of "arche-writing," tracking Derrida's traces, I came upon the following

6 The book in question is now out of print but is available as an ebook: David Farrell Krell, *Postponements: Woman, Sensuality, and Death in Nietzsche* (Bloomington: Indiana University Press, 1986). If I am not mistaken, my lecture at Yale was based on chap. 3 of this book, "Pana," which presents the unpublished notes in which Nietzsche tries to depict Zarathustra's *death,* which is indefinitely postponed.

7 Robert Bernasconi, *The Question of Language in Heidegger's History of Being* (New York: Humanities, 1985).

italicized sentence (on page 95 of the French edition, here in my desperate attempt to translate): "*In effect, the trace is the absolute origin of meaning in general. Which reverts to saying once again that there is no absolute origin of meaning in general.*" I was fine with this metaphysical winner-take-nothing until the next page, on the "hinge," or the "unhinging," or "the joint, crack, or break," which began with this: "Origin of the experience of space and time, this writing of the difference, this tissue of the trace permits the difference between space and time to articulate itself." There seemed to be a gap between these two pages, an abyss that cut between the recto and verso of a single sheet in the book, as though one would have to descend into the crevice of that single sheet to explore a great deal more this nonorigin, the trace, which becomes the origin of an experience of nothing less than space and time.

As I mentioned, I opened my copy of his book to the crevice or abyss I was asking him to explain. He replied by saying how difficult those pages—and, really, the entire first part of the *Grammatology*—had been to write. There was little more he could do at the moment; a flight to Beijing would have given us more time. In any case, before we landed, I asked him if he would inscribe something into my well-worn, heavily marked copy of the book, and he graciously complied. He took pains to make the dedication legible.

> Pour David
> si l'on peut dédicacer
> l'archi-limbo d'entre deux pages,
> avec toute mon amitié,
> Jacques D.
> en vol, *united airline*, entre
> Chicago et New York, le 25 mars 85.

On the following day, March 26, I wrote a brief note to Derrida, now addressing him by his first name, "Dear Jacques," thanking him for his generosity toward me during that entire week. I also promised to mail him the English-language volumes of Heidegger's *Nietzsche*, which I imagined would be useful for his work in the States. (Again, those two masters in his life, speaking two very different languages!) I encouraged him to go slow, take it easy, knowing he would not and could not. On March 27, if I remember correctly, I had to return to England, while Derrida remained at Yale. On that date, I entered into my journal: "Bade Derrida adieu yesterday

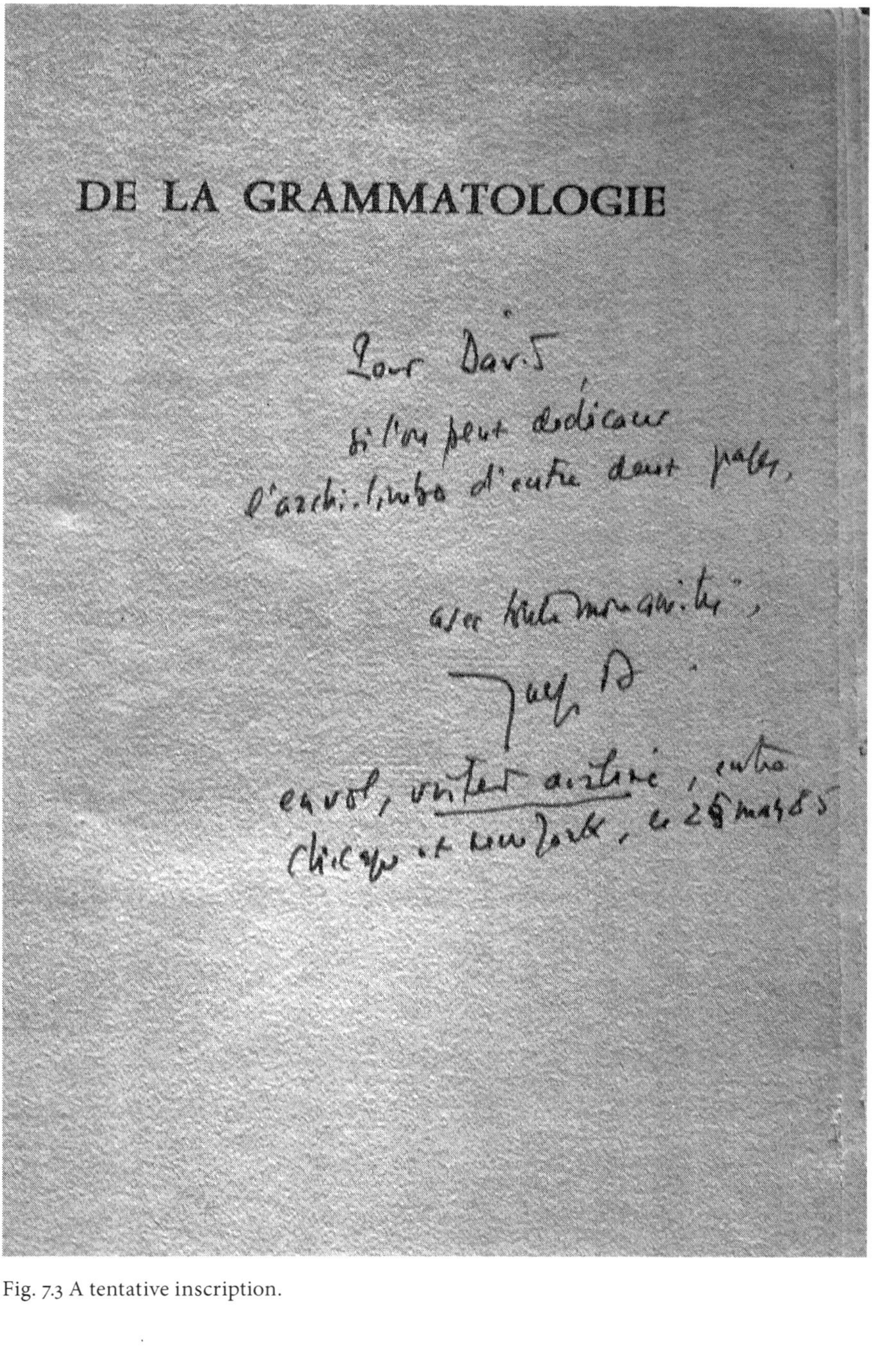
DE LA GRAMMATOLOGIE
Pour David,

Fig. 7.3 A tentative inscription.

afternoon—it was moving, as though we had known one another for some time. He seemed to take my work seriously, and to take to me kindly. Luckily, I was able to relax these past few days so that I didn't talk him to death. I imagine he was grateful for that." The note continues with a long discussion of Derrida's relationship with Michel Foucault, much in discussion at the time because of Foucault's angry response to Derrida's essay "The Cogito and the History of Madness." Foucault's response, "My Body, This Paper, This Fire," appended to the 1972 reprinting of *The History of Madness*, had long been available. Why it sparked such interest among the Yale graduate students in 1985 I cannot recall. In any case, there is no need to reproduce that part of my journal here. Benoît Peeters tells the tale in detail (BP 87, 229–30, 296–99).

In April, I sent Derrida the *Nietzsche* volumes that were available and promised to send the rest when they were reprinted. In return, I asked him to send me his book on Joyce, which we had talked about during our plane trip.[8] The Joyce book, not often discussed among philosophers, "letting punplays pass to ernest" (FW 233), immediately became one of my favorite books of his or of anyone's. Hysterically funny, astonishingly well informed, and as obsessively detailed as any text on Joyce has to be—it was an added gift from the thinker who had reshaped the Nietzsche–Heidegger confrontation for me, transforming it into an ellipse or some other weird geometric figure with four wandering foci. I imagined what it would take for me to write a book on a French writer who would be the equivalent of James Joyce, but that bout of imagination did not last long. Whether or not I told him about the "ensuance of existentiality" from *Finnegans Wake*, which I had inscribed into my copy of *Sein und Zeit*, and about my worry that Heidegger might have seen it and been puzzled by it as he was writing his own inscription, I cannot remember. "Now, just wash and brush up your memoirias a little bit" (FW 507). Yet I feel I must have told him because I can hear him laughing.

Not long after our first meeting, I was planning two conferences at which Derrida was to be the main speaker—more than that, his work was to be the focus of all the papers and the ensuing discussions: first, a meeting at the University of Essex devoted to his readings of Heidegger, the very readings I had rejected before studying them; and second, a meeting of the

---

8 Published in 1987 by Galilée in Paris as *Ulysse gramophone: Deux mots pour Joyce.*

Collegium Phaenomenologicum in Perugia, Italy, which I was slated to direct in summer 1986. At the end of April 1985, I sent him a formal invitation to "Reading Heidegger," mentioning that the office of the French cultural attaché would support the conference. I should note that this office generously supported many of our events at Essex, and that in 1988 they made me a *Chevalier de l'Ordre des Palmes Académiques*. When I asked them why they had bestowed the honor on me, they replied, "We gave you so much money, we *had* to knight you." Why can't Americans and Germans think like that?

At all events, Derrida and I eventually telephoned back and forth, trying to fix a date for the Essex meeting. Derrida's calendar was a nightmare. Before those telephone calls, he had tentatively agreed to the meeting, but it was a struggle to find a date when he would be free. On June 3, 1985, now on letterhead from the École des Hautes Études en Sciences Sociales (EHESS), he wrote:

Mon cher David,

First of all, forgive my tardiness! Since my return from the States I've been crushed with work (distraction, fatigue, harassments, etc.). I'd be very happy to receive the admirable *Nietzsche* books by Heidegger. You have done fine work there—useful also for the French, such as me for example. It is so much better than what we have here! I haven't forgotten my promise to send you the Joyce, but because it is to appear in print in September, I think it would be better to send you that rather than a sloppy manuscript. There is no urgency for you to read this little text.

But now to your lovely and generous proposal of a colloquium. My first reaction—apart from gratitude—was one of fear. For two reasons: (1) fear of not having either the time or the energy: I've already accepted too many engagements for next year, which was neither reasonable nor even serious of me to do; (2) the fear that a project so serious and so well organized, with all those competent people, could only wind up exposing to broad daylight the insufficiencies of my "readings of Heidegger."

Upon reflection, I believe that it would be neither just nor very friendly of me to compromise such a project on account of my fears. So, in principle, I am agreed. We would have to discuss the dates (as late in the spring as possible, preferably June, after my return from the States), and accepting the idea, perhaps, that I may not be in a place where I can offer significantly new work. But the participants you are thinking of inviting seem to me to be really among the most serious and most interesting people. There would be perhaps other possible participants; we'll speak about it.

Above all, I want to tell you how happy I was with our meeting in Chicago and that we were able to prolong it by "flying United" to Yale. A very fine thing, given the projected colloquium, is the prospect—for me a pleasure—of another encounter. Yours faithfully, in all friendship, etc.

I replied on June 11, 1985, saying that I took his *accord de principe* as an *accord de fait*. Discussion of dates and the possible topic of his presentation went back and forth—he might speak about the Platonic χώρα, which he was working on at this time, or add another dimension to the "Geschlecht" series, or focus on Heidegger's relation to animal life, which was occupying his thoughts increasingly—and would continue to do so for the rest of his life. Any of these topics would have pleased me: I had developed an interest in Plato's *Timaeus* and its problem of the "receptacle" or "womb" of the cosmos during my graduate school years; the "Geschlecht" series had yet to take up Trakl's poetry in an explicit and detailed way, and I was eager to see that happen; as it turned out, Derrida focused on his "hesitations" concerning Heidegger's thought, four hesitations that eventually became the four "threads" of *De l'esprit* (1987). One of those hesitations involved Heidegger's assurance that mortals could be readily distinguished from all other life-forms, a hesitation that I was beginning to share with Derrida and that would culminate in the book *Daimon Life: Heidegger and Life-Philosophy* (1992). With Derrida's encouragement, I invited Philippe Lacoue-Labarthe to join us, which inspired an unforgettable reply from him, in the tiniest script imaginable, and of course in French, "You do realize that I do not articulate a single word of English, not ever." As it turned out, neither Dominique Janicaud nor Lacoue nor Michel Haar was able to come to Essex, but in their place, we attained the incomparable Françoise Dastur.

Allow me to interrupt this chronology, however, and mention how I came to have copies of my letters to Derrida. Of course, I had kept his letters to me, but I had not made copies of mine to him, most of them, like his, handwritten. But when, in April 2012, I traveled to IMEC at Caen and worked on what became *Phantoms of the Other*, the director of the archive, Albert Dichy, walked up to my chair at the room-length desk and said with a smile, "Perhaps you may be interested in these." He had photocopied the seventeen years' worth of letters and documents from me to Derrida. I interrupted my work on *Phantoms* and leafed through these letters, now revenants, failing to recognize at first glance much of what they were about. By that time, the details were already fading. However, one document spoke to me immediately—it is important to note that Derrida kept *everything*—because it was an essay that my daughter Elena Sophia had written when she was eight and which I had sent to him for his edification. The handwriting that filled the entire page was inspirational, and the spelling, which might strike the reader as odd, represented for the most part various *phonetic* spellings of the names involved, at least for a child whose first languages were Spanish and German. For readers who may not be au courant with the essence of Nietzsche, Heidegger, and Derrida, I reproduce Elena Sophia's (untitled) essay here, which I would call

A Succinct Introduction to the Philosophies of

Nietzsche, Heidegger, and Derrida

> paper is very good for writing said niecha. we think that niecha is a very good writer and talker. Hidiger is very good to. Because of the good folosophers we become very great about niecha. I think that derida is very good at desining drawings and pronuncing talks to people like Hiedigga or niecha by these talks every one will beleve with sussess that Hiedigger is real

He kept *everything*.

* * *

In September 1985, Derrida wrote me to suggest May as the time for our "colloquium," saying that for all of June 1986, he would be at the University of Jerusalem—he had forgotten about that engagement altogether. He was on his way to the States "(Cornell, Gainesville, Emory, Rice!)" and planning a trip to South America. "*Toujours la même vie: fatigue, surcharge, dispersion, précipitation, voyages,*" a life lived, he wrote, "in great disorder." After some letters crossed, I wrote to arrange my visit to Paris in November 1985, from the eighteenth to the twenty-first. By this time, I was plotting to get him to attend the Collegium in Perugia, which he had not yet visited. Hans-Georg Gadamer had agreed to come for the first week of the four-week meeting in July and August 1986, devoted to Heidegger's Marburg lecture courses, and I hoped—successfully, as it turned out—that Derrida would come for the last week. We also fixed the dates for the Essex conference: May 16–18, 1986.

We met several times during those mid-November days, and I had supper for the first time at Ris-Orangis, where I met Marguerite for the first time. Such a gentle and wise person, such a warm yet savvy smile! I was not surprised to learn that she was a psychotherapist. The two of them were remarkably easy to be with—none of the mannerisms that mar so many academics and professional people, no self-importance, a great deal of genuine interest in others. And, of course, there were Derrida's lectures in Paris. By that time, he was lecturing in the large auditorium of the EHESS, adjacent to the Alliance Française, on the Boulevard Raspail. I have no idea how many people were present on those Wednesday afternoons, well over a hundred, in any case, probably some two hundred. Either before or after these sessions, we would meet at "La Lutèce" across the boulevard for a coffee. I remember the intensity of these conversations when it was a matter of philosophy, and a lightness of manner and mien when it was not. When the conversation became serious, he would puff on the omnipresent pipe, and his eyelids would flutter, the interval between blinks diminishing as the problem became more and more obstreperous. This "tic" of the eyelids was a constant, at least over the two decades I knew him. But back to the correspondence.

In early November 1985, I wrote him about the Essex conference but mentioned that a colleague of mine in England was also anxious to have him visit *his* university. Would that be possible? On the sixth, he replied that as usual his life was overtaxed, "the foolish and inane life that I lead," and asked me to discourage my colleague, to discourage with courtesy, promising me that he would write the colleague himself soon. I mention this because it became another constant in our relationship. A dozen colleagues cross my mind who asked me to intervene on their behalf, and these requests always put me in a difficult position. It was not a matter of jealously guarding him for myself, for his circle of friends was enormous, but of not exhausting him. Usually, the colleagues were respectful and mindful of the difficulty, but sometimes they were not. I recall one particular person at a neighboring institution in Chicago who was furious that I even *knew* Derrida and even more irate that I did not comply with the demand for assistance. It is true, as Derrida's enemies often growled, that he had become a "superstar" and that many people wanted a "piece" of him. If not the whole creature. "When a part so ptee does duty for the holos we soon grow to use of an allforabit" (FW 18–19). I recall dropping him off at an airport and remarking that he should protect himself a bit and not partition himself out so much. He laughed as he was getting out of the car.

—Don't worry, I'll save a bit for myself.

But I don't think he ever did.

In two letters from early November, I told him that I had just reread the first two "Geschlecht" papers. I encouraged him to continue the series, remarking that perhaps at Essex he could gather up the threads of these pieces, which advanced the work he had done in *Spurs*. That book had Nietzsche as its subject, of course, and not Heidegger, but it seemed to me that Derrida was circling around the same set of issues. Which issues? Perhaps Heidegger's reluctance to face the question of "truth as a woman" in Nietzsche and his inability to hear "the lunar voice of the sister" in Trakl's poetry. My letter of November 8, 1985, promised to send him some notes on the second of the *Geschlecht* papers or, rather, on the typescript that he had given the participants in the Loyola colloquium, the typescript that became the first thirty pages of "Geschlecht III." These notes, actually sent on March 5, 1986, constitute perhaps the only important document that did not wind up in the IMEC Archive—at least, it was not among the sheaf of papers that Dichy gave me.

Yet even before sending these notes to Derrida, my letter recommended that he read volume 29/30 of the Heidegger *Gesamtausgabe*, the second half of which contains "a *long* discussion of animality, but also of individuation." I adjudged Heidegger's discussion "woefully inadequate," complaining that he "allows a regressive analysis of the 'apophantic *as*' to distinguish humanity from animality" and asserting that "the text *cries* for deconstruction." To explain: the apophantic *as* is, for Heidegger, what marks human language and thought, since only the human being sees the rock *as* a rock, the sun *as* the sun, whereas the lizard merely suns itself on the rock. However, I had always been struck by Heidegger's emphasis in *Being and Time* on the *derivative* character of this apophantic *as*, which is grounded in what he called the existential-hermeneutical *as* (SZ 158). The latter, if I am right, cannot so readily be denied other life-forms than the human. Derrida began at this point to study Heidegger's account of animality in the 1929–30 lecture course, and he never tired of showing how Heidegger's account of the apophantic *as* remains classically metaphysical and even theological in its presuppositions. Indeed, Derrida devoted the very last seminar of his life to that 1929–30 lecture course.

On an attached sheet to my letter, I typed out a passage from Heidegger's "Letter on Humanism," the essay that initially irritated but later pleased Arendt, a passage that stressed the "essential remoteness" of humankind from animals. If there is a "relationship with the animal,"

MH, Die Grundbegriffe der Metaphysik: Welt - Endlichkeit - Einsamkeit (F/M: V. Klostermann, 1983). MHG 29/30.

Je t'ai écrit, Jacques, sur le cours de 1929/30 à Fribourg, un an après le "1929" de Geschlecht I. Le cours a deux divisions principales, la première cherchant l'ennui profond comme Grund-Stimmung des Daseins. La seconde -- c'est étonnante -- est une discussion très détaillée du problème de l'organisme, de la vie en tant que détermination "biologiq On peut dire peut-être que MH recherche ici ce qui aura été avan la Streuung qui est Dasein. MH prend les analyses de Welt chez les animaux qu'ont fait Uexküll et Buytendijk. C'est fa tout ça, et je ne peux pas fait une sommation. Mais l'espe le plus étonnante, c'est que MH approche quelque chose de nou sur le Todesproblem. Voici des extraits:

Sur "Geschlechtstrieb" (pp. 363-4): "Eines der frappantesten Beispiele dieses eigentümlich beseitigenden Charakters in a Benehmen [des Tieres] ist das Verhalten der Insekten innerh des Triebkreises, den wir Geschlechtstrieb nennen. Es ist daß viele Weibchen nach der Kopulation das Männchen a Nach der Kopulation verschwindet der Geschlechtscharakter, Männchen hat den Charakter der Beute und wird beseitigt.... Benehmen als solches ist in sich je ein Beseitigen." [cf. Hegel, Nature!]

Sur la mort (pp. 387-8): "Es ist der Prüfstein für die Angemessenheit und Ursprünglichkeit jeder Frage nach dem Wesen d Lebens und umgekehrt, ob sie das Problem des Todes zureichend begriffen hat und in der richtigen Weise in die Frage nach dem Wesen des Lebens hineinzunehmen vermag.... Weil zum Wesen d Tieres die Benommenheit gehört, kann das Tier nicht sterben, sondern nur verenden, sofern wir das Sterben dem Menschen zusprechen."

Mais en même temps (p. 396) MH reconnait "eine wesenha Erschütterung [im] Wesen des Tieres" (c'est MH qui souligne et qu'on ne peut pas la comprendre "solange wir nicht das dit

continué p. 27

Fig. 7.4 Page 26 of Derrida's typescript of *Geschlecht III*, with my comments on the left.

mémoire qui garde que l'animalité dont il va être question se distingue de la simple bestialité. Néanmoins cette animalité oscille encore dans une certaine indétermination (im Unbestimmten). C'est en vue de ce passage décisif que j'avais cru devoir faire précéder cette"lecture" par celle d'autres textes de Heidegger au sujet de l'animalité. L'indétermination de l'animal tient à ceci que l'animalité n'est pas encore rentrée, revenue, rassemblée(eingebracht), "recueillie" dit la traduction française, dans son essence, dans"son :être propre"(Wesen). Cet animal, poursuit alors sans hésitation Heidegger, "à savoir l'animal pensant"(nämlich das denkende), l'animal rationale, l'homme n'est ... ... selon le mot de Nietzsche, pas encore arrêté (festgestellt)". Nous reviendrons plus tard sur cette référence à Nietzsche et à tel passage de Was heisst Denken, sur le passage, précisément,(Übergang) de l'homme à l'Übermensch et sur la détermination de l'animal rationale comme homme de la saisie(vernehmen)ou, une fois de plus, de la raison saisissante (Vernunft, vernehmen). Comme dans le cas des Greiforgane du singe, la prise s'opposerait au don pour définir l'animalité. Ici, la garde de la mémoire, qui définit l'animal"pensant" et l'éloigne de la simple bestialité, ne serait pas de l'ordre de la captation, de la prise ou de l'arraisonnement.

Lorsque Nietzsche dit que l'homme n'est pas encore arrêté, fixé, festgestellt, il n'entend pas quelque chose comme: pas encore"constaté"(konstatiert). Constaté, dit Heidegger, il ne l'est que trop et de façon trop décidée. Non, cela veut dire: l'animalité de cet animal n'est pas encore parvenue à son ferme établissement (ins Feste),"c'est à dire", traduit Heidegger, "nach Haus", in das Einheimische ihres verhüllten Wesens gebracht", parvenue "chez elle", "à la maison", au foyer de son essence voilée. Un certain rapatriement n'a pas encore eu lieu, car le chemin de cette destination est un chemin de retour, même si l'avenir même, la chance de l'avenir s'y joue comme l'aventure la plus risquée. Le lexique de la maison, de la patrie ou du foyer ne donne pas lieu à des images ou à des métaphores. J'ai tenté de l'expliquer ailleurs, au titre de la catastrophe de la métaphore[1] et comme il s'agissait justement de Heidegger, je n'y insiste pas.

---

[1]

indeed, an "embodied" relationship, that kinship is "abyssal and scarcely accessible to thought."[9] I filled the rest of the sheet with handwritten notes (in German) that did not shy away from telling Derrida what to do: "You must find the way to show how—no, whether and how—for Heidegger embodiment spells downgoing or decline." It is a wonder to me still that he was so patient with me. In any case, he could see that I was excited. A second sheet typed out two long quotations from *Being and Time* (SZ 373–74) on the theme of "birth," precisely the theme that was so important for Hannah Arendt. Not only are we "born," Heidegger seems to say, but we are "borne" by our birth throughout life: we are *gebürtig* in the sense that our birth is essential to our entire stretch of life, our mortality. Who can not have known that? Certainly, there has never been a mother who was ignorant of the fact. Yet the philosophers, at least those of my acquaintance, seem to have missed its significance for a millennium or two. I was trying to learn whether Heidegger was among them, or whether, despite his overestimating the power of language as *apophansis*, he had a sense of it.

When I look back at my rather brash and pushy letters to Derrida about all this, I am secretly gratified by one thing. I think that one of his very best meditations on Heidegger, one that appeared right in the middle of his work on "Geschlecht," did manage to weave the various threads of his readings of Heidegger into a remarkable tapestry. I mean, of course, the 1987 *Of Spirit: Heidegger and the Question*. More about that book shortly.

My letter of February 1, 1986, says that I have invited Hélène Cixous to the Essex meeting as well. For reasons I cannot remember, except that there was a schedule conflict—Cixous was as much in demand as Derrida was— she was unable to come. Because I teased Queen Nefertiti at the outset of the chapter, I want to add a more serious remark here. I cannot say that we became friends, because we have seen one another so rarely over the years. But there is a closeness that I find difficult to explain, and certainly, on my part, the greatest admiration. Cixous had gotten to know Derrida in 1964, some eight years before I met her and heard her speak so glowingly of him ("very soon I was forced to realize that he was really unique" [BP 179]), and, in part because of their mutual devotion to Joyce, "between his voyous and her consinnantes!" (FW 485), they became fast friends, and for a lifetime.

---

9 Martin Heidegger, *Wegmarken* (Frankfurt am Main: V. Klostermann, 1967), 157; BW 230.

Our paths, hers and mine, crossed only on the rarest occasions, but they were always grand occasions for me. I recall an evening in London that featured two speakers on the topic of psychoanalysis. The first speaker ranted about how horrible Freud was and how he needed to be badly beaten, and she did beat him, although her weapons of choice were all too familiar, the usual polemical cudgels. Then Cixous was called on to speak. She offered us a very serious and creative approach to psychoanalysis, one deeply informed by Lacan, Derrida, and, yes, Sigmund Freud, about whom she made only one complaint, in deference to her colleague: "Yes, of course, Freud is such a terrible, terrible uncle. But what can you do, he's family."

Cixous taught at Northwestern University for a semester while my daughter Salomé was a theater student there. We were able to see her privately many times during the fall and winter of 1995–96, Salomé and I, but never enough. We both attended her remarkable lectures, and neither of us has forgotten them. A typical lecture—they were on drama and theater, aimed specifically at young playwrights—would begin with Aeschylus and end with Dostoevsky and Chekhov, and each time with originality and extraordinary depth. I recall one lecture at which a student posed a question:

—Why in all your plays are there historical persons who appear on stage as living characters—but we know that they are dead, so how *can* they appear as living characters?

Hélène thought for a few moments. Then she issued what seemed to be a command.

—In every play that you write, *every* play, no matter what the theme, you *must* introduce dead persons onto the stage—otherwise, what chance have they got?

Cixous would later speak of the "very profound connivance" that had joined her and Derrida early on. That connivance had to do with a certain fidelity to the dead, "all that is still life with death inyeborn" (FW 585), but also with the companionship of the living. "Thanks to him, I had the feeling that I did not have to live exclusively in the company of the dead, the authors of the great texts I was reading" (BP 179). I saw Cixous most recently at Brown University, where I was visiting in the German Department. She gave a paper called "The Cry of Literature." It was not so much a "paper" but rather an event, an experience of what thinking can be but rarely is. At various moments in the lecture, always when the "cries" were most intense, Derrida appeared. It had been over a decade since his death. She called him only "Jacques," as I remember, so some of her listeners would not have known who she meant. I went down to see her afterward, but she was surrounded by dozens of students. I waited a long while but saw that it was hopeless. We looked at one another and smiled a bit sheepishly, and she shook her head slowly. She was wearing her Fidel Castro cap. The smile said, "We have to start meeting like this."

My book is called *Three Encounters*, but I am beginning to see lots of other people showing up in it. Heidegger, Arendt, and Derrida drew many fine folk into their orbit, and I reaped the benefit of that draw.

* * *

On April 7, 1986, I jotted into my journal:

> Derrida will be coming here [to Essex] in mid-May for a conference on Heidegger. It is a little over a year since I met him. I've since seen him twice, for three days in Paris during November, then for one evening a week later in London. The London meeting was a total frustration: Jacques among the sycophants (like me?), himself witty yet distant. But during the days in Paris he was wonderful, inviting us out to "La Coupole" in Montmartre, meeting for lunch in "Le Pub" on Gay-Lussac, me then attending a lecture of his on χώρα in Plato's *Timaeus*, him then coming to have a coffee with us and see us off.[10]

Allow me to enter some notes on the Essex colloquium, the details of which I can recall principally because of Derrida's preserving the letters and documents that I sent him. Michel Haar and Philippe Lacoue-Labarthe had canceled by early March, so there were seven presenters: Robert Bernasconi, Françoise Dastur, Derrida, John Llewelyn, John Sallis, Jacques Taminiaux, and David Wood. And, as it turned out, I did give a presentation of some kind, one that must have had to do with what became the book *Daimon Life*. The brochure that advertised the colloquium, a conference I kept quite small, inviting only our students and no more than thirty others from the world outside, said this:

> During the past twenty years some of the most thought-provoking readings of Heidegger have emanated from the French-speaking world. Why? Why *Heidegger*? And why *reading* Heidegger? What do these readings portend for the future of Heidegger studies? More important, what paths

---

10 I am uncertain who the "we" is here, but I believe it was my brother Jonathan, now an emeritus professor of French literature at the University of Georgia. Derrida's lecture on Plato's notion of the χώρα, which was the subject of one of my first publications and an abiding interest for me, is one of Derrida's finest efforts. See Jacques Derrida, *Khôra* (Paris: Éditions Galilée, 1993).

do these readings open for the future of what Heidegger called *thinking*? These are some of the questions the participants will raise, if only by implication: for the most part they will be presenting various aspects of their own recent labors in *reading Heidegger*. These aspects, plus the questions mentioned above, they will discuss with one another and with their guests. The Colloquium schedule will be arranged in such a way as to allow for informal exchanges, teas and meals, as well as for the formal sessions.

On April 11, 1986, Derrida wrote me from Yale about his contribution to the upcoming Essex meeting:

> A word, in all haste, as usual, because of the overload and the incessant pressure I am under here, which you know about.[11]
>
> First of all, to thank you for everything you've sent and your generosity. Second, to talk about my paper in May. I have not and will not be able here to do the detailed work, the research and writing, that I hoped to do and that would be necessary in order to pursue *Geschlecht III* or Heidegger's *Chora*. Later. Maybe so much the better. That will require me—that is the decision I have just made—to prepare for your colloquium a text that is more *direct*, more open to discussion, more "macrological," on the four or five major traits of my current "questions" to Heidegger, in other words, the things that keep me in motion with respect to him. Thus, in a general fashion, the manner in which I apprehend today my "relation to Heidegger," so to speak. I'll get to it as soon as possible, but most probably I'll be sending you from Paris, the only place I can really work, either (1) bits and pieces of it or (2) the whole thing (no more than twenty pages, promise), one week before the conference. But I'll try to send you a few things from here (where I have no typewriter, however . . .).
>
> There we are, in all haste, with the "culpability" that you can imagine. But I ask myself whether the necessity, the constraints, the lack of time that oblige me to speak in a more "straightforward" fashion about all these things might be a good thing, both for the colloquium and for me.
>
> Affectionately, and till soon—I'll be returning on the morning of April 29, etc.

I mentioned earlier, and more than once, Derrida's generosity. Let me add one or two more details gleaned from his letters. First, Derrida wrote

---

11 There was not only the "good" pressure, that is, the heavy workload and the demands of students, which Derrida was always happy to accept, but also a good deal of unpleasant pressure exerted by several members of the Yale faculty. A letter of mine dated April 17, 1986, says, "We have heard here that you will be heading for Irvine, California, with Hillis. How sad for the Yale students. But Yale hasn't appreciated *your* work enough."

to recommend several of his Yale students who were applying to the Collegium Phaenomenologicum, just as he was always generous about recommendations. Second, from the moment we met, he never failed to send me his books, or to have the publishers send them, as soon as they appeared. Third, as I stressed earlier, he never spoke about honoraria—his only request for the Essex colloquium was a room at the Wivenhoe House that had a telephone, and that was easy, even though the House was quite old: it was made famous by John Constable's painting of the mansion and the surrounding ponds and gardens, "something to write hume about" (FW 606), complete with cows. The telephones came later.

The Essex meeting, if I may say so, was a success. The papers were at the level I knew they would be, and the discussions were serious though not ponderous.[12] I recall the event's most exciting moment—apart from the chamber music that was played by local musicians at each of our suppers together. As the final speaker, Derrida outlined what was to become one of his major publications, the book *Of Spirit*, published in 1987. Already a year earlier, he had worked out the four "threads" that he was trying to weave into a *Geflecht*, a "weft" or "tapestry," or, if things went awry, a "tangle." *Geflecht* was a word that he liked a lot because it "rhymed" with *Geschlecht* in more than one sense. Those four threads were: (1) the major role that "questioning" plays in Heidegger, questioning being "the piety of thinking," which is what Heidegger called it at the end of his essay "The Essence of Technology"; (2) the difficult role that "essence" plays in Heidegger's thought, whereby "essence" is meant to be taken as a verb, not a noun, thus leaving us with the conundrum as to how Heidegger can insist that the verbal "essence" of *essence* is the *essential* essence; (3) the problem of "animality" in Heidegger, whereby animality is sharply distinguished from the realm of the human being; and (4) the problematic role that "epochs" play in Heidegger's history of being or *beyng*.

During the discussion after one of the papers, a discussion in which Derrida mentioned his difficulty with Heidegger's insisting on the eminence of the question and the *piety* of questioning, Françoise Dastur posed a challenge. She pointed out that some years after Heidegger's claim that *questioning* is "the piety of thinking," he explicitly stated in an essay on language that the crucial matter is not questioning as such but the "address"

---

12 Proceedings in *Research in Phenomenology* 17 (1987), reprinted in *The Oxford Literary Review* 43, no. 1 (Edinburgh University Press, 2021): 62–74.

Fig. 7.5 The main speakers at the "Reading Heidegger" conference at Wivenhoe House, University of Essex, in May 1986. From right to left: Robert Bernasconi, David Wood, John Llewelyn, Jacques Taminiaux, Jacques Derrida, John Sallis, Françoise Dastur, the author.

of the question, or the question's "claim" on us, along with our "assent" to that address or claim. Derrida listened carefully to Dastur's remarks. So carefully, in fact, that when he revised his paper for the later Paris conference on "Open Questions" regarding Heidegger, he composed what may be the longest footnote in the history of philosophy: six pages of the ninth chapter of *De l'esprit* have only four lines of text at the top, with the rest of the page devoted to an immense footnote that responds to Dastur's question. And this longest of all footnotes is dedicated to Françoise Dastur by name as thanks for her challenge, her "address." Their exchange at the Essex conference broke a long silence between them, since Dastur had been one of Derrida's first students, but who, since that time, had gone her own way.

I also recall two other exchanges between Derrida and colleagues at the Essex colloquium, exchanges that made me laugh. The first came from a young English colleague in the audience who confessed that he was "profoundly shocked" by Derrida's presentation, shocked precisely because he believed he understood it, which was not true when he read Derrida's texts.

—That's the reason I attend colloquia, replied Derrida.

Derrida went on to say that he intended to "open up" in a "straight-forward way" a number of questions in his reading of Heidegger; a written text, he confessed, is both "more protected" and "strategically more clever, more *rusé*."

—I thought for a long time I was listening to an Oxford analytical philosopher, replied his interlocutor.

At another point in the discussion, at the very end, as I recall, a participant asked whether there could be—despite the monstrous power of the negative in both Hegel and deconstruction—a thought of unity that would not suppress differences.

Derrida smiled and responded immediately.

—That is my dream. It is what I try to think. I can't avoid dreaming, of course. . . . But I try not to dream all the time.

* * *

My journal, after the Essex event, records the following:

> May 22, 1986
>
> We have had Derrida (and many others!) here this past weekend for a colloquium, "Reading Heidegger." The event was a great success, as such meetings go. The thrill for Marta and me was to have "Monsieur Jacques" here at the house for supper on Thursday, and afterwards a little get-together with the Sallises, Robert Bernasconi, and others. Derrida, urbane, equal to every occasion, yet with a fundamental reserve, a withholding that for me is the mark of a thoughtful human being. Easy with the children—our son Davidcito was thrilled with his pipe, "The house is on fire!" he cried—and easy with the adults as well. I had Derrida out here in my study and I showed him my prize fetish, the copy of Heidegger's *Nietzsche*.
>
> Chatting with him on the phone after his return to Paris, I confessed my affection for him, unnecessarily.
>
> —I feel as though I've known you for twenty years, I said.
>
> —You have, he replied.

This jotting deserves a few comments. "Fundamental reserve, a withholding" are perhaps the wrong words. "Reticence"? It is not that he was shy or diffident, although that is what Françoise Dastur tells me he was as a young instructor. Perhaps the right way to put it is that he was always prepared first of all to *listen*. And he was genuinely interested in people, so he never found it necessary to engage in the academician's sort of chat, which is most often pompous and vacuous, *tout pour le montre*, as Sartre says. As for his ease with children, my kids loved him, and in one of the best photos I have seen of him he is squatting beside a very happy little boy named Jean-Stéphane Naas, the son of my friends Michael Naas and Pascale-Anne Brault.

Interesting that I call my inscribed copy of Heidegger's *Nietzsche* "my prize fetish." I did not call it that back in chapter 3. Some disclosures take time. As for my having known Derrida for twenty years, even after only two years had passed, that made me laugh. Yet maybe it was a mark of the friendship. Friendship needs to pass the test of time, as Aristotle affirms, but it sometimes takes hold very quickly. How exactly did I "confess" my "affection" for him? My journal remains discreet, and my memory, ever faithful, does not embarrass me by remembering. There was something "filial" about that affection, even though Derrida was only fourteen years older than I. His brilliance may have added a decade or two to the calculation, however, and there was something about his "look" and his demeanor that did remind me of my father—I remember seeing or sensing that at the very outset, on that flight from Chicago to LaGuardia. Perhaps it was simply the generosity? Or a kind of openness and affection that I felt coming from him?

No sooner did the Essex colloquium end when planning for the summer Collegium in Perugia began. The topic for that year involved the Marburg lecture courses that Heidegger gave immediately before and immediately after the publication of *Being and Time*. My next letter to Derrida, on the last day of June, thanking him again for the Essex meeting and giving him directions to Perugia, was written on "Collegium Phaenomenologicum" letterhead. Apparently, he was on his way to Glasgow, but a phone call managed to catch him at home. It was always such a pleasure to speak to him by phone, even though phone calls in French are normally a nightmare for me. My French is impeccable, to be sure, even though the French insist on pretending not to understand it; and when I'm on the phone to France, the receiver emits into my ear nothing but globules of gelatin. In any case, the June letter suggests that during the final week of the Collegium, he will give us a seminar on the "guiding principles" that Heidegger proposes toward the end of his 1928 lecture course (26:171–77), which are the statements Heidegger makes on sexuality and which had been the subject of Derrida's first *Geschlecht* article. I won't go on about that, since this is a book of mere anecdotes (he promised, his hazel eyes blinking). Instead I will tell some stories about the Collegium.

THE INTIMATE HEIDEGGER; OR, GADAMER REVEALS ALL

Hans-Georg Gadamer was eighty-six at the time of his visit to the Collegium. He was the perfect guest, without any complaints or any special needs. He had had polio as a young man and had since then walked with a cane on very weak legs. I could not help but worry about him. At one point, we were climbing one of those narrow, steep stone stairways that you find in old Italian castles and monasteries, a stairway with high risers and no banister. As we mounted, slowly, with me behind him and alert, I was thinking about the worst thing that could happen. At the very top of the stairs, he turned to face me.

—You are very kind, he said. You are afraid that I am going to fall—but I am *not* going to fall!

Gadamer was an entertaining companion at mealtimes, full of good stories, a century of good stories. I remember sitting in an outdoor restaurant high above the cathedral square of Sienna, where the Palio race is run, enjoying a dry Pinot Grigio with him. It was not there, *privatissime*, that he told the story of the intimate Heidegger, however, but before the entire assembly of Collegium participants.

He told us that he had been a student of Nikolai Hartmann in Marburg when Heidegger arrived in 1924. From that point on, Gadamer was a student of Heidegger's. Yet Heidegger's fame as a teacher did not guarantee him a professorship. He needed a book. He had been working for years on what he was calling "the fundamental ontology of Dasein," which, by 1927, would become the book *Being and Time*. But even after his 1925 lecture course on the history of the concept of time, which he appropriately called a *Prolegomena*, since less than half the project was completed, Heidegger was not ready to publish the book. So much remained to be done!

Two years after Heidegger arrived in Marburg, said Gadamer, the dean of the faculty showed up at his office unannounced. Heidegger was sitting at his desk.

—You need to publish a book. We want to promote you, but you have to have a book. Do you have a book?

Silence.

—Do you have a book *manuscript*?

Gadamer paused, noting the dramatic effect his tale was having on his audience, many of whom were young people who did not yet have a book. He then continued.

—Heidegger did not say a word. . . . The dean was waiting for his response. . . . Then Heidegger *pulled open his drawers*—and there it was!

*   *   *

Mothers often came up in Derrida's and my conversations. His mother, a very beautiful woman and a wicked poker player, was ill with Alzheimer's during the mid-1980s, and he often talked to me about her. I remember his saying that at some recent point, his mother could no longer remember his name, so he felt he had lost that name forever.

—Do you still *have* a name if your own mother cannot remember it?

This was a source of acute suffering for him, as it would be for anyone. My mother, who remained alert up to the end, was in good health both times she met Derrida, and he always asked after her when the two of us met. Not simply politely inquiring, but asking with genuine care, it seemed to me.

During Derrida's second visit to the Collegium, in 1987, under the direction of Rodolphe Gasché, he was lecturing on Hegel and on his book *Glas*, "writing *Finglas*" (FW 625). I urged my mother to sit in on the lectures, even though she feared she would understand nothing. I reminded her that she had met him the year before and had found him charming. My mother was not a philosopher, even though she was amazingly well-read. After the lecture on Hegel and the problem of transcendentality in *Glas*, she leaned over to me.

—I *think* I was able to follow, except for one thing: what is the *quasi-transcendental*?

—You're doing all right, Mom, I replied.

But that was at their second meeting. A year earlier, when I introduced her to him, Derrida heaped praise on me and on a book of mine that had recently been published, which just happened to be lying there on the table. He picked it up and opened it to the final chapter, the eleventh, which I had dedicated to him. Its theme was Heidegger's reading of Trakl's poetry, my first effort on that theme, and its title was "Strokes of Love and Death." But Derrida read aloud and without pauses the chapter number, the title, and the dedication, as though they were a single sentence.

—Eleven strokes of love and death for Jacques Derrida. . . . Frankly, I prefer the strokes of love.

We laughed, and my mother, of course, beamed.

In general, Derrida radiated a warmth, an openness, and a sense of humor that put people at their ease. He did not tear down or humble; he built up and encouraged. No touch of the professorial about him—surely one of the reasons that stuffier academics hated him.

As my mother and I left his room and were walking down the hallway, she seemed lost in thought.

—David, she said, can he really be so brilliant—he is *so beautiful!*

I was shocked, I confess, and for two reasons. First, although she was a widow, and for some years by that time, she was a very proper woman, quite reserved, and I had never heard the likes of such a remark from her before. Second, and far more egregiously shocking, was the fact that my own mother, in the presence of her son the philosopher, could think that brilliance and physical beauty would have to be strangers to one another. I pointed, modestly, but with both hands, to myself. My mother laughed.

JACQUES DERRIDA, ROGUE FOOTBALLER

An even more devastating story pertains to the year of Derrida's second visit to the Collegium, in 1987. Jean-Luc Nancy, by the way, was entirely complicit. Derrida had wanted to be a soccer player all his life. In fact, as a young man, he was a pretty good footballer. When he and Jean-Luc Nancy got together on the beautiful grounds of the Casa del Sacro Cuore in Perugia, and when a foolish student offered them a soccer ball, they could not resist starting to play. And to compete. Now, I was not the director of the Collegium in 1987, so it was not my responsibility. Yet I knew from Derrida that Nancy had a very severe heart defect, and there he was, running around like a little kid. And Derrida? He got more and more into the game, as the sportscasters say. Nancy kicked a good one; Derrida kicked a better one. Nancy kicked a hard one; Derrida kicked a harder one. Nancy lobbed a high and a far one. Derrida, calling on all his skills and all his power, kicked a high and a far and a *hard* one, not a lobber, the ball sailing off the playing field like a line drive onto the porch of the Casa. We all heard the shattering noise.

The ball struck and destroyed a huge urn the size of a burial vase, what the Greeks call a *pithos*, but this was a Roman or Umbrian urn. And it looked to be *ancient* Roman or Umbrian, Etruscan. Fortunately, there was a tree planted in this vase, not a skeleton. Or, rather, the tree had been planted in the vase; now it lay sprawling on the porch. Rodolphe Gasché, the director, was nowhere to be found. I swear he was hiding. The woman who ran the Casa was famous for being fastidious about how the property should be treated. And it was not to be treated like this. I was in a state.

Luckily, the gardener rushed onto the scene.

—Quick, she's out on some errands, she'll be back in half an hour.

—What can we do?

—We'll replace it!

—An ancient Etruscan urn? How do we replace that?

It turned out that it was not so ancient, and the local nursery had one that looked almost exactly like it. She might never know. We heaved it onto the back of the little truck, sped back, and got it into place. We swept up the dirt and the shards and bucked up the tree, which was a bit bedraggled, as best we could. I never got my money back for that urn. Yet I did escape with my life.

And Derrida? He, too, like Rodolphe, ran and hid. He was nowhere to be found. And of course, the students made lots of bad jokes about deconstruction.

*   *   *

Perhaps that errant soccer ball was an omen. Yet the first fractured urn in our relationship had come in the aftermath of the Essex colloquium, the year before. Our exchange of letters tells the story. On September 28, 1986, I wrote:

> Dear Jacques,
>
> I'll be sending you (in a separate package) an edited version of your "Hesitations" with regard to Heidegger, that is, your Essex text.[13] I did begin, faithful to your orders (!), with a brief summary, a résumé. But frankly it was *impossible*: the whole thing got lost! I have therefore proposed that we reduce the text radically (from 140 pages to 40!), simplifying the presentation. I ask you, my friend, not to be vexed with me, I've worked like a fool (no, like a sage!), like Zarathustra's camel, and the result, believe me, is very fine. It is a text that ought to be published in *Research in Phenomenology*. It contains questions, affirmations, and hesitations that are *essential* with regard to Heidegger for all "Heideggerians"!!

13 I did not keep the text in question, unfortunately, but it must have been a transcription of a conversation between Derrida and a number of Yale students and faculty. Apparently, I used only Derrida's remarks and eliminated all the other contributions and questions. Glenn Gray would have cautioned me! For a recent transcription of that Yale conversation, see *Oxford Literary Review* 43, no. 1: 1–61.

As you can see, I am anxious about your response. . . . But let's do it this way: I'll take the text to John Sallis (I'm taking a trip to the U.S. between the first and the twenty-second of October). You would have the time to read the text once again, to change this or that as you see fit, sending the changes directly to John in Chicago. And if you prefer (perversely, extremely perversely) to terminate the process of publication, well, there will be time enough for that too. (But don't do it!)

I know that [the other participants in the Yale dialogue] would not object to my work and my "eliminations": better the text should survive in this way rather than disappear. (Oh, French is impossible: I mean, they won't object to my having discretely removed them, and they would feel worse if the whole project died—the note at the bottom of the page says it all, I think.)

I received the [published form of] *Mémoires: Pour Paul de Man*, and I thank you very much for it. I read it in Perugia, as you know, but I will read it again, and many times, since memory is my favorite topic, along with mourning.

Here is a little text on Nietzsche and Hölderlin with regard to Empedocles, a mere pleasantry. Hugs, my dear Jacques, etc.

The letter sounds nervous, and it had reason to be. Here is Derrida's reply of October 13, 1986:

Dear David,

I've just returned from the States, more exhausted than ever, and plagued by various urgent matters, academic or otherwise, Parisian or otherwise. I can't go on.

I was happy to have your *Postponements*, which you showed me and let me peek into in Perugia. All these signs of commemoration moved me very much. In addition, there is your text on "Nietzsche, Hölderlin, Empedocles," which I will be happy to read soon.

But I'm writing you quickly, in spite of the overload and the fatigue, that what you thought you were allowed to do with the Essex paper is *a big surprise and a big concern* for me. I haven't read it yet, and I don't doubt that you have drawn together the best part of this singular work, but it was quite clear, I believe, that it is not at all what I had hoped and what the two of us had clearly agreed upon. I am sorry that you did not consult me before launching into the adventure of all that work. For *in no case could I agree to a text from which the contributions of my friends at Yale have been eliminated.* That would be very disloyal, altogether unjust to them. In passing let me say that it was not only [one individual] but three others who worked on the transcription, translation, and editing of the interview. I have to tell you quite clearly, and in friendship, that *I do not give my permission* to publish this text. And I prefer to tell you this now, before even having studied your version closely. It is a matter of principle, which has nothing to do with the quality of your work, which I do not doubt. I am sticking to the terms of our agreement, which were very clear: I agree to your publishing a schematic résumé (two or three pages), explaining that to the reader and the nature of my remarks. And I reserve the right to publish, later, if possible, a version of the whole thing, written by me and respecting the work with which my friends have been allied [?].

Can you send me a word about this or call me once you've returned from the States so that we can make again the agreement that I thought we already had?

Pardon me for this hasty and ill-written letter. I'm taxed, and I'm on the eve of some conferences, a trip to Berlin, etc. I'll be here, dependably here, after October 23. With affection, your friend, Jacques.

I suspect that after receiving this letter I called him immediately, although I am not sure of this. In any case, on October 30, 1986, I wrote a surprisingly relaxed reply, so I suppose we must have talked things through. "Here is the text of my brief résumé of your remarks at Essex—it has been reduced to three pages of *Research in Phenomenology*, I believe. If you have problems with it, don't hesitate to call me or write. The text of the discussion will arrive soon: John Sallis's secretary is preparing the typescript now. Your friend, etc. P.S.: I hope you will have had the time to read in my *Postponements*— I'm a bit "in suspense"! But I know that you are very, very busy!"

* * *

My journal contains some comments on the Paris conference, "Heidegger: Open Questions," at which Derrida presented his paper—no, not a paper; rather, a monograph—on "spirit" in Heidegger. Emmanuel Levinas also attended this conference and gave a paper, the final paper, I believe. Derrida and I sat together during Levinas's paper, and so both papers play a role in my note. I will try to explain some of the obscurities of the note after presenting it.

> March 15, 1987
>
> A conference at the Collège Internationale de Philosophie in Paris this week, with many excellent papers, and topped by an extraordinary paper on Heidegger by Derrida called *De l'esprit*. The Cour Poincaré was filled (five hundred people?), and the reception of the paper by the group was, I think, overwhelmingly positive. At least Michel Haar, Philippe Lacoue-Labarthe, and I thought so. Levinas, on Thursday evening, seemed weak and distracted; he presented a rehash from photocopies of already published texts.

Had lunch with Derrida on Friday. He was extraordinarily generous, as always, quite straightforward and candid. I began by asking him whether I had committed a sort of *faux pas* with Levinas the night before—Levinas was nervous and irritated when I handed him a description of our Essex meeting. [My notes say "invitation," but that is obviously a mistake; perhaps I had a sort of "poster" or printed description of the Essex meeting, which had occurred nine months earlier.] Jacques assured me that it had nothing to do with me, said that Levinas was aging, getting jumpy, unable to concentrate, and that he was disturbed by his new popularity, feeling pressed on all sides—that was Derrida's impression. He said that he had last seen Levinas that past summer and that he had sadly deteriorated in the meantime.

He described Levinas's behavior on the telephone as extraordinarily anxious: he would keep shouting *Hallo? Hallo?* as though afraid that the other party would hang up. I asked Derrida whether he had been thinking of Levinas while describing Bloom waiting on the phone or, earlier on in *Ulysses*, trying to call from that phone—*"Bloom is at the telephone, he said"*—and he laughed warmly but said firmly *no*, he had not been thinking of Levinas.

The tone of our conversation lightened as we spoke of other less interesting characters.

I interrupt to say that I remember this conversation about "other less interesting" people quite clearly. He mentioned the name of a philosopher in the English-speaking world whom he had recently encountered, one whom I have always regarded, charitably, as a dolt. Did I know him?

—Yes, I replied.

And he:

—*Mais, David, il est mauvais!*

And I:

—*Oui, Jacques, je sais!*

And he:

—*Mais, David, il est simplement mauvais!*

And I:

—*Oui, oui, il est mauvais! Aussi très ambitieux.*

And he:

—*Mais, il est mauvais!*

I believe that because the dolt in question and I both shared the English language, Derrida anticipated that I would rise to his defense. He continued to say the same thing, "Bad! bad! he's simply bad," but he never did tell me what unfortunate occurrence lay behind this newly won insight of his. I could only imagine. But a thousand possibilities did occur to me. I am certain that Derrida did not mean that this colleague had merely presented a bad paper at some conference or other. We all do that. No, there was at least the suggestion of a kind of pomposity, charlatanism, or bad faith. In any case, I return now to my notes, which continue to be mildly critical of others:

> We also spoke of *x*, who had offered an absurd display of empty talk at the conference. Derrida portrayed him as a juggler of concepts desperately trying to rearrange things in order to make a space for himself. Jacques illustrated by manically, hysterically, shuffling about every object on the table—beer bottles, glasses, forks, knives, and spoons, first here then there then back to their original place. He kept it up for a long time, reducing me to hysteria as well. When I went to take a sip of my beer, I paused in confusion.
>
> —Hey, is this *my* beer?
>
> —I make no guarantees!
>
> His lecture at the amphitheater Poincaré—about three hours and ten minutes long—was masterful. Intense, subdued at first, rising to dramatic heights when the "quotation marks" surrounding the words *Geist* and *geistig*, "spirit" and "spiritual," lift after 1927 [that is, after *Being and Time*], rising like a stage curtain in the 1933 Rectorate Address upon the drama of the spiritual-historical *Führer* principle. His voice weakened just a bit at the end, his mouth obviously dry, but his energy never flagged. The intensity of a thinking in full command of itself—but as far removed from dogmatism as a sense of humor alone can take us.

Some explanations. First of all, concerning my reaction to "Of Spirit," I wrote Derrida on March 16, saying "for me, your paper wasn't exactly a paper but one of the greatest events of my life." Even in retrospect, that does not seem like hyperbole. I knew that Lacoue-Labarthe shared my enthusiasm. As for Michel Haar's becoming convinced about the quality of Derrida's work, let me tell the rather complicated story.

Jealousy is a Terrible Thing

Michel Haar was a careful scholar of Heidegger's and Nietzsche's works, and his books are still among the best that we have.[14] For a long time, he

---

14 See, for example, Michel Haar, *Heidegger and the Essence of Man*, trans. William McNeill (Albany: State University Press of New York, 1993); Michel Haar, *The Song of the Earth: Heidegger and the Grounds of the History of Being*, trans. Reginald Lilly (Bloomington: Indiana University Press, 1993); Michel Haar, *Nietzsche and Metaphysics*, trans. Michael Gendre (Albany: State University Press of New York, 1996).

resisted affirming the same of Derrida, and this had created tension between us. About a year before the Paris conference, I had joined him and a third interlocutor in an exchange about Derrida. Michel and the other colleague were scornful, saying that Derrida was simply dying to be Maurice Blanchot, but that he could not be, so his entire life was a failure. On and on in that vein. I remained silent for a long time. They finally asked me what I thought, and I gave my response only after some hesitation.

—Jealousy is a terrible thing.

Both men immediately understood what I meant—and that I was not referring to Derrida and Blanchot. Michel was upset, and the other conversant never spoke to me again for the rest of his life. Michel and I patched things up, so when Derrida's lecture "Of Spirit" was scheduled for an evening of the "Open Questions" conference, he agreed, after some initial resistance, to attend it with me. We sat together, alongside Lacoue-Labarthe. If I remember correctly, only one of the five hundred people in attendance left the hall before Derrida's lecture ended.

After those three hours and ten minutes, or perhaps four hours and ten minutes, I no longer recall, Michel and I were walking back to his residence in the sixth arrondissement. On the way there, not yet speaking with one another, really a bit stunned, we were crossing a street that opens onto the Place du Panthéon. Crossing, I have to say, and risking our lives—the traffic was horrendous and insanely speedy. Normal Parisian traffic, in other words. Right in the middle of that street, Michel stopped, cars whizzing by him left and right, honking but otherwise perfectly willing to take his life. He stood there for a long time—meanwhile, I had found my way to safety. When he finally joined me on the curb, his head dropped to his chest. He spoke very quietly.

—*Bon. Bon. . . . Il est un génie.*

*   *   *

A further word about Levinas, whom I had not met before. On the last day of the "Open Questions" conference, as Derrida and I entered the hall, he was already seated at the table up on stage. But when he saw Derrida, he got up from his chair and rushed off the stage and stormed up to him.

—What are you doing here? What are you doing here? You should be at home working!

Derrida smiled sheepishly and shrugged his shoulders. He introduced me, and Levinas greeted me and shook my hand but immediately went back to scolding Derrida. It seemed more than the usual way one scolds a colleague, letting them know that they should not be wasting their time attending a paper of yours but also that you are secretly happy to see them there. Clearly, Levinas *was* happy to see him, but the scolding was nonetheless intense.

The meeting got underway. Levinas presented his remarks. Among the points he made, a familiar one was that Heidegger was so concerned about one's *own* existence—since Dasein is *in each case my own*—that he was never able to develop the idea of *sacrifice* for the sake of another human being. After the paper, Derrida raised his hand to ask a question. Levinas recognized him. Derrida asked his question in the style he regularly employed, respectful, slow, carefully formulating the matter, although not taking an eternity and four hands to do it. He asked, if I may reduce the question here to its simplest form, whether *sacrifice* could have any meaning at all, any *value* at all, if existence were not indeed in each case *my own*. Is not what Heidegger calls *Jemeinigkeit* actually at the heart of any possible sense of sacrifice?

Levinas's response was astonishing. He smiled broadly, bobbed his head up and down, swiveled back and forth in his chair. And said nothing. Finally, he raised his two hands, palms upward. It was the most eloquent answer to a question I have ever seen.

There is one more exchange I ought to report. A young woman who was seated in the same row as Derrida and I, but farther over to the right, began her question with a long comment. She started by castigating Heidegger in a way that by that time had become familiar, citing his involvement in National Socialism, his silence after the war, his complicity, and her question was whether anyone should bother reading Heidegger any longer.

This time Levinas did not swerve and bob. He spoke sharply, even aggressively. I cannot put English words into his mouth, but he said in no uncertain terms that Heidegger was *the* great thinker of the twentieth century and that she should be careful about consigning him to oblivion. He went on in that vein, and I remember looking over and seeing the questioner distraught, even trembling. It had been one of those questions a young person asks when they want to ingratiate themselves with a speaker, and it is a terrible thing for them when the question backfires or boomerangs. Levinas's ethics of the other clearly did not mean letting the other get away with what he judged to be disrespect.

I asked Derrida about this incident afterward, flummoxed by Levinas's desire to *protect* Heidegger from the sort of sacrifice the young woman was making of him, and I remember Derrida's saying that there were "a lot of Levinases," a remark he would have grounds to repeat to me later that year.

* * *

While I am on the theme of ingratiating questions that boomerang and hurt the questioner, my journal encourages me to digress, because the very next entry, dated May 8, 1987, continues on that same theme of boomerangs. It is about the then-recent visit to Essex of Luce Irigaray. She had come to give us a paper on Levinas. The paper was sharply critical of Levinas's treatment of sex and gender issues, a treatment that she felt was far too restrictive and far too patriarchal. What struck me most about her paper was its emphasis, not so much on the feminine as such, but on the role of the *flesh* in general: protect the memory of the flesh! she seemed to cry. My notes say, "to create an alchemy of representations beyond both patriarchy and matriarchy, to find divinity in the carnal encounter of the lovers, *l'amant* et *l'amante*, not the *aimée*." The plea was to allow women as well as men to be active lovers, and not merely to be consigned to the passive "beloved." My notes say that her paper was "remarkably strong and beautiful." Beautiful, too, and memorable were the breakfasts I had with Irigaray at the Wivenhoe House over the several days that followed her paper. Among the things we talked about was her book on Heidegger, *Oblivion of the Air*. The book poses many questions and challenges to Heidegger, among them questions about his interpretation of "boyhood" in his second Trakl essay, "Language in the Poem." Yet what struck me during our breakfast conversations was not the challenges posed in her book but her account of the book as a work of mourning. That was her word: *le deuil*. She told me that she began to write the book on the very day she learned of Heidegger's death on May 26, 1976. The book did not appear until several years later, but for her it remained a kind of critical eulogy and, above all else, a work of mourning.

That is the necessary presupposition for understanding what happened at a supper we arranged for Irigaray after her paper at Essex. Robert Bernasconi and I invited some colleagues to join us who we knew were dedicated to Irigaray's work. Among them was a professor of French at a neighboring institution. At one point in the table talk, the professor made a frivolous remark about Heidegger—presumably to ingratiate herself with Irigaray, whom she took to be irate about men like Heidegger. I cannot remember either the context or the precise remark, but I remember that it was the sort of supercilious observation that academics often believe they can make with impunity.

Irigaray put down her fork and knife. She asked the woman whether she was familiar with Heidegger's work. The woman explained that her field was French studies, not Heidegger studies. Irigaray replied that it is invariably a good idea not to comment on things one knows nothing about. Robert and I pushed the peas around on our plates.

These French folk can be pretty tough. Yet also very kind and very generous. Irigaray wrote me a long and gracious letter on January 13, 2000, thirteen years after our Essex breakfasts. I had written to invite her to address the Society for Phenomenology and Existential Philosophy at its next meeting. Unfortunately, I no longer have a copy of my letter, but I must have referred in some detail to our conversations about Heidegger and her work of mourning for him. She reconfirmed her critique of Levinas in the letter ("he does not *really* appreciate the other very much," she wrote) and her appreciation of Heidegger. She was thinking, she said, of beginning yet another text on Heidegger's thinking. As for the invitation to fly to the States, she graciously declined for the reason that she had decided—for ecological concerns—to stop flying altogether. "I am certain that someone who appreciates Heidegger won't reproach me for wanting to respect the sky! And, since making that decision, I love the sky more and more—how can I ever get on another airplane?"

Irigaray's contribution to feminist theory has remained powerful over the past half century, although it has encountered strong criticism along the way. Some critics decided that she was an "essentialist" and that she, presumably like Derrida in this respect, was "not political enough." It is true that Irigaray has always tried to touch on "essential" differences between women and men, and those differences are so much of the *flesh*, so much about the body, especially the female body and all its remarkable lips and folds, that I cannot help but think that our Anglo-American Puritanism, concealing itself behind something more intellectually respectable, once again has gotten the better of us. As for being "not political enough," it strikes me that Irigaray is a philosopher, a genuine philosopher, the real thing, along with being a poetic and powerful writer. That seems to me enough for one person.[15]

15 As I was writing these remarks, on August 14, 2020, some twenty years after our last communication—those two decades intervening not because of any difficulty between us but simply because life (= everydayness) swallows us all—Luce Irigaray wrote me to ask if I would join her and several other philosophers in a project challenging the role of the "neuter" and the "neutral" in philosophy, with special emphasis on Heidegger. Of course, I said *yes*. Irigaray continues to be one of the most remarkable voices in contemporary European thought. See her *Challenge to a Fictitious Neutrality: Responses to Heidegger* (London: Palgrave Macmillan, 2022).

Fig. 8.1 Derrida at DePaul University, Chicago, in April 1991. He is sixty-one. Photo by Amy Rothblatt.

8

LIFEDEATH—OR, FOLLOWING
THE ANIMALS

In May 1987, I received from Derrida a copy of *Feu la cendre*, both as a printed text and in recorded form, read by him and Carole Bouquet. I was very moved by this theme of cinders, the most friable form of the trace, perhaps because it reminded me so much of Nietzsche's speculations on the cosmos as consisting of the ashes of once-living things. In my letter responding to the gift of *Feu la cendre*, I cited a number of passages from Nietzsche's unpublished notes, notes taken up into the book *Postponements* that developed the thought of ashes. I seem to have forgotten that by 1980, in the *Envois* of Derrida's *Post Card*, the theme of conflagration, cinders, and ash had already come to the fore. In any case, Derrida seemed to be increasingly occupied with Nietzsche's notes on the fundamental ambiguity of life and death in the universe—of what Yeats had called "death-in-life and life-in-death," and what one might even dare to call *lifedeath*, "my life in death companion," as though life and death were fused or could be confused with one another.[1]

The companionship of life and death is not merely a bookish invention, even though books also seem to tell the tale. In February 1987, the faculty of the University of Essex nominated Derrida to become a "Doctor of the University," along with the renowned Mexican writer Carlos Fuentes. (As it turned out, the two men had never met, and they spent the entire awards day in June conversing with one another like old friends.) My journal records a few aspects of Derrida's visit, but it does not mention a birthday gift

---

1 See William Butler Yeats, "Byzantium," in *Complete Poems*, 243; and for "my life in death companion," see FW 201.

that I presented him with on that occasion—a first edition of Heidegger's *Sein und Zeit*, one of two that I had managed to acquire many years earlier. I decided that it should go to the best reader of that book I had ever known. It was strangely moving for me when, quite recently, I saw the book once again at an exhibition of Derrida's personal library organized by Katie Chenoweth at Princeton University. I remembered that Derrida had said very little when I gave it to him. He knew full well how rare the book was, and "the economy of the gift" was something that had haunted him for decades. Having that volume in my hands again so many years after Derrida's death, then surrendering it to the collection once again became for me in an uncanny way a marker of my own death. Although I had not really thought it through, that first edition of *Sein und Zeit*, the very book Heidegger gave to his mother as she lay dying, reminded me of my signed copy of the book: my children would have to figure out how to deal with it and with all those books of mine. How to dispose of them? Would they go to some library? But libraries do not accept books anymore: they are removing books and bookshelves to make space for computers and carrels and coffee corners. *La fin du livre*. The book itself as a marker of the end, the last page, full stop, *finis*. Unless: "You do not have heard? It stays in the book of that which is" (FW 570).

But my mind wanders. Here is the journal note about Derrida's visit to Essex for the conferral of the honorary degree:

> July 16, 1987
>
> Jacques arrived yesterday, the day of his fifty-seventh birthday, for today's degree conferment as "Doctor of the University." On the way home from Heathrow I was doing my best to avoid the lorries on the M25 (the "M" stands not for Motorway but "Murder Way"), when he told me something extraordinary.
>
> I had asked him about *Mutterbindung*, "the maternal bond," thinking of what Goethe says about the importance of that relation for the artist, the mother's unwavering support. He told me about certain of his own obsessions—that was his word—in this regard. His own relation to his mother, who has never had any understanding at all of his academic work, he thinks may be dominated by the fact that his mother lost an infant boy (at several months of age) a year or so before his own birth. Jacques is therefore a sort of *Ersatz* son, threatening to disappear too at any moment. He remembers a very beautiful figure hovering over him as the doctors threatened to operate on his mastoid bone after a series of bad ear infections. He remembers her tears and lamentations and—after the operation is postponed—her rejoicings. Ever since his youth Jacques thinks of himself at least once a day, or

several times, especially when driving, in the future perfect tense: his own death in the eyes of others, he the bereaving-bereaved.

He also told me a more complicated story, a story of pipes that were not pipes (as in Magritte's "Ceci n'est pas une pipe"), pipes that passed in some way between fathers and sons, pipes that were lost or broken, pipes that were repaired and "replaced" by simulacra, which were of course not the originals. The one detail I recall is that one day his favorite pipe (was it a gift from his father? from his son?) disappeared from his study—disappeared forever, as it turned out. That was the day he learned of his father's death.

A note sketched two weeks later expands this last story a bit:

> Perugia, July 25, 1987
>
> The story of paternal death, continued. I talked with Jacques about mourning (Rebecca Comay tells me I must read *Fors* immediately!) and about my not having seen my father in my father's corpse. [I arrived late, from Germany, after my father's death in the States; when I first saw him, what I saw was his oldest brother, my Uncle Nick; it was as though my father were wearing a mask, the "Krell" mask, the same for all the brothers.] Jacques told me of his own father's death in Algeria—of the body being laid out on the stone floor in order to finish the dying; he told me of the sheet covering the body and of the rabbis who stopped him when he bent over to raise the sheet from his father's face. The implication of the story was that his was an *unsuccessful* mourning, involving incorporation rather than introjection. Yet this is the only mourning that respects otherness, therefore the only *successful* mourning.

My journal note is, of course, quite mistaken. Derrida's father died in Nice, not in Algeria. Aimé Derrida died of pancreatic cancer on October 18, 1970, after two wretched months of misdiagnosed illness. Benoît Peeters notes the uncanny happenstance that Derrida himself would die of the same disease at exactly the same age as his father (BP 273). Am I therefore also to doubt the story of the stone floor and of the veil that dare not be raised? I do not know. But what remains strong in my memory is the devastation in the son as he recounted to me, years and years after the fact, the death of his father. It was a prime case of impossible mourning, which, in Derrida's view, is the only faithful mourning—hence, whatever Freud may say, the only "successful" mourning.

* * *

The year 1987 was filled with controversies. There was the revelation of the late Paul de Man's early journalistic writings, which contained antisemitic slurs of the worst kind, slurs the enemies of "deconstruction" were elated to find. De Man's Yale students were distraught over this, as was Derrida. For in the intervening years, Paul de Man had become an intimate friend of Derrida's (BP 405). Simultaneously came Farías's publication of *Heidegger and Nazism*, which unleashed yet another phase of the Heidegger Scandal. The Heidegger discussion was in full swing already by March of that year, when the colloquium "Heidegger: Open Questions" was held in Paris.

Derrida's relation to de Man was surely not "filial," and yet de Man's death, soon followed by those disclosures of his early antisemitism, was a severe blow for Derrida. This I remember clearly. Closer to a son-father relationship was his bond with Levinas. It therefore became a problem between us that I was so negative about Levinas's philosophy. I had attended at Essex the sympathetic and insightful lectures by Robert Bernasconi on Levinas and had tried to read Levinas's *Totality and Infinity* and *Otherwise than Being*, without much success. What others took to be an ethics of the face-to-face encounter, I took to be the usual sort of moralizing and policing typical of ethical discourses. In other words, I could feel the violence coming down "from on High," so that I could not accept the putative "peace" and ostensible "nonviolence" of the "face-to-face" encounter that others were celebrating.

A disagreement ensued between Derrida and me over Levinas's work—or at least over the work's intentions—during a meeting at Vanderbilt University sponsored by Charles Scott. Scott had invited me to attend the conference on Levinasian ethics, which was scheduled for the first week of October 1987. I tried to get out of it, explaining to Scott my inability to read Levinas with sympathy, but he insisted.

—Krell, I invited you—you comin' or ain'tcha?

Three weeks before the conference, I had the double pleasure of being in Paris and having lunch with Derrida and some members of his family. After lunch, I lowered the tenor of the conversation by rehearsing all my difficulties with the Levinasian text and what I take to be its characteristic forms of "religious" violence. Derrida listened quietly, drew slowly on his pipe, nodded sympathetically, noncommittally. My tirade abated, the confession ceased. I waited, knowing that good counsel would be forthcoming. Derrida smiled his imp-of-the-perverse smile and said, "You have three weeks, David, what are you going to do?"

What I did was to prepare a slideshow of Michelangelo's "The Last Judgment" and a text I called "Infinite Violence." (Before my departure on September 26, I sent Derrida a copy of my paper, albeit without the slides.) Neither the paper nor the slideshow was ever published. I suppose that is fortunate, even though Michelangelo's fresco still enthralls me, and the paper, alas, still convinces me. "The Last Judgment" shows all the saints, including Peter and Paul, in terror, as the Judge threatens to send every soul to Hell. One of those saints, Bartolomeo, holds in his left hand the flayed skin—ostensibly his own—that seems to be a portrait of Michelangelo and that does not look at all like Bartolomeo. The bartering saint wields in his right hand the flaying knife in a gesture that seems to threaten the Judge or even the Judge's demure Mother—precisely as the Judge's raised right hand seems to be threatening *all* souls with damnation. The scene, in other words, is one of infinite violence. The fresco encapsulated for me the meaning of all religions of the Book: in this case, the Book of the Damned, as Michelangelo depicted it, looked like the New York City telephone directory, whereas the Book of the Saved was a Lilliput Edition. To make matters worse, or better, I used Derrida's "Violence and Metaphysics" to support my argument, used it one-sidedly, namely, at those moments where the essay worries about the violence of every "vertical," every appeal to the "on High." For to follow the commands issuing from "on High," the human head has to be jerked back violently at the neck—*à la nuque rompue* was Derrida's phrase.

My underlying thesis was that ethicoreligious discourse is invariably characterized by rancor and reaction, indeed, that it is *infinitely* reactive. As for "Violence and Metaphysics," I stressed the way, for Derrida, philosophical questioning involves a "double affirmation," that is, an anticipatory "yes" to the "yes, I am asking you to respond." Yet can affirmation really have anything to do with submission to the law, to summons, command, and commandment? Perhaps the boldest or most outrageous claim of the paper was that the so-called face-to-face encounter in Levinas cannot be face-to-face if the heads of the two are jerked back by a command from the "Most High." Such a face-to-face would in fact be a perversion, a defacement—in some frightening way portrayed in the flayed skin by which Bartolomeo is trying to barter the skin of an other for his own salvation.

Not wanting to be entirely negative at a conference on ethics, and in the company of friends, I decided to propose a different sort of ethical discourse, one that did not subject human beings to the commandments of some vertical power. I cited the "desperado philosophy" of Melville's Ishmael and the ethics that such a philosophy could affirm, along with a more ecstatic vision of ethical discourse, from chapter 94, "A Squeeze of the Hand." The discussion after my paper and slideshow was heated, to say the least, whether because of my accusation of "defacement" against Levinas or my Melvillean alternative, I do not know. I was roundly condemned by the Christian clergy who were present, and Derrida, while not condemning, was nonetheless worried by the way I had made him complicit in my analysis. Charles Scott took detailed notes during the discussion between Derrida and me after the paper, and, thanking Scott, I reproduce them here in abbreviated form. They show Derrida's evident consternation—even if he begins with a squeeze of the hand:

> You say we will not agree, will not be able to agree—but I do agree: let's squeeze hands. Squeeze! But who is perverse? You are the one who is using a logic of perversity. You use only my text on Levinas. You have no face-to-face with Levinas himself. Now I begin to feel responsible for Levinas! You use me to charge Levinas so terribly. The logic is very, very perverse. Squeeze!
>
> You prefer the ruse of the artist over the ruse of the priest. How are we to understand that? Do we understand the artist and the priest? I will return to this question.
>
> A word about affirmation and the question. For me, *double* affirmation is the structure of affirmation itself. There is no affirmation without the possibility of questioning, and questioning involves some degree of faithfulness to the question. In the case of Heidegger, for example, the *Zu-sage* is in language itself, in the very acceptance of language. My own affirmations are ways of keeping the questions.
>
> But to return now to the artist and the priest. You use Nietzsche and Bataille to break the circle of reappropriation, to break the return to the same, the closed circle. Levinas too wants to break closed circles. Is the priestly Levinas the only Levinas? Is it fair to remain with the rejection of the priestly Levinas? There are many Levinases.
>
> Is it not the case that infinite violence as such is not flat and boring, but, on the contrary, devilish and interesting? Isn't this dimension of Levinas interesting—and not so uninteresting as you charge his work to be? As the piety turns into the opposite of piety—that is interesting! Levinas's violence cannot be reduced, but it can be turned. . . .
>
> What in Levinas's text can be assimilated to the figure of the priest? He intends to leave no possibility for the priest in the face-to-face. We need to find out what the place of the priest is in Levinas's text, that is, of the Jewish priest—which is a very different matter from the Christian

priest. Levinas attempts to overcome inwardness and interiority in the face-to-face. In that sense, he is in league with Nietzsche. At all events, is there not a limit to genealogical critique, which is precisely a critique of interiority?

As to the question of sacrifice: first, are you, David, against any sacrifice at all? second, in Levinas isn't there a sacrifice of God? Is not God otherwise than being? Is not this sacrifice interesting and worth pursuing? Do not forget that there are many who regard Levinas as an atheist. I read Levinas with the hypothesis in mind that he sacrifices God.

Finally, with regard to the logic of infinite violence: What can "infinite reaction" mean? Is not all reaction finite? The logic of reactivity cannot be applied to the "infinite" in Levinas's sense. Furthermore, Levinas's infinite is of the relation with the other—it is not Bataille's infinite. And in any case, in Bataille there must be commandment and law, for there is pardon.

And so, I do agree. Let's squeeze hands. I am interested in Levinas precisely because I am interested in these violent passions.

I have no idea how I may have replied to any of these responses on the spur of the moment. We continued to talk about it all back at the hotel. He said he understood completely what my worries were, and that he shared those worries. But he repeated that there were many Levinases, and that I had to be fair to all of them. Levinas was not really interested in *ethics*, Derrida repeated. He was interested in *sanctity*.

That word did not help me, especially because the Judge, at least in Michelangelo's version, was sending all the sanctified to Hell, or so it seemed to this observer. In my jaded (or realistic) view, all the talk in Levinas of widows and orphans and goodness and sanctity amounted to the usual clichés of organized religions everywhere, whereas what underlay it all was the hand that grips the head of the others *à la nuque rompue*. *Cliché* was the word I had used repeatedly in my paper, which complained that the bland piety of religious discourses could not conceal their violence. It was this accusation of *cliché* that most disturbed Derrida, and he forced me to admit that "infinite violence" would certainly take us beyond the realm of platitudes.

Our discussion, Derrida's and mine, never really came to an end. After receiving Charles Scott's notes, I sat down to write out some thoughts, which I need not present here. Clearly, I did mail them to Derrida, because in his next letter to me he refers to my desire, as my final paragraph says, to "drop the knife," meaning both the flaying knife of Bartolomeo and my attack on Levinas's "face-to-face" as defacement.

The next letter from him, on November 7, 1987, takes up the themes of the de Man and the Heidegger scandals, along with our discussion of Levinas's thought.

> Thank you, dear David, for having written—and for what you write. A word, first of all, about the subject of Paul de Man: after long and difficult discussions [*tractations*] with the "friends" of de Man who were not present in Alabama,[2] we are finding our way to a solution: divide the materials into two different time frames and into two volumes, the one dedicated to the calm and clear publication of texts by de Man, the other dedicated to an open discussion (including those who take themselves to be "enemies"). But I cannot go into detail here about the whole process so far, up to the moment. If something serious comes up (. . . . .).[3]
>
> I'm very happy for your having responded so patiently and so generously on the subject of Levinas, or, rather, of your having taken the trouble to prolong our discussion and my rather impulsive and not very coherent remarks improvised at Nashville. I believe I understand, and I myself am quite split, quite divided. If "goodness," with Levinas, were simply a cliché, do you think his discourse would seem so fascinating at least to those people who are not the sort of amateurs who deal in clichés?
>
> Reading you, I ask myself, What does he mean by "soon," when he says, "the only difference is that I will *soon* drop it (the knife)." How soon? When? At the end you do drop it, at least you say you drop it, at least for me, at last: thank goodness! No difference any more. But we will continue this *Gespräch* [conversation] without letters. Letters are becoming impossible for me.
>
> Do you know about the "media war" that is taking place in France on Heidegger and Nazism? concerning the book by a certain Farías and my own book [i.e., *De l'esprit*]? If you can find this week's *Nouvel Observateur*, there is an interview with me on the subject. If you can't find it, I'll try to send it to you. I was happy to be able to travel with you in America: what good luck![4] Hugs, your friend, etc.

Not long after this, on February 15, 1988, I wrote Derrida about the Farías book and his own *Of Spirit*. I had already seen that the work of Hugo Ott and Bernd Martin in Freiburg had made the Farías book irrelevant, even though Jürgen Habermas had granted it his *Imprimatur*, knowing

---

2 Discussions had already started at a conference in Tuscaloosa some weeks earlier.

3 The meaning of this last phrase, "S'il y a quelque chose de grave (. . . . .)," is unclear to me. Perhaps he simply means he will keep in touch with me about the matter as things develop.

4 Unfortunately, I cannot recall what these "travels" were, although they were presumably in the United States at about the time of the Vanderbilt conference. My journal remains silent.

full well that the book was seriously flawed. I was certain that *Of Spirit*, along with Dominique Janicaud's *L'Ombre de cette pensée*, would overshadow Farías's "exposé." I turned out to be wrong about this: Rüdiger Safranski's biography of Heidegger, for example, while a serious effort, one I have benefited from, is not always well informed. It uses Farías uncritically and mentions neither Derrida nor Janicaud, who would have made his account so much more thought-provoking than it is. At all events, I wrote to Derrida:

> I was very much heartened by the review of *De l'esprit* by Roger Pol-Droit. You remember that when I visited Paris last March and we had lunch together I told you that your own reception in France was changing for the better. I am certain that I was right, and events since then confirm what I said. You remember Roger Pol-Droit's concluding words to his review: "And what would happen if the French really discovered Jacques Derrida?" I am enclosing another review from Germany, from the *Frankfurter Allgemeine Zeitung.* I have read through the whole thing, and while I don't think you have to do so, I did want to tell you what an excellent review it is. Just take a look at its concluding words and you will see why I am sending it to you.
>
> My impression is that this whole terrible episode involving Farías's book will actually have one very good consequence: people will recognize the importance of your own reading of Heidegger, which is both highly critical and profoundly appreciative. I was also very pleased to see the excellent articles by Levinas, Blanchot, and Lacoue-Labarthe in the *Nouvel Observateur.* . . .
>
> Needless to say, it would be great to see you. I am at the moment writing the final chapter of my memory book, which is all about mourning in the sense that you have developed in your recent work. I'd actually like to have a chance to sit down with you . . . and talk about some of these very profound puzzles. Take good care, greet Marguerite for me, etc.

The review by Roger Pol-Droit for *Le Monde* treated both *De l'esprit* and *Psychè: Inventions de l'autre.* It seemed to me to indicate a turning point in the French reception (or avoidance) of Derrida. I remember being particularly struck by Pol-Droit's concluding words about the French possibly "discovering Jacques Derrida" (BP 470).

That the de Man scandal continued to cause Derrida great suffering during 1988 is suggested by my February 24 letter to him. I had sent him some damning newspaper accounts, adding, "Again, I feel a bit helpless, and I don't know what to do or say—or write. And I wish I could spare you all this ugliness."

* * *

A surprise in my correspondence with Derrida comes with the revelation that I was planning yet another Essex colloquium for May 1987. The occasion was the hundredth anniversary of Nietzsche's *Genealogy of Morals*, and the Essex philosophy department was planning an entire year of courses and guest lectures, with Lacoue-Labarthe, Luce Irigaray, Rodolphe Gasché, Charles Scott, Alphonso Lingis, John Sallis, Ernesto Laclau, and others. Apparently, funding for the meeting—this time from the Germans, who had a great deal more money than the French—fell through, so the colloquium did not take place. My letter to Derrida proposes something bizarre, perhaps as a result of my experience in the aftermath of the 1986 meeting, or as a result of my *in*experience. On November 10, 1987, I wrote suggesting that *I* write a paper on *his* uses of genealogy, to which *he* could then reply. The ostensible idea was to save him a certain amount of work, but it looks to me now like my own megalomania. In any case, this whole project never got underway.

Mrs. Thatcher's England, meanwhile, was becoming tiresome to me, and Derrida and I talked about my applying to Irvine for a position—a letter to him on February 4, 1988, reveals this to me now, even if I had in the meantime totally forgotten about it. Nothing ever came of such an idea. But I soon had a year-long sabbatical that I spent in Greece (beneath Mount Pelion, not far from Mount Olympus) and then, over the winter, in Cuernavaca (under the volcano). From there, I went on to Chicago and DePaul University.

Before returning to the theme of lifedeath and the animals, allow me to add two snippets from my letters to Derrida and a postcard from him. On July 30, 1988, from Perugia, thanking the Derridas for a visit with them in Paris on our way to Italy, "Perugia is again wonderful: Nietzsche gives to our days the sharpness of suspicion, to our nights the sweetness of Zarathustran songs. Naturally, we miss you, precisely because you are so present!" And, from Greece, "My dear Jacques, autumn comes to Greece also: it is a bit chilly when I go into the sea mornings. But still the days are golden here, and I feel very fortunate, especially when I think of you without sabbaticals, ever! If it were not for my family, I would give you mine! or we could both escape into les Alpes Maritimes and live like hermits!" And, from him, an undated postcard sent from Morocco to Mexico. Its final lines are reminiscent of something he had written not long before to another friend, referring to "a grave *epistolarophobia,* a true malady of body and soul," which was affecting him—his inability to keep up with the correspondences in which he had been engaged for years and years (BP 533). Derrida, oppressed by the brevity of life and the long list of people to write, wrote from Morocco:

> My dear David, will you still pardon these silences? This voyage is over (the end of a visit, plenty of papers presented here, where strange things are happening among the intelligentsia, fascinating, moving things. . . .) I am speaking about friendship, yes. . . . Your project for the Collège [a proposed course on Hölderlin's *The Death of Empedocles*] is perfect. I hope to be able to follow at least the first few sessions. . . . I have news of you, I mean in addition to what you write in your letters, from John Sallis. Above all, I want what is best for you, but the English, the Continentals, among them myself, will regret losing you.
>
> Thank you for all you've told me, for all you are doing, all you are writing. You know that in spite of my chronic "mailophobia," which is getting worse, I am thinking of you, hoping to see you soon. Hugs to all the family.

*   *   *

If the 1980s were the years of *Geschlecht* for Derrida, at least for the Derrida I knew, one might say that the 1990s were the years of "animality," or of all the words and worlds of animals. At least, that theme emerged fully during the 1990s and became ever stronger in his life and in mine—in his, up to and including his last seminar in Paris, the astonishing seminar that followed the equally astonishing *Death Penalty* seminar of 1999–2001, namely, *The Beast and the Sovereign,* taught during 2001–2003.[5] As for me, *Daimon Life: Heidegger and Life-Philosophy,* published in 1992 and dedicated to Derrida, was the result of work begun in the 1980s; *Derrida and Our Animal Others,* published in 2013, was the culmination of work that began in the 1990s.

. 5 The transcripts of both seminars have been published in French and English. See Jacques Derrida, *Séminaire: La peine de mort,* 2 vols., ed. Geoffrey Bennington, Marc Crépon, and Thomas Dutoit (Paris: Galilée, 2015 [2012]); Jacques Derrida, *The Death Penalty,* English trans. Peggy Kamuf and Elizabeth Rottenberg (Chicago: University of Chicago Press, 2017 [2014]). And Jacques Derrida, *Séminaire: La bête et le souverain,* 2 vols., ed. Michel Lisse, Marie-Louise Mallet, and Ginette Michaud (Paris: Galilée, 2008); Jacques Derrida, *The Beast and the Sovereign,* English trans. Geoffrey Bennington (Chicago: University of Chicago Press, 2011 [2009]).

It is not as though the theme of "animality" was a new departure for either of us. A letter of mine from Cuernavaca on April 10, 1989, asks about a reference he had made in *The Post Card* to "the first loop" of a seminar taught in 1975–76, *La vie la mort* ("Life Death").[6] The "loop" in question involved contemporary biology and genetics, and I wanted to delve into that theme for *Daimon Life*. At least I was *thinking* about beginning to write such a book, since I mention the title to him, even though that sabbatical year was devoted entirely to a novel about the last ten years of Nietzsche's life, the years of his illness and death. That novel would have run parallel to the *second* loop of Derrida's "Life Death" seminar, had I known about it at the time, since it takes up the theme of autobiography, with Nietzsche's *Ecce Homo* as Derrida's principal text.

One of the tasks I undertook during 1989 was to read Nietzsche's correspondence, all of it, which took up a large chunk of the year. Like every correspondence, Nietzsche's was full of serendipity and occasional silliness, and I copied for Derrida one snippet from Nietzsche's letter to Erwin Rohde from August 26, 1872. Nietzsche had recently read a friend's *Habilitationsschrift* on the theme of "Kant and the Essence of Things," in which, naturally, Kant's famous *Ding-an-sich* emerged as the principal problem. Nietzsche tells Rohde that he has decided to alter Kant's expression to capture the genuine sense of it, namely, its universality *and* radical undecidability; he employs an "utterly abstract series of particles in order to designate what in terms of content is purely indeterminate."[7] Nietzsche calls "the thing-in-itself" *das Derdiedas*. For reasons I cannot explain, if only because I have only now noticed it, Derrida (or Derdiedas) wrote at the top of this letter of mine a reference to "Tracings Without Wax," which became a chapter of my memory book that dealt with his own early work on "the trace" and "arche-writing." Perhaps *das Derdiedas* reminded him of that arche-limbo of deconstruction we had talked

---

6 This seminar, too, is available now in both French and English. See Jacques Derrida, *La vie la mort: Séminaire 1975–1976*, ed. Pascale-Anne Brault and Peggy Kamuf (Paris: Seuil, 2019); in English translation, *Life Death*, trans. Pascale-Anne Brault and Michael Naas (Chicago: University of Chicago Press, 2020). See also the excellent commentary on this seminar by Dawne McCance, *The Reproduction of Life Death: Derrida's* La vie la mort (New York: Fordham University Press, 2019).

7 Friedrich Nietzsche, *Sämtliche Briefe Kritische Studienausgabe*, 8 vols., ed. Giorgio Colli, Mazzino Montinari, and Helga Anania-Heß (Berlin and Munich: Walter de Gruyter and Deutscher Taschenbuch Verlag, 1986), 4:47. I will cite the letters as "KSAB" with volume and page.

about while flying United, a limbo to which this chapter of the memory book also referred.[8]

Derrida soon replied to his "Mexican friends" in Cuernavaca with a picture postcard of Goya's "Colossus," saying that he knew about my upcoming move to the United States, that is, to DePaul University in Chicago, and that this would both separate us and bring us closer together—by that time, his own life was fairly evenly split between the US, where he had many friends, and France, where the friends were few and far between, at least in the academy. Apparently, I had sent him some papers of mine that were to appear in the memory book, or perhaps in *Daimon Life*, and I want to cite his response to these even if it seems self-serving. His response reveals something about his own reticence, perhaps even diffidence, when it came to his work. As for his praise of me, I will caution the reader as I caution myself: Derrida was always generous, overgenerous, in fact, if that is a word or a concept (is not all generosity over the top?), so that the praise has to be taken cum grano salis. On November 20, 1989, he wrote:

> Dear David, your texts are too beautiful! This generosity (excessive, as generosity must be) in your gift of friendship makes me think, among other things, something I will confide to you: I become aware, whenever I am read, heard, divined, and preceded [?] *in this fashion*, that something in me defends itself against the best readings of what I have written, as though I were reassured, as though I could win a little more time, whenever I can see, as I so often do, that the majority of those who read me don't *read* me (to say nothing about those who do not read me!). The kinds of readings, so rare, such as yours, make me a little afraid, and this fear gets mixed in at the same time with the singular gratitude that you can imagine. At bottom, it is ridiculous to admit it, but the "current" sorts of readings, whether good or bad, protect me from the most lucid readings, like yours; they allow my texts to sleep peacefully, and I become aware that someone inside me prefers that these texts sleep in peace, prefers that they will leave me in peace. Things aren't that simple, of course, but what I'm saying isn't false. For example, I catch myself protecting myself by forgetting (as in the case of *Glas*, for example, or *The Post Card*) about the things that came to me there [?]. I am sure you will not be so surprised about this being the case for me.
>
> How brief, how minuscule our "real" meetings (for example, in Chicago) will seem in comparison with what goes on in reading. . . . But the meetings do me good nevertheless, just as, at the end of the day, your terribly friendly lucidity is beneficial for me. . . . *Thank you.*

8 See Krell, *Of Memory, Reminiscence, and Writing: On the Verge*, 175–76.

> Yes, about sacrifices. . . . I am teaching about sacrifice this year, based on the text of "Eating the Other" or "Loving-Eating the Other" (once again Penthesilea and some others. . . .)[9]
>
> Till soon. I'm thinking of you, etc.

"Yes, about sacrifices. . . ." I am uncertain about what he means to say here. I believe he is referring to my constant warning to him not to expend or "sacrifice" too much of himself. Of course, he did not need me to tell him to protect himself. During his midthirties, apparently troubled by heart palpitations, he consulted a number of physicians. One of them, perhaps the wisest, said to him, "Your life in the world seems to me the ransom you are paying for your newfound glory. Each causes the other to augment, but you'll have to defend yourself against the one in order to preserve the other" (BP 206).

Or it may be that the phrase "Yes, about sacrifices" alludes to the troubling theme of blood sacrifice in the history of religions and the history of philosophy—troubling for him because sacrifice is always caught up in an economy of substitution and exchange, and thus an economy of violence. The fact that philosophers from Kant and Hegel through Heidegger and Levinas were thinkers of *sacrifice* was a nightmare from which, like Dedalus, he was trying to awake. It is no accident that at the time of this letter, Derrida chose to teach a course on "eating the other" or "loving-eating-the other."[10] There would be further reflection on sacrifice a decade later in the seminar on the death penalty, which in his view was the principal scene of sacrifice in our time, a scene, if not of bloodshed, then certainly of *Grausamkeit*, "atrocity."

The need for self-protection in what otherwise seems a rather innocent occupation or profession, spending one's life in a Socratic "think tank" or in the archive and in the classroom, is intriguing, and even if I do not understand it well, I surely share it—the desire and the need that one's own work be left in peace, and that one's own self be left in peace. I realize that

---

9 Does he mean Kleist's *Penthesilea*, on the theme of her self-sacrifice for the sake of Achilles? I do not know, although I was reading Kleist at the time, and we may have spoken about Penthesilea's sacrifice. I look forward to the publication of the seminars from 1989 to 1991!

10 Derrida also refers to this important seminar in his *Circonfession*, or *Circumfession*. See Geoffrey Bennington and Jacques Derrida, *Jacques Derrida* (Paris: Seuil, 1991); in English, *Jacques Derrida*, trans. Geoffrey Bennington (Chicago: University of Chicago Press, 1993), 154/164. I will refer to this important work as "C," with the French/English pagination, in the body of my text.

disputatio has always been a part of academic life, and that it plays a particularly important role in philosophy. Yet I have always hated and feared
it. I became good at it, I have to say, during my high school and university
years: as a debater, I won a number of state and national championships. It
was perfect training in sophistry, but for a philosopher, it was malpractice. I
suppose that is why "analytical" philosophy, which has often been fittingly
compared to the Cambridge Debating Society, insofar as its sole purpose is
to give each philosopher the chance to prove that he or she is the cleverest
person in the room, has always seemed to me such an unpleasant bore and
a misuse of time and energy. Such "analytical" philosophy is unfortunately
gaining ground in France and Germany these days, and throughout Europe
generally. This partly has to do with the Europeans' having lost confidence
in their own traditions, although the principal reason is their desire to dip
into the excess capital enjoyed by the major American universities. To cash
in and cash out, one must learn to play the game called "Imagine a world
in which. . . ."

So-called analytical philosophers would be the first to complain about
Derrida's "obscurity," taking his reticence and the need to protect his work
as "obscurantism." As direct descendants of Descartes, prizing "clear and
distinct ideas" above all else, the analyticals will have nothing to do with a
philosopher who takes the unconscious seriously and who understands that
philosophy is also rhetoric and literature, not merely a logic that is "too-too-
logical" (FW 468). I will have to return to this need Derrida confesses in
his letter, the need to protect his work, in my concluding reflections, because
it manifests what I take to be one of his major contribution to philosophy,
namely, his profound understanding of the importance of biography and
autobiography—as heterothanatography—for thinking as such.

At all events, I replied to Derrida's excessively generous letter on January 9, 1990, assuring him that "lucidity" was not my forte. "The fact is that I
read like a blind man who has fallen asleep, both eyes closed, full of dreams
and desires." I ought to have been satisfied to be either blind or asleep, but
I went for both.

The letter also speaks of a paper I had given at the Collège Interna-
tionale de Philosophie on Schelling's freedom essay, and it mentions that
I was planning to offer at the Collège a course on Hölderlin's tragedy, or
"mourning-play," (*Trauerspiel*), *The Death of Empedocles*. Derrida put
me in touch with Michel Deguy, then the director of the Collège, and the

course became a reality. My semester-long visit to Paris in the fall of 1990 and a conference on architecture held at DePaul at the end of April 1991 were decisive events in my friendship with Derrida.

The course of ten lectures at the Collège, from November 15 to December 21, 1990, was called "The Voices of Empedocles," *Les voix d'Empédocle.* Derrida, as I recall, could be present for only a few of them, but I had the benefit of Françoise Dastur's presence for all of them. Françoise and I had fruitful discussions—Hölderlin was one of her major interests, and her books on the great German poet are among the best that I know—which became important for me years later when I was translating the three versions of *Der Tod des Empedokles* into English.[11] On Wednesday afternoons, the two of us would hie off to the EHESS auditorium on the Boulevard Raspail for Derrida's seminar. His theme that year was "The Rhetoric of Cannibalism," a continuation of his "Eating the Other" from the previous year.[12] The seminar dealt with a wide range of remarkable discourses on eating, speaking, swallowing, defecating, vomiting, and kissing, not necessarily in that order. Among the books Derrida was reading was an edition of Novalis's "scientific notes" on these various subjects, among the strangest and most thought-provoking texts in the German language, or in any language for that matter. "Who would not be pleased," asked Novalis, "with a philosophy whose germ is a first kiss?"[13] What I remember most vividly about these lectures were Derrida's imaginative yet quite concrete references to what are usually called "bodily functions." I had always felt that Maurice Merleau-Ponty's philosophy of the flesh had somehow been left in abeyance by deconstruction, but the flesh came back with a vengeance in Derrida's lectures on eating, and it would continue to come back throughout this decade dedicated to "animality." Also vivid in my memory was

11 I will cite only one of Françoise Dastur's books here: *Hölderlin: le retour natal, et autres essais* (Paris: Les Belles Lettres, 2013), the expanded edition of a work published by Encre Marine in 1997. For my translation, see Friedrich Hölderlin, *The Death of Empedocles: A Mourning-Play* (Albany: State University of New York Press, 2008).

12 There is some confusion about the titles of these two seminars, precisely because the theme is continuous. The title that might embrace them both is *Aimer-manger l'autre* ("To Love-To Eat the Other"). See David Farrell Krell, "All You Can't Eat: Derrida's Lecture Course *Rhétorique du cannibalisme* (1990)," the Derrida Memorial Issue of *Research in Phenomenology* 36 (2006): 130–80.

13 See David Farrell Krell, *Contagion: Sexuality, Disease, and Death in German Idealism and Romanticism* (Bloomington: Indiana University Press, 1998), 36. Here, I am quoting Novalis's "Preliminary Sketches of 1798."

my astonishment over his familiarity with Novalis: I had been working on these scientific notebooks for several years by that time, and they were quite familiar to me. Yet once again, Derrida managed to excavate gems that I somehow had missed, so that a certain irritation concerning my own opacity accompanied my admiration of Derrida's perspicuity. I do not believe it is disingenuous of me to claim that we were never in competition with one another, even though so many of our interests intersected. For my part, it was in each case admiration and even wonderment that won out over the irritation; better, it was the shared dedication to the work, to the thinking that brushed aside any sense of competition. He consistently called me back to what Husserl liked to call "the things themselves," which for the two of us always involved *texts*.

It is difficult to describe the intensity of these "seminars." As I mentioned in the previous chapter, they were held on Wednesday afternoons from five till seven in the large auditorium. They were actually formal lectures, each one beautifully prepared and typed. (I remember asking my friend Michael Naas why it was that we never found the time or the energy to prepare our classes in that way. We knew half the answer, which was that teaching in the US is valued for its "spontaneity" and its "dialogue," not its careful formulations based on the reading of texts, but the other half remained elusive.) Derrida sat at a large desk down front, a stack of books off to the side, books from which he would cite long passages during the lecture. From time to time, he would look up from a tome or his own text and formulate a phrase or two that would capture the gist of what he was so painstakingly developing. Or he might look up to make a word-play or a little joke—sprays of chuckles were always rising from his audience—which I often was unable to hear or understand. (Françoise would explain it to me after the session.) These "asides" were often extremely helpful, however, so that the transcription of the seminars really must, and usually do, retain them when audiotapes make this possible. The actual typescripts of Derrida's seminars that I have worked on are filled with marginal notes of his, many of them illegible to all but him, or with key words circled many times and often the command-to-self, "Comment on this." Comment he did, and always masterfully. I have heard quite a few impressive lecturers in my lifetime, but never anyone remotely like Derrida. Not that he was out to make an effect or put on a show. Quite the contrary: he allowed the *work* to take center stage, and he invited his students to be rapt to, or wrapped up in, the *work*.

How to describe that work? He posed his questions carefully and from many different perspectives, some of them seemingly far afield, at least at first. He never fell back on accepted notions, never bandied about mere concepts. (I find myself here echoing Hans Jonas's description of Heidegger's lectures in Marburg!) One of the most illuminating remarks he ever made about philosophical concepts was that whenever a traditional concept rose to meet him, offering itself as the obvious concept, the only available one, hence the inevitable one, he said he felt like a fly who sensed danger in that honeyed strip of paper hanging from the ceiling. "I've always had the reflex to flee, as though even with the initial contact, even just to *name* these concepts, I would find myself, like a housefly, with my feet stuck in the goo of the flypaper: captive, paralyzed, trapped, hostage to a program" (BP 599). He used his enormous writerly gifts, his imagination, his perspicuity, and his vast library of reading to formulate anew every set of problems that presented itself to him. None of this, nor all of it together, can explain his originality. Yet he was, as they say, unmistakably "an original." He was seldom grave but always serious, even when he made us laugh. He took no long pauses during the lectures, no breaks, no concessions to the bladder or to text-messaging, so that over the years I have heard many people complain about the relentlessness and above all the length of his presentations. I never understood these complaints. For me, the time was always a singular moment of focused concentration, a moment of philosophical work at its very best, week after week. Françoise Dastur, a student of his early on, one who continued to follow Derrida's lectures whenever she was in Paris, put it best: "During the years I followed his seminars, between 1987 and 1994, I was present for something quite rare: a thinking in process of creation, and a thinking, as it were, without safety nets" (BP 544–45).

* * *

In addition to my lectures at the Collège—how I slaved over them to bring Hölderlin's German, which itself responded to Empedocles's Greek, into my own primitive French!—and Derrida's lectures on "The Rhetoric of Cannibalism," an exhibition at the Louvre, "Memoirs of the Blind," generated the greatest excitement during those weeks in Paris.[14] The very concept behind

---

14 See Jacques Derrida, *Memoirs of the Blind: The Self-Portrait and Other Ruins,* beautifully translated by Pascale-Anne Brault and Michael Naas (Chicago: University of Chicago Press, 1993). The exhibition in the Napoléon Hall took place from October 6, 1990 to January 21, 1991.

the exhibition was inspired. The curators of the Louvre, realizing that their basement was crammed full of fine art that was not being exhibited due to lack of space, decided to ask a select group of laypersons to rummage through the basement and come up with an exhibition. Derrida was the first person they asked. Because he had recently suffered a facial nerve infection that blinded his left eye and disfigured his face for some weeks, Derrida decided to organize an exhibition of paintings and drawings on the theme of blindness.

I visited the exhibition many times, sometimes with my daughter Salomé, who had accompanied me to Paris for these weeks, sometimes alone. The works were powerful, and equally powerful were the "captions" composed by Derrida to accompany each artwork—except for one drawing, which received no commentary from him.

The exhibition catalog, *Memoirs of the Blind*, became one of my favorite books by Derrida. It is impossible for me to describe all its themes—vision, blindness, tears of imploring and deploring, the impossible gaze that self-portraiture requires (making it akin to autobiography, perhaps), prosthetic aids such as eyeglasses and monocles, the gaze of Narcissus and the cries of Echo—based on works of art many of which I had never seen before. Among these works that I did not know was the one that lacked a caption. In the catalog, it is number 37, Félicien Rops's *Woman with Monocle*. It is not a monocle, actually, but a pince-nez hanging by a cord around the neck of a gaunt yet very striking woman. Her face has turned to the left, rapidly, it seems, since her pince-nez and loop earring, along with the black veil covering yet revealing her shadowy face, are still reeling as a result of her motion. Art historians imagine that she is a woman of the demimonde, perhaps a cabaret singer or dancer, although the details of her costume do not seem to jibe with that description. One evening, while at supper in Ris-Orangis, I asked Derrida why he had left this drawing alone without commentary. He was puzzled.

—There's no commentary? he asked.

—None at all, I replied.

He shrugged his shoulders and shook his head, nonplussed. I did not hesitate to tease him.

—It's a great exhibit. You should go see it.

To celebrate the appearance of their translation of the Louvre catalog, Michael Naas and Pascale-Anne Brault sponsored a conference at DePaul on February 5, 1994, "Drawing from Philosophy: Derrida's *Memoirs of the*

Blind." Michael Fried, an art historian captivated by the theme of the *theatricality* of the spectator's gaze, provided an insightful analysis of this particular drawing, perhaps in response to a question from me. I mentioned to Michael Naas my conversation with Derrida—his being flummoxed by the absence of caption or commentary for this piece. Naas thought about it for a while, then came up with an astonishing idea.

—Of course, he can't really provide a commentary on this drawing, because it is a portrait of his mother.

He was no doubt thinking of the famous "winter garden" photograph of Roland Barthes's *Camera obscura*. That photograph, as Derrida emphasized, is of Barthes's mother as a young woman; it is the one photo that Barthes refuses to reproduce in his text. I never dared to report this conversation with Michael Naas to Derrida, nor would Michael, I think, have wanted me to, especially if the art historians are right about the demimonde. Mothers, as I mentioned earlier, were a perpetual theme between Derrida and me. All of these mothers, Derrida's, Barthes's, Michael's, my own, perhaps Rops's, were, as Faust says, a mystery. *Die Mütter! Mütter!—'s klingt so wunderlich!* ("The mothers, mothers—how wondrous it sounds!").

Having mentioned Salomé's presence in Paris with me, I will allow myself some digressions. One involves the Louvre exhibition itself. Because I had forgotten how complicated the entrances to the Louvre are, and there are many of them, I gave Salomé some sloppy directions about where we would meet. We wound up searching for one another for over an hour, an upsetting hour for both father and daughter. Lost in Paris! Otherwise, it was a special "bonding" time, Salomé fourteen years old and thrilled by her first extended stay in Paris—climbing the Tour Eiffel, which I had never done, meandering through the Galéries Lafayette, which I also had never done, watching the fantastically skilled boule players in the Jardin du Luxembourg, which I always do—all the wonders of Paris at her disposal. And among those wonders,

LA GALANTERIE FRANÇAISE

We met "Monsieur Jacques" one day for lunch. Salomé was surely in awe of him, though not in terror. Years earlier, during one summer evening at his house in Ris-Orangis, the children had played ping-pong at his outdoor table while the adults talked philosophy. They played so enthusiastically that they blasted a dozen ping-pong balls high over the hedge into his neighbor's property—until there were none left. For months afterward, they were afraid that the master of deconstruction would discover their misdeed. Of course, he never seemed to have noticed. In any case, that may have been on her mind as we arrived for our luncheon date with Derrida. He opened the door of the bistro, and my daughter immediately started to enter. Derrida stopped her and admonished her.

—No, no! In France I have to go in first! I have to go in, look around, and make sure it's safe for you.

He entered the restaurant, which did not *seem* to be dangerously demi-monde, at least from the outside, and heroically scouted out the premises.

—It looks okay, he said. Come on in.

* * *

During those weeks in Paris, I was also participating in an architecture workshop at the Laboratory of Primary Studies in Architecture, directed by Donald L. Bates, now a professor of architecture at the University of Melbourne. My interest in architectural theory was sparked during the 1980s through contact with Don Bates and Peter Davidson of LAB Architectural Studios in London, and Ben Nicholson in Chicago. In July 1988, I met Daniél Libeskind for the first time. He invited me to give a paper, "Ecstatic Spatiality," at his Intermundium Summer Studio of Architecture at the Villa Olmo in Como. Not long after that, Libeskind began his work on the Jewish Museum of Berlin, originally an "extension" to the Berlin Museum. His project, "Between the Lines," was one of the most remarkable texts I had ever seen: the plans for the museum were superimposed on musical composition paper on which portions of Arnold Schönberg's *Moses and Aaron* appeared in the background as a subtext. I wrote a layman's response to the plans, and from that moment on, I was determined that Derrida and Libeskind should meet.[15]

Derrida had in the meantime gotten to know Bernard Tschumi and Peter Eisenman, so that his own interest (and participation) in architecture

---

15 See David Farrell Krell, "'I Made It on the Verge': A Letter to Daniél Libeskind on the Jewish Museum in Berlin," *Assemblage: A Critical Journal of Architecture and Design Culture* 12 (MIT Press, August 1990): 52–57. "Ecstatic Spatiality" appears as the second chapter in David Farrell Krell, *Archeticture: Ecstasies of Space, Time, and the Human Body* (Albany: State University of New York Press, 1997). The word *archeticture*, from the Greek ἀρχή and τίκτω, the latter word meaning "to procreate," is spelled correctly!

was growing. My letters to him in spring 1990 suggested a conference at which he and Libeskind would meet. Derrida called to say yes, indeed, a double-yes, and confirmed his acceptance in a letter of July 6, 1990.

The conference, "*Das Unheimliche*: Philosophy, Architecture, and the City," took place at DePaul on April 25–27, 1991. The dates had been coordinated with Tom Mitchell, who had arranged for Derrida to be at the University of Chicago around that time. The German word *unheimlich* meant to refer to Freud's famous essay of 1917 and to Heidegger's use of that same word in early drafts of *Being and Time*, where "anxiety" is discussed as a subordinate theme of *Unheimlichkeit*, understood as the not-being-at-home of human being as such. Finally, the reference to the "unhomelike" meant to indicate the homelessness that was plaguing thousands of people—now tens of thousands—in all the cities of the United States, including the city of Chicago. Peter Eisenman came in from New York, Don Bates from London, Stanley Tigerman and Ben Nicholson of Chicago also presented, and the final session was with Libeskind, who presented his Jewish Museum project, and Derrida, who responded to "Between the Lines."

I opened that final session by reciting some lines from Jeremiah (12:7–12) that Libeskind had inscribed in Hebrew letters into a number of corners of his "Between the Lines." I knew theoretically what a "Jeremiad" was, but I had never experienced the original, which has many more barbs and double edges than I had imagined. I found the passage in my Luther Bible, and, although nervous about how problematic the move from the Hebrew to the German was, put them into what I called English "variations":

> I had to forsake my house,
> I had to spurn my heritage,
> I had to hand over my sweet soul to my enemies.
>
> My heritage is to me a lion in the wood; it roars against me.
> My heritage tears at my heart.
> I hate it! I hate it!
>
> My heritage is a speckled bird; other birds gather round,
> Speckled birds of prey: so be it.
> Let them come and devour me.
>
> Many shepherds have ruined my vineyard, trampled my field,
> Turned my pleasant portion into a desolate wilderness.
> Already I see, and I lament: a wasteland, the whole country devastated.

Fig. 8.2 Derrida in Chicago in spring 1991 with Michael Naas, Pascale-Anne Brault, and Janet Rabinowitch, philosophy editor and later president of Indiana University Press. Photo by Amy Rothblatt.

> Desolate, it mourns. I hear it.
> Yet no one will take it to heart.
> No one will take it to heart.

From the outset, I had been struck by the difficulty of Libeskind's task: to "extend" or "expand" (*Erweiterung* was the word used by the Berlin government to describe the project) the Berlin Museum with a Jewish Museum. What could such an "extension" or "expansion" be after the Extermination? That question was doubtless at the center of Libeskind's plans, and it was also at the core of Derrida's remarks and his questions to Libeskind. Derrida cited the view of the neo-Kantian philosopher Hermann Cohen to the effect that the Jewish and the German cultures were inherently *one*, and that since antiquity they had been destined to be at the forefront of Western civilization; he then cited the contrary view of Gershom Scholem, namely, that the very idea of such a German-Jewish unity was a myth, an empty dream, a delusion. In earlier chapters of this book, we heard Arendt's adamant refusal to be denied her original language and her beloved German literature, no matter how tarnished and twisted the language had become.

German remained the language of Benjamin, that exquisite stylist, and of Kafka, who wrote in neither Hebrew nor Czech nor Yiddish but only in German. Neither Libeskind nor Derrida hesitated to speak of "the end of history" when referring to the Holocaust, so that the very language of ends and means, articulated in *any* language, appeared to be shattered. Derrida asked Libeskind where, between the conflicting views of Cohen and Scholem, he would place his project. Libeskind spoke of a museum that could no longer be reconciled with "theoretical utopias" of any kind, and Derrida wondered aloud whether any *discourse* could be equal to what Libeskind was attempting to design "between the lines." He posed some quite "practical" questions about the discourse of Libeskind's proposal, which the architect had to address to the city fathers of Berlin, as it were, to those who would likely have little or no understanding of architecture. The politics of such architectural competitions, followed by the politics of building, with constant negotiations between architect and engineers, fire and safety experts, financiers, and so on—Derrida asked about all these incredibly complex negotiations. Libeskind described how disarmed the city officials had been by the fact that "Between the Lines" appeared on musical notepaper, remarking that Schönberg's never-completed *Sprechoper* was surely known to only a few of them.

Libeskind noted that he had organized his basic design, which involved one straight line and a zigzag line intersecting the straight line at irregular intervals, as "lines around a void," turning that void into an impenetrable crypt. Derrida, after remarking that the "zigzag" reminded him of Jean-Claude Lebensztein's work of perpetual zigzag, asked many questions about that "void," distinguishing it from the Platonic χώρα, the "receptacle," inasmuch as Libeskind's void is meant precisely *not* to be available as an exhibition space—it is meant to contain nothing at all. The extension to the Berlin Museum, radically destabilized and destabilizing, with each of its windows differing in shape and dimensions from every other window, with rising and falling ramps that do not seem to lead anywhere (I walked through the building with Daniél Libeskind when only the rough structure was completed, then once again when the building was finished but still empty of exhibits and displays, experiencing both times the disquieting and uncanny effects of the constantly shifting perspectives), was clearly made to be beyond commemoration, beyond customary ritual, beyond every economy of exchange, beyond sacrifice.

What was it, then? Derrida, recalling the disputed and fractious discourses of the German-Jewish relationship, called Libeskind's museum "a ghostly gift" to Berlin and to a Germany now united, Germany as a whole. Lines that fall apart and disengage even as they intersect, relentlessly forming an impenetrable void that runs through the building, lines of a *time* that is no longer punctual, interrupted time, frustrated convergence, postponed intersection. . . . If these lines represented a time of ecstatic rapture, as the Heidegger of *Being and Time* would have insisted, then it would be a time of *ruptured* rapture, a kind of *Ruinanz*. If it is not a "memorial" for or a "monument" to the Holocaust, and it is not, it seems nonetheless to issue a stark command: remember to remember what took place in Berlin but remember to forget whatever you thought remembering was; remember that what took place took all possible places and spaces and times with it, so that you will always be *only on the verge* of remembering events that never dare be forgotten.

I cannot pretend to recall the exact words spoken by either Libeskind or Derrida, but my notes tell me that this was the tenor of their exchange. The intellectual energy that passed back and forth between the two was intense, and as far as I know, the two men remained in touch with one another after that evening, even though each was insanely busy. It is not too much to say that Libeskind's plan for the Jewish Museum, with its lightning bolt passing through the structure of the museum—those who have visited the building will confirm that they never get over the jolt—and his presentation of his plan that evening in Chicago had an appropriately electrifying effect on everyone present. Derrida's questions to Libeskind, which I do not believe he ever published, conducted that energy along his own lines of genius, discerning in Libeskind's design something like a "memory" of the Shoah, but a memory that could only be, to repeat, a *ruined* memorial, an anguished monument to what Derrida called "impossible mourning."

Their encounter reminded me of the kind of energy that had flowed at the "Open Questions" meeting in Paris four years earlier. In both cases, I was willing to grant Hegel his sighting of the World Spirit on horseback, posing as Napoleon, near Jena. These two meetings, one in Paris, the other in Chicago, were drama enough for me.

*   *   *

Other conferences during the early 1990s were less satisfactory, usually because of the large number of people involved and the resulting lack of focus and dispersion of energy. True, it was exciting to be at Cerisy-la-Salle in Normandy from July 11 to 21, 1992, for the *Décade* on Derrida, one of many, this one under the title "Passage des frontières: sur Jacques Derrida."[16] What made the event pleasurable for me was the presence of Michael Naas and Pascale-Anne Brault. We entertained one another while the sponsors of the *Décade* kept Derrida so busy that we scarcely had time to greet him. Yet the thrilling part of the event was Derrida's paper, "Aporias: To Die— Waiting at the 'Limits of Truth.'"[17]

Here once again, Derrida turned to Heidegger as the central figure of his address—as he had done five years earlier with *Of Spirit*. And once again, I was astonished by what he elaborated, even though I venture to say that Heidegger's existential analysis of death, the death of Dasein, was a familiar theme for me. I had been teaching *Being and Time* for years and had written about it often. I realized that there were problems with Heidegger's account—he had once referred to "the difficult problem of death," a mild understatement. I had also worried for a long time about Heidegger's insistence that death, as one's *"ownmost* possibility," *die* eigenste *Möglichkeit,* had to be met "appropriately" or "authentically," *eigentlich.* There was something about "authenticity" that smacked of an ethical imperative hiding within an ostensibly ontological discourse. Moreover, that imperative seemed to reflect a "factical ideal," as Heidegger himself conceded (SZ 310), that is, an ideal that had been inherited from a long-standing theological tradition. Beyond this, Derrida was quite aware that Heidegger's effort to write about the death that "in each case" is "my own" found itself at a certain limit—indeed, at the limit of truth. What can I know of "my own death"? Can I even speak or write about it without crossing a frontier that does not permit me to emerge on the other side?

Derrida chose the word *aporia* for a serious reason. It is the negative of "finding one's way through or across." An "impasse," as many

16 At this meeting, I presented a paper ("Passage à la soeur: Autour de Trakl, Heidegger et 'Geschlecht'") that became important for my work on *Geschlecht*. It became the fourth chapter of my *Lunar Voices* and remained important for *Phantoms of the Other* and even some more recent papers on the poetry of Georg Trakl.

17 Jacques Derrida, *Apories: Mourir—s'attendre aux "limites de la vérité"* (Paris: Galilée, 1996); trans. Thomas Dutoit as *Aporias: Dying—Awaiting (One Another at) the "Limits of Truth"* (Stanford, CA: Stanford University Press, 1993). I will cite first the French then the English pagination, after the code "A," in parentheses in my text.

languages say. Derrida made us all laugh when, about a third of the way through his paper, he uttered an aside that appears in parentheses in the published text: "Whenever someone suggests to you a solution for escaping an impasse, you can be almost sure that he has ceased to understand, assuming that he has understood anything up to that point" (A 65/32). In a sense, that aside characterizes Derrida's entire career: he was only ever interested in impasses and double binds, "undecidables," as it were, that philosophers were constantly scrambling to avoid or escape. Heidegger was fond of saying that the only philosophical thinking that is worthy of the name is the one that suffers "genuine shipwreck," *echtes Scheitern.* In his *Aporias,* Derrida seems to be piloting Heidegger toward such shipwreck—not as an act of cruelty but as an affirmation of Heidegger's radicality. When Heidegger declares that death is "the possibility of the sheer impossibility of being-there" (SZ 250), Derrida wonders, with Maurice Blanchot, whether "my" death may be the sheer *impossibility of possibility.* Perhaps there is only the "wait," *l'attente,* when it comes to death. But then the postulated distinction between human dying and animal "perishing" might not hold. And what becomes of the hope for "authenticity" or for an "appropriation" of one's own dying? Finally, toward the end of his address to us, Derrida said something that would continue to obsess him for the rest of his days: if "my" death does not come to appear as such, if there is no crossing that frontier much less any return from it, no retrospect on being-in-the-world *as such,* this means "nothing less than the end of the world, with each death, each time." (A 131/75). Yet another aporia: How can the death of a single person be the end of the entire world? Or, given Heidegger's analysis of the worldhood of the world, how can it *not* be? What *is* world? Heidegger never tired of asking that question, and Derrida, in that respect at least, never tired of Heidegger. And yet I recall Derrida's words to me after an exhausting conference, as we were on our way to an airport.

—Heidegger: we will never be rid of his corpse.

A large conference that autumn in the United States was considerably more disappointing than Cerisy had been. Even though Derrida and I had some time together before the session, the session on his work was so disjointed and unsubstantial that I felt we owed him an apology: my letter of November 1, 1992, is both scathing and apologetic. He replied nine days later, blaming himself for "having agreed to improvise (in English!)," lamenting his own "poor response," and saying a few kind things about my contribution—the usual generosity on his part.

In general, it has to be said that Derrida's work is so difficult, so demanding that it is easy to utter inanities about it, and that seems to happen a lot. Certainly, it has happened to me. Perhaps it is a blessing that fewer and fewer "papers" on Derrida are delivered at mass meetings of philosophers nowadays. There is a strong preference now, it seems, for what my friends Elizabeth Rottenberg and Peg Birmingham call "poppy topics." Perhaps this is the requiescat that, as we heard, Derrida sometimes wished for his work. Or it may be the "eclipse" that he said philosophers such as Heidegger often go into—and then come out of, each time different, each time unique.

My paper at the Society for Phenomenology and Existentialism that year eventually became chapter 6 of *The Purest of Bastards*.[18] Because the society has a membership with widespread interests, from Husserl and Heidegger studies, through contemporary French philosophy, to social-critical and political philosophy, I tried to address as many of these interests as I could. The principal text for the paper was Derrida's recently published *Cinders*, which I mentioned briefly in the foregoing chapter. *Feu la cendre* is a "polylogue" on the theme of mourning, *le deuil*, which became for me perhaps the central theme of Derrida's thought. Even though the thought of cinder and ash as the most ephemeral form of the trace was a thought unique to Derrida, I tried to seek out hints of it in phenomenology and existentialism generally. For example, Husserl's *Analyses of Passive Synthesis* suggested that there was a "zero-point" on the horizon of our remote or long-distance memories, a point at which all memory "founders" and all memories themselves are no more than funereal figures—mere shades, as Husserl says, "*in der 'toten' Gestalt*."[19] This language of the crypt seemed strange in the otherwise optimistic Husserl. In any case, these figures or traces of ash in classical phenomenology certainly merited our attention. It was less surprising to see such figures in Merleau-Ponty, whose notions of "ambiguity" and "adversity" at least suggested a relation to mourning, to cinder and ash. In his classic *Phenomenology of Perception*, Merleau had

---

18 David Farrell Krell, *The Purest of Bastards: Works of Mourning, Art, and Affirmation in the Thought of Jacques Derrida* (University Park: Penn State University Press, 2000).

19 On this entire issue, see Edmund Husserl, *Analysen zur passiven Synthesis*, Husserliana, vol. 11, ed. Margot Fleischer, derived from lecture and research manuscripts dating from 1918 to 1926 (The Hague: M. Nijhoff, 1966), esp. 172–222 and 364–85.

invoked "the feeling of my contingency, the anxiety of my being *dépassé*, so that even if I do not think my death I live in an atmosphere of death in general, and there is something like an essence of death that is always on the horizon of my thoughts."[20] Nor was it far-fetched to find the theme of cinder and ash in the scarcely heard voices of the weak and the defeated in Walter Benjamin's "Concept of History," or in Heidegger's notion of pain (*der Schmerz*), as well as in Luce Irigaray's notion of "embrasure," in Nietzsche's unpublished notes on the cosmos as the ash of once-living beings, and in Hélène Cixous's experience of writing as "delirium, cinder or ashes, in every direction."[21]

Derrida's response to the paper during the discussion period, whatever his own doubts, was, as always, more than stimulating. He began by making some general remarks on the nature of *surprise* and of the *secret—* the secret encrypted in a text, assuredly in his own *Feu la cendre* but also in every other text, which surprises us by retaining its secret, keeping the secret secret. The text *Feu la cendre*, he said, involved the mourning of a loss, of a radical destruction beyond mere repression, with no possible return. The secret of the *Cinders* text, which doubtless related it to my own, might be encrypted in a proper name that the text itself contains but also conceals, keeps as a secret—for example, as an anagram of I.L.Y.A.L.C., "*Il y a là cendre.*" That might be an anagram of his own "sacred" name, Eliahu or Elijah. The effect of such secrecy is to close the very space of philosophy, especially the institutional space of a meeting of professional philosophers.

Turning specifically to my paper, he commented on the importance of the theme of *impossible* mourning for him. He reasserted his conviction that the work of introjection, as Freud defines it, namely, the work of successfully withdrawing one's "investment" from the defunct other, must come to a halt if respect for the departed other is to be preserved. He then turned to the sections of my paper on Husserl and Heidegger. He observed that to a significant extent Husserl is a life-philosopher, emphasizing as he does the importance of the "living present" for all phenomenology. It is therefore all the more important to take into account the figures of death

<hr>

20 Maurice Merleau-Ponty, *Phénoménologie de la Perception* (Paris: Gallimard, 1945), 418.

21 Hélène Cixous, *Neutre* (Paris: Grasset, 1972), on the opening page after the epigraphs. For the references to Benjamin, Heidegger, Nietzsche, and Irigaray, see the notes to chap. 6 of *The Purest of Bastards*.

in Husserl's philosophy of life. Heidegger apparently reverses priorities, inquiring into the possible impossibility of Dasein, the death of mortal Dasein, but leaving all discussion of the *life* of Dasein in abeyance. However, inasmuch as Heidegger remains faithful to Husserlian life-philosophy as such, hence to a phenomenology of eidetic essences—and he does this when he excludes the animal from world-relations—Heidegger is closer to Husserl than first appears. Nevertheless, both the phenomenological project of *Being and Time* and the later thinking of Heidegger are alike threatened when, as it turns out, the analysis of the *as such*, that is, of the apophantic "as," the "as" of expressions such as "being *as* being," "death *as* death," cannot be maintained.

Finally, Derrida commented briefly on Jean-Paul Sartre's ironic phrase in *Les mots*, "We keep everything." I had cited the phrase in my paper, noting that Sartre was using it parodically. Derrida remarked that the confidence that underlay the phenomenological project of the recuperation of evidence and the restitution of all things past to presence, in other words, the project devoted to keeping everything, was a confidence that both Merleau-Ponty's philosophy of ambiguity and his own *Feu la cendre* were dedicated to undermining.

He then told us a story about his recent visit to Cornell University, a story, he said, he was trying to repress, trying to forget. For it was an indication of the hopeless complexity of thinking the impossible possibility of death and the impossible mourning of one's own death and the deaths of others. He had given a lecture at Cornell on Heidegger's analysis of death in *Being and Time* (it was most likely a section of the Cerisy lecture, "Aporias"). After the lecture, a young woman approached him and asked him how to spell "Heidegger." She then asked whether this Heidegger was another French philosopher. A dozen such queries followed. Derrida imagined that she was an earnest but ill-informed undergraduate. The next day, an article appeared in the local newspaper under her byline. Headline: Prof Shares Optimistic Views of Life and Death.

* * *

In his letter to me of November 10, 1992, Derrida complains that he is having trouble phoning me. While at Caen, I saw at the top of one of my letters to him my telephone number, scrawled in his handwriting but missing the final number! Eventually, we straightened it out. I mention this only to say that as the nineties went on, we talked more by phone, as the letter-writing and even the postcards dwindled. "I can't write any more, dear David, because I'm too tired and busier than ever. Since my return from Boston I haven't stopped for a second (Hungary for a week, Nice, Strasbourg for a colloquium on who knows what, plus my seminar, plus plus plus . . .)."

Apropos of the difficulty of Derrida's thought, and the difficulty of responding to it adequately, I sent him the syllabus of a graduate course that my colleague Stephen Houlgate and I had designed for the winter and spring of 1993: "Derrida's *Glas*: What [Are the] Remains of Absolute Knowing?" Stephen taught Hegel's *Phenomenology of Spirit* during the fall, with me sitting in, and I took on the role of seminar leader for the rest of the year. We were following the model that Michael Naas and I had developed a year or two earlier with a course on Plato's *Phaedrus*, followed by Derrida's "Plato's Pharmacy." As I mentioned in the foregoing chapter, it was the model I had used at Essex when teaching Derrida's *Of Grammatology* with Gabriel Pearson of the Literature Department. Each time Derrida's *Grammatology* would mention "the book of nature," Gabriel would recite by heart a stirring passage from Spenser's *Faerie Queene* that demonstrated the point perfectly. In each case—whether with Gabriel, or Michael, or Stephen, or even back in Mannheim where I team-taught courses with Ulrich Halfmann—the result of such team efforts was more than rewarding: team-teaching is never half the work but always double the work and treble the quality of the outcome. When I look back, these are clearly the courses from which I learned the most. The syllabus for the *Glas* course was five single-spaced pages, and, as I look at it now, it reminds me of the kind of detailed work that Derrida's texts always require.

That said, I seem to have been growing weary of academic life, while Derrida himself was exhausted by it. On June 1, 1993, I proposed that Derrida and a small group of friends meet for some more or less informal discussions in my Black Forest village. I suggested as our theme the title of a section from Heidegger's *Contributions to Philosophy*, namely, "The Futural Ones," *Die Zukünftigen*, perhaps with a mind to Derrida's emphasis on the aleatory and ever-unpredictable *l'a-venir*, the "to-come." Derrida replied by postcard from Iceland on September 9, 1993:

> Dear David, pardon, pardon once again, this long silence. Since your last letter times have been so busy that I could not give a single thought to "Die Zukünftigen," even though I've been thinking and writing about this subject alone in order to give a true response to your letter—so amiable,

so lovely, so generous—and to your St. Ulrich project. I still do not know whether or when it is possible, or even whether it is desirable. . . . We will talk it over soon. . . .

But I could not allow this culpable silence to last any longer. I am here for a week before heading for New York. Your friend, etc.

As it happened, an unpredicted illness and a surgery that September prevented me from pursuing the plan. Derrida and I must have talked over the phone about the now doubtful possibility of such a meeting, since a letter of mine from November 1 replies with a health update.

Derrida next wrote sometime in January 1994 to wish the family a happy New Year, saying how much he had enjoyed his days in Chicago and Evanston. I can no longer remember what the occasion of this visit might have been, but he remarked how much he had enjoyed his time with Pascale-Anne Brault, Michael Naas, Bill Martin, and my family. For all of us, he wrote, "I have as much affection as I do admiration, and I think with a touch of nostalgia and melancholy how seldom and how brief such moments of joy are, their being-already-gone, moments when there is no divorce between heart and thought." Again he mentions his impossible schedule, adding a remark about what must have been an odd flight from New York to Paris: "On the two days following my return from New York, on an airplane in which they couldn't find the pilot (!), I had three different meetings. Then I was off to . . . Naples, Capri,[22] Oxford, my seminar, conferences on Levinas and Sarah Kofman, and in two weeks I'm off to India. Okay, enough." From February to December 1994, I was planning an event at DePaul, "Mourning (and) the Political," which did not take place until October 7, 1996, twenty months later! That was the way his schedule worked. A letter of mine dated January 15, 1996, proposes a number of possible dates; the margins are filled with handwritten notes of his that try to "coordinate" the DePaul event with other commitments.

Politiques de l'amitié had appeared in 1994, *Spectres de Marx* a year before that. These and other texts were discussed at the DePaul meeting in papers by Peg Birmingham, Pascale-Anne Brault, Will McNeill, Bill Martin, and Michael Naas, with Derrida offering comments on each paper and posing questions to each participant. The "mourning" in question had also

---

22 The reference to Capri is presumably to the colloquium on religion in February 1994, at which Derrida presented the original form of his text *Faith and Knowledge*.

become an issue in Derrida's life: so many of his friends and colleagues had passed by the beginning of 1996, among them Roland Barthes, Louis Marin, Paul de Man, and Emmanuel Levinas, that his own thoughts around this time centered more than ever on questions of mourning. In addition to his work at the conference—and this was true of each of his visits to both Essex and DePaul—he arranged to stay an extra day or at least some extra hours to meet with graduate students. He was at his best at such sessions. Even though he hated to "improvise" at professional meetings, he never objected to discussing the widest possible range of issues with students. And not only graduate students: I remember his taking time in March 1990 to sign a book of his, *De l'esprit*, that we were giving as a book prize to an outstanding undergraduate. I knew how busy Derrida was, but I didn't hesitate to ask, and he didn't hesitate to reply and comply. *Every* time he visited DePaul, I repeat, he took time to meet with our philosophy majors and graduate students for several hours. His replies to questions that were coming out of all sorts of philosophic nooks and crannies showed how agile his mind was, how thorough his education and his reading were, how humorous he could be, and how modest he always was. If he had "star quality," as his enemies often bitterly complained, he never acted like a star.

*   *   *

About that "star" quality. I recall a time, perhaps in the early 1990s, when our paths crossed in an unexpected way, and the results of that meeting disconcerted me. For reasons I can no longer remember, I was attending a large conference at the University of California at Irvine. Derrida was at Irvine at the time, offering the equivalent of his Paris seminar, something he had been doing for many years, first at Yale, now at Irvine. I did not have time to let him know I was coming to California, so he did not expect to see me. I "cut" the part of my conference that conflicted with his course; probably I was not alone in doing that, but I remember sitting alone toward the back of the large lecture hall.

Derrida was setting up the pile of books to which he would refer during the lecture. It was a constant with him, as I have mentioned, to read and comment on passages from various works, sometimes very long passages, and, rather than type these out, he simply brought the books with him, as most lecturers do. Yet most lecturers do not have to do this in two or three different languages, with multiple piles of books. In any case, he was setting up, then greeting the American students—when he looked up and saw me in the back of the room. He stopped and made his way to the back. *Bisous* on both cheeks followed by the question of how I happened to be there. We talked for only half a minute, fixing a time when we could meet afterward.

He returned to his desk and began the class. What I found strange, even disconcerting, was the way students turned back to stare at me from time to time throughout the lecture, to the point where I wanted to hide. I could see, or thought I could see, people whispering to their neighbor.

—So, who the hell is that guy?

I wanted to reply as Odysseus did to Polyphemus.

—I'm Nobody, Nobody at All, my name is Οὖτις, stop gaping at me and pay attention!

A silly story, but it tells something about the pluses and minuses of friendship with Derrida, and many others of his friends would, I think, be able to confirm this. He really was a sort of "superstar," an academic "celebrity," and that in itself seemed so unexpected in the staid and stolid academy. Among the philosophers that I knew, he was perhaps the most difficult to read with understanding; he should have been the wallflower of all wallflowers, the nerd of nerds, the geek of geeks. I remember, from the dreary years I spent in England, how the Oxbridge "dons" despised him for his dapper style of dress and his good looks: that shock of white hair, the dark teint of the face and hands, the undeniable physical "presence" of the man who sought to undercut the metaphysics of presence—there was so much to hate. And there were surely more bookish reasons to object to him: I could well understand the furious envy of the world's greatest Rousseau expert, or, paraphrasing *Little Miss Sunshine*, the world's *second*-greatest Rousseau expert, after said expert happened to read Derrida's "deconstruction" of their private hero and their own commentaries on that hero. The list of "turfs" and "fiefdoms" in which Derrida intervened with unnerving expertise would begin with Plato and Aristotle and run through Kant and Hegel to Nietzsche and Heidegger, and the list of writers and poets would extend at least as long. And, to top it all, beyond the literature of his own language, the list would include Trakl, Celan, Shakespeare, Defoe, and the "Vary vary Finny" Joyce (FW 519). There was good reason for scholars to bristle. A poster for the Kirby Dick and Amy Ziering-Kofman film asks, "What if someone came along who changed not the way you think about everything but everything about the way you think?" The answer is that you would be upset. And the more learned you were, the more upset you would be. Add to this the fact that this thinker of extraordinary breadth and depth was *not* dowdy, *not* Melville's modestly dusting "sub-sub-librarian," and you have good grounds for all the uproar and upset.

* * *

There are several letters of mine after 1996, some of them arranging meetings between us in Paris, but no replies from Derrida that have been preserved, and I did try to preserve everything. As I mentioned, we often exchanged telephone calls during the mid-to-late nineties. On July 29, 1999, he wrote from Istanbul in reply to my having mentioned that my book on mourning and affirmation in his thought was about to appear. He arranged a meeting between us for September and noted above the date, "As you see I am in Turkey; before that it was Greece, England, and California—all in the same month!" He was on his way to Australia and New Zealand, and, after that, some vacation time with the family in Nice-Èze and Villefranche.[23] Three days later, he had to write again, saying that he had made a mistake about the September date. Marguerite had reminded him of a conflict, and so he invited me out to the house for supper on the new date. I remember asking Marguerite at one point, "Why does he do this to himself?" She smiled her ever-warm and ever-savvy smile and said, "I guess he needs it."

Derrida ventured a guess about what might be behind this incessant traveling. It reminded him of his father's constant road trips for his work as a sales rep in Algeria. "Am I by chance doing what he did, after having protested all my life against his being so enslaved? Could this being on tour from conference to conference be a theatrical version, a distinguished, sublimated version of a humiliated father?" (BP 528). One cannot help but think of "A Disturbance of Memory on the Acropolis," in which Freud is caught short by an experience of guilt, the absurd but profound guilt over having professionally surpassed, outstripped, and out-traveled the father. And I, who once did get around but am now so sedentary? My own father passed up a promotion at his firm to avoid the excessive travel it demanded.

---

23 Nice meant a lot to me because of the presence of Dominique Janicaud and Françoise Dastur there. Èze was important to me because of the *Chemin Nietzsche*, which I had ascended many times. Derrida himself traveled to Èze each year so that he could send a postcard from there to Maurice Blanchot, who had lived there for many years (BP 536). Èze is important to me now because of Janicaud's death there on August 18, 2002. Readers who have not yet climbed the Nietzsche path at Èze may enjoy looking at the photographs in Krell and Bates, *The Good European: Nietzsche's Work Sites in Word and Image*, 188 and 222.

Yet I have wound up speaking the language he had heard and spoken at home as a small boy.

A whole year passed before another letter arrived. Even the telephone conversations dwindled by the start of the new millennium. My last visit with him was in late October of 2000 when he came to the University of Chicago to give a seminar on "The Death Penalty," which was the subject of his seminar that year in Paris. The session at Hyde Park was more than memorable. The United States played a privileged role in the death penalty seminar, not only when he presented a version of it to his American audience but also in the Paris lectures themselves, "privileged" insofar as the USA joined its declared enemies across the world in retaining capital punishment. Indeed, America seemed to be more avidly in favor of the death penalty than any other nation, and its president, "Dubya," held the world record in refusals to commute the sentences of condemned criminals, no doubt many of them falsely convicted. The principal theme of Derrida's seminar was not "justice" but "cruelty," from *cruor,* "I bleed," even if the Supreme Court had ruled that capital punishment was no longer "cruel": it could be administered now with two pricks of a syringe, one to sedate, the other to kill. What remained was *Grausamkeit,* systematic atrocity—which Derrida argued was, if not "cruel," then in many respects certainly "unusual." And Derrida was an expert when it came to the unusual. I distinctly recall that a number of the faculty who were present bristled to hear a Frenchman citing statistics about executions—the majority of them of black males— in a nation, *their* nation, which regarded itself as "advanced." During the discussion, a small group became sardonic and aggressive, perhaps in an effort to rattle this famous and controversial French philosopher. It did not work. Derrida stuck to his arguments and his carefully accumulated facts and figures, remained calm and earnest—as one must when discussing life- and-death issues—and entirely convincing. By the time it was over, the only ones who were rattled were his listeners. Me, for example. When I had the chance to read the two-volume transcript of his Paris seminar a decade later, the death penalty became the theme of one half of my own book, *The Cudgel and the Caress: Reflections on Cruelty and Tenderness.*[24]

I believe it was during this October 2000 visit to Chicago that a group of Derrida's DePaul friends had lunch with him, a lunch at which Derrida

---

24 Published by State University of New York Press, Albany, in 2019.

raised a question to a friend and colleague of mine that is worth reporting. Indeed, it is worth reporting in story form, if only to offer some relief from the gravity of the death penalty discussion. The story might be called, as many stories now are, especially after Stuart Smalley's "Daily Affirmations" interview with Michael Jordan,

Denial Ain't Just a River in Egypt

Kids Say the Darndest Things was a popular television show during my youth, one I hope I never watched, but then how would I be able to remember the name of the show? The kid in question for the present story was not one of those bratty Art Linkletter sorts of kids, however, but Clare Birmingham, the daughter of DePaul's Peg Birmingham.

Peg told us a fascinating story, a family story, about Clare. It may seem odd that a group of philosophers would tell family stories, as we often did when meeting with Derrida, instead of talking about Kantian hypotyposis, which is a kind of disease philosophers suffer from—the need to categorize and subsume every thing under some other thing. But Derrida believed that families were essential and that even Hegel's pure spirit was in the family way, so to speak. In any case, Peg told the following story.

She had a relative or friend, who, driving down an icy Pennsylvania highway with her young daughter tightly strapped into her child seat in the back, suddenly found her car spinning out of control and flipping over. Mother and daughter hung suspended in their seatbelts for what seemed hours, topsy-turvy on the verge of the highway, until rescuers arrived, forced open the doors, and removed them to safety. They were shaken but unharmed.

Peg said that this story so impressed her daughter Clare, who was wide-eyed when she heard it, that one day many months later, Clare said to her mother, "Mom, remember that time our car flipped over and we were hanging from our seatbelts?" Peg, astonished, had to explain to Clare that it was not *they* who had undergone that trauma, but others, those relatives or friends. Clare was not easily convinced, but she finally accepted her mother's assurances.

Peg remarked to all of us who were sitting around the table that she had never seen such an astonishing interiorization or projection or whatever it was. We all shared her amazement, but Derrida turned to Peg and spoke in a gentle and supportive voice, the velvety voice of an experienced therapist.

—Peg, when are you going to stop denying that terrible accident you had with Clare?

*   *   *

While I am in the story-telling mood, "O hell, here comes our funeral! O pest, I'll miss the post!" (FW 190), Benoît Peeters tells one about Derrida and Sam Weber that I am going to steal from both of them—in the hope of a double pardon. My version of the story may contain a few "stretchers," as Huck Finn says of the author of *The Adventures of Tom Sawyer*, but I will try to stick to the facts. Yet before I relate Sam's story, I want to recount my own, since both stories are about meeting Derrida at airports. With Arendt, it was train stations, with Derrida airports.

I had promised to pick him up at Chicago's O'Hare, but I must have been running late. I parked my forest-green Honda Civic in one of the five or six parking garages at O'Hare. Each garage has many floors, and each floor hundreds of parking spaces. I hurried off to meet him, and I made it just in time. He was tired from the trip, and so we made our way directly to the parking garage. I was fairly certain which one held my Honda. The elevator took us to what surely was the approximate floor, but when we arrived there, I realized that I had not jotted down the number of the space. In those days, there were no smartphones with cameras that can photograph the space, the floor, the building, the works. I wrote down my license plate number for him, described the vehicle, and sent him off in one direction, me in the other. I am not sure how many floors or buildings through which we had to perambulate, nor do I remember which of us found the wayward, uncivil Civic, but we found it, and he was very kind, not a peep of complaint.—But here is a story, Sam's story, from decades earlier and an ocean away, at Berlin-Tegel.

Doctor Derrida and Mr. Hyde

Peter Szondi had invited Derrida to present a paper to his institute at the Free University of Berlin. He dispatched a young Sam Weber to meet Derrida, whom Sam did not yet know, at the airport, to conduct him to his hotel. A friend who *had* met Derrida advised Sam to be on the lookout for someone who looked more like a rocker than a professor. He might be wearing a motorcycle jacket, like Marlon Brando in *The Wild One*, but without the silly cap. Sam had been reading Derrida's texts, and so he imagined how the revolutionary thinker might look.

Sam arrived at the waiting hall. He immediately espied a man who looked like the Italian film star Vittorio Gassman, if not Brando himself. He was wearing a velvety sort of shirt with several buttons open at the top and carrying some illustrated weeklies under his arm. Sam was surprised a bit by the décolleté, although other French intellectuals, on the model of Austin Powers, were far more explicit than this man both then and now.

—There he is, the philosopher of the future, I guess, mused Sam, no doubt thinking of Nietzsche's *Beyond Good and Evil*, albeit surprised by the leisurely and stylish attire.

Sam greeted him shyly and said that he had been appointed to get him to his hotel.

—Very kind of you, said Derrida.

On the way to the car, Derrida asked whether there was a pool at the hotel. Sam, nonplussed, said he did not know, but that the conference would be starting soon, so there might not be time for a swim.

—Conference? said Derrida. I'm here to produce some films.

Both men, both Sam and "Derrida," realized the mistake. The two of them, Sam and the Derrida impersonator, returned to the main entrance of the airport, the producer to find a cab, Sam to find the philosopher of a different future. Outside the revolving door, Sam saw a man in a gray suit looking a bit lost, a bit sheepish, really, searching in vain for a ride. When Derrida saw the two men approaching, with Sam now the one looking sheepish, he realized what had happened—clearly, one of those innocent cases of misidentification. Derrida and Sam bade the impersonator, the unwitting impersonator, a fond farewell. As the authentic Derrida settled into Sam's car, he could not forbear, he had to ask.

—So, how could you have confused that guy with me?

—Well, um . . . er . . . you know, violence and metaphysics and all that, said Sam.

It seemed that Derrida was a bit piqued. Or it may have been gentle irony.

—Violence, perhaps, but not *brutality*, he said, probably closer to pique.

Like all good stories, however, this one has an O'Henry twist at the end. When Sam took Derrida back to the airport after the conference, whom should they see lounging at the bar in the waiting hall but the faux Derrida, surrounded by a bevy of what Sam would later describe as "superb" young women. Clearly, the producer had assembled them for the film or films he was producing. What sorts of films, one would like to have known, but did not ask.

There is no need to think anything unseemly, however. I myself once spent an evening in one of the famous Munich beer halls with Federico Fellini at the next table, he, too, surrounded by a group of very striking men and women. At a certain point in the evening, I confronted him, saying, also more than a bit sheepishly, that I admired his films. He smiled and shrugged.

—*É mi lavoro.* It's my job, said Fellini.

The Derridean producer at the Berlin-Tegel bar waved to Sam and to his doppelgänger as they passed through the hall, then entertained the starlets with a succinct account of the mistaken identity. They laughed charmingly.

Sam would later explain that in those early days, Derrida—the authentic one—dressed quite conservatively, like a normal academic. Only gradually would he eschew that gray suit and don more proper attire, which, however, would never run to motorcycle jackets.

* * *

In August 2000, two letters from Derrida arrived in rapid succession, one at Chicago, the other at St. Ulrich, saying that he had tried to reach me by phone many times, but again without success. It was, if I remember correctly, difficult to reach me during those years, even if one dialed all the numbers. I was going through a divorce in Chicago and spending as much time as I could in Germany.

He wanted me to know that he had received a copy of *The Purest of Bastards*, and that he was reading it. As usual, his praise was over the top, and while I decline to cite very much of it, there are one or two things that say something about him. First of all, he denied that the book was really "about" him, or "about" me, for that matter. Or, if it *was* about him, then, as he wrote, it was "not only 'about' me and about the least readable things about me" but also "a book signed by your most intimate, most singular signature." He used the word *generosity* to describe it, which is the word that I perpetually ascribe to him. Finally, he called the book "a treatise on *love*, on the 'too much of love' that inundates our life with its 'not enough,' 'not enough of life. . . .'" ("*un traité de* l'amour, *du 'trop d'amour' qui inonde notre vie de son 'pas assez,' 'pas assez de vie.'*"), saying once again that he was reading it "as though you were not talking about either you or me." In the second letter—or perhaps the first, since one had been sent to Chicago, the other to Germany—he wrote that the book had "gone beyond him," if that is the sense of "*me dépassé*," and that he loved being understood that way, "from all sides" and "also in the sense of overflowing" ("*au sens du débordement aussi*").

I need to add a word about the strange title of my Derrida book, which might easily be misunderstood. I must have sent him many years earlier my initial paper of that title, "The Purest of Bastards," a title based on a remark of his in the *Envois* of *The Post Card*: "This chance [affirmation without issue] can come to us only from you, do you hear me? Do you understand me? [. . .] And I, the purest of bastards, leaving all sorts of bastards just about everywhere." I was struck by this confession, if that is what it is, quite early in the process of writing the book *The Purest of Bastards*, which did not appear until 2000. In a letter of July 6, 1990, that is, ten years before the book was published, he had written a brief note thanking me for something "on behalf of the purest (well, in the end . . .) of bastards." He was reminding me that the very first time we had discussed bastardy—philosophic bastardy—was in connection with Plato's *Timaeus*. The discussion took place at the Collegium in 1986 at Perugia, and it involved Giorgio Agamben, Derrida, and me. The gist of that discussion is this: when Timaeus finds it necessary to talk about *that in which* beings are produced by the Demiurge, the "in which" that he calls "the receptacle" and "the nurse of becoming," he uses the word χώρα, which seems to be something between "space" and "matter"; in so doing, Timaeus confesses that he can speak about this receptacle or cosmic womb only by way of "a bastard reasoning," or an "illegitimate" kind of thinking. For reasons I cannot recall, I volunteered the suggestion that Timaeus was a "pure bastard." Derrida immediately replied.

—Pure? What can *pure* mean in that case, the case of bastardy?

Later, when I read his reference to himself (in *The Post Card*) as "the purest of bastards," I decided to make that the title of my book. I recall an English reviewer who was puzzled about why I would insult Derrida so terribly, what did I have against him, why was I impugning his legitimacy, and so on. Yet Derrida loved the title: he loved those crooked lines of descent on the sinister side of every family escutcheon, the "bar sinister" marking some unexpected intrusion into the life of the family proper, whether it involved people or texts, so that for him the title was a fitting compliment.

I do not want to say much about the book, except that its long gestation manifests the development of my reading of Derrida. The middle section of the book deals with some of my first preoccupations with Derrida's thought. For example, I became interested in what I called "engorged philosophy," as a response to what Derrida describes as "hearing and understanding oneself while speaking," the *s'entendre parler*. Derrida examines philosophy's long-standing confidence that the *voice* in dialogue with itself, but especially in *silent* communion with itself, is perfectly present to its innermost thoughts. Yet the fact that we hear our own voice, our engorged voice, eerily otherwise than the way others hear it, implies that a certain kind of exteriority invades even the presumed interiority of thinking. That exteriority or alterity of the voice becomes evident the first time we hear a recording of our voice—and are repulsed by the sound of it. "Engorged philosophy," in other words, had to do with the flesh of the voice, and I followed Derrida—who himself followed Novalis and Nietzsche—in examining what one might call "systems of the mouth."[25] That interest spilled over into a broader interest in Novalis, especially his ideas concerning "contagion," one of Derrida's most common themes, to wit, the mutual contamination of supposed "opposites." I also continued to take an interest in the problem of *time* in Derrida's work, including his preference for the "future anterior" tense, that is, the future perfect, which will have characterized his entire career of thought and much of my own. Philosophical treatments of *memory* had long been important to me, none of them more important to me than Derrida's constant involvement with issues of memory and anniversary. The entire second part of my earlier memory book, *On the Verge*, had engaged with Derrida's various accounts of memory—and especially memory as *mourning*—during the 1980s. *The Purest of Bastards* tried to recapture all of these ideas and develop them a bit further.

The final two chapters of *The Purest of Bastards*, the last to be written, take up the matter of mourning, first of all in Hegel, then in Augustine. Derrida's early piece on Hegel, "The Pit and the Pyramid," struck me as the best analysis I had seen of Hegel's "semiology," and his monumental work *Glas* seemed to me the single work that would change Hegel studies forever. My chapter on it in *Purest*, under the title "Knell," a word that was

---

25 See David Farrell Krell, *Infectious Nietzsche*, chap. 9 (Bloomington: Indiana University Press, 1996).

proximate to my signature, since, like everyone, "I sign myself" (FW 454), was probably the most difficult chapter for me to write. That was partly because of Hegel, who is nothing if not difficult, and partly because of Derrida, who is always as difficult as any figure he may be reading, and partly also because of the formidable theme of mourning as such.

It strikes me that virtually every book I have written in the intervening years, at least those that involve themselves with philosophy, are not only "touched" by Derrida but also have aspects of his thinking at their core. His importance for my work, all of its "scribbledehobbles" (FW 275), became only greater after Derrida's death, as the transcripts of his seminars began to appear in book form. By that time, I was either planning my retirement or was already retired, hoping to devote the rest of my days to fiction. Yet, one by one, these published seminar transcripts overwhelmed whatever plans I had. "The Beast and the Sovereign," his final seminar, "The Death Penalty," his penultimate seminar, the recently published *Geschlecht III*, to mention only a few—these instances of extraordinary teaching continued to teach me, and I found I had to write about them.

I will add only that I feel almost certain that every novel, short story, or play I have ever written would show the impact as well, perhaps a bit disguised, but nonetheless haunting it all as "a slip of the time between a date and a ghostmark" (FW 473). But let me bring this chapter to a close, in order to take up Benoît Peeters's excellent biography of Derrida, which contains more than a few surprises for me.

On August 18, 2000, I responded to Derrida's letter(s) from earlier that month, the last letters I would receive from him. I want to cite my letter, because it introduces the next chapter, the last apart from some concluding reflections:

> Sometimes you must wonder what your own voyage of thought has been all about: it has caused such anger and jealousy that you must feel battle-weary sometimes, or simply surprised by all the furor. Yet those of us who have *read* you are so grateful, so much in your debt, and those of us who have the privilege of knowing you are so fortunate!
>
> Once again I want to say how beautiful a book your book on *mourning* is—the book that Michael and Pascale-Anne have just finished translating [eventually called *Chaque fois unique, la fin du monde* ("Each Time Unique—The End of the World")]. *That* is the great book! My *Purest* is quite simply a modest commentary—but I love it because it puts me in close touch with your thinking.

Fig. 9.1 Derrida in 1991. Photo by Amy Rothblatt.

9

EACH TIME UNIQUE

At the end, as in the beginning, I can see that much of my friendship with Derrida and my involvement in his work circled about the theme of mourning and the mother, or, as I was inclined to write it, mourning the (m)other. To be sure, in any given life, many other "others" in addition to the mother are mourned. Fathers, for instance. Lovers and friends, for example. In this chapter, I want to read Benoît Peeters's biography of Derrida once again, read it alongside Derrida's own *Circumfession*, trying to think a bit more about this confusing and fraught intersection—this Place du Panthéon with its exuberant, death-dealing traffic—of philosophy, biography, and auto-hetero-bio-thanato-graphy, especially when these discourses confront love, friendship, and mourning the (m)other.

If biographies and even autobiographies usually begin with the *birth* of their subject, then it may not be surprising that mothers play an important role in these genres. Much of what Peeters tells us about Georgette Sultana Esther Safar I had already heard from Derrida himself. Yet the view from outside, from a third party, puts things in a way the son would never put them. Well-nigh the first thing Peeters relates about her is that "she was famous for her wild laughter and her coquetry" (BP 27). An avid poker player, Georgette was reluctant to surrender a good hand—even when the contractions came to announce "Jackie's" impending arrival. Her son could play poker before he could read, his dexterity matching that of a casino dealer.

Yet Lady Luck was not always with Sultana Esther. Her second son, Paul Moïse, died at three months, less than a year before "Jackie" was born— "Jackie" because of *The Kid*, featuring child star Jackie Coogan (BP 23). In his *Circumfession*, Derrida remarks that he may have merited his religious name, Élie or Eliahu, since he was the one who came to fill the empty place, the place left by Paul Moïse, at the table. Already before the beginning, then, an uncanny mix of life and death—what I will later in the chapter discuss in terms of Derrida's notion of *ob-sequence*—marks Derrida's own life. The liveliness of life is everywhere haunted by terrors of death, whether in oneself or in one's (m)other. And more disasters follow: a young cousin is hit by a car and killed in the street in front of his house; later, doctors announce that Jackie will have to undergo a serious surgery on his mastoid bone, his mother is in tears; meningitis kills his younger brother Norbert when Jackie is ten, so that one death (Paul Moïse) lies immediately ahead of him and another (Norbert) follows close behind; or, on the plain of the more mundane necessities that every mother's child must face, the need to leave the house every morning and go to school. I remember Derrida telling me what I later read, namely, that he never crossed the threshold of an educational institute of any sort without a rising of the gorge and a hollowing in the pit of his stomach. Years later, when he was failing the entrance exams for admission to the École Normale Supérieure, the trauma of separation from the mother was still working its effects.

I recall Hegel's insisting that whereas women may play a role during the first several years of a boy's life, a father must rescue his son from the effects of their coddling, "the pathological bloating and the inertia and apathy of spirit" that their care may well induce.[1] Likewise, after the first few years of schooling, where the women continue to prevail, the schoolmistresses must be left behind and the child placed in the ruder hands of men. Hegel is hardly alone in having this view of the proper education of boys. Part of Derrida's effort in *Glas*, I believe, with the book's references to Maria Magdalena (the name of Hegel's mother) and to Hegel's sister Christiana, is to expose the scarcely concealed misogyny of spirit itself—a misogyny that nonetheless fails to obliterate the fact that spirit *remains* familial, is *of* the family, persists *in the family way*, as it were.

I am haunted by a memory of one of my earliest days at kindergarten, an institution I never stopped fearing and fleeing. For reasons I do not remember, my father did not have to go to work that day—the only time I remember his not leaving early for work and coming home late in the day—whereas I was compelled to attend kindergarten. Not a garden for children,

---

1 G. W. F. Hegel to Johanna Frommann, letter dated Nürnberg, May 18, 1811, concerning his illegitimate son, Louis, the son of spirit.

really, if the truth be told, but a life-threatening jungle. I had to clamber up a wooded hill to get to the schoolhouse, and I can still see the sky beyond the limbs and the crowns of the trees as I looked up and screamed my lungs out, both beseeching and cursing the heaven that had defrauded me. Little Oedipus, betrayed and bereft. I wonder when some nation, grown wise, will choose as its national anthem the only possible natal hymn, "Sometimes I Feel Like a Motherless Child"? As Ishmael would ask, how long will we have to wait for that form of wisdom, d'ye think?

There does not seem to be an Oedipal strain in Derrida's "fusion" with his mother, at least if that strain produces strife with the father. In fact, the boy often accompanied his father on his salesman's route, traveling across the Algerian landscape from town to town, taking orders for the wine merchant who was Aimé's employer. And is that not a strange name for a man, Aimé? "Beloved." Later in his life, Derrida was fascinated by the word for "magnetism" in French, *aimance*, related to or even derived from the *aimer* of loving. Peeters cites a detail that Derrida never mentioned to me: for a good part of Derrida's adolescence, the boy was furious with his mother for putatively failing to appreciate sufficiently Aimé's exhausting labors on her and the children's behalf. "He is sacrificing himself for us," Derrida pleaded on behalf of this *père voûté*, "stooped with age and weariness." (That conflict with the mother ended when, toward the end of his high school years, she had to undergo a serious surgery: the old tenderness between them returned and endured.) As for Aimé, I remember asking Derrida why his *Circumfession* had so little to say about his father. That is when he told me the stories of the pipes and of the veil or sheet that he was not permitted to lift from his dead father's face. Often on the drive between Paris and Ris-Orangis, years later, Derrida would scratch a note or two on a pad held against the steering wheel (a practice no one should imitate, please), and each of these notes must have been at least in part a recollection of his father at the wheel, interminably at the wheel of his blue Citroën, perhaps taking notes on orders (BP 38–39).

Even though Georgette's father was profoundly religious and her mother the enforcer of tradition, neither Georgette nor Aimé was particularly dedicated to the practice of Judaism. It was not until the Vichy-controlled government of Algiers forced Derrida's removal from school at age ten, and not until he heard the cry "Jew" from his schoolmates as a term of opprobrium, that Derrida's Jewishness became relevant for him. However, when the Jewish community established a makeshift school of its own, Derrida found it equally intolerable (BP 28–29, 33). For the rest of his life, Derrida's Jewishness seems to have resembled Freud's: only when the Jewish people were under attack, and that was often enough, was the identification deeply felt. Otherwise, the word "community" sparked an allergic reaction in Derrida. Nor is it impossible to relate his situation to that of the young Hannah Arendt, even though the catastrophic disruption of her life in 1933 made her identification with the community much stronger than his. In any case, for the two of them, there was a strong resistance to the Zionist goal of a nation-state in Palestine; both were fierce advocates of a two-state solution for Israel and Palestine. Both states would have to confront what Derrida took to be the central paradox, dilemma, or double bind of democratic states: there can be no nation-state without some form of communitarian identity, but there can be no *democratic* nation-state without unreserved respect for and hospitality offered to the other, the outsider. Derrida puts it this way, a way that is perhaps especially pertinent for a nation one half of which does not shy away from separating "outsider" children from their parents and keeping them in cages: "No democracy without respect for singularity or irreducible alterity, but no democracy without a community of friends, . . . without the calculation of majorities based on stabilizable, representable, identifiable subjects who are equal among themselves. These two laws are irreducible to one another. They are tragically irreconcilable and they always lacerate. The wound itself gapes with the initial necessity of one's having to *count* one's friends, count the others, in an economy of what is ours, there where every other is altogether other."[2]

One of the criticisms of Derrida that I was hearing a decade or two ago and that is sometimes repeated today is that "Derrida is not political enough." I always felt, and still feel, that he went to the core of "the political," so that we have more to learn from him about our fractured polis and our fractious politics than from anyone else. And this brings him closer to Hannah Arendt than most would have suspected. When I read the following words by Jerry Kohn concerning Arendt, I could not help but think of Derrida's critique of sovereignty as well: Kohn says that in Arendt's view, the genuine American "innovation" in politics "was the consistent abolition of sovereignty within the body politic of the Republic, the insight

---

2 Jacques Derrida, *Politiques de l'amitié* (Paris: Galilée, 1994), 40.

that in the realm of human affairs sovereignty and tyranny are the same" (YB xxxiii).[3]

* * *

On November 12, 1994, I wrote Derrida a newsy letter, but some of that news astonishes me now on account of its chutzpah:

> To a small group of very bright undergraduates at DePaul I taught a course on Augustine's *Confessions* and your *Circumfession*. We first read Geoffrey [Bennington]'s text, then Augustine's, then your own. It was an extraordinary experience for these young people—as for me. They were deeply into the texts and wrote wonderful papers. I imagine that you were not thinking of such young students when you wrote your text—giving your contemporaries the slip by writing one of your most difficult texts. But you would be amazed to know how moved the students were: I knew I was taking a risk in having them read it, the risk that they would be lost and troubled, but the response was overwhelmingly positive. We are *all* lost and troubled, of course, and *Circumfession* helped them and me to get accustomed to it!

My description of the course here is incomplete: a fourth part of it was a reading of Nietzsche's third treatise in the *Genealogy of Morals*, "What Do Ascetic Ideals Signify?" The tenor of the course is probably reflected in what became the eighth chapter of *The Purest of Bastards*, "Mourning Monica, Our (M)Other." The handling of Augustine there (and presumably in the course I taught) is not very gentle.

What has always intrigued me about Augustine's "memorial" to his mother, the "altar" that he erects for her in and as his *Confessions*, is that it is not as pious as one might have thought. Not only does the son spot "the relic of Eve" that is concealed in his mother's heart, not only does he confess—on her behalf—that she had a weakness for wine, but he also loudly deplores her flow of tears over him, tears that drench the ground on which they both have to stand.[4] Mired in this swampland at their feet, she shares with her son—at least according to his memories or fantasies—some details

---

3 I do not know of any full-length study of Arendt and Derrida, but there certainly needs to be one. For the moment, see Peg Birmingham's forthcoming article "Light without Glory: Arendt and Derrida on Witnessing, Poetic Sovereignty, and a Non-Sovereign Politics."

4 Regarding confessing "on behalf of" the mother, Derrida writes: "I confess my mother, one always confesses the other, I confess (myself) means I confess my mother means I own up to making my mother own up, I make her speak in me, before me, whence all the questions at her bedside as though I were hoping to hear from her mouth the revelation of the sin at last" (C 139–40/147–48). Derrida then proceeds to mention Augustine's "confession" of his mother's "surreptitious" weakness for wine, if not for coquetry and poker.

of the sexual indignities to which Patricius, Augustine's earthly father, has subjected her, while he shares with her his thoughts about the ladder of love that rises from fornication and "the birdlime of concupiscence" to the fecund seas of heavenly ἀγάπη. Monica, evidently a gripping conversationalist, is nonetheless wildly inconsistent in her behavior: she sends Augustine's concubine of thirteen years back to Africa, the nameless concubine who has given him a son, Adeodatus, a gift from God given back to the Father, and yet she encourages him to marry and to give her more grandchildren, legitimate ones. In general, she cleaves to her son in the physical, animal way that mothers are wont to cleave to sons. Meanwhile, as he relates in Book V, he promises her he will stay with her, will never leave her, then he sneaks away in the night to the harbor at Carthage and boards a ship bound for Ostia and Rome. Even though his vessel is well underway across the Mediterranean, he can still see her, at least in his mind's eye, making a terrible fuss on the shore. However, his betrayal will not deter the mother; she will soon follow in his wake. Speaking of wakes, *"Qui quae quot at Quinnigan's Quake!"* (FW 496–97), one might say that she prepares her son's wake before arranging her own, so that the converted son soon enough follows in his saintly mother's wake, or she in his, it is difficult to say.

Monica, of course, was not Derrida's mother, even if she, Derrida's mother, weeps as desperately as Monica did over each of her son's departures (C 166/177). Derrida finds himself in Santa Monica, of all places, writing about his dying mother, and it can be verified that his family lived for a time when he was a child on the rue St. Augustin. Every reader of Derrida's *Circumfession* is bound to complain that it is filled with such matters of sheer coincidence, mere chance, serendipity, accident—for example, the fact that Jackie physically resembles his mother more than his father. What matters in a life, Hegel would counter, is essence rather than accident, and essence is what a man *does*, what he accomplishes for civil society and the state, not what he looks like. When the community raises a stone for that man on his death, the monolith records what he has *achieved*, not the thousands of accidents, many of them unsavory, that admittedly constitute so much of that life. The stone symbolizes the *spirit* that a man's life yields by way of his deeds, and to that monolithic spirit, a real man must yield. Anxieties, nightmares, phobias, loves, false steps—these pertain to infancy and childhood, and they deserve the oblivion that soon swallows them. I cannot remember that earliest period of my life, says Augustine, and so it must have pertained to someone else. Nietzsche adjudged that claim naive if not disingenuous.

Derrida, for his part, stubbornly sticks with accidents over essences. To be sure, in his reading of texts, he looks for "laws" and quasitranscendentals (which I prefer to call *queasy* transcendentals), so that "deconstruction" can go to the heart of every text while keeping its head. The reading is nothing if not rigorous. Even so, it is the obliques that intrigue Derrida, all those things that come storming in from left field, as it were, the uncanny *sinistra* of a life and a thinking.

One of the "laws" that he discovers early on in his reading of Nietzsche's autobiography is the law of *obsequence*. He finds it at work in Nietzsche's account, in "Why I Am So Wise," of his "dual inheritance": as his father, Nietzsche is "already dead"; as his mother, he is "still alive and is growing old" (KSA 6:264). The title of Nietzsche's autoheterobiothanatography, in translation, is Pontius Pilate's *Behold the Man.* By the time of his mother's death in 1894—his father died in 1849, when Fritz was not yet five—Nietzsche is submerged in the night of his illness. We cannot be certain whether he was even aware of her passing; for him, she may have passed well before her death, after the onset of his own slow demise. In any case, the "sequence" of mourned deaths in any given life is jumbled and uncertain.

Likewise, if one remembers only one thing about Rousseau's *Confessions* it is his father's remark to the boy that each time the father looks at his son, he sees the son's resemblance to the mother. For she died giving birth to him. She is the mother whose life the son unwittingly took. A chance remark, perhaps not even a cruel accusation but merely an observation of father to son—yet one that might be engraved on the tombstone of Rousseau's entire life and death: Here lies the boy who was the death of his mother. . . . For what face would Rousseau have seen for the rest of his life gazing back at him from the mirror? In all the writers and thinkers that intrigue Derrida, or at least a good many of them, it is difficult to determine the *sequence* of the generations in their lives, hard to determine who follows whom and what generates what. *Ob-sequence*: the *ob* is an abbreviation of *obiit*, "he or she died," or a preposition meaning either "following behind" or "heading toward," or, most tellingly, an exchange, "this for that," tit for tat, a life for a life, which of course means that death, each time unique, is each time manifold and overdetermined.

*   *   *

Other details of Derrida's youth, as Benoît Peeters portrays it, enlarge the picture I have of the man: his love of the movies, no matter what was playing, the cinema opening up to the boy life in *la métropole*, that is, in mainland France, and life in the dreamworld of Hollywood; his family's "adoption" of an American GI toward the end of the war, one among *les Amerloques*, who were the liberators of the Jewish population of Algeria (BP 35). Derrida's contact with the United States thus goes much farther back than I knew. His love of soccer was familiar to me, ever since the Umbrian urn incident, but I did not know about his deep connection with his football *shoes*, something that touched me because of my own little fetish, during my teenage years, involving my baseball "spikes." As for his teenage exploits, which Derrida liked to paint as those of a *voyou* or "rogue" long before he philosophized about so-called rogue-states, that is, states accused "of estreme voyoulence" (FW 432), Peeters is probably right to be skeptical. It is true that the disruption of his studies during the war left a wound and resulted in gaps in the boy's education and even in his *desire* for schooling. Yet Derrida was no delinquent. His biographer follows the traces of Albert Camus—who comes up many times in the biography, always in an admirable way, and who is an author Derrida will read quite sympathetically in his penultimate seminar on the death penalty—when he describes the fantasy of an entire generation of Algerian lads: "Doubtless, Jackie and his friends all played the part of 'Clark' [Gable, of course], as evoked by Camus, 'harmless adolescent boys who go to great trouble to look like bad boys,' trying to seduce their 'Marlène' [Dietrich, of course]" (BP 37).

However disrupted his schooling, it is clear that Derrida was reading voraciously from early on, poring over not the easiest of texts. Gide, Rousseau, and Nietzsche, the latter two "my two positive heroes," as he calls them (C 127/133), Valéry, Camus, Artaud—the list goes on, and it is extraordinary. Little wonder that Derrida will find himself forever on the threshold between philosophy and literature. A cousin, Micheline Lévy, tells him that she prefers him to become a writer, not a professor; she looks forward to reading his "novels" (BP 105). I recall a scene much later in his life when a nervous young student tells him how excited she is to meet him because she has read and admired his "novels." (Perhaps she was mistaking him for Blanchot?) Instead of chiding her and saying that she is obviously confusing him with someone else, however, Derrida replies reassuringly.

—Thank you, you are very kind.

An aspect of Derrida's secondary school education that interests me in particular is his early introduction to and fascination with Heidegger. In Derrida's final year of high school, a teacher named Jan Czarnecki, otherwise unknown to me, spoke about the German philosopher. Derrida then read the only volume of Heidegger's writings that was available in French, a selection translated by Henry Corbin that included Heidegger's inaugural address at Freiburg, "What Is Metaphysics?" I myself used Corbin's translation decades ago while preparing my translation of that address for *Basic Writings*. Even though Derrida later became famous for his translation of and commentary on Husserl's *Origins of Geometry*, it was in fact Heidegger who introduced Derrida to phenomenology (BP 47–49). Camus was already familiar to him during his high school years, and Sartre's series of *Situations* introduced him to Maurice Blanchot, Francis Ponge, and Georges Bataille; Sartre's *Being and Nothingness* no doubt fortified the interest in Heidegger, especially the Heidegger for whom "the nothing" is more powerful than mere negation (ibid.). More powerful than logical or grammatical negation is this strange-sounding "nihilation," which is fundamentally *uncanny* in its pervasiveness. Heidegger writes, "For negation cannot claim to be either the sole or the leading nihilative behavior in which Dasein remains shaken by the nihilation of the nothing. Unyielding antagonism and stinging rebuke have a more abysmal source than the measured negation of thought. Galling failure and merciless prohibition require some deeper answer. Bitter privation is more burdensome" (BW 105).

Peeters observes that if Derrida "reverberates" with these words, as Derrida himself confesses, it is doubtless because of the catastrophe of World War II for Europeans and North Africans alike (BP 48). Yet even a baby boomer such as myself, born at the very end of the conflict and on another continent, never yet the victim of catastrophe, can come to "reverberate" with these same words. Without that shared sympathy for what Heidegger was trying to get at in "What Is Metaphysics?" Derrida and I would have never encountered one another.

*   *   *

The title of this chapter, "Each Time Unique," is all about mourning. It is the first half of the title Derrida chose for one of his last books: *Each Time Unique, the End of the World*. The book has an odd history. In the late 1990s, Michael Naas and Pascale-Anne Brault, on the urging of Peg Birmingham, determined to publish in a single volume a number of eulogies that Derrida had written over the years, beginning in 1981 with the death (or "deaths") of Roland Barthes. The University of Chicago Press published *The Work of Mourning* in 2001.[5]

It was an excellent idea, partly because the eulogies themselves are testimonies to the life *and* work of each deceased individual, testimonies profoundly thought and deeply felt. An excellent idea also, however, because mourning had been a *philosophical* theme of Derrida's from the outset. The subtitle of my own book about his thought, *Works of Art, Mourning, and Affirmation*, chose the word "mourning" as its central theme. Derrida had become well aware of the centrality of mourning for him, and so he agreed to a French edition of Michael and Pascale-Anne's collection, now with two additional eulogies, those for Gérard Granel and Maurice Blanchot. However, because of Derrida's problems with Freud's notion of the "work" of mourning, "work" that can be putatively either "successful" (introjective) or "unsuccessful" (incorporative), he chose the title *Each Time Unique, the End of the World.*

Does the entire world come to an end with the death of each unique individual? Derrida insisted, yes, the entire world, once and for all, one more time. "Once and for all, one more time": that was Derrida's way to translate Nietzsche's most exalted thought, the eternal recurrence of the same. In his preface to the French edition of his eulogies, Derrida wrote, "Death declares each time *the end of the world in totality*, the end of every possible world, and *each time the end of the world as a totality that is unique, hence irreplaceable, and hence infinite.* . . . But death, death itself, if there is such a thing, leaves no place, leaves not the slightest chance for either the replacement or the survival of the sole and unique world, of the 'sole and unique' that makes of everything that lives (animal, human, or divine) a sole and unique living entity."[6]

The paradox that each time something living leaves the world it takes the entire world with it is similar to or perhaps identical to the need to think Nietzsche's eternal return of the same once and for all one more time. One is never done with this dizzying truth.

5 Jacques Derrida, *The Work of Mourning*, ed. Pascale-Anne Brault and Michael Naas (Chicago: University of Chicago Press, 2001). The editors' introduction, "To Reckon with the Dead: Jacques Derrida's Politics of Mourning," demonstrates the *philosophical contours* of mourning in Derrida's thought. I can add no more to what is said there so well.

6 Jacques Derrida, *Chaque fois unique, la fin du monde*, ed. Pascale-Anne Brault and Michael Naas (Paris: Galilée, 2003), 9–11.

Pierre Klossowski explains it in a fascinating way.[7] He says that because the thought of eternal return elates us each time we think it, it must strike us as a novel idea each time it occurs to us and astonishes us, which suggests that in the meantime we have forgotten it. Life runs on a cycle of anamnesis and amnesia. For Derrida, the cycle has to do with the periodic appearance of *finitude* in our lives, not the finitude that acknowledges our own demise but the one that announces itself in the deaths of others. For Derrida, finitude expresses itself in our mourning of people *and* their world. He was struck by Paul Celan's line *Die Welt ist fort, ich muss dich tragen*, "The world is gone, I must carry you." In every eulogy that he delivered, Derrida bore witness to the fact that the *world* had disappeared and that only the mourner was left to bear the dead one. But on what ground does such a mourner stand? The captious critic might take that question to be a clever refutation, but the loss of ground is precisely what the mourner undergoes.

That thought, *each time unique, the end of the world*, develops along two lines of resistance, one toward Freud, the other toward Heidegger. If Freud found it unhealthy to incorporate the deceased other, no matter how beloved, Derrida argues that loyalty itself demands something like incorporation. If that sounds like melancholia, that is because our mortal existence *is* melancholic. In his seminar on the death penalty, Derrida insists that the execution of a condemned criminal, even if the criminal is "justly" condemned, guilty as charged, means the end of the world. If Kant insisted that harm done to others invariably recoils on the one who does the harm, Derrida finds that this is especially true when the state coolly and with malice aforethought snuffs a life. As for the resistance to Heidegger, it involves a radical extension of Heidegger's thesis concerning the difference between the unliving and the living. The stone, says Heidegger, has no "world," the animal is "poor in world," and the human being (alone among all beings) "shapes" or "forms" a world. As I mentioned earlier, Derrida counters that every living thing "traces" its life, "secretes" its life, and in so doing shapes a world. Shapes *the* world, one must say, even if the definite article collapses the proffered distinction between the human "world" and the vegetal or animal "environment," and even if it makes of "the world" a forfeit for each living being.

---

7 Pierre Klossowski, *Le cercle vicieux*, chap. 3, "The Experience of Eternal Return," rev. ed. (Paris: Mercure, 1969).

For Derrida, this unique concept of "world" is simply a consequence of Heidegger's insistent question "What *is* world?" Even when Heidegger seems to be sure about the distinction between stone, animal, and human being, Derrida suspects that he is entirely unsure about *how* the "world" is formed. For Derrida, I imagine, this thought about the demise of the cosmos with the death of each living thing has to do with Heidegger's "eschatology of being." The Greeks thought about the end of the world as ἐκπύρωσις, universal conflagration or holocaust, the consummation of the world. Derrida seems to combine the early with the late, seeing in cinders or ash a friable trace of the living totality of the world. When Freud says that successful mourning marks a loss to the ego but not a loss of the world, that the world remains intact, Derrida counters that loss is loss, so that the dream of compensation—the compensation being that the mourner *survives*—evanesces in the face of a darker truth: the loss is not only *to* the world but also *of* the world, *each time unique* and yet *each time universal—*a *finitude* that each time is *infinite* in its consequences.

When Zarathustra loses his first and only human friend, the tightrope walker who falls to his death while crossing over the bridge to the future, he carries the dead friend on his back wherever he goes, searching for a place to bury him. Zarathustra carries his burden for the longest time, precisely because the world has vanished. The hollow tree in which he finally inters his friend is indeed hollow, has no pith, is the mere shadow of the trees that used to populate the world that once was. That is why Nietzsche felt that he would have to write a fourth, fifth, and even sixth part of *Thus Spoke Zarathustra*, so that he could finally allow his hero to die—and to let the world of Zarathustra collapse (KSAB 6:557).

This all seems a wild fancy, not serious thought, but I swear it is how I felt after Derrida's death, and not only his. The end of the world. The melancholy that settled in after his death had strange effects. For years afterward, I could not go to Paris. The city no longer existed for me; there was no way to get there. And there was no there there, at least until my younger brother took me by the ears and dragged me back to the city we both love. But even he had to admit that the world had gone missing after the death of a friend of his and a fond acquaintance of mine, Michel Tournier. As for the world of philosophy in general, I had trouble finding it again. It seemed to have gone up in smoke. I held out for a few more years, then retired, in search of another world. Not another planet, but another cosmos, another jewel, since that other world had foundered.

As for the absurdity of this fantasy, the foundering of the entire world when each "someone" dies, I suddenly remember mentioning such a thought to my mother during my high school years, the thought that when someone dies, the world comes to an end. My mother discouraged that thought. She did so to protect me, I am certain, just as, when I was five and we were returning from the funeral of a young playmate who, because he had done something unforgivable, leaped to his death from the roof of his house, she took my hand and told me very earnestly—it was our first adult conversation—that no matter what I might ever do, I must never hurt myself. She knew, I think, that the world hung in the balance.

*   *   *

Does the world hang in the balance? Perhaps that is the meaning of a dream I had, the only dream I have ever had in which Derrida has appeared, as far as I know. I recorded it in a small notebook that I carry on my travels, then expanded on it days later in a journal:

> August 24, 2007. Last week, in Prague, I was thinking of Marguerite and Jacques. [Marguerite had lived in Prague as a child, and Derrida had been arrested there during one of their visits to the city.] I dreamt that he had published a new book. He was there; he showed it to us. It was gigantic book, dwarfing Arno Schmidt's *Zettels Traum*. The book lay there on a table—it measured perhaps four-by-six feet. It was an atlas, a book of maps, printed in the most brilliant colors, especially the blazing blue of the seas. With both of his outstretched arms, Derrida turned the pages, which were like heavy vellum sheets. On the verso side of one of the maps were bits of text. I recognized on one page the word *Quoniam*, "since" or "because," printed in red in a medieval script. A day or two after the night I had the dream, the word leapt out at me from a page of Lucretius, which I had been reading and admiring—even *before* having had the dream.

More fitting than my allusion to Lucretius would be a reference to Augustine's *Confessions*. There the word *quoniam*, as "since" or "because," introduces a raft of specious causal connections (*verlogen*, "deceitful," says Nietzsche, such that "philosophical value = zero"). The word appears in three of Derrida's many brief quotations from Augustine in his *Circonfession*.[8] In any case, it was an oddly moving dream, as absurd as it may seem, as all dreams do, and I had no trouble remembering it even days afterward, something that is extremely rare with me.

---

8 The three passages I am referring to here may be found at C 130/137, 201/216, and 248/268.

What can it mean? Is it about *L'autre cap* ("The Other Heading"), with the Mediterranean in blazing azure? I believe it was clear to me in the dream that he had returned from the dead, from the bourn of that undiscovered country, to show us this new *opus posthumum* of his. He was proud of it. And we were all gripped by its enormity in both size and content. An atlas is a book of the world—Atlas supporting on his shoulders and with his spine the entire world. Derrida brought back with him the book of the entire world, with which he had absconded.

*   *   *

All this talk of mourning and melancholy would make one think that Derrida was morose and that contact with him was drear. That would be a mistake. Happy-go-lucky would not be the way to describe him, of course, but Stephen Dedalus's "morose delectation" would be even farther from the truth. And yet the best friend of Derrida's youth, Michel Monory, recollects that the tone of Derrida's letters to him reflected a temperament that tended to be "somber and melancholy" (BP 71). One of the most moving facets of Peeters's biography is his account of Derrida's friendship with Monory, whom he befriended at lycée Louis-le-Grand. The friendship endured for at least a decade, and the letters between the two were regular, sometimes almost daily exchanges, and always candid and intimate. Monory recalls in particular that even though their correspondence was regular, Derrida would always beg forgiveness for his "silences," a trait that I saw in virtually every note I received from him. At a particularly low point in Derrida's life, he wrote to Monory, "I am leading here a very sad life. Some day I will give you the details. . . . I can no longer shed tears about it . . . weep for the world, cry after God. I can't go on much longer. Michel, pray for me" (BP 64, citing Derrida). That from a boy who, although he cherished his maternal grandfather's prayer shawl, was not a frequenter of the temple.

Peeters remarks that the correspondence between Monory and Derrida deserves to be published in full, and one may hope that someday this will happen (BP 63). I mention the correspondence, which is such an important source for the biography, because it reminds me of the kinds of exchanges that were common during the eighteenth and nineteenth centuries, especially during the Romantic period. Derrida does not shy away from expressing his deepest anxieties, frustrations, and hopes during those early years in Paris, nor does he shy away from expressing his deeply felt affection for Monory. I think especially of Hölderlin's correspondence, and even of his epistolary novel, *Hyperion,* both of which contain this sort of impassioned prose. Likewise, what would we know of Nietzsche's life without the eight volumes of his wonderful letters? and what would go missing from our appreciation of his *thought* if those volumes of letters were not available? I think, too, of Freud's letters, not only to Wilhelm Fliess but also to family, friends, and colleagues written much later in his life. Freud's letters are scattered in numerous volumes published by disparate publishers, so that they are difficult to track down—they cry for a complete historical-critical edition.

These sorts of revelatory letters remained an important part of Derrida's life, even given his waxing "mailophobia." It strikes me how rare such correspondences have become. It is not simply that email and "texting" have displaced the post, although that is part of the story. Am I right in thinking that as communication becomes immediate, instantaneous, the depth of feeling in it dies? Many critics have observed how tenuous and how easily misunderstood the "tone" of our hastily dispatched emails can be. So often the writer appears to be ill-tempered, simply because the medium itself is not a well-tempered clavier.

Yet it is not merely a matter of email technology, "Speak to us of Emailia" (FW 410), to say nothing of tweets and Instagram posts. It may be that some early letters of mine to cousins and friends had the sort of depth I long for and miss, although those productions of mine would never have been as articulate and as eloquent as Derrida's letters to Monory. However, I suspect that I was never capable of writing such letters, certainly not day-by-day and over years and years. Why? There is something about the culture in which I grew up, something about its Puritanism and its need to show a brave face, which does not permit exchanges of the heart. I think of my correspondence with J. Glenn Gray, one of the great exceptions to the rule of impoverished correspondences in my own life. My letters to and from Derrida, no matter how much the "everyday" dominates them, have at least for me the quality of a genuine correspondence, exchanges of head and heart—that is part of what has gone missing from my world since his death.

* * *

Another theme of Peeters's biography that comes up repeatedly is Derrida's star-crossed relationship with the French academic system, no matter on which side of the desk he sat. I believe it is safe to say that his teachers generally saw the young man's brilliance ("excellent in every respect; very fine philosophical qualities," "results constantly brilliant; assuredly a philosophical personality"), but the advice he received on one of his written exams for entry into the École Normale Supérieure (ENS) seems to be typical: "Come back when you are ready to play by the rules; don't try to *invent* when what you must do is *inform yourself.* A failing grade like this ought to provide a service to this candidate" (BP 68). Even a friendly and supportive teacher, Maurice de Gandillac, felt compelled to give similar advice. "Play the game," he recommended, "*scolariser un peu,*" which sounds a bit like "try to become more like a schoolboy" (BP 98). As for "invention," decades later Derrida would subtitle one of his largest collections of articles, *Psyche*, "Inventions of the Other." Asking him not to invent was like handing him the knife for seppuku.

Soon after graduating from the ENS, however, Derrida produced articles and books that stunned Parisian intellectual circles. It is quite astonishing in retrospect to see that virtually everyone recognized that his translation of and commentary on Husserl's *Origins of Geometry* was a work of genius, one destined to change the history of phenomenology in France. For the problem with the *origins* of geometry, as Derrida showed, was "an originary complication of the origin, an initial contamination of the simple" (BP 93, quoting Derrida's *Origins*). Years earlier, when Louis Althusser received an essay on Freud from his student, he had to be nonplussed by the level of sophistication manifested by declarations like this one, expressing a lifetime commitment to the study of psychoanalysis: "The unconscious, when it ceases to be a reproach to philosophy, merely becomes philosophy's form of repentance" (BP 96). Althusser was not at all surprised by the brilliant pieces that began to appear in the mid-1960s, and his praise of Derrida's work remained vocal and unstinting.

What seems incredible is that both before and during this time of initial publication and immediate public recognition, Derrida was busy teaching courses at the Sorbonne and at the ENS, courses visited by dozens of students, the most serious students of philosophy, the best and the brightest in France. For the word had spread. Just as Hannah Arendt and her friends made their way from Königsberg to Marburg and Heidegger in 1924, so countless students found their way into Derrida's classrooms and into his office hours during the early to mid-1960s. About the latter, one student recounts the following: "Everything that emanated from him, his gestures, his verbal responses, was lively and at the same time extremely focused.

Never a mere approximation, never a moment of relaxation. Very often, pauses. He was in front of you, already at that time, like a block of capability and memory [*comme un bloc de puissance et de mémoire*]" (BP 345). Another student remarks on his "remarkable manner of entering into the ,argumentation of others" (ibid.).

I remember quite vividly one of the first times I heard Derrida in discussion and "argumentation." He had been asked about a pair of conceptual opposites that seemed unshakable in their difference. Derrida took the time to show—in a way that admittedly I could but barely follow—how and why these "opposites" actually "came down on one side, the identical side" of their supposed opposition. It was not like observing a clever dialectician at work, since there was no "determinate third object" that blossomed forth from his demonstration, as there is in Hegel. What resulted from it was the insight that one could no longer be sure about the status of either of these apparent "opposites" or even about the very meaning of "opposition." My first research paper in graduate school had been on the ταναντία ἀπάντα, the "opposites" and "oppositional thinking" among the early Greek thinkers. I now needed to start over again.

I have had many conversations with Françoise Dastur about him as a teacher, so I can confirm Peeters's account: Derrida taught in the Salle Cavaillès of the Sorbonne, which could hold a hundred and fifty auditors, but his courses were so over-subscribed that he had to divide the class in two, teaching the same material twice, even though his schedule was already impossible. As if that were not enough, Derrida organized a number of *Arbeitsgemeinschaften* each semester with his more advanced students, each group consisting of five or six individuals. Often their work involved translating texts of Husserl's that were not yet available in French. Derrida would visit each group at least three times per semester to see how the work was progressing and to lend assistance. I recall being astonished by this, so I asked Françoise whether this was common practice, whether other professors repeated courses to accommodate students or organized work groups to help them progress. It was done by no one else, she assured me. It was done by no one else, she assured me. Peeters cites an interview that Françoise Dastur had with the late Dominique Janicaud, and I will refer to it here: Dastur talks about the difference between Derrida's masterful performance as a teacher, highly disciplined and quite focused on the works under discussion, and the rather shy but helpful mentor that she met during office hours: "He seemed timid and even a bit awkward" (BP 147). By the time I met him, decades later, he was of course quite polished and apparently at ease in person, anything but maladroit. As for the Sorbonne courses back in the early 1960s, Dastur describes them as "truly magnificent." She mentions the courses "Method and Metaphysics" and "Theology and Teleology in Husserl," but I have heard her laud in the same way Derrida's first Heidegger course at the ENS, "Heidegger: The Question of Being and History."[9]

But to return to those earliest publications by Derrida and the responses they garnered. Concerning Derrida's long introduction to the Husserl text on the origins of geometry, which in effect offers a commentary on all of Husserlian phenomenology, the well-known philosopher of science Georges Canguilhem writes to the neophyte Derrida:

> It has been a long time—more than a few months—since I've been able to suspend all other things and read a book all the way through, at one fell swoop. That is how I measure the quality of your work, because I read your introduction to *The Origin of Geometry* without interruption and with unaccustomed intellectual satisfaction. . . . My first glance at the book, comparing the dimensions of the introduction [by Derrida] with [Husserl's] text itself, made me smile. But I'm no longer smiling: on the contrary, I am rejoicing that the introduction is as long as it is, because in the end everything there is necessary. Not a "filler" word to be found. . . . I am not the first one to have had confidence in you; that was Jean Hippolyte. My confidence followed upon his, but now it has found its justification. (BP 163–64)

Derrida's work on Husserl did not cease with this first publication, however. Françoise Dastur has told me many times about the work groups that Derrida formed to translate Husserl's *Ideen II* and *Krisis*. And during the remarkable year 1967, during which three books by Derrida were published by various houses in Paris, so that his own situation, as Peeters writes, "evolved in a spectacular fashion" (BP 165), the third to appear was *Voice and Phenomenon: An Introduction to the Problem of the Sign in Husserl's Phenomenology*. In later years, Jean-Luc Nancy singled out this work on Husserl for special praise: "In my eyes, *Voice and Phenomenon* remains the most masterful of his books, the one that induces in me the greatest

---

9 This last, a truly remarkable first effort, has been published, and I have noted it earlier in the book: Jacques Derrida, *Heidegger: la question de l'Être et l'Histoire; Cours de l'ENS-Ulm 1964–1965*, ed. Thomas Dutoit with Marguerite Derrida (Paris: Galilée, 2013).

enthusiasm, because it contains the heart of his entire operation: taking distance from self-presence, and differance with an *a*, in the difficult relationship between infinite and finite. That is for me the true core, the motor, the energy of his thought" (BP 224).

It was this book, after Derrida's reading of Nietzsche and Heidegger in *Spurs*, that fascinated me most, principally, as I have said, because of its account of "hearing and understanding oneself while speaking," *le s'entendre-parler*, but also its account of Husserl's desire for an infinitely expanding "living present" and what Derrida called the finitude of the "testamentary ego." Only after struggling with these issues did I turn to the second publication of 1967, the remarkable *Of Grammatology*; and I am still trying to catch up with the studies gathered in *Writing and Difference*, which extend from Artaud and Bataille to Levinas and Freud—among others. Concerning the Freud essay, which appears to be based on one unpublished piece and one curiosity by Freud, but which then goes on to confront crucial issues for all of psychoanalysis, Roland Barthes comments in a letter to Derrida, "More and more—what would we do without you?" (BP 206). American literary critic David Carroll, after attending a seminar with Derrida in the fall of 1967, a seminar for a small group of scholars in Paris organized by Paul de Man, summarizes the general reception of Derrida's work in 1967 by telling Benoît Peeters, "After that, nothing was the same" (BP 229). Perhaps the most wonderful praise and acknowledgment, however, comes from the scholar who supervised Derrida's degree program at the ENS, Jean Hippolyte.

—When you supervise a philosopher like that, said Hippolyte, all you can do is follow (BP 234).

I will not continue with these *éloges*, since there are too many of them, but will close with two that are especially remarkable. They come from two other teachers of Derrida, Paul Ricoeur and Louis Althusser, each of whom doubtless had significant philosophical differences with him. However, each of them remarks, toward the close of his own life, on Derrida's exceptional achievement. Ricoeur: "Me, I had talent; Derrida, he had genius" (BP 643). Althusser: Derrida is "the most radical of all . . . the sole Great of our time, and perhaps for a long time to come, the last Great" (BP 509). Althusser here is quoting, almost word for word, Heidegger on Nietzsche.

The only exceptions to the rule of universal acclaim among French intellectuals are two: first, the academic philosophers of the Association of French Philosophy, who find all these publications by Derrida too radical, upsetting an august tradition as they invariably do, and second, the psycho-analyst Jacques Lacan, who finds that Derrida has "stolen" all his ideas. An instantaneous and mutual dislike, one that never abates, is all that one can say about these two major theoreticians of psychoanalysis after Freud, Jung, Adler, and Klein. As for the first group, they see to it that the doors of the distinguished academies—the Sorbonne, the ENS, the Collège de France, the Académie Française—remain closed to Derrida for the remainder of his life. I recall a conversation with Françoise Dastur in which she reported that one of the least interesting philosophers whom the two of us knew had recently been elected to one of these august bodies. Election there amounted to something like the attainment of knighthood, which included investiture with a ceremonial sword. But this pathetic fellow, upon his election, was thrilled to wear his swashbuckler sword instead of being embarrassed by the anachronism. Françoise roared with laughter when she told me. We then tried to imagine Derrida with a sword at his side, and the laughter became hysterical.

In terms of the French academic system, Derrida was and would remain an outsider, someone who had come from another "cape," *l'autre cap*, from another headland and under another heading. A similar sort of split would occur in England and the United States: whereas the logical positivists and analytical philosophers of all stripes rent their tweeds over Derrida, the "Continental" philosophers, along with many leading literary critics, art critics, legal scholars, architects, and others were convinced that something revolutionary had happened.

With the publication of the *Grammatology*, Derrida became, and not only for me, the thinker who had taken on the full burden of both Nietzsche's and Heidegger's responses to the entire tradition of metaphysics and morals, and that distinction endured for the rest of his life. Derrida and Heidegger never met, even though Pierre Aubenque reports that in 1967, Heidegger expressed a desire to meet Derrida, intrigued as he was by the notion of *différance* (BP 232). Because the French word means both the German *Differenz* and *Verschiebung*, "difference" and "deferral," Heidegger was forced to admit, perhaps for the first and only time in his life, that the French language—to say nothing of the Latin *differre*, Latin being the language that in Heidegger's view invariably misconstrues the Greek—could do something that the German could not do. Heidegger was notorious for having said that when his French friends were *thinking*, they had to speak German. Derrida often commented that he did not know whether to laugh or cry at such a remark, as naive as it was arrogant. An intense ambivalence regarding Heidegger, admiration mixed with all sorts of doubts and hesitations, characterized Derrida's response to him. It was an ambivalence more intense than my own, yet there is no doubt that the more I studied Derrida's work, the greater my distance from Heidegger became.

In an early interview, Derrida offers a very clear account of his ambivalence: "Nothing of what I am trying to do would have been possible without the questions that Heidegger opened up. . . . Yet, despite this debt to Heidegger's thought, or rather because of this debt, I am trying to recognize in the Heideggerian text, which, no more than any other text, is not homogeneous, continuous, and everywhere equal to the greatest force and the full consequences of its questions, the signs of its belonging to metaphysics or to what he calls onto-theology" (BP 231). I do not know whether Derrida ever got wind of Heidegger's concession to Pierre Aubenque concerning *différance*, to wit, his admission that for once in his life, he and his friends would have to think in French. Derrida certainly would have smiled.

*   *   *

Amid these detailed accounts of Derrida's astonishing production of works published between 1967 and 1972, Benoît Peeters changes the subject. He reminds us of Sam Weber's *conclusion* to his airport story, which I have saved for this moment. Sam avers, at least as Peeters cites him, "It was only little by little that he [Derrida] liberated himself, inventing his public persona and the erotic form that was proper to him" (BP 238). What was the "erotic form" that was "proper" to Derrida? And did he "invent" his "public persona"? Here I run up against the limits of my own encounter with Derrida. The most erotic discussion we ever had was about Heidegger's treatment of Georg Trakl's poetry. And my affection for him did not seem to be a result of an invention on his part.

"The frontiers between the public life and the private life," writes Peeters, "pose one of the most delicate questions that the biographer confronts" (BP 303). That is the way he opens his cautious discussion of a long love relationship outside of his marriage that Derrida had from 1972 until around 1984, which was when I met him. The relationship with Sylviane Agacinski—a name I knew from her published work but a name Derrida never mentioned to me—had serious consequences, including the birth of a son, consequences that troubled him up to the time of his death. Yet I knew as much about that relationship as I did about Heidegger's and Arendt's, to wit, nothing at all. If the present book is "autobiographical," and it is, then it ought to say nothing about the relationship. Yet if a reader were to ask me whether such relationships are of no significance in a life, I would object in the strongest terms. True, Aristotle was born, worked, and died. Yet there is that tradition about Phyllis, or perhaps her name was Stella, and the tradition has its charm. Many friends of Derrida's heard him say at one time or another that he would love to know about the love life of Hegel and Heidegger—to say nothing of Kant, who, remarkably, was found to have been buried with another human being, the two of them intimately interred in the same coffin, apparently "categorically unimperatived by the maxims" (FW 176). Sometimes I believe that the only honest biography or autobiography would consist solely of accounts of the subject's dream life and love life, letting all the rest go. Whether one loves, how one loves, whom one loves, and about what one dreams when aching for love—what could be more significant for a life than that? Yet Freud himself, in his *Interpretation of Dreams*, which is heavily autobiographical, does not tell us much about his love life. Quite daring in theory and quite open concerning his humiliating bouts of professional envy and ambition, the theoretician of the soul remains reticent about his loves.

One can understand the reticence. If love is, as Freud elsewhere says, the outstanding instance of the collapse of those frontiers that protect the ego, who will want to blather about such a collapse or submit to others' blathering? With whom will one want to share these risky revelations? In the culture in which I grew up, for which love was met with either prudery or vulgarity, a culture that has now advanced beyond prudery to litigation and public humiliation, although the vulgarity remains a constant, who would want to treat such matters? And are philosophers any more reflective than others are in this respect? I wonder. Is there a matter more crucial to the "meanderthalltale" (FW 19) of lifedeath? I wonder. What about the philosophical tradition and its archive? Plato? Surely it depends on whether one heeds Plato's Aristophanes or Plato's Pausanias. Augustine? Soon after his conversion, they tell us, he lost his teeth, his lungs went bad, and he was at last alone with his God. And Kant? What wisdom, no matter who he was buried with, does the pragmatic bachelor share with us? And what has

Hegel's "spirit" to tell us about love's "contradictions," which matrimony alone will presumably unravel? And is Heidegger's "neutral Dasein" also neutered, transcendentally speaking? "O love it is the commonknounest thing how it pashes the plutous and paupe" (FW 269). The other animals seem to be a lot savvier about all this than the philosophers.

Benoît Peeters, beginning his discussion of Derrida's love relationship, cites the "liaison" between Heidegger and Arendt, about which, to repeat, I knew nothing at the time we worked together—except for the fact that the loyalty and the friendship, for all the intervening catastrophes, never came to an end. To that, I was a witness. Peeters alludes to their relationship because Derrida himself refers to it in a 1995 lecture course. Derrida says the following to his students, and one may suppose that he had thought long and hard about it before saying anything:

> I think that one day, with regard to Arendt and Heidegger, we will have to speak openly, in a dignified way, philosophically, with the proper elevation and staking out the appropriate dimensions; we will have to speak of the great passion that bound the one to the other during what one calls "an entire life," across or beyond continents, wars, the Holocaust. This singular passion, the archive of which, if one can put it this way, is being uncovered little by little, with its innumerable historical threads, public and private, manifest or secret, academic and familial . . . this passion of a life merits something better than what generally surrounds it, namely, embarrassed or ashamed silence on the one hand and, on the other hand, vulgar rumor or whisperings in the corridors of academe. (BP 305)

Once again, I recall Derrida's aside during an earlier seminar that *l'amour* was all he ever talked about.[10] Peeters, in a long note, speculates that the enormous correspondence between Derrida and Agacinski is extant, that neither partner destroyed the letters, even if the whereabouts of the letters are as yet unknown (BP 304n.). I mention this not to claim that for Derrida "love," just like everything else, "is a text," although there is something to be said for that. After all, how can so much of our literature be about love

---

10 Benoît Peeters cites the opening remark as follows—and I will leave it in the French—commenting that it reminds Peeters of the way Lacan captivated his listeners with the opening words of each lecture: "*Ceci sera, comme d'habitude, comme auront dû l'être, comme auraient dû tous mes séminaires, un court traité de l'amour.*" Yet it won't be the usual demagoguery about love, Derrida continues, not the usual serenade, even if it is five in the afternoon and the sun is down; in fact, it will be a seminar that might scare people off as much as draw them in, since it will be treating the entire "system of the mouth" (BP 543).

if love is not already a text? I recall Robert Musil's rumination on love and talk, and on the remarkable "volubility" of lovers:

> The human being, quite properly the speaking animal, is the only being that needs conversations in order to reproduce. And not merely because he or she will speak in any case, as though by the way, but rather because his or her delight in loving [*Liebseligkeit*] is apparently bound up essentially with delight in talking [*Redseligkeit*], so secretly and so profoundly that it reminds us of the ancients, according to whose philosophy God, human beings, and the things all came to be out of "Logos," by which they meant either the Holy Ghost, reason, or speech. Now, not even psychoanalysis or sociology has taught us anything essential about this connection, although these two newest sciences allow themselves to compete with Catholicism in rummaging through everything that is human. One has to discover for oneself the reason why conversations play a greater role in love than almost anything else. Love is the most loquacious of feelings; for the most part it consists almost entirely of volubility. If the human being is young, these wide-ranging conversations pertain to the phenomena of growth; if he or she is mature, they form the peacock's tail, which, even though it consists of nothing but plumage, unfolds all the more splendidly when it does so quite late in the day. The reason may lie in the awakening of contemplative thinking by feelings of love, and in contemplation's constant connection with such feelings. Of course, that would only postpone the answer to the question, for even if the word *contemplation* is used almost as often as the word *love*, it is not any more transparent in meaning.[11]

Derrida was not reluctant to speak of love, and he never stopped writing about it. Is it not generally true that love loves to exchange written exhalations and exaltations, producing text, leaving traces? Love is also *schreibselig*, Musil would have conceded, even if the word is a barbarism. Is this still so, however, even in the age of emails and tweets? What brusque exchanges these electronic exaltations are! Can there be *contemplative* emails? Is a lover ever inspired to save them on a USB stick or to send them soaring into the Cloud?

Earlier on in the book, I had some fun with Tom Joad's defrocked preacher friend, who explains somewhat more candidly than either Hegel or Heidegger how things must go with spirit. In Derrida's case, the fun is more difficult to find. When he insists that autobiography is auto-hetero-bio-thanato-graphy, he is very much in earnest, even and especially when a love story is to be recounted. In any life, I believe he would say, passionate

---

11 Robert Musil, *Der Mann ohne Eigenschaften*, ed. Adolf Frisé (Reinbek bei Hamburg: Rowohlt Verlag, 1978), 1219–20.

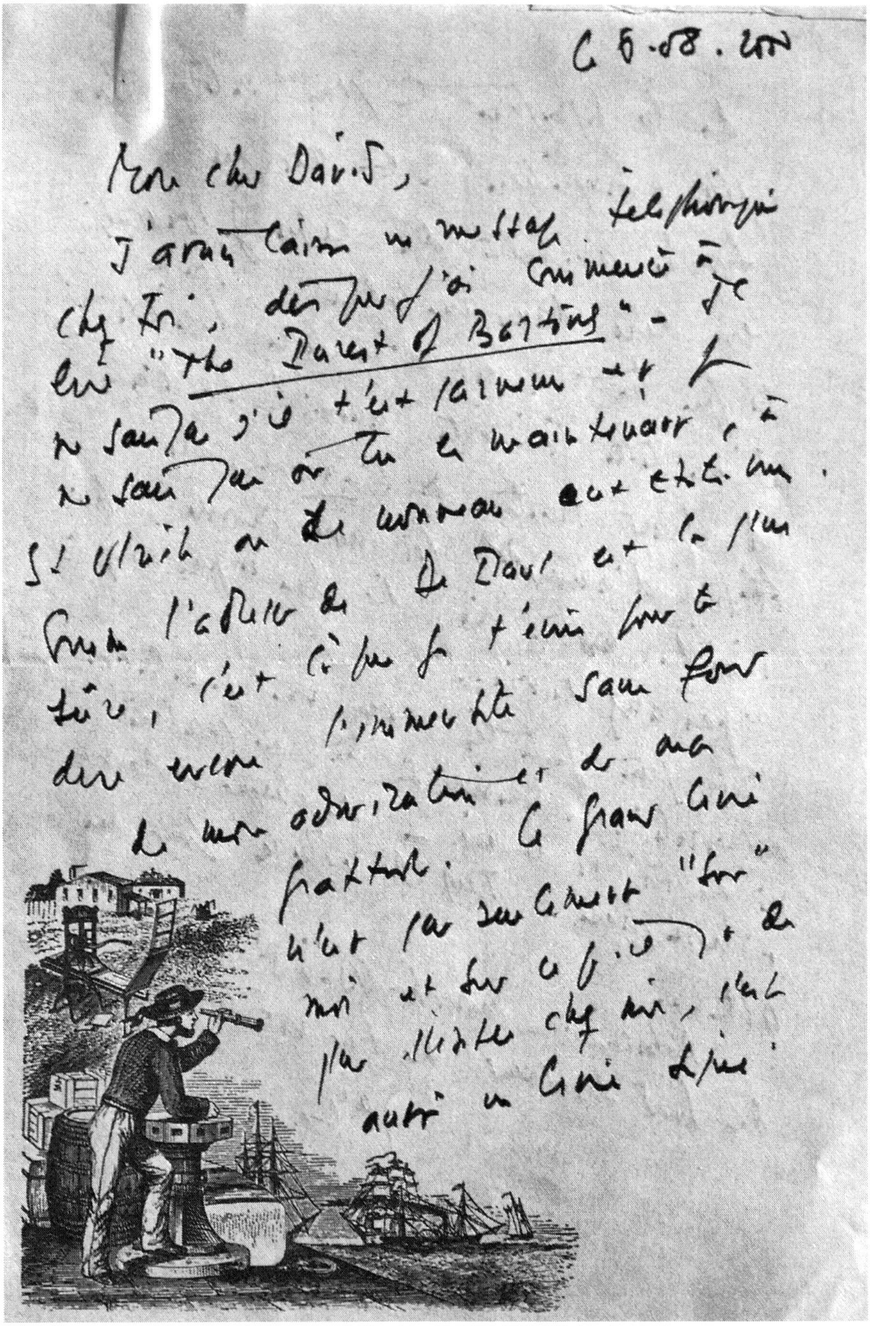

Fig. 9.2 Derrida's letter to me of August 6, 2000, in which he acknowledges receipt of the book *The Purest of Bastards*.

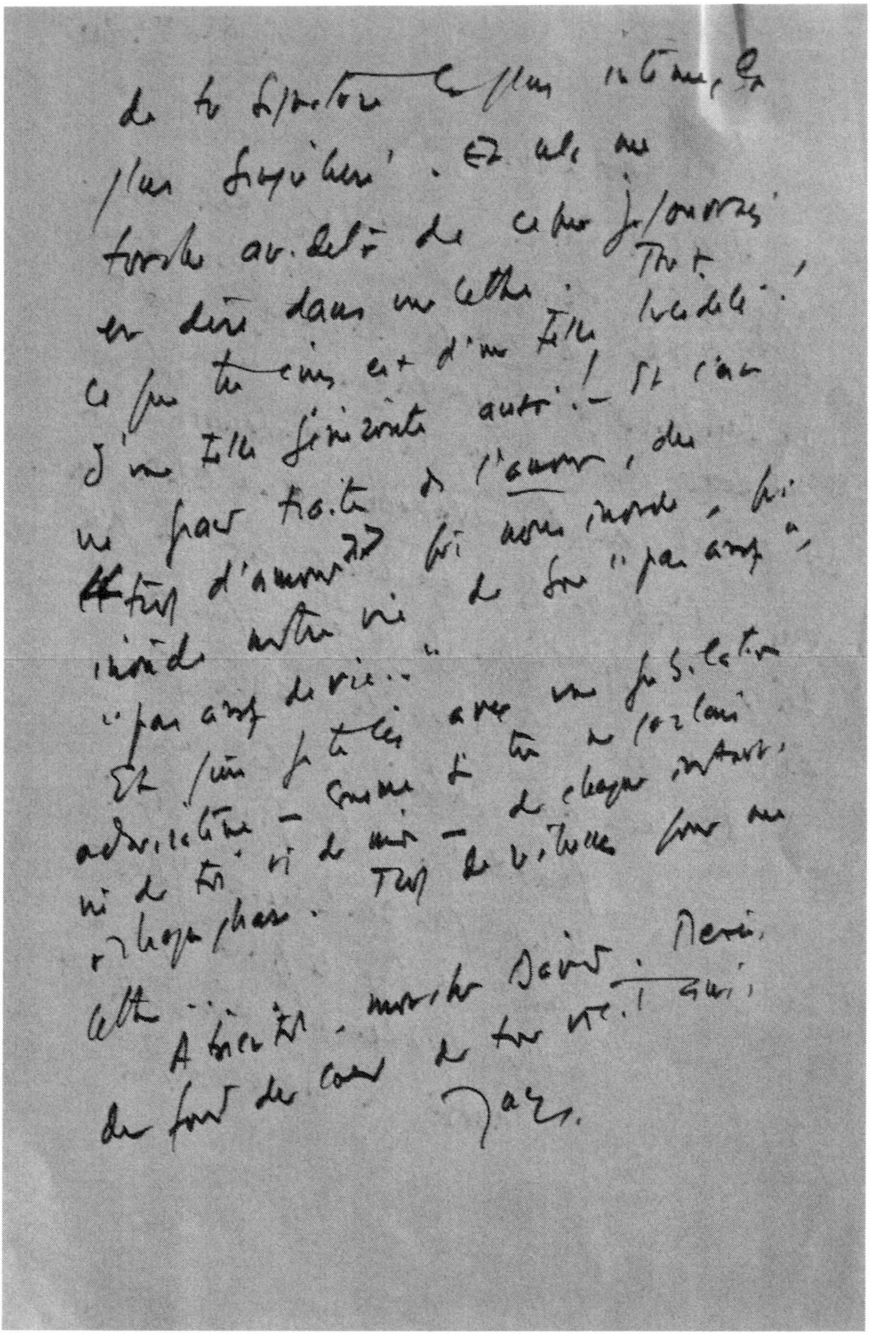

Fig. 9.3 "And it is a grand treatise of *love*, of the 'too much love' that inundates our lives with its 'never enough,' 'never enough of life.'"

love is a matter of alterity and death—passion, therefore—and *mourning* invariably supervenes long before the demise of the lovers or the friends. "A hunddred cares, a tithe of troubles and is there one who understands me?" (FW 627). Glenn Gray wrote to me after the death of Arendt, to whom he felt very close, that it was strange that Heidegger and the French existentialists focused so much on one's own death and not the deaths of others we love. Derrida, with strong support from Levinas and Blanchot, resists this focus on one's own death. As I have already said, but it bears repeating, for Derrida each death means the end of the world, and with the death of someone we love, Celan put it best: "The world is gone, I'll have to carry you." And even in those cases, not rare, where love explodes into quarrel and fury, ending in bitterness and the taste of wetted ashes, does the "carrying" of the other ever stop? Does the burden grow lighter after such an explosion? "We have to move on" is the desperate pronouncement of the war-wounded who have not yet seen the extent of the damage they have suffered. Each time unique, this loving, the end of the world.

Again I have to say that the dilemma or double bind of all discourse on love stuns me. Nothing is more worthy of recounting than what used to be called "the affairs of the heart." These recountings are the tales that form our literature, the literatures of all languages, by a kind of slow accretion over centuries, as with coral reefs. Yet when philosophers touch them, the reefs disintegrate, and when gossips plunder them, the waters are contaminated. I myself, even at my most voluble, am reduced to a kind of stutter—except perhaps when I am writing fiction, and only if the writing goes well. As for pronouncing judgments about love relationships from the outside, or from some presumed superior vantage point, the only judgment I can come up with is this: I am happy when lovers survive, "Try not to part! Be happy, dear ones!" (FW 627), ecstatic when they thrive and awed when the least possible amount of hurt is done; and I am wretched when love galls and bitterness and *mille regrets* must be endured. As for the gossips, let them get a life, as the American language says so aptly, and let them practice benign neglect when it comes to the lives and loves of others. In my judgment, Antonia Grunenberg and Benoît Peeters are particularly remarkable biographers precisely for their having written about these matters of love so well, with such justice, empathy, and sympathy. And, for all his ironizing, Rüdiger Safranski is not far behind them. I am a bit surprised by my own reticence, and I do not know whether to attribute it to embarrassment or a desire to respect the friendships—and to admit that since I knew nothing about these matters of love in the case of all three encounters nothing is what I should report. Except to say that I could see and sense in all three a kind of *vitality* and *generosity* that is difficult to account for without invoking Eros.

* * *

Benoît Peeters reproduces a "Questionnaire de Proust" to which Derrida subjected himself in 1992 (BP 510–11). Although the interview with Osvaldo Muñoz that contains it was to be published in *El Pais*, it never appeared in print. Yet it offers—as such questionnaires have done since their origin as a parlor game in England, immensely popular throughout Europe at the end of the nineteenth century—a portrait of Derrida that is both humorous and apt. Derrida must have loved the catechetical nature of the questionnaire, if only because it reminded him of the "Ithaca" episode of Joyce's *Ulysses*.

> *What is, for you, the very depths of misery?* Loss of memory.
> *Where would you love to live?* In a place to which I could always return, that is to say, a place I could always leave.
> *For what fault do you have the greatest indulgence?* Keeping a secret that one should not keep.
> *Your favorite hero in a novel?* Bartleby.
> *Your favorite heroines in real life?* There I will keep the secret.
> *Your favorite quality in a man?* Knowing how to admit his fear.
> *Your favorite quality in a woman?* Thought.
> *Your favorite virtue?* Fidelity.
> *Your favorite occupation?* Listening.
> *Who would you love to be?* Someone else who would remember me a bit.
> *The principal trait of your character?* A certain lightness [*légèrté*].
> *Your dream of happiness?* Continuing to dream.
> *What would be your greatest unhappiness?* Dying after those I love.
> *What you would like to be:* A poet.
> *What do you detest above all?* Complacency and vulgarity.
> *The reform that you most admire:* The one touching sexual difference.
> *The gift of nature that you would most love to possess:* Musical genius.
> *How you would prefer to die:* By absolute surprise.
> *Your motto?* Prefer saying yes.

Peeters comments: "The convictions and the aporias, the anxieties, the hopes and the flaws, the will to occupy all places, poesy, memory, and the secret—in a sense, it's all there" (BP 511). Of all the aporias, I would emphasize this one: I would prefer not to, although I prefer saying yes. "You've surpassed yourself! Be introduced to yes!" (FW 465). My personal favorite, concerning the dream of continuing to dream, would repeat the words spoken at Essex: "I can't avoid, dreaming, of course. . . . But I try not to dream all the time."

*   *   *

What can one say about Derrida's extravagant "autobiography," *Circumfession*, if "autobiography" is what it is? Benoît Peeters describes the role it plays, printed on a gray band at the bottom of each page of Geoff Bennington's formidable account of deconstruction, the "Derridabase," in the following way: "Disquieted at seeing himself boxed in, Derrida wants to write a text that escapes the systematic cartography established by Bennington" (BP 495). In all fairness, one must admit that Geoff was delighted to collude with Derrida's "escape" from the system that never was a system.

Fifteen years before his *Circumfession*, during the winter holidays of 1976, Derrida equipped himself with two notebooks that became the journals that went into the making of *Circumfession*. Yet the oldest notes from these "intimate" journals go back twenty years to the period of his first visit to New York City. He describes the idea of such a journal in the same way that he describes his admiration of Joyce's *Ulysses*, the novel in which, as Joyce himself said, we learn more about a human being, "Our national umbloom!" (FW 467), over a mere twenty-four-hour period than we know about anyone living or dead. Derrida writes—and once again it involves the dream:

> If there is a dream that has never left me, in terms of what I have written, it is to write something in the form of a journal. At bottom, my desire to write is the desire for an exhaustive chronicle. What is going through my head? How can I write fast enough so that everything that is going through my head can be preserved? It so happened that once again I took up notebooks and journals, but each time I abandoned them. . . . But that is the regret of my life, because the thing I would most love to write would be that: a "total" journal. (BP 359)

Of the two notebooks whose contents go into *Circumfession*, one is "the book of Elijah," and its subject is circumcision, a word that in Hebrew, transcribed as *milah*, oddly coincides with the word for "word"; the other, untitled, was undertaken not long after the death of Aimé, Derrida's father. There is less about the father in *Circumfession* than one might have expected, although Augustine's father, Patricius, has also been all but outshouted by a divine Father. "Loud hear us!" (FW 258). In Derrida, there is more about sons and a brotherhood of fathers, that is, uncles, but most about mothers. The dream behind these notebooks is that Derrida can free himself from the rigorous discourses of philosophy and "tell lots of stories," that he can release the handbrake that is impeding his progress and devote himself absolutely to "anecdote" (BP 361). The worries that I was having about this "memoir," which caused me, as I relate in the preface, to put it off for many years, above all the worry that the book would be based on anecdotes and therefore would be irresponsible, even frivolous, in fact mirror Derrida's own frustrations and worries: "Independently of the content, and whether it be more or less interesting, this *relationship to the anecdote* is itself what has to be transformed. *With me* it is strangled; I tense up, repress. All the 'good reasons' for this repression ought to fall under suspicion. What is involved in this hiding, this prohibition? Fear of the physician: what is he going to uncover? And I mean the classic physician, not even the psychoanalyst" (ibid.).

No doubt, the *Envois* of *The Post Card* are a huge step in the direction of a discourse that has liberated itself from the rhetoric and logic of philosophy and become narrative, even anecdote, met with passionate affirmation and not shame—even if these "dispatches" are sent in the direction of a forbidden love, and even if "the voice," *la voix*, is that forbidden love of the writer. In *Circumfession*, Derrida confesses that his thinking often takes its start from a single word and that it remains captive to this word, for example, the Hebrew word for "word." "In the beginning is the woid" (FW 378). He offers another example out of the blue, namely, the word "cascade." Now, this is the word that captivated Arendt as we were searching for words to render the *Gefälle* of Heidegger's "Anaximander" essay. She rolled the word around in her mouth several times, while I spoke about a particular spot on one of my walks where the water cascades trippingly down a steep hillside. Derrida writes the following about "cascade": "[N]ow this morning it seems to me I am seeing a word, 'cascade,' for the first time, as happens to me so often, and each time it's the birth of a love affair, the origin of the earth . . . and a few times that I have thought I was, like a cascade, falling in love, I began to love each word again . . . but the word cascade . . . I do not see, it falls under my eyes" (C 247/266–67). Derrida would have loved the fact that in English and even in American, according to the *Oxford English Dictionary*, "cascade" is also a colloquial or even vulgar verb, now obsolete, for "to vomit." That would of course have caused him to love the word even more. Hannah would have scowled at first but then laughed, then scowled again.

The dream that drives Derrida's *Circumfession* is that the writer will find the *vein*, "the crural vein," which is not so easy to reach, so that his pen, having transformed itself into a syringe, will deftly enter, and his narrative flow like blood into a test tube. It is the dream of finding a certain raw and even bloody word or phoneme, perhaps "the hygienic gllll" (FW 54) of *Glas*, unrefined, unfiltered, uncooked, and therefore innocent of every system and program. Blood had already been a metaphor for ink, or ink a metaphor for blood, in the *Grammatology*; later, in his seminar on the death penalty, Derrida pursues a *history* of blood, especially the bloodletting of sacrifice and the bloodshed and cruelty that dominate human history, which no one understands very well, not even the psychoanalysts. (Benjamin saw a reaction to the raw cruelty of history in the facial expression of Klee's *Angelus novus*, the new angel that gazes aside in horror.) Cruelty will be the theme of Derrida's address to the Estates General of Psychoanalysis in July 2000, the *Grausamkeit* of Freud's "destruction and death drives," which he tells the psychoanalysts they must study if their art and science are to have any future at all. In the *Circumfession*, circumcision is one of the marks or wounds of cruelty, the sign of a god who insists on blood sacrifice. That same god, preferring Abel's bloody sacrifice over Cain's vegetal offering, also has a horror of fornication, a horror that preoccupies him to the point of obsession. If fornication has anything at all to do with love, then one may say that Derrida's focus in his *Circumfession* is on the circulation of blood, the mark of circumcision, the family, love, and sex.

Yet the initial appearance of blood in this text, if only by way of periphrasis or circumvention, is about not cruelty but appeasement—that "glorious appeasement" or light-headedness that supervenes if an excess of blood is drawn, the anemia inducing a swoon. If Geoff Bennington ("Geoff" pronounced as *djef*, which looks like an ancient etymon of *dieu*) knows all about Derrida and deconstruction, if he is absolutely able to reduce every aspect of Derrida's thinking to a logic and a system, Derrida feels compelled to find the vein that cannot be systematized even if it is essential to circulation. It is, if I may say so when Derrida does not, the dream of Empedocles, who knew that thought flows not through the brain in the head but through the blood that washes like a sea in and around the heart. (The sea does play multiple roles in Augustine's *Confessions*, however, and Derrida cites many of them.) Without ever writing the name of the ancient Greek philosopher from Agrigent, Derrida practices *pericardial* thinking.

Augustine's *Confessions* are a major inspiration, if only because of Augustine's fixation on Monica, his mother. At the time Derrida is writing his own circuitous confession, during 1988–89, his own mother is, to all appearances, adrift in Alzheimer's disease, neither recognizing her son nor pronouncing his name, which he therefore feels he has lost. She utters impossible sentences about her own mother, slipping into hopeless obsequence; she shows herself to her son in impossible disclosures, as though in mockery of Augustine's intimate chats with Mom. Derrida's mother also suffers from bedsores, since she has long been bedridden, and some of the cruelest passages of *Circumfession* describe these "red and blackish volcanoes, enflamed wounds, crusts and craters, signifiers like wells several centimeters deep, opening here, closing there" (C 79/82). They are volcanoes of the flesh, a ghastly allusion perhaps once again to Empedocles on the rim of Etna, confronting his own death. It is as though the writer is in a race with his own mother to die, to upset the generations and affirm the obsequence of all obsequies. What will she know of it if he should die first? What harm would there be in it?

What has all this to do with "deconstruction"? The reader has the right to ask this impatient question. And the answer is: nothing and everything. Nothing insofar as Derrida is precisely "giving Geoff the slip," indeed, giving all his contemporaries the runaround. The Seuil series in which the French *Circonfession* is published is called "Les Contemporains," and the Chicago series in which *Circumfession* is published is the "Religion and Postmodernism Series," and there can be no doubt that Derrida, this "purest of bastards" who here calls himself "the truest of false prophets" (C 208/225), wants to give them all the slip. And yet. As a teacher and lecturer, Derrida never wanted to skip town, even if, as a writer, he knew a thing or two about concealments and ruses. Even so, "deconstruction" has everything to do with these stories and histories of blood, of the family, of love and of sex—and not for purposes of evasion. The dynamism of "deconstruction" is pericardial, always was, always will be. Try to reduce it to a system or a method, drawing it all out, down to the last drop, and you collapse the vein. Contusion, even more than confusion, is the result. Derrida's effort here, if I am right, is to find the vein, to get into the vein, to let the ink flow, to allow secrets to be secreted, both secréted and sécreted, as though remembering Heidegger's *bergen*, which means both to safeguard and—at least if *ver-bergen* is bound up with it—to conceal. Not for the sake of some willful obscurantism, since our confidence that declarative sentences tell the truth about lives is the worst obscurantism, but for the sake of the important stories, the life and death stories. For example, departing for a moment from Derrida's text, this next one.

THE GODMOTHERS—HOW WONDROUS IT SOUNDS!

The last ten years of the life of my godmother, my aunt Catherine, were spent in the final stages of Alzheimer's. My godfather and uncle, her husband, would ask me to visit with her whenever I happened to be in the States. She was in a wheelchair by that time, her hands, reduced to claws, gripping the armrests, her face contorted in agony. He would feed her vanilla ice cream, she would mumble it, losing a great deal of it down her bibbed front. After that, he would get very close to her face and call out her name.

—Catherine! Catherine!

She would make what seemed to me the effort of an entire lifetime to announce something to the world; from her lungs a moan or an animal noise of some kind would rise. My uncle, defeated, would finally relent from what Georgette Safar's doctor once called "therapeutic harassment" (C 167/179), always well intended, always a catastrophic failure.

My role then was to lay my hands on hers and tell her to stop trying, that it was okay, she should simply stay where she was. My uncle, although defeated, always felt that in these moments I was in fact "reaching" her in a way that he could not. There was no way to tell, but each time I traveled to the States, I made a point of visiting them, repeating the ritual, until she died.

During my childhood, she was such a godly godmother, serene and loving, hence the name "godmother," I suppose. She was the head librarian at her local public library. She taught me never to dog-ear a book but to have respect. When I see a library book in which some idiot has made underlinings and scribbled his idiotic notes, I go into a silent rage. The copies of Barrett's *Irrational Man* and Heidegger's *Introduction to Metaphysics* were my own: I was allowed to inscribe my *idiotises*. And in any case, I never dog-eared them. I have an enviable collection of bookmarks.

My mother, like her eldest sister an avid reader, suffered greatly on account of Catherine's fate, and she was haunted by the fear that the same lay in store for her. Yet she remained alert until the early morning hour when she died in her sleep. The private caretakers who had nursed her in her own home had needed to retire, and so my mother was moved to an old-age home in another part of the country. Her doctor warned the children that when a person of that age is removed from familiar surroundings, death often advenes promptly. My mother endured the nursing home for three days.

The strange thing about such family stories, sometimes strikingly similar even if quite unique, is that anyone can tell them, so that virtually everyone can understand the stories. There is nothing obscure about them, even though the events they recount are never "clear and distinct." They are recounted not by the brain but pericardially, by the heart's blood, which perhaps explains their hue. Derrida's *Circumfession* is one of those stories— one where the revelations are often excruciating but also where the sheltering or safeguarding is highly developed. Even so, I am not convinced that he wants to give anyone the slip. "O foetal sleep! Ah, fatal slip!" (FW 563).

* * *

Derrida loves the association in Augustine's *Confessions* of writing and fornicating, at least if fornicating is evil, for "writing is interesting only in proportion to and in the experience of evil" (C 48/47). He also loves the urge to confess guilt and the impossible avowal—what he also calls "the ruse of avowal" (C 201/216)—in circumfession. God himself, writes Derrida, is "coming to circulate among the unavowables, unavowable as he remains himself, like a son not bearing my name, like a son not bearing his name, like a son not bearing a name, and . . . I write that there is *too much* love in my life, emphasizing the *too much*, the better and the worse, that too would be true, love will have got the better of me, my faithfulness stands any test, I am faithful even to the test that does harm, to my euthanasias" (C 147–48/156–57). He loves Augustine's holding back his tears at his mother's deathbed, but he loves even more Augustine's confession of his sin, to wit, that after his mother's death he hid for an hour and wept copious tears— the reader of his *Confessiones*, Augustine begs, should not be hard-hearted about that surreptitious sin of "sweet tears."

Derrida also loves the ambiguity of who it is that requires circumcision of the infant males: the women are kept at bay during the ritual, which is all about potent fathers and submissive sons, and yet Moses's Zipporah seems to have wielded the knife on their own sons when her husband was too weak-kneed to do so. There are many moments in *Circumfession* when Derrida seems to hold his mother or womankind in general responsible for the wound on his sex: "*Imagine the loved woman herself circumcising (me), as the mother did in the biblical narrative*" (C 202–203/217–18). There are even more moments, however, when he sees his mother banished from the ritual act, banished and weeping over her infant's wailing. There are many moments when the pathos of Derrida's intense response to his mother's slow dying (C 196–97/211: "That my fear of death will only have reflected her own, I mean my death *for her* whose anxiety I perceived each time I was ill") brings back to me the fifth stanza of Yeats's unforgettable "Among School Children":

> What youthful mother, a shape upon her lap
> Honey of generation had betrayed,
> And that must sleep, shriek, struggle to escape
> As recollection or the drug decide,
> Would think her son, did she but see that shape
> With sixty or more winters on its head,
> A compensation for the pang of his birth,
> Or the uncertainty of his setting forth?[12]

One of the strangest parallels that Derrida draws in his *Circumfession* is that between circumcision and flaying, for, as Derrida writes, "never will the man flayed alive that I am have written like this." He continues, "The death of my mother, Sultana Esther Georgette Safar Derrida, would come to sculpt the writing from the outside, give it its form and its rhythm from an incalculable interruption, never will any of my texts have depended in its most essential inside on such a cutting, accidental and contingent outside, as though each syllable . . . were preparing itself to receive a telephone call, the news of the death of one dying" (C 192–93/206–207). Derrida later refers to "de-skinning" himself, "tearing off" his skin (C 222–23/240). Such flaying is reflected in the many poems composed by Michelangelo Buonarroti, which I read at the time I was preparing my "slideshow" for "Infinite Violence." He begs God to cut into him, flay him, so that he can step out of the skin of his self.

And yet Derrida does not shrink from speculating on various forms of glorious appeasement, even fellative appeasement, that may have followed and palliated the bloodshed of circumcision. Something other than piety pervades these speculations, most of which involve women rather than

---

12 From *The Tower* (1928), in Yeats, *The Collected Poems*, 213–14.

men, even though the women are said to have been banished from the rite of circumcision. Likewise, if his religious name, *Élie*, should cause him to believe that he is among the "elect," that name, under the form *Éliahu*, the name of the uncle who holds the infant Jackie on his lap for the performance of circumcision, will come to be associated with cinder and ash, *il y a là cendre*. If, now that his own mother cannot speak his name, the son searches for some reassuring identity in the mirror of his family, the mirror returns to him a Cyclops eye—an eye that is blinded by a facial nerve paralysis that causes the entire left side of his face to droop.

The testimony of the body is so present in this text, so powerfully present in what Derrida now writes as "the uninterrupted[13] autobiothanatoheterographical opus" (C 198/213), that again I have to think of Merleau-Ponty's *corps propre*. Strangely, it is here that Derrida refers to both Merleau-Ponty and Roland Barthes, who were very close to their mothers, and *Circumfession* is written around the time of *Memoirs of the Blind*, where Merleau plays an important and positive role.[14] Yet Derrida's body is perhaps more reminiscent of Bataille and Genet than of Merleau-Ponty. It is a body of sensations, sensibilities, dejections, pulsations, and ecstasies. At one point,

13 The English has "interrupted," a serious error but one that is so easy to make, given the *inin-* of *ininterrompu*. It is good to know that *dieu/djef* slips on occasion, albeit rarely. Years ago, in Geoff's presence, I referred several times to "the omniscient author," whereupon Geoff remarked, rather archly, on my malapropism: "I've heard of an omniscient *narrator*," he said, "but never an omniscient *author*." As usual, he was correct.

14 I feel constrained to add a long footnote on Merleau-Ponty. Benoît Peeters makes much of the fact that Derrida "saw" Maurice Merleau-Ponty only one time in his life, at the time of his oral exam for entry into the École Normale Supérieure (BP 60; cf. 83–84, 162). I am uncertain about the truth of this. I remember many conversations with Derrida about Merleau-Ponty, whose work I was devoted to and on which I had published some articles early in my career. It had struck me that Derrida's emphasis on the "body" of writing, the materiality of ink and blood, semen and saliva, made for a more positive connection with Merleau's *corps propre* or "lived body" than Derrida was willing to admit. Many of these conversations about Merleau-Ponty took place around the time of the Louvre exhibition, "Memoirs of the Blind," whose catalog offers a sympathetic account of the remarkable phenomenologist who died in 1961, far too soon. Indeed, I mentioned to Derrida that I regretted never having had the chance to *meet* Merleau-Ponty. I remember Derrida's telling me, in response to this, that even though he never studied with Merleau-Ponty, he and his circle of friends at the ENS remained informed about him. They were too proud to be seen at the Collège de France, where Merleau-Ponty was teaching, but at least one of the group would attend the lectures and report back to the others in the group. Peeters reports these deputations in the case of Foucault, who was still teaching at the ENS at the time, but he does not mention Merleau-Ponty. Yet, unless my memory is playing tricks on me, I remember Derrida including Merleau-Ponty in this story of "deputations." And this suggests, at least to me, that Derrida would have been deputized to attend at least some of Merleau's remarkable lectures and lecture courses at the Collège. I do not know whether or where I can find corroboration of this—Françoise Dastur was unable either to

following "the traces of blood" in his life, Derrida recounts his reaction to an accident he witnessed as a boy—his cousin hurt by the pedal of a scooter. Her bleeding from the accident (which he mistranslates as *Verfall*, "corruption," rather than *Unfall*, "accident," although the mistranslation may actually be a reference to Hegel, who regards *all of nature* as the realm of accident [*Unfall, Zufall*] and hence corruption [*Verfall, Abfall*]) causes a stir in the pit of his stomach—rather, "the first phantom sensation, that algic sympathy around my sex," a sensation that is so difficult to describe. I know that I have felt "algic sympathy" in vertigo, when out on a ledge in high mountains, or on a high bridge, but I have no idea how the physiologists describe or explain it. In any case, autobiography, in Derrida's case, is also *hematological*. This body, our body of flesh and blood, following the animals, is found everywhere, if discretely, circumspectively in all the works of deconstruction, whether the subject be Rousseau or Hegel or even Heidegger.

Among the body fluids that flow in *Circumfession*, blood and tears are the privileged ones. As for tears, they are a constant in his life, "weepy and pusillanimous son that I was, . . . who was always to weep over himself with the tears of his mother," weeping "over the child whose substitute I am" (C 114–15/118–19); yet these tears are also those he imagines that his sons will shed at his gravesite. One may say that tears alone constitute the form of *avowal* that Derrida accepts as genuine. As in the case of Monica, these tears are often wept by Georgette. Yet they are just as often wept by her son. Which does not mean that his life was entirely wretched. Here is Derrida's remarkable avowal, his circumspect confession, to wit,

> that not only do I not know anyone, I have not met anyone, I have had in the history of humanity no idea of anyone, wait, wait, anyone who has been happier than I, and luckier, euphoric, this is *a priori* true, isn't it?,

confirm or disconfirm it—but my recollection is strong enough that I want to report it here. Yet at the end of the day, Peeters is right when he says that Derrida and Merleau-Ponty never became close. Merleau's early death might explain this, at least in part. But it is also true that Derrida always felt that Merleau's reading of Husserl, especially of the unpublished manuscripts, was insufficiently critical. And neither Merleau-Ponty's *Phenomenology of Perception* nor *The Visible and the Invisible* became important texts for him—at least until the time of the Louvre exhibition and the later book on Jean-Luc Nancy. Françoise Dastur joins me, as I am certain others do, in being perplexed by long-lasting distance taken on Merleau-Ponty. It therefore comes as a great relief to me when I finally read Derrida's appreciation of Merleau-Ponty's *The Visible and the Invisible*, a book that "remains still open, a work-in-progress," its pages "so powerful, so alive, pages that will have done so much to open a path of thinking for his time and for our own." See Jacques Derrida, *Le toucher, Jean-Luc Nancy* (Paris: Galilée, 2000), 242.

drunk with uninterrupted enjoyment, "All these things we see, and they are very good; for [*quoniam*] Thou seest them in us" (*Conf.*, XIII, xxxiv, 49), but that if, beyond any comparison, I have remained, me the counterexample of myself, as constantly sad, deprived, destitute, disappointed, impatient, jealous, desperate, negative and neurotic, and that if in the end the two certainties do not exclude one another for I am sure they are as true as each other, simultaneously and from every angle, then I do not know how still to risk the slightest sentence without letting it fall to the ground in silence, to the ground its lexicon, to the ground its grammar and its geologics, how to say anything other than an interest as passionate as it is disillusioned for these things, language, literature, philosophy, something other than the impossibility of staying still, as I am here, me, I sign. (C 248–49/268–70)

And yet, even as he signs, especially as he signs, closing the band of his autoheterobiography, he wonders whether what he has performed in these pages for the *dieu* who is *djef* is simply *Everybody's Autobiography*, Finnegans's "here comes everybody," which means "that you will never have had any witness, *ergo es* ['therefore you are'], in this very place, you alone whose life will have been so short, the voyage short, scarcely organized, by you with no lighthouse and no book, you the floating toy at high tide and under the moon, you the crossing between these two phantoms of witnesses who will never come down to the same" (C 291/314–15). Who these two "phantoms of witnesses" may be remains unclear, perhaps because they are multiple and always in disguise. Yet one hears throughout these pages the echo "Pity poor Haveth Childers Everywhere with Mudder!" (FW 535).

* * *

Who will be surprised that the most beautiful meditation on Derrida's *Circonfession* and its "two phantoms of witnesses" comes from Hélène Cixous? Her *Portrait de Jacques Derrida en Jeune Saint Juif* gleans a handful of the fifty-nine sections of Derrida's text but reads them *joyceously*, down to the phoneme and the letter, with all the tenderness that a friend-in-connivance can muster. I do not know whether her book has been translated into English, and I do not know how it could be. For example, this: "Who I am (or follow), me, me in my proper place in my proper presence where I never ever was, impossible question, cut in two, I and me, insatiable pain of the foundling, pain of the double, double pain. *Élie* his name, the odd one out, uncomprehended by the family. A phantom deprived of all the qualities of

Fig. 9.4 and 9.5 Derrida and the author in spring 1991 at DePaul University. Photos by Amy Rothblatt.

the phantom. An infantom of the phantom. What the devil! he would say, derridevilishly."[15]

* * *

My last letter to Derrida, sent with a copy of my stage play on the lives of Grete and Georg Trakl, "To My Sister," is dated August 29, 2003. He had a little over a year to live. Michael and Pascale-Anne had told me about the diagnosis—pancreatic cancer—and I knew how deadly that form of cancer is. I mention to him in my letter my own bout with a far less dangerous cancer eleven years earlier and encourage him to "fight," to "resist." "Our world is becoming more and more stupefying: we are in need of your light and your vitality." I mention that I have seen the *Derrida* film by Kirby Dick and Amy Ziering-Kofman, and that it made me feel quite close to him and Marguerite. It was true. There were some silly efforts to play at "deconstruction" in the film, putting questions to Derrida that the filmmakers hoped would unsettle him, even rattle him, but whenever they let Derrida speak, the result was always humorous and insightful.

Benoît Peeters, through his interviews with Marguerite and others, is able to add some details about Derrida's final days. I will truncate the chapter after citing these few details, if only because death itself is so abrupt.

The cancer and the chemotherapy, that deathly double bind that always does its work, have weakened him visibly. He is in the clinic. The pain patches and the morphine induce hallucinations or at least haunting visitations from his childhood. "Who is playing that music? Is there a cabaret close by?" It is Maghreb or Berber music he hears, the music, Cixous would say, of Élie-Baba. He complains of strange odors emanating from the kitchen. Sometime later, three men dressed in black enter his room and begin to rummage about. Another drug is administered to banish these confusions. He can no longer eat: an intestinal blockage, diverticulitis, a six-hour surgery. He survives. He comes to and teases Jean-Luc Nancy, who has had a heart transplant years earlier, joking that now he has an incision that is

---

15 Hélène Cixous, *Portrait de Jacques Derrida en Jeune Saint Juif* (Paris: Galilée, 2001), 24: *"Qui je suis, moi, moi à ma propre place en ma propre présence où je ne fus jamais, question impossible, coupée en deux, je et moi, douleur insatiable de l'enfant-trouvé, douleur du double, double douleur. Élie son nom d'intrus, l'incompris de la famille. Un fantôme privé de toutes les qualités du fantôme. Un enfantôme de fantôme. Diable, disait-il, derridiablement."* Samir Haddad, who has helped my own book along in so many ways, informs me that Hélène's book has indeed been translated: see Hélène Cixous, *Portrait of Jacques Derrida as a Young Jewish Saint*, trans. Beverley Bie Brahic and Hélène Cixous (New York: Columbia University Press, 2004). My apologies to the translator and to H. C.!

just as impressive. That night, October, 8–9, 2004, he slips into a coma and dies before Marguerite can reach the hospital. He is four months into his seventy-fourth year.

His son Pierre reads the message his father has asked him to read at his interment. A friend had sent me these words soon after the burial, and so I have known of them for a long time now, and they still seem to me the perfect words. Benoît Peeters (BP 660) reports Pierre's saying the following:

> Jacques wanted neither a ritual nor speeches. He knew from experience how hard it would be for the friend who was charged with the task. He asked me to thank you for coming, to bless you, to ask you not to be sad, to think only of the many happy moments you've given him, the moments you were able to share.
>
> He says, Smile on me as I will have smiled on you up to the end. Always prefer life and do not cease to affirm survival. . . .
>
> I love you and I smile on you from wherever I am.

10

CONCLUDING REFLECTIONS

> No common-place is ever effectually got rid of, except by essentially emptying one's self of it into a book; for once trapped in a book, then the book can be put into the fire, and all be well. But they are not always put into the fire; and this accounts for the vast majority of miserable books over those of positive merit. Nor will any thoroughly sincere man, who is an author, ever be rash in precisely defining the period, when he has completely ridded himself of his rubbish, and come to the latent gold in his mine. It holds true, in every case, that the wiser a man is, the more misgivings he has on certain points.
>
> —Herman Melville, *Pierre, or, The Ambiguities*

It is time to face up to the misgivings I expressed in my preface. Letting the reader decide about the value of these recollections still seems like a subterfuge on my part—although it is also an inevitability for every book, is it not? Even so, my sense of the "traps" in autobiographical discourse is perhaps even more highly developed now than it was at the outset. I confess that it was in the writing of the little stories or anecdotes involving my three subjects that I felt both the greatest pleasure and the best assurance that the project was worthwhile. In any case, the misgivings persist, and I want to dedicate a few paragraphs to them.

An editor of Rousseau's *Confessions* alludes to a remark by Georges Gusdorf to the effect that every novel, and presumably every piece of fiction, is "an autobiography by means of interposed personages"; likewise, "inversely," a writer of autobiography, no matter how sincere he or she may be or pretend to be, finds it "difficult to avoid playing with" his or her own personage.[1] That same editor does not hesitate to observe, specifically with

---

1 See Jean-Jacques Rousseau, *Les confessions*, ed. Jacques Voisine (Paris: Garnier, 1964), xv. I will cite this work as "R," with page numbers. The remark by Georges Gusdorf, not footnoted, presumably appears in Gusdorf's "Conditions et limites de l'autobiographie," in Fritz Neubert, ed., *Formen der Selbstdarstellung* (Berlin, 1956).

respect to Rousseau, *sa coquetterie d'écrivain*, which he elaborates in this way: "Every autobiography is a work of art. Its approximation to the truth is constantly menaced, not only by the inevitable partiality of the observer, but also by the literary deformation of the writer (based on the simple pleasure of writing), a deformation that transforms the data of memory or supplements the absence of data as the occasion requires" (R lxxiii). To be sure, Derrida's *Grammatology* makes us suspicious of this ancient complaint concerning writing and writers, who live a life of "pleasure," a "deformed" life, in which truth is perpetually "menaced" by the deleterious "supplement" of inscription. That would be the traditional complaint of philosophers, who insist that one must *speak* from the soul and not *write* with a sordid ink-stained hand. Even the loquacious soul has its ruses that the reason does not know. Nevertheless, it is also Derrida who warns his readers and himself against overconfidence and complacency when it comes to *writing* life stories.

Those "interposed personages" mentioned a moment ago, by which the writer of fiction conceals the autobiography, make me think of Maurice Blanchot's apparently innocent remark that fiction begins when the pronoun "I" becomes a "he" or a "she," or, more accurately, the neutral and neuter "it." Surely, storytelling is like dreaming: as the experienced therapist tells us, *every* character in the dream is the dreamer himself or herself. After all, out of what other stuff would such personages be formed, out of what reservoir drawn? Yet the obverse is equally true: when I dip into the well of the presumably nonfictional "self," the sole self that is ostensibly *my* self, what a host of personages and masks I draw to the surface, such that *none* of those *larvae*, taken alone, *is* the self. Perhaps each is a mere remnant and residue of the sundry personages and personae that constitute the self. It is as though the αὐτός, the one and only "me," were all the players of *War and Peace*, if not an entire menagerie in dispersion, as in Yeats's "Circus Animals' Desertion." It is as though the "intentional fallacy" never looms larger than when an author writes "autobiographically."

What we best remember after reading Rousseau's autobiographical works—the *Confessions*, the *Dialogues*, and the *Promenades*—are his claims of sincerity and absolute transparency. In the ninth book of the *Confessions*, he writes, "I have seen, during the entire course of my life, that my heart, transparent as crystal, never knew how to hide for an entire minute a feeling of even minimal vitality that had sought refuge there" (R 527–28).

However, one of the longest of the "Neuchâtel variants," namely, a variant of the opening pages of the *Confessions*, is quite revealing in this respect. After affirming that the life of a man can be written only by himself, since his "interior being" and "veritable life" can be known only to himself, Rousseau confesses that "in writing" such a life, the writer in fact "disguises that life." He elaborates in this way: "In the name of his life, he makes his apology; he shows himself as he wants to be seen, but not at all as he is. The most sincere among us are true at most in what they say, but in what they are reticent about they lie, and what they silence changes so much of what they are feigning to avow that in saying only part of the truth they in fact say nothing" (R 787). This variant Rousseau, as it were, pledges to paint his self-portrait by "going to work in the dark": *Je vais travailler . . . dans la chambre obscure* (R 790).

I believe things would go better for the truth if one could project auto-biography into fiction, if one could translate every "I" into a "he," "she," or "it." And I also suspect that the meaning of a text lies outside the circumference of its narration and beyond the scope of its narrator, as Blanchot insists it does, so that the "author" has only a limited sense of it all and the reader quite possibly a much greater sense, hence greater "authority."

As for that adolescent I complained about earlier, the one lurking in my early journals and letters and book margins, I suppose I will have to let him be. Old age yields to the foolishness that forgives the foolishness of youth. I hope that for the most part, I have let the irony go, the irony that tries to protect the writer from what is too close and so banishes the best things. On the *verge* of memory, "on the verge of selfabyss" (FW 40), is where I still feel I am, not at the heart of memory, even as I affirm again that *pericardial* thinking is the only real thinking. At all events, I hope that there is very little polemic left in the book.

I have remarked several times on the fact that I entered into the lives of Heidegger and Arendt quite late, really at the end of their lives. The same is true, to my surprise, with Derrida. The only part of Peeters's biography that is familiar to me is the third and final part, "Jacques Derrida 1984–2004," as though 1984 were the year of his birth—or of mine. And even then the word "familiar" has to be taken with a grain of salt: much of his intense life of study, teaching, writing, and travel, but also much of the more intimate life, was revealed to me by Peeters's book, just as the books by Safranski, Grunenberg, and Young-Bruehl taught me so much about Heidegger and

Arendt. If my preface began with excessive doubts and suspicions concerning the genre of biography, let these "Concluding Reflections" declare my gratitude to all four of my principal sources. As for the more problematic genre of autobiography as autoheterobiothanatography, that will be a longer story.

Let me abide by gratitude, however, a moment longer. So many students of Heidegger, Arendt, and Derrida have over the years become friends who have enriched my life. That may sound sentimental, but I mean to say that all three thinkers attracted so many gifted students to themselves, intellectually gifted but also positive and generous hearts, that my life is much the better and much the happier for these encounters. Especially with Derrida, whom I knew best and longest, one was always in good company, and one is still in good company even in his absence. I tried in a first draft of this "conclusion" to list some of this company, but it became the overflowing pot of "The Sorcerer's Apprentice," and so I now let the list go with this universal declaration of thanks.

* * *

As I was reading through the drafts of this book, I "starred" several paragraphs that seemed to me especially worth remembering in my "Concluding Reflections." A number of themes, at least in immediate retrospect, leaped out at me. Allow me to go through these "starred items" to see if some general conclusions can be drawn. The themes appear here more or less in chronological order by chapter.

First, setting aside "Before the Beginning," which seemed to me to contain reminiscences from a prior life, some general reflections about translation occurred to me. Much of this autoheterobiothanatography of mine is taken up with my duties as a translator, especially of Heidegger. Benoît Peeters reports two sides of the challenges of translation—the case in question being Derrida's *Carte postale*. One translator of that work, Alan Bass, reports how impossibly difficult the book was to translate, offering this detail: how does one render the question *Est-ce taire un nom*? One has little difficulty in rendering it as "Is silence a name?" or "Is 'to be silent' a name?" Yet what if *Est-ce taire* is homophonic with the name *Esther*, so that the phrase has a biblical echo, an echo of Purim (CP 79–81)? And what if *Esther* is also one of the author's mother's names, her "religious" name, a name that her son is "not ready to divulge" (CP 239), a name therefore that he is *silencing*? Can *those* echoes be saved in a translation? These are the sorts of challenges that condemn translators to sleepless nights. At the same time, however, a good translator may challenge the "original" and its author. Derrida responds as follows to the German translator of *La Carte postale*, Hans Joachim Metzger, who in the course of his labors posed a whole range of questions to the author: "When I read your questions I see once again that you have read the text better than I have. That is why a translator is absolutely unbearable, and the better he is the more afraid he makes me: he is the superego in person" (BP 387). I never really had the chance to become unbearable to Derrida, at least not in this respect, and I came close to being so for Heidegger only once—recall the story about the sentence from *Was heisst Denken?* that I could not understand, so that when I asked Heidegger about it, he took several minutes to pore over the sentence and then shook his head and told me to translate what he *meant*. I rarely had the chance to be Heidegger's superego, so I remember finding modest joy in that one incident.

Second, right from the start, and even "before the beginning," my enthusiasm for Heidegger's work, especially in connection with Nietzsche's thinking, was intense. And yet my relation to Heidegger's work was, also right from the start, strained by whatever I knew of his politics. In general, Heidegger's militancy, and sometimes his outright militarism, was quite remote from my formation during the years of desperate opposition to the Vietnam War. His "decisionism" in matters of thinking and willing opened a distance between us that never really closed. Hannah Arendt, both loyal and critical, critical "from the inside," as it were, was the model for me in this as in so many respects. And Derrida, too, banned from his school at the age of ten along with the other Jewish pupils, became a model: I knew few others who took Heidegger's thought so seriously, affirming it as an epoch-making and epoch-ending event in the history of philosophy—and yet who were able to take critical distance from that thinking to the point of challenging the very sense of "epochality." I was a witness to the intense and conflicted encounters of the three of them.

In terms of the kindnesses of all three to me, I would like to note what I recently called an "indefensible idea" about polemic and criticism in general. That indefensible idea has to do with the relationship of generosity to scholarly work and to thinking in general. Heidegger made much of the apparent etymological connection between *gedanc* ("thought") and *Dank* ("thanks"). For him, and for Arendt as well, the word "thoughtful" meant not only "full of thought" but also—and this is its ordinary, everyday sense in English—"considerate," "mindful." And generosity, as I have mentioned, was both crucial to Derrida's method of "double reading" and a mark of the man himself. My "indefensible idea" is that an inconsiderate person *cannot* write a book that is worth reading. Indefensible! many will cry, because think of all the famous writers who, according to all reports, were entirely unpleasant characters, extremely difficult persons, obstreperous, bitter, and caustic curmudgeons. I accept the reproof. But I have decided that I will drive a taxi or plant potatoes or do any number of things if being a scholar means that I must give the books of the ungenerous a chance. There is doubtless some seedy, sentimental humanism at the bottom of my refusal, the idea that at least in the "humanities" there has to be a modicum of the humane. If that idea does turn out to be indefensible, I will renew my chauffeur's license, I will fetch my pick and shovel.

Third, I find that I am moved repeatedly by the shadow of Eros in Hölderlin's, Nietzsche's, Heidegger's, Arendt's, and Derrida's lives—and, emphasizing now the negative, I continue to be disturbed by the apparent inability of Heidegger to allow the erotic to enter into and even shape "the thought-provoking." I regret that there seems to be no room in his thinking for a "history of Eros," but only for a "history of beyng." True, he has those passages in the *Beiträge* that speak of Eros in terms of εὐδαιμονία, and such "happiness," understood as a life blessed by the "good daimons," surely has to do with what Heidegger calls the δαιμόνιον. The latter is both divine and anxiety-producing, and it ought to have led him to a full discussion of ἔρως, and not merely as an accident that happens to his thinking, not merely as an ecstasy that diverts him into "mere sensuality." Likewise, in his *Nietzsche*, he comments on Plato's *Phaedrus*, which tells us that being is ἐρασμιώτατον, the most erotic—but Heidegger leaves it at that. I was therefore particularly excited to find him taking up *amor fati*, "love of fate," in a 1938–39 workshop on Nietzsche. Indeed, he called Nietzsche's yes-saying thought, that is, his affirmation of the fundamental "innocence" of becoming, Nietzsche's "basic metaphysical position"; neither will to power nor eternal recurrence now occupied that place, but a word and a thought that would immediately have captured the attention of both Arendt and Derrida. Indeed, it may be here, more than with the notions of "pluralism" or "birth" or "the public space" that the influence of Arendt on Heidegger is most powerfully felt—here, that is to say, in a philosophy of *amor*, even if he is otherwise incapable of responding creatively to that influence.

Heidegger's failure to *think* the erotic may have had enormous political consequences. His inability to protect his students, particularly his Jewish students, "Whose dolour, O so mine!" (FW 588), along with his stubborn silence after World War II, are failures of both loving and thinking; better, they are failures to let the one shape the other. Arendt, though always discreet, is quite aware of this failure on Heidegger's part. And Derrida, perhaps most conspicuously of the three, because he thinks about Eros all the time, feels compelled to develop what he calls "the politics of friendship," in which Heidegger does not play much of a role. I also recall Luce Irigaray's cry, as I formulated it in my notes after her Essex paper, to protect the memory of the flesh, to create an alchemy of representations beyond both patriarchy and matriarchy, to find divinity in the carnal encounter of the lovers. I remember that cry and her celebration, decades ago, of the only tenderness there is. Make no mistake, both Irigaray and Derrida remain devoted to Heidegger, as Arendt remained devoted, and yet all three seem to despair over this flaw or lack in his thinking, just as Jaspers, toward the end of his life, recognized it and rued it. It was perhaps indiscreet of me to introduce John Steinbeck's defrocked preacher as an exemplar of this need of "sperit" to reflect on the sensual and sexual, and yet fiction does seem to be able to go where philosophers, for the most part, fear to tread.

Fourth, staying with the "political," but now regarding my own comments on the Extermination, it occurs to me that one of the differences between biography and autobiography, especially in my encounters with both Heidegger and Arendt, is that the bulk of my remarks on the issues of antisemitism and the Holocaust occur in my reading of Safranski, Grunenberg, and Young-Bruehl. This surprises me, because as a history major I had done specialized research into the Third Reich and its crimes. I carried that knowledge with me when I met Arendt and Heidegger, and yet these things did not assume center stage in my work with them. Perhaps this is one of the most painful demonstrations of the need for biography to supplement the gaps in every autobiography. In particular, my work with Heidegger was protected from all the details that the biographers reveal—or at least from a good many of them. Was this the result of my own tendency to idealize? Was it a form of self-protection? I do not know, but I have to worry.

Fifth, I was very moved by Derrida's letter to me in which he wrote about the need to hide, to give his contemporaries the slip—better, the need to protect his *work*, his texts, from the scrutinizing eye, the need to leave his work in peace. Such a strange idea! And yet how well I understand it! To be sure, like the rest of us, he *published* his work, and *public* works expose themselves necessarily to every eye. Nevertheless, and here polemic makes its return, there are so many in the academic crowd—*mauvais! mauvais! simplement mauvais!*—from whom one wants to *protect* the work. Not only that, however, but even the discerning eye of a lucid friend may seem "unbearable." The more intrepid the work, the more it exposes the life of the worker, and the more both the work and the life need safeguarding. This reminds me of Heidegger's romance with *bergen*, the need he too felt to develop a language of safeguarding rather than a conceptuality that drags everything into the merciless light. Arendt also, with her insistence on *thoughtfulness*, was pointing to this need to protect, safeguard, and shelter our thoughts, all the more so as our *vita* becomes increasingly *activa*. And perhaps especially when these thoughts of ours open themselves to the barbs of Eros, to the barbs or the gentle limbs of Eros, depending on how things go.

Sixth, for reasons I cannot explain, I remember over and over again my question to Marguerite Derrida, who, terribly, died only recently, a victim of the COVID-19 pandemic, "Why does he do this to himself?" I meant, of course, Derrida's frenetic travel schedule. Marguerite answered, "I guess he needs it." What I remember is the tone of her voice and the smile. Tone and gesture—maybe these are the things that make encounters what they are, which is something different from books. In her case, the tone and gesture, the voice and the smile, along with the sparkling intelligence of her eyes, remind me once again of a theme that has come up many times in this book. I mean the theme of *tenderness*. We heard the word from the young Arendt, the author of "Shadow," who invoked the "diffident and palpating tenderness toward the things of the world." We then saw it in her nondedication of *Vita activa* to Heidegger: *My confidant, / To whom I have remained faithful / And not remained faithful, / And both in love,* that most tender and lucid dedication. We searched for it in Heidegger's halting and abashed responses to Arendt early and late. We found it in the obsessions of a man with a mother who can no longer speak her son's name, a man who tries to write from the vein. I found it in every letter or note from Derrida, perhaps especially that note in which he expresses his fear of the perspicuous reader, the reader that he himself was, and his desire to protect his work from too much sun.

Hölderlin once wrote to Schiller that in his presence he felt like a seedling that is exposed to excessive sunlight: you have to cover a seedling during the afternoon hours, he wrote, when the light and heat are most intense. Hölderlin was obsessed with the theme of tenderness, perhaps because he found so little of it in his culture and in his own life. After his journeys to Bordeaux and back home again, much of them on foot, he wrote to his friend Böhlendorff that he believed he had found in the South of France the secret of ancient Greek civilization: it lay in the "heroic bodies" of the Greeks, their "athletic" bodies, "which seem so full of life." And what is the secret of the vital, heroic, athletic body? It has to do with "the intellect," not in the sense of a calculating cleverness but as "supreme understanding." He describes such understanding as a "force of reflection." And the secret of that force? "It is tenderness," he says.

Heroic bodies and tenderness? His contemporaries have no idea what he is talking about. And that is what makes him sad.

Seventh, and I will stop with the sacred number, which is also the number of the deadly sins, I have been trying the entire time to think a bit more about this confusing and fraught intersection—this Place du Panthéon with its insane traffic—of philosophy, biography, and autoheterobiothanatography, especially when these discourses confront love, friendship, and mourning. Auto-hetero-bio-thanato-graphy: an awful concoction, may Glenn and Hannah and all lovers of the English language forgive me, but ultimately quite simple in its sense: no same without the other to "guide them through the labyrinth of their samilikes and the alteregoases of their pseudoselves" (FW 576); no life without dying; as for "graphy," the unsettling implications and imbrications of same and other, life and death, are what writing is all about. Especially, I think, the writing of anecdotes, the telling of stories. I felt confirmed and heartened by Derrida's desire to "tell lots of stories," to fill notebooks with stories in such a way that "this *relationship to the anecdote*" is transformed. Even when my anecdotes seemed silly, that is what they were aiming at, on the oblique: the fraught intersection.

*   *   *

It is folly to speculate on the future of any thought or any thinker. Yet I cannot help but believe that these three encounters of mine involve thinkers who—even if we avoid talk of a canon—form at least part of a long-lasting trajectory in philosophy and letters. I find myself repeating lists of names, lists that are absurd, all of them, because of the names they *fail* to include. Yet they are lists that for me have a certain staying power: Anaximander

Empedocles Plato Aristotle Augustine Aquinas Descartes Kant Fichte Hegel Schelling Hölderlin Nietzsche Heidegger Derrida. And Arendt? That would require an amended list, adding names like More Machiavelli Hobbes Locke Rousseau Marx Benjamin Adorno Arendt. As I say, this is all folly, and I ought to drop these lists too, since there is no authority that can pronounce on such lasting trajectories. Even without authority, however, one has experiences of reading and thinking, very limited experiences, to be sure; one also has, added to this, the very limited experience of persons, exceptional persons, and so one continues to muse and to compose sundry lists of names for the future, even if it be foolishness. "That's enough, genral, of finicking about Finnegan and fiddling with his faddles" (FW 531).

These lists, if not sober judgments of history, are billets-doux. In the face of these billets, my misgivings about autobiography, at least the part that can speak of these three encounters, may be overdrawn—or, if not overdrawn, beside the point. What seems more telling is my good fortune. For which one should never hesitate to express gratitude once and for all one more time.

ILLUSTRATIONS

Figure 1.1 Not all my books have survived my moves back and forth across the Atlantic. This one has.

Figure 1.2 Another survivor from my library. To be recommended. Fits nicely into a hymnal.

Figure 2.1 The first two hardbound volumes of Heidegger's *Nietzsche* in English, published in 1979 and 1984, respectively, were joined as one volume in the paperback edition of 1991, pictured here.

Figure 3.1 "David and Goliath."

Figure 3.2 The notebook in which I recorded my sessions with Heidegger.

Figure 3.3 Two inscriptions in my copy of *Sein und Zeit*, the first unfortunately in my own hand, the second not.

Figure 4.1 Stephanie Richter took this photo of the Todtnauberg *Hütte* or cabin during a recent visit. My thanks to her.

Figure 4.2 The *Hütte* at Todtnauberg was always shuttered when I visited it, usually in the company of friends who wished to see it. I took the lower photo, using slide film, when Alphonso Lingis accompanied me there in the late 1970s. The cabin faces south, receiving the sunlight in winter; Heidegger's workspace was behind the window on the right.

Figure 4.3 The "star" fountain and water trough at Todtnauberg. Photo by Stephanie Richter.

Figure 5.1 A letter from Hannah Arendt in 1975.

Figure 5.2 Notes on Hannah Arendt's second visit from another of my journals.

Figure 7.1 This, I believe, is the only photograph of Derrida I ever took. It is from the summer of 1987 at the Collegium Phaenomenologicum in Perugia, Italy. Derrida had attended the Collegium in 1986, on my invitation, and returned once again in 1987, on the invitation of Rodolphe Gasché.

Figure 7.2 A recto page from *De la grammatologie* and the "limbo" it opened for me.

Figure 7.3 Derrida inscribed my copy of the *Grammatology* during our flight to LaGuardia not long after our first meeting in Chicago.

Figure 7.4 A page from Derrida's *Geschlecht III* typescript, with my comments, on DIN A3–sized paper. On the right is page 26 of the typescript, with comments from me on the left. My notes concern the recently published Heidegger *Gesamtausgabe* volume 29/30, which will become important for Derrida's lectures on "the beast and the sovereign."

Figure 7.5 The "Reading Heidegger" colloquium at Essex. Photographer unknown, unfortunately. My thanks to whoever took it and to the Special Collections and Archives, DePaul University Library, Chicago, Illinois, for preserving it.

INDEX

DAVID FARRELL KRELL is Emeritus Professor of Philosophy at DePaul University, Chicago, and Brauer Distinguished Visiting Professor of German Studies at Brown University, Providence. He also teaches at the University of Freiburg, Germany. His most recent scholarly books include *The Sea: A Philosophical Encounter* and *The Cudgel and the Caress: Reflections on Cruelty and Tenderness*. He has also published a number of translations, short stories, and three novels.